To Audrey

With all my Love.

Wishing you much happy reading

4th Feb 1953

John.

EDINBURGH
from the Calton Hill.

TRADITIONS OF EDINBURGH

By

ROBERT CHAMBERS, LL.D.

Illustrated by

JAMES RIDDEL, R.S.W.

W. & R. CHAMBERS, LIMITED
EDINBURGH AND LONDON

Latest Reprint, August 1949

Printed in Great Britain
by T. and A. CONSTABLE LTD., Hopetoun Street,
Printers to the University of Edinburgh

CONTENTS.

CONTENTS.

COLOUR PLATES.

TRADITIONS OF EDINBURGH

EDINBURGH : 1745–1845.

EDINBURGH was, at the beginning of George III.'s reign, a
picturesque, odorous, inconvenient, old-fashioned town, of
about seventy thousand inhabitants. It had no court, no factories,
no commerce; but there was a nest of lawyers in it, attending
upon the Court of Session; and a consider-
able number of the Scotch gentry—one of
whom then passed as rich with a thousand a year—gave it the benefit of
their presence during the winter.
Thus the town had lived for some
ages, during which political
discontent and division had
kept the country poor. A
stranger approaching the city,
seeing it piled 'close and
massy, deep and high' — a
series of towers, rising from
a palace on the plain to a
castle in the air—would have
thought it a truly romantic
place; and the impression
would not have subsided much
on a near inspection, when he
would have found himself
admitted by a fortified gate
through an ancient wall, still
kept in repair. Even on entering the one old street of which
the city chiefly consisted, he would have seen much to admire—

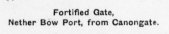

Fortified Gate,
Nether Bow Port, from Canongate.

houses of substantial architecture and lofty proportions, mingled
with more lowly, but also more arresting wooden fabrics ; a huge
and irregular, but venerable Gothic church, surmounted by an
aërial crown of masonry ; finally, an esplanade towards the Castle,
from which he could have looked abroad upon half a score of
counties, upon firth and fell, yea, even to the blue Grampians.
Everywhere he would have seen symptoms of denseness of
population ; the open street a universal market ; a pell-mell of
people everywhere. The eye would have been, upon the whole,
gratified, whatever might be the effect of the *clangor strepi-
tusque* upon the ear, or whatever might have been the private
meditations of the nose. It would have only been on coming
to close quarters, or to quarters at all, that our stranger would
have begun to think of serious drawbacks from the first impression. For an inn, he would have had the White Horse, in
a close in the Canongate ; or the White Hart, a house which
now appears like a carrier's inn, in the Grassmarket. Or, had
he betaken himself to a private lodging, which he would have
probably done under the conduct of a ragged varlet, speaking
more of his native Gaelic than English, he would have had to
ascend four or five stories of a common stair, into the narrow

chambers of
some Mrs
Balgray or
Luckie Fer-
gusson, where
a closet-bed
in the sitting-
room would
have been
displayed as
the most com-
fortable place
in the world ;
and he would
have had, for
amusement, a
choice be-
tween an ex-

House-tops.

tensive view of house-tops from the window and the study of a
series of prints of the four seasons, a sampler, and a portrait of
the Marquis of Granby, upon the wall.

On being introduced into society, our stranger might have discovered cause for content with his lodging on finding how poorly off were the first people with respect to domestic accommodations. I can imagine him going to tea at Mr Bruce of Kennet's, in Forrester's Wynd—a country gentleman and a lawyer (not long after raised to the bench), yet happy to live with his wife and children in a house of fifteen pounds of rent, in a region of profound darkness and mystery, now no more. Had he got into familiar terms with the worthy lady of the mansion, he might have ascertained that they had just three rooms and a kitchen; one room, 'my lady's'—that is, the kind of parlour he was sitting in; another, a consulting-room for the gentleman; the third, a bedroom. The children, with their maid, had beds laid down for them at night in their father's room; the housemaid slept under the kitchen dresser; and the one man-servant was turned at night out of the house. Had our friend chanced to get amongst tradespeople, he might have found Mr Kerr, the eminent goldsmith in the Parliament Square, stowing his *ménage* into a couple of small rooms above his booth-like shop, plastered against the wall of St Giles's Church; the nursery and kitchen, however, being placed in a cellar under the level of the street, where the children are said to have rotted off like sheep.

But indeed everything was on a homely and narrow scale. The College—where Munro, Cullen, and Black were already making themselves great names—was to be approached through a mean alley, the College Wynd. The churches were chiefly clustered under one roof; the jail was a narrow building, half-filling up the breadth of the street; the public offices, for the most part, obscure places in lanes and dark entries. The men of learning and wit, united with a proportion of men of rank, met as the *Poker Club* in a tavern, the best of its day, but only a dark house in a close, to which our stranger could scarcely have made his way without a guide. In a similar situation across the way, he would have found, at the proper season, the *Assembly*; that is, a congregation of ladies met for dancing, and whom the gentlemen usually joined rather late, and rather merry. The only theatre was also a poor and obscure place in some indescribable part of the Canongate.

The town was, nevertheless, a funny, familiar, compact, and not unlikable place. Gentle and semple living within the compass of a single close, or even a single stair, knew and took an interest in

each other.* Acquaintances might not only be formed, Pyramus-
and-Thisbe fashion, through party-walls, but from window to
window across alleys, narrow enough in many cases to allow of
hand coming to hand, and even lip to lip. There was little
elegance, but a vast amount of cheap sociality. Provokingly
comical clubs, founded each upon one joke, were abundant. The
ladies had tea-drinkings at the primitive hour of six, from which
they cruised home under the care of a lantern-bearing, patten-shod
lass ; or perhaps, if a bad night, in Saunders Macalpine's sedan-
chair. Every forenoon, for several hours, the only clear space
which the town presented—that around the Cross—was crowded
with loungers of all ranks, whom it had been an amusement to
the poet Gay to survey from the neighbouring windows of Allan
Ramsay's shop. The jostle and huddlement was extreme everywhere. Gentlemen and ladies paraded along in the stately attire
of the period ; tradesmen chatted in groups, often bareheaded,
at their shop-doors ; caddies whisked about, bearing messages,
or attending to the affairs of strangers ; children filled the kennel
with their noisy sports. Add to all this, corduroyed men from
Gilmerton, bawling coals or yellow sand, and spending as much
breath in a minute as could have served poor asthmatic Hugo
Arnot for a month ; fishwomen crying their caller haddies from
Newhaven ; whimsicals and idiots going along, each with his or
her crowd of listeners or tormentors ; sootymen with their bags ;
town-guardsmen with their antique Lochaber axes ; water-carriers
with their dripping barrels ; barbers with their hair-dressing
materials ; and so forth—and our stranger would have been
disposed to acknowledge that, though a coarse and confused, it
was a perfectly unique scene, and one which, once contemplated,
was not easily to be forgotten.

A change at length began. Our northern country had settled
to sober courses in the reign of George II., and the usual results
of industry were soon apparent. Edinburgh by-and-by felt much
like a lady who, after long being content with a small and inconvenient house, is taught, by the money in her husband's pockets,
that such a place is no longer to be put up with. There was a

---

* Mr W. B. Blaikie (*The Book of the Old Edinburgh Club*, vol. ii.) gives a
list of the occupants of a first-class tenement some years subsequent to the
'45 Rebellion : 'First-floor, Mrs Stirling, fishmonger ; second, Mrs Urquhart,
lodging-house keeper ; third-floor, the Countess Dowager of Balcarres ; fourth,
Mrs Buchan of Kelloe ; fifth, the Misses Elliot, milliners and mantua-makers ;
garrets, a variety of tailors and other tradesmen.'

wish to expatiate over some of the neighbouring grounds, so as to get more space and freer air; only it was difficult to do, considering the physical circumstances of the town, and the character of the existing outlets. Space, space!—air, air! was, however, a strong and a general cry, and the old romantic city did at length burst from its bounds, though not in a very regular way, or for a time to much good purpose.

A project for a new street on the site of Halkerston's Wynd, leading by a bridge to the grounds of Mutrie's Hill, where a suburb might be erected, was formed before the end of the seventeenth century.* It was a subject of speculation to John, Earl of Mar, during his years of exile, as were many other schemes of national improvement which have since been realised—for example, the Forth and Clyde Canal. The grounds to the north lay so invitingly open that the early formation of such a project is not wonderful. Want of spirit and of means alone could delay its execution. After the Rebellion of 1745, when a general spirit of improvement began to be shown in Scotland, the scheme was taken up by a public-spirited provost, Mr George Drummond, but it had to struggle for years with local difficulties. Meanwhile, a sagacious builder, by name James Brown, resolved to take advantage of the growing taste; he purchased a field near the town for £1200, and *feued* it out for a square. The speculation is said to have ended in something like giving him his own money as an annual return. This place (George Square) became the residence of several of the judges and gentry. I was amused a few years ago hearing an old gentleman in the country begin a story thus: ' When I was in Edinburgh, in the year '67, I went to George Square, to call for Mrs Scott of Sinton,' &c. To this day some relics of gentry cling to its grass-green causeways, charmed, perhaps, by its propinquity to the Meadows and Bruntsfield Links. Another place sprang into being, a smaller quadrangle of neat houses, called Brown's Square.† So much was thought of it at first that a correspondent of the *Edinburgh Advertiser*, in 1764, seriously counsels his fellow-citizens to erect in it an equestrian statue of the then popular young king, George III.! This place, too, had some distinguished inhabitants; till 1846, one of the houses continued to be nominally the town mansion of a venerable judge, Lord Glenlee. We pass willingly from these traits of grandeur to dwell on the fact of its having

* Pamphlet *circa* 1700, Wodrow Collection, Adv. Lib.

† Brown Square finally disappeared with the making of Chambers Street.

been the residence of Miss Jeanie Elliot of Minto, the authoress of the original song, *The Flowers of the Forest;* and even to bethink ourselves that here Scott placed the ideal abode of Saunders Fairford and the adventure of Green Mantle. Sir Walter has informed us, from his own recollections, that the inhabitants of these southern districts formed for a long time a distinct class of themselves, having even places of polite amusement for their own recreation, independent of the rest of Edinburgh. He tells us that the society was of the first description, including, for one thing, most of the gentlemen who wrote in the *Mirror* and the *Lounger.* There was one venerable inhabitant who did not die till half the New Town was finished, yet he had never once seen it !

The exertions of Drummond at length procured an act (1767) for extending the royalty of the city over the northern fields ; and a bridge was then erected to connect these with the elder city. The scheme was at first far from popular. The exposure to the north and east winds was felt as a grievous disadvantage, especially while houses were few. So unpleasant even was the North Bridge considered that a lover told a New-Town mistress —to be sure only in an epigram—that when he visited her, he felt as performing an adventure not much short of that of Leander. The aristocratic style of the place alarmed a number of pockets, and legal men trembled lest their clients and other employers should forget them if they removed so far from the centre of things as Princes Street and St Andrew Square. Still, the move was unavoidable, and behoved to be made.

It is curious to cast the eye over the beautiful city which now extends over this district, the residence of as refined a mass of people as could be found in any similar space of ground upon earth, and reflect on what the place was a hundred years ago. The bulk of it was a farm, usually called Wood's Farm, from its tenant (the father of a clever surgeon, well known in Edinburgh in the last age under the familiar appellation of *Lang Sandy Wood).* Henry Mackenzie, author of the *Man of Feeling,* who died in 1831, remembered shooting snipes, hares, and partridges about that very spot to which he alludes at the beginning of the paper on Nancy Collins in the *Mirror* (July 1779) : ' As I walked one evening, about a fortnight ago, *through St Andrew Square,* I observed a girl meanly dressed,' &c. Nearly along the line now occupied by Princes Street was a rough enclosed road, called the *Lang Gait* or *Lang Dykes,* the way along which Claverhouse went with his troopers in 1689, when he retired in disgust from the Convention, with the resolution of raising a rebellion in the Highlands. On the site of the present Register House was a hamlet or small group of houses called *Mutrie's Hill;* and where the Royal Bank now stands was a cottage wherein ambulative citizens regaled themselves with fruit and curds and cream. Broughton, which latterly has been surprised and swamped by the spreading city, was then a village, considered as so far afield that people went to live in it for the summer months, under the pleasing idea that they had got into the country. It is related that Whitefield used to preach to vast multitudes on the spot which by-and-by became appropriated for the *Theatre Royal.* Coming back one year, and finding a playhouse on the site of his tub, he was extremely incensed. Could it be, as Burns suggests,

'There was rivalry just in the job!'

James Craig, a nephew of the poet Thomson, was entrusted with the duty of planning the new city. In the engraved plan, he appropriately quotes from his uncle:

'August, around, what PUBLIC WORKS I see!
Lo, stately streets! lo, squares that court the breeze!
See long canals and deepened rivers join
Each part with each, and with the circling main,
The whole entwined isle.'

The names of the streets and squares were taken from the royal family and the tutelary saints of the island. The honest citizens had originally intended to put their own local saint in the foreground; but when the plan was shown to the king for his approval, he cried: 'Hey, hey—what, what—*St Giles Street!*—never do, never do!' And so, to escape from an unpleasant association of ideas, this street was called *Princes Street,* in honour of the king's two sons, afterwards George IV. and the Duke of York. So difficult was it at the very first to induce men to build that a premium of twenty pounds was offered by the magistrates to him who should raise the first house; it was awarded to Mr John Young, on account of a mansion erected by him in Rose Court, George Street. An exemption from burghal taxes was granted to the first house in the line of Princes Street, built by Mr John Neale, haberdasher (afterwards occupied by Archibald Constable, and then as the Crown Hotel), in consequence of a bargain made by Mr Graham, plumber, who sold

this and the adjoining ground to the town.* Mr Shadrach Moyes,
when having a house built for himself in Princes Street, in 1769,
took the builder bound to rear another farther along besides his,
to shield him from the west wind! Other quaint particulars are
remembered; as, for instance: Mr Wight, an eminent lawyer,
who had planted himself in St Andrew Square, finding he was in
danger of having his view of St Giles's clock shut up by the
advancing line of Princes Street, built the intervening house
himself, that he might have it in his power to keep the roof low
for the sake of the view in question; important to him, he said,
as enabling him to regulate his movements in the morning, when
it was necessary that he should be punctual in his attendance at
the Parliament House.

The foundation was at length laid of that revolution which has
ended in making Edinburgh a kind of double city—*first*, an
ancient and picturesque hill-built one, occupied chiefly by the
humbler classes; and *second*, an elegant modern one, of much
regularity of aspect, and possessed almost as exclusively by the
more refined portion of society. The New Town, keeping pace
with the growing prosperity of the country, had, in 1790, been
extended to Castle Street; in 1800 the necessity for a second
plan of the same extent still farther to the north had been felt,
and this was after acted upon. Forty years saw the Old Town
thoroughly changed as respects population. One after another,
its nobles and gentry, its men of the robe, its ' writers,' and even
its substantial burghers, had during that time deserted their
mansions in the High Street and Canongate, till few were left.
Even those modern districts connected with it, as St John Street,
New Street, George Square, &c., were beginning to be forsaken
for the sake of more elegantly circumstanced habitations beyond
the North Loch. Into the remote social consequences of this
change it is not my purpose to enter, beyond the bare remark
that it was only too accordant with that tendency of our present
form of civilisation to separate the high from the low, the intelligent from the ignorant—that dissociation, in short, which would
in itself run nigh to be a condemnation of all progress, if we
were not allowed to suppose that better forms of civilisation are
realisable. Enough that I mention the tangible consequences of
the revolution—a flooding in of the humbler trading classes where
gentles once had been; the houses of these classes, again, filled

* Mr William Cowan, in vol. i. of *The Book of the Old Edinburgh Club*, says
this exemption applied to the three eastmost tenements in Princes Street.

NEWHAVEN FISHWIFE.

DUKE OF GORDON'S HOUSE.

Page 18.

with the vile and miserable. Now were to be seen hundreds of instances of such changes as Provost Creech indicates in 1783 : 'The Lord Justice-Clerk Tinwald's house possessed by a French teacher—Lord President Craigie's house by a rouping-wife or salewoman of old furniture—and Lord Drummore's house left by a chairman for want of accommodation.' 'The house of the Duke of Douglas at the Union, now possessed by a wheelwright !' To one who, like myself, was young in the early part of the present century, it was scarcely possible, as he permeated the streets and closes of ancient Edinburgh, to realise the idea of a time when the great were housed therein. But many a gentleman in middle life, then living perhaps in Queen Street or Charlotte Square, could recollect the close or the common stair where he had been born and spent his earliest years, now altogether given up to a different portion of society. And when the younger perambulator inquired more narrowly, he could discover traces of this former population. Here and there a carved coat-armorial, with supporters, perhaps even a coronet, arrested attention amidst the obscurities of some *wynd* or court. Did he ascend a stair and enter a floor, now subdivided perhaps into four or five distinct dwellings, he might readily perceive, in the massive wainscot of the lobby, a proof that the refinements of life had once been there. Still more would this idea be impressed upon him when, passing into one of the best rooms of the old house, he would find not only a continuation of such wainscoting, but perhaps a tolerable landscape by Norie on a panel above the fireplace, or a ceiling decorated by De la Cour, a French artist, who flourished in

Carved Armorial, with Supporters.

Edinburgh about 1740. Even yet he would discover a very few relics of gentry maintaining their ground in the Old Town, as if faintly to show what it had once been. These were generally old people, who did not think it worth while to make any change

till the great one. There is a melancholy pleasure in recalling
what I myself found about 1820, when my researches for this
work were commenced. In that year I was in the house of
Governor Fergusson, an ancient gentleman of the Pitfour family,
in a floor, one stair up, in the Luckenbooths. About the same
time I attended the book-sale of Dr Arrot, a physician of good
figure, newly deceased, in the Mint Close. For several years later,
any one ascending a now miserable-looking stair in Blackfriars
Wynd would have seen a door-plate inscribed with the name
MISS OLIPHANT, a member of the Gask family. Nay, so late as
1832, I had the pleasure of breakfasting with Sir William Macleod
Bannatyne in Whiteford House, Canongate (afterwards a type-
foundry), on which occasion the venerable old gentleman talked
as familiarly of the levees of the *sous-ministre* for Lord Bute in the
old villa at the Abbey Hill as I could have talked of the affairs
of the Canning administration; and even recalled, as a fresh
picture of his memory, his father drawing on his boots to go
to make interest in London in behalf of some of the men in
trouble for the Forty-five, particularly his own brother-in-law,
the Clanranald of that day. Such were the connections recently
existing between the past system of things and the present. Now,
alas! the sun of Old-Town glory has set for ever. Nothing is
left but the decaying and rapidly diminishing masses of ancient
masonry, and a handful of traditionary recollections, which be
it my humble but not unworthy task to transmit to future
generations.*

---

* The late Bruce J. Home drew up in 1908 'A Provisional List of Old Houses
Remaining in High Street and Canongate,' which was printed, with accompanying map, in the first volume of *The Old Edinburgh Club Book*. The statement
is therein made 'that since 1860 two-thirds of the ancient buildings in the Old
Town of Edinburgh have been demolished.' The map showed, coloured in red,
the remaining buildings of the Old Town which had survived until the beginning
of the twentieth century.

THE CASTLE-HILL.

Hugo Arnot—Allan Ramsay—House of the Gordon Family—Sir David Baird—Dr Webster—House of Mary de Guise.

THE saunter which I contemplate through the streets and stories, the lanes and legends, of Old Edinburgh may properly commence at the Castle-hill, as it is a marked extremity of the city as well as its highest ground.

The Castle-hill is partly an esplanade, serving as a parade-ground for the garrison of the Castle, and partly a street, the upper portion of that vertebral line which, under the various names of Lawnmarket, High Street, and Canongate, extends to Holyrood Palace. The open ground—a scene of warfare during the sieges of the fortress, often a place of execution in rude times—the place, too, where, by a curious legal fiction, the Nova Scotia baronets were enfeoffed in their ideal estates on the other side of the Atlantic—was all that Edinburgh possessed as a readily accessible promenade before the extension of the city. We find the severe acts for a strict observance of the Sabbath, which appeared from time to time in the latter part of the seventeenth and early part of the eighteenth century, denouncing the King's Park, the Pier of Leith, and the *Castle-hill* as the places chiefly resorted to for the profane sport of walking on 'the Lord's Day.' Denounce as they might, human nature could never, I believe, be altogether kept off the Castle-hill; even the most respectable people walked there in multitudes during the intervals between morning and evening service. We have an allusion to the promenade character of the Castle-hill in Ramsay's city pastoral, as it may be called, of *The Young Laird and Edinburgh Katy*—

> ' Wat ye wha I met yestreen,
>   Coming down the street, my jo?
> My mistress in her tartan screen,
>   Fu' bonny, braw, and sweet, my jo.
>
> "My dear," quoth I, "thanks to the night,
>   That never wished a lover ill,
> Since ye 're out o' your mother's sight,
>   Let 's tak' a walk up to *the hill*." '

A memory of these Sunday promenadings here calls me to introduce what I have to say regarding a man of whom there used to be a strong popular remembrance in Edinburgh.

HUGO ARNOT.

The cleverly executed *History of Edinburgh*, published by Arnot in 1779, and which to this day has not been superseded, gives some respectability to a name which tradition would have otherwise handed down to us as only that of an eccentric gentleman, of remarkably scarecrow figure, and the subject of a few *bon-mots*.

He was the son of a Leith shipmaster, named Pollock, and took the name of Arnot from a small inheritance in Fife. Many who have read his laborious work will be little prepared to hear that it was written when the author was between twenty and thirty; and that, antiquated as his meagre figure looks in Kay's Portraits, he was at his death, in 1786, only thirty-seven. His

body had been, in reality, made prematurely old by a confirmed asthma, accompanied by a cough, which he himself said would carry him off like a rocket some day, when a friend remarked, with reference to his known latitudinarianism: 'Possibly, Hugo, in the contrary direction.'

Most of the jokes about poor Hugo's person have been frequently printed—as Harry Erskine meeting him on the street when he was gnawing at a spelding or dried haddock, and congratulating him on *looking so like his meat;* and his offending the piety of an old woman who was cheapening a Bible in Creech's shop, by some thoughtless remark, when she first burst out with: 'Oh, you monster!' and then turning round and seeing him, added: 'And he's an anatomy too!' An epigram by Erskine is less known:

R.

Hugo Arnot, looking so like his meat.

'The Scriptures assure us that much is forgiven
    To flesh and to blood by the mercy of Heaven;
But I've searched the whole Bible, and texts can find none
    That extend the assurance *to skin and to bone.*'

Arnot was afflicted by a constitutional irritability to an extent which can hardly be conceived. A printer's boy, handing papers to him over his shoulder, happened to touch his ear with one of them, when he started up in a rage, and demanded of the trembling youth what he meant by insulting him in that manner! Probably from some quarrel arising out of this nervous weakness —for such it really was—the Edinburgh booksellers, to a man, refused to have anything to do with the prospectuses of his *Criminal Trials*, and Arnot had to advertise that they were to be seen in the coffee-houses, instead of the booksellers' shops.

About the time when he entered at the bar (1772), he had a fancy for a young lady named Hay (afterwards Mrs Macdougall), sister of a gentleman who succeeded as Marquis of Tweeddale, and then a reigning toast. One Sunday, when he contemplated making up to his divinity on the Castle-hill, after forenoon service, he entertained two young friends at breakfast in his lodgings at the head of the Canongate. By-and-by the affairs of the toilet came to be considered. It was then found that Hugo's washerwoman had played false, leaving him in a total destitution of clean linen, or at least of clean linen that was also *whole*. A dreadful storm took place, but at length, on its calming a little, love found out a way, by taking the hand-ruffles of one cast garment, in connection with the front of another, and adding both to the body of a third. In this eclectic form of shirt the meagre young philosopher marched forth with his friends, and was rewarded for his perseverance by being allowed a very pleasant chat with the young lady on 'the hill.' His friends standing by had their own enjoyment in reflecting what the beauteous Miss Hay would think if she knew the struggles which her admirer had had that morning in preparing to make his appearance before her.

Arnot latterly dwelt in a small house at the end of the Meuse Lane in St Andrew Street, with an old and very particular lady for a neighbour in the upper-floor. Disturbed by the enthusiastic way in which he sometimes rang his bell, the lady ventured to send a remonstrance, which, however, produced no effect. This led to a bad state of matters between them. At length a very pressing and petulant message being handed in one day, insisting that he should endeavour to call his servants *in a different manner*, what was the lady's astonishment next morning to hear a pistol discharged in Arnot's house! He was simply complying with the letter of his neighbour's request, by firing, instead of ringing, as a signal for shaving-water.

ALLAN RAMSAY.

On the north side of the esplanade—enjoying a splendid view of the Firth of Forth, Fife and Stirling shires—is the neat little villa of Allan Ramsay, surrounded by its miniature pleasure-grounds. The sober, industrious life of this exception to the race of poets having resulted in a small competency, he built this odd-shaped house in his latter days, designing to enjoy in it the Horatian quiet which he had so often eulogised in his verse. The story goes that, showing it soon after to the clever Patrick, Lord Elibank, with much fussy interest in all its externals and accommodations, he remarked that the wags were already at work on the subject — they likened it to a goose-pie * (owing to the roundness of the shape). 'Indeed, Allan,' said his lordship, 'now I see you in it, I think the wags are not far wrong.'

Allan Ramsay's Villa.

The splendid reputation of Burns has eclipsed that of Ramsay so effectually that this pleasing poet, and, upon the whole, amiable and worthy man, is now little regarded. Yet Ramsay can never be deprived of the credit of having written the best pastoral poem in the range of British literature—if even that be not too narrow a word—and many of his songs are of great merit.

Ramsay was secretly a Jacobite, openly a dissenter from the severe manners and feelings of his day, although a very decent and regular attender of the Old Church in St Giles's. He delighted in music and theatricals, and, as we shall see, encouraged the Assembly. It was also no doubt his own taste

* This jest was doubtless based on Swift's famous poem on Vanbrugh's house (1704). The peculiar architectural features of Allan's 'goose pie' have been almost entirely obliterated by recent alterations. Only the two circular upper stories remain in their original form.

which led him, in 1725, to set up a circulating library, whence he diffused plays and other works of fiction among the people of Edinburgh. It appears, from the private notes of the historian Wodrow, that, in 1728, the magistrates, moved by some meddling spirits, took alarm at the effect of this kind of reading on the minds of youth, and made an attempt to put it down, but without effect. One cannot but be amused to find amongst these self-constituted guardians of morality Lord Grange, who kept his wife in unauthorised restraint for several years, and whose own life was a scandal to his professions. Ramsay, as is well known, also attempted to establish a theatre in Edinburgh, but failed. The following advertisement on this subject appears in the *Caledonian Mercury*, September 1736 : 'The New Theatre in Carrubber's Close being in great forwardness, will be opened the 1st of November. These are to advertise the gentlemen and ladies who incline to purchase annual tickets, to enter their names before the 20th of October next, on which day they shall receive their tickets from Allan Ramsay, on paying 30s.—no more than forty to be subscribed for ; after which none will be disposed of under two guineas.'

The late Mrs Murray of Henderland knew Ramsay for the last ten years of his life, her sister having married his son, the celebrated painter. She spoke of him to me in 1825, with kindly enthusiasm, as one of the most amiable men she had ever known. His constant cheerfulness and lively conversational powers had made him a favourite amongst persons of rank, whose guest he frequently was. Being very fond of children, he encouraged his daughters in bringing troops of young ladies about the house, in whose sports he would mix with a patience and vivacity wonderful in an old man. He used to give these young friends a kind of ball once a year. From pure kindness for the young, he would help to make dolls for them, and cradles wherein to place these little effigies, with his own hands.* But here a fashion of the age must be held in view ; for, however odd it may appear, it is undoubtedly true that to make and dispose of dolls, such as children now alone are interested in, was a practice in vogue amongst grown-up ladies who had little to do about a hundred years ago.

* 'My mother was told by those who had enjoyed his plays, that he had a child's puppet stage and a set of dressed dolls for actors, which were in great favour with old and young.'—C. K. Sharpe's note in Wilson's *Reminiscences*.

Ramsay died in 1757. An elderly female told a friend of mine that she remembered, when a girl, living as an apprentice with a milliner in the Grassmarket, being sent to Ramsay Garden to assist in making *dead-clothes* for the poet. She could recall, however, no particulars of the scene but the roses blooming in at the window of the death-chamber.

The poet's house passed to his son, of the same name, eminent as a painter—portrait-painter to King George III. and his queen —and a man of high mental culture; consequently much a favourite in the circles of Johnson and Boswell. The younger Allan enlarged the house, and built three additional houses to the eastward, bearing the title of Ramsay Garden. At his death, in 1784, the property went to his son, General John Ramsay, who, dying in 1845, left this mansion and a large fortune to Mr Murray of Henderland. So ended the line of the poet. His daughter Christian, an amiable, kind-hearted woman, said to possess a gift of verse, lived for many years in New Street. At seventy-four she had the misfortune to be thrown down by a hackney-coach, and had her leg broken; yet she recovered, and lived to the age of eighty-eight. Leading a solitary life, she took a great fancy for cats. Besides supporting many in her own house, curiously disposed in bandboxes, with doors to go in and out at, she caused food to be laid out for others on her stair and around her house. Not a word of obloquy would she listen to against the species, alleging, when any wickedness of a cat was spoken of, that the animal must have acted under provocation, for by nature, she asserted, cats are harmless. Often did her maid go with morning messages to her friends, inquiring, with her compliments, after their pet cats. Good Miss Ramsay was also a friend to horses, and indeed to all creatures. When she observed a carter ill-treating his horse, she would march up to him, tax him with cruelty, and, by the very earnestness of her remonstrances, arrest the barbarian's hand. So also, when she saw one labouring on the street, with the appearance of defective diet, she would send rolls to its master, entreating him to feed the animal. These

Happy.

Contented.

Repose.

Convivial.

peculiarities, although a little eccentric, are not unpleasing; and I cannot be sorry to record them of the daughter of one whose heart and head were an honour to his country.

[1868.—It seems to have been unknown to the biographers of Allan Ramsay the painter that he made a romantic marriage. In his early days, while teaching the art of drawing in the family of Sir Alexander Lindsay of Evelick, one of the young ladies fell in love with him, captivated probably by the tongue which afterwards gave him the intimacy of princes, and was undoubtedly a great source of his success in life. The father of the enamoured girl was an old proud baronet; her mother, a sister of the Chief-Justice, Earl of Mansfield. A marriage with consent of parents was consequently impossible. The young people, nevertheless, contrived to get themselves united in wedlock.

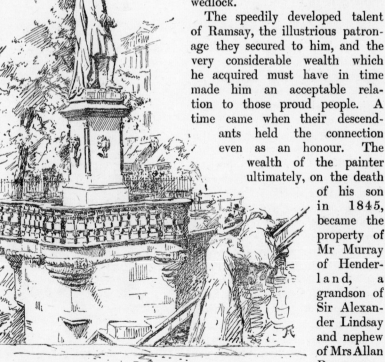

Allan Ramsay's Monument, Princes Street Gardens.

The speedily developed talent of Ramsay, the illustrious patronage they secured to him, and the very considerable wealth which he acquired must have in time made him an acceptable relation to those proud people. A time came when their descendants held the connection even as an honour. The wealth of the painter ultimately, on the death of his son in 1845, became the property of Mr Murray of Henderland, a grandson of Sir Alexander Lindsay and nephew of Mrs Allan Ramsay;

thence it not long after passed to Mr Murray's brother, Sir John
Archibald Murray, better known by his judicial name of Lord
Murray. This gentleman admired the poet, and resolved to
raise a statue to him beside his goose-pie house on the Castle-
hill; but the situation proved unsuitable, and since his own
lamented death, in 1858, the marble full-length of worthy
Allan, from the studio of John Steell, has found a noble
place in the Princes Street Gardens, resting on a pedestal,
containing on its principal side a medallion portrait of Lord
Murray, on the reverse one of General Ramsay, on the
west side one of the General's lady, and on the east similar
representations of the General's two daughters, Lady Campbell
and Mrs Malcolm. Thus we find—owing to the esteem
which genius ever commands—the poet of the *Gentle Shepherd* in the immortality of marble, surrounded by the figures
of relatives and descendants who so acknowledged their aristocratic rank to be inferior to his, derived from mind alone.]

HOUSE OF THE GORDON FAMILY.

Doorway of Duke of Gordon's House.
Now built into School in Boswell's Court

Tradition points out, as the
residence of the Gordon family, a
house, or rather range of buildings, situated between Blair's and
Brown's Closes, being almost the
first mass of building in the
Castle-hill Street on the right-
hand side. The southern portion
is a structure of lofty and massive
form, battlemented at top, and
looking out upon a garden which
formerly stretched down to the old
town-wall near the Grassmarket,
but is now crossed by the access
from the King's Bridge.* From
the style of building, I should be
disposed to assign it a date a little
subsequent to the Restoration.
There are, however, no authentic

* King's Bridge crosses King's Stables
Road, and the access from it is Johnston
Terrace.

memorials respecting the alleged connection of the Gordon family with this house,* unless we are to consider as of that character a coronet resembling that of a marquis, flanked by two deer-hounds, the well-known supporters of this noble family, which figures over a finely moulded door in Blair's Close.† The coronet will readily be supposed to point to the time when the *Marquis of Huntly* was the principal honour of the family—that is, previous to 1684, when the title of Duke of Gordon was conferred.‡

In more recent times, this substantial mansion was the abode of

* When Mrs Cockburn, author of 'Flowers of the Forest,' entered on occupation of the house in 1756, it was described in the Baird titles as 'my lodging in the castle-hill of Edinburgh, formerly possessed by the Duchess of Gordon.'

† A Board-school now occupies the site of the mansion. The doorway referred to is rebuilt into the school-house.

‡ George, sixth Earl of Huntly, took his last illness, June 1636, in 'his house in the Canongate.' George, the first duke, who had held out the Castle at the Revolution, died December 1716, at his house in the Citadel of Leith, where he appears to have occasionally resided for some years. I should suppose the house on the Castle-hill to have been inhabited by the family in the interval. The Citadel seems to have been a little nest of aristocracy, of the Cavalier party. In 1745 one of its inhabitants was Dame Magdalen Bruce of Kinross, widow of the baronet who had assisted in the Restoration. Here lived with her the Rev. Robert Forbes, Episcopal minister of Leith [afterwards Bishop of Orkney], from whose collections regarding Charles Edward and his adventures a volume of extracts was published by me in 1834. [The *Lyon in Mourning* is here referred to, from which Dr Chambers published a number of the narratives in his *Jacobite Memoirs* (1834), and from which he also utilised some information of the Rebellion of 1745 in the preparation of his *History of the Rebellion.* At his death he bequeathed the work to the Advocates' Library, Edinburgh, where it now remains. It consists of eight small octavo volumes of manuscript of about two hundred pages, each bound in black leather, with blackened edges, and around the title-page of each volume a deep black border. The collection was the work of the Rev. Robert Forbes, a clergyman of the Episcopal Church of Scotland, who became in 1762 Bishop of Ross and Caithness. It was treasured by his widow for thirty years, and then bought by Sir Henry Stewart of Allanton in 1806. Dr Robert Chambers unearthed it for historical purposes, and later purchased it from Sir Henry Stewart. Some relics which Forbes succeeded in obtaining from his correspondents—such as a piece of the Prince's garter, a piece of the gown he wore as Betty Burke, and of the string of the apron he then had on, a fragment of a waistcoat worn by the Prince, and other things—were preserved on the inside of some of the boards of the volumes. The *Lyon in Mourning* was edited by Mr Henry Paton from the manuscript in the Advocates' Library, and published in three volumes by the Scottish History Society (1895).] Throughout those troublous days, a little Episcopal congregation was kept together in Leith ; their place of worship being the *first floor* of an old, dull-looking house in Queen Street (dated 1615), the lower floor of which was, in my recollection, a police-office.

Mr Baird of Newbyth ; and here it was that the late gallant Sir
David Baird, the hero of Seringapatam, was born and brought up.
Returning in advanced life from long foreign service, this distinguished soldier came to see the home of his youth on the Castle-
hill. The respectable individual whom I found occupying the
house in 1824 received his visitor with due respect, and after
showing him through the house, conducted him out to the garden.
Here the boys of the existing tenant were found actively engaged
in throwing cabbage-stalks at the tops of the chimneys of the
houses of the Grassmarket, situated a little below the level of the
garden. On making one plump down the vent, the youngsters
set up a great shout of triumph. Sir David fell a-laughing at
sight of this example of practical waggery, and entreated the
father of the lads ' not to be too angry ; he and his brother, when
living here at the same age, had indulged in precisely the same
amiable amusement, the chimneys then, as now, being so provokingly open to such attacks that there was no resisting the
temptation.'

The whole matter might have been put into an axiomatic form
—Given a garden with cabbage-stalks, and a set of chimneys
situated at an angle of forty-five degrees below the spot, any boys
turned loose into the said garden will be sure to endeavour to
bring the cabbage-stalks and the chimneys into acquaintance.

DR WEBSTER.

An isolated house which formerly stood in Webster's Close,* a
little way down the Castle-hill, was the residence of the Rev. Dr
Webster, a man eminent in his day on many accounts—a leading
evangelical clergyman in Edinburgh, a statist and calculator of
extraordinary talent, and a distinguished figure in festive scenes.
The first population returns of Scotland were obtained by him in
1755 ; and he was the author of that fund for the widows of the
clergy of the Established Church which has proved so great a
blessing to many, and still exists in a flourishing state.† He was

* Webster's Close became Brown's Close when the property changed hands,
and two brothers of that name occupied the house. To Brown's Close the
recently formed Society of Antiquaries of Scotland removed in 1794 from
Gosford's Close, because the latter was too narrow to admit of the members
being carried to the place of meeting in sedan-chairs.

† Before the Government bounty had supplemented the poor stipends of the
Scotch Church up to £150, many of them were so small that the widow's
allowance from this fund nearly equalled them. Such was the case of Cran-

also deep in the consultations of the magistrates regarding the New Town.

It is not easy to reconcile the two leading characteristics of this divine—his being the pastor of a flock of noted sternness, called, from the church in which they assembled, the *Tolbooth Whigs;* and his at the same time entering heartily and freely into the convivialities of the more mirthful portion of society. Perhaps he illustrated the maxim that one man may steal horses with impunity, &c.; for it is is related that, going home early one morning with strong symptoms of over-indulgence upon him, and being asked by a friend who met him ' what the Tolbooth Whigs would say if they were to see him at this moment,' he instantly replied : ' They would not believe their own eyes.' Sometimes he did fall on such occasions under plebeian observation, but the usual remark was : ' Ah, there 's Dr Webster, honest man, going hame, nae doubt, frae some puir afflicted soul he has been visiting. Never does he tire o' well-doing ! ' And so forth.

The history of Dr Webster's marriage is romantic. When a young and unknown man, he was employed by a friend to act as go-between, or, as it is termed in Scotland, black-fit, or black-foot, in a correspondence which he was carrying on with a young lady of great beauty and accomplishment. Webster had not acted long in that character, till the young lady, who had never entertained any affection for his constituent, fell deeply in love with himself. Her birth and expectations were better than his ; and however much he might have been disposed to address her on his own behalf, he never could have thought of such a thing so long as there was such a difference between their circumstances. The lady saw his difficulty, and resolved to overcome it, and that in the frankest manner. At one of these interviews, when he was exerting all his eloquence in favour of his friend, she plainly told him that he would probably come better speed if he were to speak for himself. He took the hint, and, in a word, was soon after married to her. He wrote upon the occasion an amorous lyric, which exhibits in warm colours the gratitude of a humble lover for the favour of a mistress of superior station, and which is perhaps as excellent altogether in its way as the finest compositions

shaws, a pastoral parish among the Lammermoor Hills. A former minister of Cranshaws having wooed a lass of humble rank, the father of the lady, when consulted on the subject, said, 'Tak' him, Jenny; he 's as gude deid as living ! ' meaning, of course, that she would be as well off as a widow as in the quality of a wife.

of the kind produced in either ancient or modern times. There is one particularly impassioned verse, in which, after describing a process of the imagination by which, in gazing upon her, he comes to think her a creature of more than mortal nature, he says that at length, unable to contain, he clasps her to his bosom, and—

'Kissing her lips, she turns woman again!'

HOUSE OF MARY DE GUISE.

The restrictions imposed upon a city requiring defence appear as one of the forms of misery leading to strange associations. We become, in a special degree, sensible of this truth when we see the house of a royal personage sunk amidst the impurities of a narrow close in the Old Town of Edinburgh. Such was literally the case of an aged pile of buildings on the north side of the Castle-hill, behind the front line of the street, and accessible by Blyth's, Nairn's, and Tod's Closes, which was declared by tradition to have been the residence of Mary de Guise, the widow of James V., and from 1554 to 1560 regent of this realm.

Ancient Pile of Buildings, North Side of Castle-Hill.

Descending the first of these alleys about thirty yards, we came to a dusky, half-ruinous building on the left-hand side, presenting one or two lofty windows and a doorway, surrounded by handsome mouldings; the whole bearing that appearance which says: 'There is here something that has been of consequence, all haggard and disgraced though it now be.' Glancing to the opposite side of the close, where stood another portion of the same building, the impression was confirmed by further appearances of a goodly style of architecture. These were, in reality, the principal portions of the palace of the Regent Mary; the former being popularly described as her *house*, the latter as her *oratory* or chapel. The close terminated under a portion of the building; and when the visitor made his way so far, he found an exterior presented northwards, with many windows, whence of old a view must have been commanded, first of the gardens descending to the North Loch, and second, of the Firth of Forth and Fife. One could easily understand that, when the gardens existed, the north side of the house might have had many pleasant apartments, and been, upon the whole, tolerable as a place of residence, albeit the access by a narrow alley could never have been agreeable. Latterly the site of the upper part of the garden was occupied by a brushmaker's workshops and yard, while the lower was covered by the Earthen Mound. In the wall on the east side there was included, as a mere portion of the masonry, a stray stone, which had once been an architrave or lintel; it contained, besides an armorial device flanked by the initials A. A., the legend NOSCE TEIPSUM, and the date 1557.

Reverting to the door of the queen's house, which was simply the access of a common stair, we there found an ornamented architrave, bearing the legend,

LAUS ET HONOR DEO,

terminated by two pieces of complicated lettering, one much obliterated, the other a monogram of the name of the Virgin Mary, formed of the letters M. R.* Finally, at the extremities of this stone, were two Roman letters of larger size—I. R.—doubtless the initials of James Rex, for James V., the style of cutting being precisely the same as in the initials seen on the palace built by that king in Stirling Castle; an indirect proof, it may be remarked, of this having been the residence of the Regent Mary.

Passing up a spiral flight of steps, we came to a darksome lobby, leading to a series of mean apartments, occupied by persons of the

---

* 'The monograms of the name of our blessed lady are formed of the letters M. A., M. R., and A. M., and these stand respectively for Maria, Maria Regina, and Ave Maria. The letter M. was often used by itself to express the name of the Blessed Virgin, and became a vehicle for the most beautiful ornament and design; the letter itself being entirely composed of emblems, with some passage from the life of our lady in the void spaces.'—*Pugin's Glossary of Ecclesiastical Ornament and Costume*, 1844.

humblest grade. Immediately within the door was a small recess in the wall, composed of Gothic stonework, and supposed by the people to have been designed for containing holy-water, though this may well be matter of doubt. Overhead, in the ceiling, was a round entablature, presenting a faded coronet over the defaced outline of a shield. A similar object adorned the ceiling of the lobby in the second floor, but in better preservation, as the shield bore three *fleurs de lis*, with the coronet above, and the letters H. R. below. There was a third of these entablatures, containing the arms of the city of Edinburgh, in the centre of the top of the staircase. The only other curious object in this part of the mansion was the door of one of the wretched apartments—a specimen of carving, bearing all the appearance of having been contemporary with the building, and containing, besides other devices, bust portraits of a gentleman and lady. This is now in the possession of the Society of the Antiquaries of Scotland.

A portion of the same building, accessible by a stair nearer the head of the close, contained a hall-like apartment, with other apartments, all remarkable for their unusually lofty ceilings. In the large room were the remains of a spacious decorated chimney, to which, in the recollection of persons still living, there had been attached a chain, serving to confine the tongs to their proper domain. This was the memorial of an old custom, of which it is not easy to see the utility, unless some light be held as thrown upon it by a Scottish proverb, used when a child takes a thing and says he found it : ' You found it, I suppose, where the Highlandman found the tongs.' In the centre of almost all the ceilings of this part of the mansion I found, in 1824, circular entablatures, with coats of arms and other devices, in stucco, evidently of good workmanship, but obscured by successive coats of whitening.

The place pointed out by tradition as the queen-regent's oratory was in the first-floor of the building opposite—a spacious and lofty hall, with large windows designed to make up for the obscurity of the close. Here, besides a finely carved piscina, was a pretty large recess, of Gothic structure, in the back-wall, evidently designed for keeping things of importance. Many years ago, out of the wall behind this recess, there had been taken a small iron box, such as might have been employed to keep jewellery, but empty. I was the means of its being gifted to Sir Walter Scott, who had previously told me that ' a passion for such little boxes was one of

THE BOWHEAD.

PAGE 27.

GRASSMARKET
from west end of Cowgate.

those that most did beset him ; ' and it is now in the collection at Abbotsford.

The other portions of the mansion, accessible from different alleys, were generally similar to these, but somewhat finer. One chamber was recognised as the *Deid-room;* that is, the room where individuals of the queen's establishment were kept between their death and burial.

It was interesting to wander through the dusky mazes of this ancient building, and reflect that they had been occupied three centuries ago by a sovereign princess, and one of the most illustrious lineage. Here was the substantial monument of a connection between France and Scotland, a totally past state of things. She whose ancestors owned Lorraine as a sovereignty, who had spent her youth in the proud halls of the Guises in Picardy, and been the spouse of a Longueville, was here content to live—in a *close* in Edinburgh ! In these obscurities, too, was a government conducted, which had to struggle with Knox, Glencairn, James Stewart, Morton, and many other powerful men, backed by a popular sentiment which never fails to triumph. It was the misfortune of Mary to be placed in a position to resist the Reformation. Her own character deserved that she should have stood in a more agreeable relation to what Scotland now venerates, for she was mild and just, and sincerely anxious for the good of her adopted country. It is also proper to remember on the present occasion that ' in her court she maintained a decent gravity, nor would she tolerate any licentious practices therein. Her maids of honour were always busied in commendable exercises, she herself being an example to them in virtue, piety, and modesty.' * When all is considered, and we further know that the building was strong enough to have lasted many more ages, one cannot but regret that the palace of Mary de Guise, reduced as it was to vileness, should not now be in existence. The site having been purchased by individuals connected with the Free Church, the buildings were removed in 1846 to make room for the erection of an academical institution or college for the use of that body.†

* Keith's History.
† The New College and Assembly Hall of the (United) Free Church.

THE WEST BOW.

[The West Bow has long since disappeared as a street ; see note on p. 54.]

IN a central part of Old Edinburgh—the very Little Britain of our city—is a curious, angular, whimsical-looking street, of great steepness and narrowness, called the West Bow. Serving as a connection between the Grassmarket and Lawnmarket, between the Low and the High Town, it is of considerable fame in our city annals as a passage for the entry of sovereigns, and the scene of the quaint ceremonials used on those occasions. In more modern times, it has been chiefly notable in the recollections of country-people as a nest of the peculiarly noisy tradesmen, the white-iron smiths, which causes Robert Fergusson to mark, as one of the features of Edinburgh deserted for a holiday :

> 'The tinkler billies * o' the Bow
> Are now less eident † clinkin.'

Another remarkable circumstance connected with the street in the popular mind is its having been the residence of the famed wizard, Major Weir. All of these particulars serve to make it a noteworthy sort of place, and the impression is much favoured by its actual appearance. A perfect Z in figure, composed of tall antique houses, with numerous dovecot-like gables projecting over the footway, full of old inscriptions and sculpturings, presenting at every few steps some darksome lateral profundity, into which the imagination wanders without hindrance or exhaustion, it seems eminently a place of old grandmothers' tales, and sure at all times to maintain a ghost or two in its community. When I descend into particulars, it will be seen what grounds there truly are for such a surmise.

To begin with

---

* Fellows.   † Busy.

THE BOWHEAD.

This is a comparatively open space, though partially straightened again by the insertion in it of a clumsy, detached old building called the *Weigh-house*, where enormous masses of butter and cheese are continually getting disposed of. Prince Charles had his guard at the Weigh-house when blockading the Castle; using, however, for this purpose, not the house itself, but a floor of the adjacent tall tenement in the Lawnmarket, which appears to have been selected on a very intelligible principle, in as far as it was the deserted mansion of one of the city clergy, the same Rev. George Logan who carried on a controversy with Thomas Ruddiman, in which he took unfavourable views of the title of the Stuart family to the throne, not only then, but at any time. It was, no doubt, as an additional answer to a bad pamphlet that the Highlanders took up their quarters at Mr Logan's.

ANDERSON'S PILLS.

In this tall *land*, dated 1690, there is a house on the second-floor where that venerable drug, Dr Anderson's pills, is sold, and has been so for above a century. As is well known, the country-people in Scotland have to this day [1824] a peculiar reverence for these pills, which are, I believe, really a good form of aloetic medicine. They took their origin from a physician of the time of Charles I., who gave them his name. From his daughter, Lillias Anderson, the patent came to a person designed Thomas Weir, who left it to his daughter. The widow of this last person's nephew, Mrs Irving, is now the patentee; a lady of advanced age, who facetiously points to the very brief series of proprietors intervening between Dr Anderson and herself, as no inexpressive indication of the virtue of the medicine. [Mrs Irving died in 1837, at the age of ninety-nine.] Portraits of Anderson and his daughter are preserved in this house: the physician in a Vandyke dress, with a book in his hand; the lady, a precise-looking dame, with a pill in her hand about the size of a walnut, saying a good deal for the stomachs of our ancestors. The people also show a glove which belonged to the learned physician.

[1868.—In 1829 Mrs Irving lived in a neat, self-contained mansion in Chessels's Court, in the Canongate, along with her son, General Irving, and some members of his family. The old lady, then ninety-one, was good enough to invite me to dinner, when I likewise found two younger sisters of hers, respectively eighty-nine and ninety. She sat firm and collected at the head of the table, and carved a leg of mutton with perfect propriety. She then told me, at her son's request, that in the year 1745, when Prince Charles's army was in possession of the town, she, a child of four years, walked with her nurse to Holyrood Palace, and seeing a Highland gentleman standing in the doorway, she went up to him to examine his peculiar attire. She even took the liberty of lifting up his kilt a little way; whereupon her nurse, fearing some danger, started forward for her protection. But the gentleman only patted her head, and said something kind to her. I felt it as very curious to sit as guest with a person who had mingled in the Forty-five. But my excitement was brought to a higher pitch when, on ascending to the drawing-room, I found the general's daughter, a

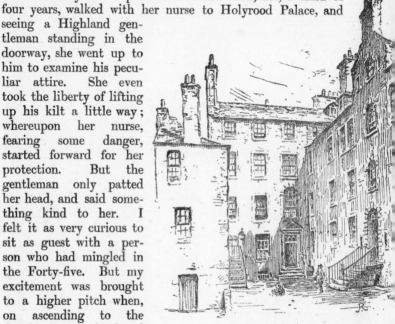

Chessels's Court, Canongate.

pretty young woman recently married, sitting there, dressed in a suit of clothes belonging to one of the nonagenarian aunts— a very fine one of flowered satin, with elegant cap and lappets, and silk shoes three inches deep in the heel—the same having been worn by the venerable owner just seventy years before at a Hunters' Ball at Holyrood Palace. The contrast between the former and the present wearer—the old lady shrunk and taciturn, and her young representative full of life and resplendent in joyous beauty—had an effect upon me which it would be impossible to describe. To this day, I look upon the Chessels's Court dinner as one of the most extraordinary events in my life.]

ORATORIES—COLONEL GARDINER.

This house presents a feature which forms a curious memorial of the manners of a past age. In common with all the houses built from about 1690 to 1740—a substantial class, still abundant in the High Street—there is at the end of each row of windows corresponding to a separate mansion, a narrow slit-like window, such as might suffice for a closet. In reality, each of these narrow apertures gives light to a small cell—much too small to require such a window—usually entering from the dining-room or some other principal apartment. The use of these cells was to serve as a retreat for the master of the house, wherein he might perform his devotions. The father of a family was in those days a sacred kind of person, not to be approached by wife or children too familiarly, and expected to be a priest in his own household. Besides his family devotions, he retired to a closet for perhaps an hour each day to utter his own prayers ; * and so regular was the custom that it gave rise, as we see, to this peculiarity in house-building. Nothing could enable us more clearly to appreciate that strong outward demonstration of religious feeling which pervaded the nation for half a century after the agonies of 'the Persecution.' I cannot help here mentioning the interest with which I have visited Bankton House,† in East Lothian, where, as is well known, Colonel Gardiner spent several years of his life. The oratory of the pious soldier is pointed out by tradition, and it forms even a more expressive memorial of the time than the closets in the Edinburgh houses. Connected with a small front room, which might have been a library or *study*, is a little recess, such as dust-pans and brooms are kept in, consisting of the angular space formed by a stair which passes overhead to the upper floor. This place is wholly without light, yet it is said to have been the place sacred to poor Gardiner's private devotions. What leaves hardly any doubt on the matter is that there has been a wooden bolt within, capable only of being shot from the inside, and therefore unquestionably used by a person desiring to shut himself

---

* Not improbably this was done in a spirit of literal obedience to the injunction (Matthew vi. 6) : 'Thou, when thou prayest, enter into thy closet.' Commentators on this passage mention that every Jewish house had a place of secret devotion built over the porch.

† When Colonel Gardiner occupied it the house was known as Olive Bank. It was later changed to Bankton House by Andrew Macdowall, who, when raised to the Bench in 1755, took the title of Lord Bankton.

in. Here, therefore, in this darksome, stifling little cell, had this extraordinary man spent hours in those devotional exercises by which he was so much distinguished from his class.*

BOWHEAD SAINTS—SEIZERS—A JACOBITE BLACKBIRD.

In the latter part of the seventeenth century, the inhabitants of the West Bow enjoyed a peculiar fame for their piety and zeal in the Covenanting cause. The wits of the opposite faction are full of allusions to them as ' the Bowhead Saints,' ' the godly plants of the Bowhead,' and so forth. [This is the basis of an allusion by a later Cavalier wit, when describing the exit of Lord Dundee from Edinburgh, on the occasion of the settlement of the crown upon William and Mary :

> ' As he rode down the sanctified bends of the Bow,
> Ilka carline was flyting, and shaking her pow ;
> But some young plants of grace, that looked couthie and slie,
> Said : "Luck to thy bonnet, thou bonnie Dundee ! " '

It is to be feared that Sir Walter has here shown a relenting towards the ' young plants,' for which they would not have thanked him.] All the writings of the wits of their own time speak of the system to which they were opposed as one of unmitigated sternness. It was in those days a custom to patrol the streets during the time of divine service, and take into captivity all persons found walking abroad ; and indeed make seizure of whatever could be regarded as guilty of Sabbath-breaking. It is said that, led by a sneaking sense, the patrol one day lighted upon a joint of meat in the course of being roasted, and made prize of it, leaving the graceless owner to chew the spit. On another occasion, about the year 1735, a capture of a different kind was made. ' The people about that time,' says Arnot, ' were in use to teach their birds to chant the songs of their party. It happened that the blackbird of an honest Jacobitical barber, which from his cage on the outside of the window gave offence to the zealous Whigs by his songs, was neglected, on a Saturday evening, to be brought within the house. Next morning he tuned his pipe to the usual air, *The king shall enjoy his own again.* One of the *seizers*, in his holy zeal, was enraged at this manifestation of impiety and treason in one of the feathered tribe. He went up to the house, seized the bird and the cage, and with much solemnity lodged them in the

---

* Bankton House has been burned down and rebuilt since this was written.

City-Guard.' * Pennycook, a burgess bard of the time, represents the officer as addressing the bird:

> 'Had ye been taught by me, *a Bowhead saint*,
> You 'd sung the Solemn League and Covenant,
> Bessy of Lanark, or the Last Good-night;
> But you 're a bird prelatic—that 's not right. . . .
> Oh could my baton reach the laverocks too,
> They 're chirping *Jamie, Jamie*, just like you:
> I hate vain birds that lead malignant lives,
> But love the chanters to the Bowhead wives.'

MAJOR WEIR.†

It must have been a sad scandal to this peculiar community when Major Weir, one of their number, was found to have been so wretched an example of human infirmity. The house occupied by this man still exists, though in an altered shape, in a little court accessible by a narrow passage near the first angle of the street. His history is obscurely reported; but it appears that he was of a good family in Lanarkshire, and had been one of the ten thousand men sent by the Scottish Covenanting Estates in 1641 to assist in suppressing the Irish Papists. He became distinguished for a life of peculiar sanctity, even in an age when that was the prevailing tone of the public mind. According to a contemporary account: 'His garb was still a cloak, and somewhat dark, and he never went without his staff. He was a tall black man, and ordinarily looked down to the ground; *a grim countenance, and a big nose*. At length he became so notoriously

Major Weir's House.

* *History of Edinburgh*, p. 205, note.

† Before Major Weir took up house in the West Bow he is said to have lodged in the Cowgate, where he had as a fellow-lodger the fanatic Mitchell (Ravaillac *redivivus*), who attempted to shoot Archbishop Sharpe.

regarded among the Presbyterian strict sect, that if four met together, be sure Major Weir was one. At private meetings he prayed to admiration, which made many of that stamp court his converse. He never married, but lived in a private lodging with his sister, Grizel Weir. Many resorted to his house, to join him and hear him pray; but it was observed that he could not officiate in any holy duty without the black staff, or rod, in his hand, and leaning upon it, which made those who heard him pray admire his flood in prayer, his ready extemporary expression, his heavenly gesture; so that he was thought more angel than man, and was termed by some of the holy sisters ordinarily *Angelical Thomas.*' Plebeian imaginations have since fructified regarding the staff, and crones will still seriously tell how it could run a message to a shop for any article which its proprietor wanted; how it could answer the door when any one called upon its master; and that it used to be often seen running before him, in the capacity of a link-boy, as he walked down the Lawnmarket.

After a life characterised externally by all the graces of devotion, but polluted in secret by crimes of the most revolting nature, and which little needed the addition of wizardry to excite the horror of living men, Major Weir fell into a severe sickness, which affected his mind so much that he made open and voluntary confession of all his wickedness. The tale was at first so incredible that the provost, Sir Andrew Ramsay,* refused for some time to take him into custody. At length himself, his sister (partner of one of his crimes), and his staff were secured by the magistrates, together with certain sums of money, which were found wrapped up in rags in different parts of the house. One of these pieces of rag being thrown into the fire by a bailie, who had taken the whole in charge, flew up the chimney, and made an explosion like a cannon. While the wretched man lay in prison, he made no scruple to disclose the particulars of his guilt, but refused to address himself to the Almighty for pardon. To every request that he would pray, he answered in screams: 'Torment me no more—I am tormented enough already!' Even the offer of a Presbyterian clergyman, instead of an established Episcopal minister of the city, had no effect upon him. He was tried April 9, 1670, and being found guilty, was sentenced to be strangled and burnt between

* Sir Andrew Ramsay was provost of the city, first from 1654 till 1657, and then continuously for eleven years, 1662-73. It was he who obtained from the king the title of Lord Provost for the chief magistrate, and secured precedence for him next to the Lord Mayor of London.

Edinburgh and Leith. His sister, who was tried at the same time, was sentenced to be hanged in the Grassmarket. The execution of the profligate major took place, April 14, at the place indicated by the judge. When the rope was about his neck, to prepare him for the fire, he was bid to say: 'Lord, be merciful to me!' but he answered as before: 'Let me alone—I will not—I have lived as a beast, and I must die as a beast!' After he had dropped lifeless in the flames, his stick was also cast into the fire; and, 'whatever incantation was in it,' says the contemporary writer already quoted,* 'the persons present own that it gave rare turnings, and was long a-burning, as also himself.'

The conclusion to which the humanity of the present age would come regarding Weir—that he was mad—is favoured by some circumstances; for instance, his answering one who asked if he had ever seen the devil, that 'the only feeling he ever had of him was in the dark.' What chiefly countenances the idea is the un-equivocal lunacy of the sister. This miserable woman confessed to witchcraft, and related, in a serious manner, many things which could not be true. Many years before, a fiery coach, she said, had come to her brother's door in broad day, and a stranger invited them to enter, and they proceeded to Dalkeith. On the way, another person came and whispered in her brother's ear something which affected him; it proved to be supernatural intelligence of the defeat of the Scotch army at Worcester, which took place that day. Her brother's power, she said, lay in his staff. She also had a gift for spinning above other women, but the yarn broke to pieces in the loom. Her mother, she declared, had been also a witch. 'The secretest thing that I, or any of the family could do, when once a mark appeared upon her brow, she could tell it them, though done at a great distance.' This mark could also appear on her own forehead when she pleased. At the request of the company present, 'she put back her head-dress, and seeming to frown, there was an exact horse-shoe shaped for nails in her wrinkles, terrible enough, I assure you, to the stoutest beholder.'† At the place of execution she acted in a furious manner, and with difficulty could be prevented from throwing off her clothes, in order to die, as she said, 'with all the shame she could.'

The treatise just quoted makes it plain that the case of Weir

* The Rev. Mr Frazer, minister of Wardlaw, in his *Divine Providences* (MS. Adv. Lib.), dated 1670.

† *Satan's Invisible World Discovered.*

and his sister had immediately become a fruitful theme for the imaginations of the vulgar. We there receive the following story: 'Some few days before he discovered himself, a gentlewoman coming from the Castle-hill, where her husband's niece was lying-in of a child, about midnight perceived about the Bowhead three women in windows shouting, laughing, and clapping their hands. The gentlewoman went forward, till, at Major Weir's door, there arose, as from the street, a woman about the length of two ordinary females, and stepped forward. The gentlewoman, not as yet excessively feared, bid her maid step on, if by the lantern they could see what she was; but haste what they could, this long-legged spectre was still before them, moving her body with a vehement cachinnation and great unmeasurable laughter. At this rate the two strove for place, till the giantess came to a narrow lane in the Bow, commonly called the Stinking Close, into which she turning, and the gentlewoman looking after her, perceived the close full of flaming torches (she could give them no other name), and as if it had been a great number of people stentoriously laughing, and gaping with tahees of laughter. This sight, at so dead a time of night, no people being in the windows belonging to the close, made her and her servant haste home, declaring all that they saw to the rest of the family.'

For upwards of a century after Major Weir's death, he continued to be the bugbear of the Bow, and his house remained uninhabited. His apparition was frequently seen at night, flitting, like a black and silent shadow, about the street. His house, though known to be deserted by everything human, was sometimes observed at midnight to be full of lights, and heard to emit strange sounds, as of dancing, howling, and, what is strangest of all, spinning. Some people occasionally saw the major issue from the low close at midnight, mounted on a black horse without a head, and gallop off in a whirlwind of flame. Nay, sometimes the whole of the inhabitants of the Bow would be roused from their sleep at an early hour in the morning by the sound as of a coach and six, first rattling up the Lawnmarket, and then thundering down the Bow, stopping at the head of the terrible close for a few minutes, and then rattling and thundering back again—being neither more nor less than Satan come in one of his best equipages to take home the major and his sister, after they had spent a night's leave of absence in their terrestrial dwelling.

About fifty years ago, when the shades of superstition began universally to give way in Scotland, Major Weir's house came to be regarded with less terror by the neighbours, and an attempt was made by the proprietor to find a person who should be bold enough to inhabit it. Such a person was procured in William Patullo, a poor man of dissipated habits, who, having been at one time a soldier and a traveller, had come to disregard in a great measure the superstitions of his native country, and was now glad to possess a house upon the low terms offered by the landlord, at whatever risk. Upon its being known that Major Weir's house was about to be reinhabited, a great deal of curiosity was felt by people of all ranks as to the result of the experiment ; for there was scarcely a native of the city who had not felt, since his boyhood, an intense interest in all that concerned that awful fabric, and yet remembered the numerous terrible stories which he had heard respecting it. Even before entering upon his hazardous undertaking, William Patullo was looked upon with a flattering sort of interest, similar to that which we feel respecting a regiment on the march to active conflict. It was the hope of many that he would be the means of retrieving a valuable possession from the dominion of darkness. But Satan soon let them know that he does not tamely relinquish any of the outposts of his kingdom.

On the very first night after Patullo and his spouse had taken up their abode in the house, as the worthy couple were lying awake in their bed, not unconscious of a certain degree of fear —a dim, uncertain light proceeding from the gathered embers of their fire, and all being silent around them—they suddenly saw a form like that of a calf, which came forward to the bed, and, setting its forefeet upon the stock, looked steadfastly at the unfortunate pair. When it had contemplated them thus for a few minutes, to their great relief it at length took itself away, and, slowly retiring, gradually vanished from their sight. As might be expected, they deserted the house next morning ; and for another half-century no other attempt was made to embank this part of the world of light from the aggressions of the world of darkness.

It may here be mentioned that, at no very remote time, there were several houses in the Old Town which had the credit of being haunted. It is said there is one at this day in the Lawnmarket (a flat), which has been shut up from time immemorial. The story goes that one night, as preparations were making for a supper-party, something occurred which obliged the family, as well as all the assembled guests, to retire with precipitation, and lock up the house. From that night it has never once been opened, nor was any of the furniture withdrawn: the very goose which was undergoing the process of being roasted at the time of the occurrence is still at the fire! No one knows to whom the house belongs; no one ever inquires after it; no one living ever saw the inside of it; it is a condemned house! There is something peculiarly dreadful about a house under these circumstances. What sights of horror might present themselves if it were entered! Satan is the *ultimus hæres* of all such unclaimed property!

Besides the many old houses that are haunted, there are several endowed with the simple credit of having been the scenes of murders and suicides. Some contain rooms which had particular names commemorative of such events, and these names, handed down as they had been from one generation to another, usually suggested the remembrance of some dignified Scottish families, probably the former tenants of the houses. There is a common-stair in the Lawnmarket which was supposed to be haunted by the ghost of a gentleman who had been mysteriously killed, about a century ago, in open daylight, as he was ascending to his own house: the affair was called to mind by old people on the similar occasion of the murder of Begbie. A deserted house in Mary King's Close (behind the Royal Exchange) is believed by some to have met with that fate for a very fearful reason. The inhabitants of a remote period were, it is said, compelled to abandon it by the supernatural appearances which took place in it on the very first night after they had made it their residence. At midnight, as the goodman was sitting with his wife by the fire reading his Bible, and intending immediately to go to bed, a strange dimness which suddenly fell upon his light caused him to raise his eyes from the book. He looked at the candle, and saw it burning blue. Terror took possession of his frame. Turning away his eyes, there was, directly before him, and apparently not two yards off, the head as of a dead person, looking him straight in the face. There was nothing but a head, though that seemed to occupy the precise situation in regard to the floor which it might have done had it been supported by a body of the ordinary stature. The man and his wife fainted with terror. On awaking, darkness pervaded the room. Presently the door opened, and in came a hand holding a candle. This came and stood—that is, the body supposed to be attached to the hand stood—beside the table, whilst the terrified pair saw two or three couples of feet skip along the floor, as if dancing. The scene lasted a short time, but vanished quite away upon the man gathering strength to invoke the protection of Heaven. The house was of course abandoned, and remained ever afterwards shut up. Such were grandams' tales at no remote period in our northern capital :

> 'Where Learning, with his eagle eyes,
> Seeks Science in her coy abode.'

TULZIES.

At the Bowhead there happened, in the year 1596, a combat between James Johnston of Westerhall and a gentleman of the house of Somerville, which is thus related in that curious book, the *Memorie of the Somervilles.*

' The other actione wherein Westerhall was concerned happened three years thereftir in Edinburgh, and was only personal on the same account, betwext Westerhall and Bread (Broad) Hugh Somervill of the Writes. This gentleman had often formerly foughten with Westerhall upon equal termes, and being now in Edinburgh about his privat affaires, standing at the head of the West Bow, Westerhall by accident comeing up the same, some officious and unhappy fellow says to Westerhall : "There is Bread Hugh Somervill of the Writes." Whereupon Westerhall, fancying he stood there either to waitt him, or out of contempt, he immediately marches up with his sword drawen, and with the opening of his mouth, crying : "Turne, villane ; " he cuttes Writes in the hint head a deep and sore wound, the foullest stroak that ever Westerhall was knoune to give, acknowledged soe, and much regrated eftirwards by himself. Writes finding himself strucken and wounded, seeing Westerhall (who had not offered to double his stroak), drawes, and within a short tyme puttes Westerhall to the defensive part ; for being the taller man, and one of the strongest of his time, with the advantage of the hill, he presses him sore. Westerhall reteires by little, traverseing the breadth of the Bow, to gain the advantage of the ascent, to supply the defect of nature, being of low stature, which Writes observeing, keepes closse to him, and beares him in front, that he might not quyte what good-fortune and nature had given him. Thus they continued neer a quarter of ane hour, clearing the callsay,* so that in all the strait Bow there was not one to be seen without their shop doores, neither durst any man attempt to red them, every stroak of their swords threatening present death both to themselves and others that should come neer them. Haveing now come from the head of the Bow neer to the foot thereof, Westerhall being in a pair of black buites, which for ordinary he wore closse drawen up, was quyte tyred. Therefore he stepes back within a shop doore, and stood upon his defence. The very last stroak that Writes gave went neer to have brocken his broad sword in peaces, haveing hitt the lintell of the door, the marke whereof remained there a long tyme. Thereftir, the toune being by this tyme all in ane uproar, the halbertiers comeing to seaze upon them, they wer separated and privatly convoyed to ther chambers. Ther wounds but slight, except that which Writes had upon his head proved very dangerous; for ther was many bones taken out of it; however, at lenth, he was perfectly cured, and the parties themselves, eftir Hugh Lord Somerville's death, reconcealled, and all injuries forgotten.'

In times of civil war, personal rencontres of this kind, and even skirmishes between bands of armed men—usually called tulzies—were of no unfrequent occurrence upon the streets of Edinburgh. They abounded during the troublous time of the minority of James VI. On the 24th of November 1567, the Laird of Airth and the Laird of Wemyss met upon the High Street, and, together with their followers, fought a bloody battle, 'many,' as Birrel the chronicler reports, 'being hurte on both sides by shote of pistoll.' Three days afterwards there was a strict proclamation, forbidding 'the wearing of guns or pistolls, or aney sick-like fyerwork ingyne, under ye paine of death, the king's guards and shouldours only excepted.' This circumstance seems to be referred to in *The Abbot*, where the Regent Murray, in allusion to Lord Seyton's rencontre with the Leslies, in which Roland Græme had borne a distinguished part, says: 'These broils and feuds would shame the capital of the Great Turk, let alone that of a Christian and reformed state. But if I live, this gear shall be amended; and men shall say,' &c.

On the 30th of July 1588, according to the same authority, Sir William Stewart was slain in Blackfriars Wynd by the Earl

---

* The causeway. A skirmish fought between the Hamiltons and Douglases, upon the High Street of Edinburgh, in the year 1515, was popularly termed *Cleanse the Causeway.*

of Bothwell [the fifth earl], who was the most famed disturber of
the public peace in those times. The quarrel had arisen on a
former occasion, on account of some despiteful language used by
Sir William, when the fiery earl vowed the destruction of his enemy
in words too shocking to be repeated; 'sua therafter rancoun-
tering Sir William in ye Blackfriar Wynd by chance, told him he
vold now . . . ; and vith yat drew his sword; Sir William standing to hes defence, and having hes back at ye vall, ye earle mad
a thrust at him vith his raper, and strake him in at the back and
out at the belley, and killed him.'

Ten years thereafter, one Robert Cathcart, who had been
with the Earl of Bothwell on this occasion, though it does
not appear that he took an active hand in the murder, was
slain in revenge by William Stewart, son of the deceased, while
standing inoffensively at the head of Peebles Wynd, near the
Tron.

In June 1605, one William Thomson, a dagger-maker in the
West Bow, which was even then remarkable for iron-working
handicraftsmen, was slain by John Waterstone, a neighbour of
his own, who was next day beheaded on the Castle-hill for his
crime.

In 1640, the Lawnmarket was the scene of a personal combat
between Major Somerville, commander of the forces then in the
Castle, devoted to the Covenanting interest (a relation of Braid
Hugh in the preceding extract), and one Captain Crawfuird,
which is related in the following picturesque and interesting
manner by the same writer: 'But it would appear this gentleman
conceived his affront being publict, noe satisfactione acted in a
private way could save his honour; therefore to repair the same,
he resolves to challange and fight Somervill upon the High
Street of Edenburgh, and at such a tyme when ther should be
most spectators. In order to this designe, he takes the occasione,
as this gentleman was betwext ten and eleven hours in the
foirnoon hastily comeing from the Castle (haveing been then
sent for to the Committie of Estates and General Leslie anent
some important busines), to assault him in this manner; Somervill being past the Weigh-house, Captaine Crawfuird observeing
him, presentlie steps into a high chope upon the south side of
the Landmercat, and there layes by his cloak, haveing a long
broad sword and a large Highland durke by his side; he comes
up to Somervill, and without farder ceremonie sayes: "If you
be a pretty man, draw your sword;" and with that word pulles

out his oune sword with the dagger. Somervill at first was somewhat stertled at the impudence and boldnesse of the man that durst soe openly and avowedly assault him, being in publict charge, and even then on his duty. But his honour and present preservatione gave him noe tyme to consult the conveniency or inconveniency he was now under, either as to his present charge or disadvantage of weapons, haveing only a great kaine staff * in his hand, which for ordinary he walked still with, and that same sword which Generall Rivane had lately gifted him, being a half-rapper sword backed, hinging in a shoulder-belt far back, as the fashion was then, he was forced to guaird two or three strokes with his kaine before he got out his sword, which being now drawne, he soon puts his adversary to the defencive part, by bearing up soe close to him, and putting home his thrusts, that the captaine, for all his courage and advantage of weapons, was forced to give back, having now much adoe to parie the redoubled thrusts that Somervill let in at him, being now agoeing.

'The combat (for soe in effect it was, albeit accidental) begane about the midle of the Landmercat. Somervill drives doune the captaine, still fighting, neer to the goldsmiths' chops, where, fearing to be nailled to the boords (these chops being then all of timber), he resolved by ane notable blow to revenge all his former affronts ; makeing thairfor a fent, as if he had designed at Somervill's right side, haveing parried his thrust with his dagger, he suddenly turnes his hand, and by a back-blow with his broadsword he thought to have hamshekelled † him in one, if not both of his legges, which Somervill only prevented by nimbly leaping backward at the tyme, interposeing the great kaine that was in his left hand, which was quyte cut through with the violence of the blow. And now Providence soe ordered it, that the captaine missing his mark, overstrake him-self soe far, that in tyme he could not recover his sword to a fit posture of defence, untill Somervill, haveing beaten up the dagger that was in the captaine's left hand with the remaineing part of his oune stick, he instantly closes with him, and with the pummil of his sword he instantly strikes him doune to the ground, where at first, because of his baseness, he was mynded to have nailled him to the ground, but that his heart relented, haveing him in his mercy. And att that same instant ther happened several of his oune soulders to come in, who wer soe incensed, that they

* Cane.   † Hamstringed.

wer ready to have cut the poor captaine all in pieces, if he had not rescued him out of theire hands, and saw him safely convoyed to prisone, where he was layd in the irones, and continued in prisone in a most miserable and wretched condition somewhat more than a year.' *

THE TINKLARIAN DOCTOR.

In the early part of the last century, the Bowhead was distinguished as the residence of an odd, half-crazy varlet of a tinsmith named William Mitchell, who occasionally held forth as a preacher, and every now and then astounded the quiet people of Edinburgh with some pamphlet full of satirical personalities. He seems to have been altogether a strange mixture of fanaticism, humour, and low cunning. In one of his publications—a single broadside, dated 1713—he has a squib upon the magistrates, in the form of a *leit*, or list, of a new set, whom he proposes to introduce in their stead. At the end he sets forward a claim on his own behalf, no less than that of representing the city in parliament. In another of his prose pieces he gives a curious account of a journey which he made into France, where, he affirms, ' the king's court is six times bigger than the king of Britain's ; his guards have all feathers in their hats, and their horse-tails are to their heels ; and their king [Louis XV.] is one of the best-favoured boys that you can look upon—blithe-like, with black hair ; and all his people are better natured in general than the Scots or English, except the priests. Their women seem to be modest, for they have no fardingales. The greatest wonder I saw in France, was to see the braw people fall down on their knees on the clarty ground when the priest comes by, carrying the cross, to give a sick person the sacrament.'

The Tinklarian Doctor, for such was his popular appellation, appears to have been fully acquainted with an ingenious expedient, long afterwards held in view by publishers of juvenile toy-books. As in certain sage little histories of Tommy and Harry, King Pepin, &c., we are sure to find that ' the good boy who loved his lessons' always bought his books from ' kind, good, old Mr J. Newberry, at the corner of St Paul's Churchyard, where the greatest assortment of nice books for good boys and girls is always to be had '—so in the works of Mr Mitchell we find some sly encomium upon the Tinklarian Doctor constantly peeping forth ; and in the pamphlet from which the above extract is made, he is

* *Memorie of the Somervilles*, vol. ii. p. 271.

not forgetful to impress his professional excellence as a whitesmith. 'I have,' he says, 'a good pennyworth of pewter spoons, fine, like silver—none such made in Edinburgh—and silken pocks for wigs, and French white pearl-beads; all to be sold for little or nothing.' *Vide* 'A part of the works of that Eminent Divine and Historian, Dr William Mitchell, Professor of Tinklarianism in the University of the Bowhead; being a Syze of Divinity, Humanity, History, Philosophy, Law, and Physick; Composed at Various Occasions for his own Satisfaction and the World's Illumination.' In his works—all of which were adorned with a cut of the Mitchell arms —he does not scruple to make the personages whom he introduces speak of himself as a much wiser man than the Archbishop of Canterbury, all the clergymen of his native country, and even the magistrates of Edinburgh! One of his last productions was a pamphlet on the murder of Captain Porteous, which he concludes by saying, in the true spirit of a Cameronian martyr: 'If the king and clergy gar hang me for writing this, I'm content, because it is long since any man was hanged for religion.' The learned Tinklarian was destined, however, to die in his bed—an event which came to pass in the year 1740.

The profession of which the Tinklarian Doctor subscribed himself a member has long been predominant in the West Bow. We see from a preceding extract that it reckoned dagger-makers among its worthy denizens in the reign of James VI. But this trade has long been happily extinct everywhere in Scotland; though their less formidable brethren the whitesmiths, copper-smiths, and pewterers have continued down to our own day to keep almost unrivalled possession of the Bow. Till within these few years, there was scarcely a shop in this street occupied by other tradesmen; and it might be supposed that the noise of so many hammermen, pent up in a narrow thoroughfare, would be extremely annoying to the neighbourhood. Yet however dis-agreeable their clattering might seem to strangers, it is generally admitted that the people who lived in the West Bow became habituated to the noise, and felt no inconvenience whatever from its ceaseless operation upon their ears. Nay, they rather experi-enced inconvenience from its cessation, and only felt annoyed when any period of rest arrived and stopped it. Sunday morning, instead of favouring repose, made them restless; and when they removed to another part of the town, beyond the reach of the sound, sleep was unattainable in the morning for some weeks, till they got accustomed to the quiescence of their new neighbourhood.

An old gentleman once told me that, having occasion in his youth to lodge for a short time in the West Bow, he found the incessant clanking extremely disagreeable, and at last entered into a paction with some of the workmen in his immediate neighbourhood, who promised to let him have another hour of quiet sleep in the mornings for the consideration of some such matter as half-a-crown to drink on Saturday night. The next day happening (out of his knowledge) to be some species of Saint Monday, his annoyers did not work at all; but such was the force of a habit acquired even in a week or little more, that our friend awoke precisely at the moment when the hammers used to commence; and he was glad to get his bargain cancelled as soon as possible, for fear of another morning's want of disturbance.

OLD ASSEMBLY-ROOM.

At the first angle of the Bow, on the west side of the street, is a tall picturesque-looking house, which tradition points to as having been the first place where the fashionables of Edinburgh held their dancing assemblies. Over the door is a well-cut sculpture of the arms of the Somerville family, together with the initials P. J. and J. W., and the date 1602. These are memorials of the original owner of the mansion, a certain Peter Somerville, a wealthy citizen, at one time filling a dignified situation in the magistracy, and father of Bartholomew Somerville, who was a noted benefactor to the then infant university of Edinburgh. The architrave also bears a legend (the title of the eleventh psalm):

IN DOMINO CONFIDO.

Ascending by the narrow spiral stair, we come to the second floor, now occupied by a dealer in wool, but presenting such appearances as leave no doubt that it once consisted of a single lofty wainscoted room, with a carved oak ceiling. Here, then, did the fair ladies whom Allan Ramsay and William Hamilton celebrate meet for the recreation of dancing with their toupeed and deep-skirted beaux. There in that little side-room, formed by an *outshot* from the building, did the merry sons of Euterpe retire to *rosin their bows* during the intervals of the performance. Alas! dark are the walls which once glowed with festive light; burdened is that floor, not with twinkling feet, but with the most sluggish of inanimate substances. And as for the fiddlers-room —enough :

' A merry place it was in days of yore,
  But something ails it now—the place is cursed.' *

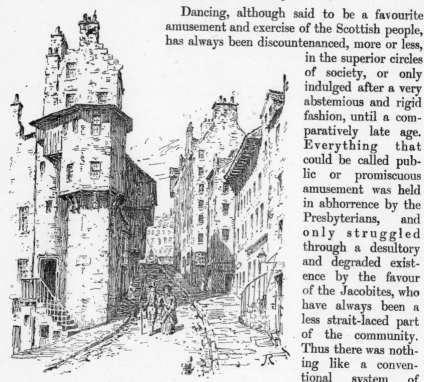

Old Assembly-Room.

Dancing, although said to be a favourite amusement and exercise of the Scottish people, has always been discountenanced, more or less, in the superior circles of society, or only indulged after a very abstemious and rigid fashion, until a comparatively late age. Everything that could be called public or promiscuous amusement was held in abhorrence by the Presbyterians, and only struggled through a desultory and degraded existence by the favour of the Jacobites, who have always been a less strait-laced part of the community. Thus there was nothing like a conventional system of dancing in Edinburgh till the year 1710, when at length a private association was commenced under the name of ' the Assembly ; ' and probably its first quarters were in this humble domicile. The persecution which it experienced from rigid thinkers and the uninstructed populace of that age would appear to have been very great. On one occasion, we are told, the company were assaulted by an infuriated rabble, and the door of their hall perforated with red-hot spits.† Allan Ramsay, who was the friend of all amusements, which he conceived to tend only to cheer this sublunary scene of care, thus alludes to the Assembly :

* This house was demolished in 1836.
† Jackson's *History of the Stage*, p. 418.

'Sic as against the Assembly speak,
  The rudest sauls betray,
When matrons noble, wise, and meek,
  Conduct the healthfu' play ;
Where they appear nae vice daur keek,
  But to what's guid gies way,
Like night, sune as the morning creek
  Has ushered in the day.

Dear E'nburgh, shaw thy gratitude,
  And o' sic friends mak sure,
Wha strive to mak our minds less rude,
  And help our wants to cure ;
Acting a generous part and guid,
  In bounty to the poor :
Sic virtues, if right understood,
  Should every heart allure.'

We can easily see from this, and other symptoms, that the Assembly had to make many sacrifices to the spirit which sought to abolish it. In reality, the dancing was conducted under such severe rules as to render the whole affair more like a night at La Trappe than anything else. So lately as 1753, when the Assembly had fallen under the control of a set of directors, and was much more of a public affair than formerly, we find Goldsmith giving the following graphic account of its meetings in a letter to a friend in his own country. The author of the *Deserted Village* was now studying the medical profession, it must be recollected, at the university of Edinburgh :

'Let me say something of their balls, which are very frequent here. When a stranger enters the dancing-hall, he sees one end of the room taken up with the ladies, who sit dismally in a group by themselves ; on the other end stand their pensive partners that are to be ; but no more intercourse between the sexes than between two countries at war. The ladies, indeed, may ogle, and the gentlemen sigh, but an embargo is laid upon any closer commerce. At length, to interrupt hostilities, the lady-directress, intendant, or what you will, pitches on a gentleman and a lady to walk a minuet, which they perform with a formality approaching to despondence. After five or six couple have thus walked the gauntlet, all stand up to country-dances, each gentleman furnished with a partner from the aforesaid lady-directress. So they dance much, and say nothing, and thus concludes our Assembly. I told a Scotch gentleman that such a profound silence resembled the ancient procession of the Roman matrons in honour of Ceres ; and the Scotch gentleman told me (and, faith, I believe he was right) that I was a very great pedant for my pains.'

In the same letter, however, Goldsmith allows the beauty of the women and the good-breeding of the men.

It may add to the curiosity of the whole affair, that when the Assembly was reconstituted in February 1746, after several years of cessation, the first of a set of regulations hung up in the hall * was : ' *No lady to be admitted in a night-gown, and no gentleman in boots.*' The eighth rule was : ' No misses in skirts and jackets, robe-coats, nor stay-bodied gowns, to be allowed to dance in country-dances, but in a sett by themselves.'

In all probability it was in this very dingy house that Gold-smith beheld the scene he has so well described. At least it appears that the improved Assembly Room in Bell's Wynd (which has latterly served as a part of the accommodations of the Commercial Bank) was not built till 1766.† Arnot, in his *History of Edinburgh,* describes the Assembly Room in Bell's Wynd as very inconvenient, which was the occasion of the present one being built in George Street in 1784.

PAUL ROMIEU.

At this angle of the Bow the original city-wall crossed the line of the street, and there was, accordingly, a gate at this spot,‡ of which the only existing memorial is one of the hooks for the suspension of the hinges, fixed in the front wall of a house, at the height of about five feet from the ground. It is from the arch forming this gateway that the street takes its name, *bow* being an old word for an arch. The house immediately *without* this ancient port, on the east side of the street, was occupied, about the beginning of the last century, and perhaps at an earlier period, by Paul Romieu, an eminent watchmaker, supposed to have been one of the French refugees driven over to this country in consequence of the revocation of the Edict of Nantes. This

* See *Notes from the Records of the Assembly Rooms of Edinburgh.* Edinburgh : 1842. In the eighteenth century a lady's ' night-gown' was a special kind of evening-dress, often of silk brocade, &c., other than full dress ; and a gentleman's night-gown was a dressing-gown, not a bed-garment.

† It was a ball in the room of the Old Assembly Close building which Goldsmith describes in the letter quoted, and in which public assemblies were revived in 1746. The new rooms in Bell's Wynd were opened in 1756.

‡ Called the ' Ovir Bow Port.' It stood about the line of the present Victoria Terrace.

is the more likely, as he seems, from the workmanship of his watches, to have been a contemporary of Tompion, the famous London horologist of the reign of Charles II. In the front of the house, upon the third story, there is still to be seen the remains of a curious piece of mechanism—namely, a gilt ball representing the moon, which was made to revolve by means of a clock.*

'HE THAT THOLES OVERCOMES.'

Pursuing our way down the steep and devious street, we pass an antique wooden-faced house, bearing the odd name of the *Mahogany Land*, and just before turning the second corner, pause before a stone one of equally antiquated structure,† having a wooden-screened outer stair. Over the door at the head of this stair is a legend in very old lettering—certainly not later than 1530—and hardly to be deciphered. With difficulty we make it out to be:

HE YT THOLIS OVERCVMMIS.

He that tholes (that is, bears) *overcomes;* equivalent to what Virgil says:

'Quidquid erit, superanda omnis fortuna ferendo est.'
Æneid, v.

We may safely speculate on this inscription being antecedent in date to the Reformation, as after that period merely moral apothegms were held in little regard, and none but biblical inscriptions were actually put upon the fronts of houses.

Mahogany Land, West Bow.

On the other side of the street is a small shop (marked No. 69), now occupied by a dealer in small miscellaneous wares,‡ and which was, a hundred years ago, open for a nearly similar kind of business, under the charge of a Mrs Jeffrey. When, on the night of the 7th September 1736, the rioters hurried their victim Porteous down the West Bow, with the design of executing him in the Grassmarket, they called at this shop to provide themselves

---

* This house was demolished in 1835, to make way for a passage towards George IV. Bridge.
† Taken down in 1839.   ‡ Demolished in 1833.

with a rope. The woman asked if it was to hang Porteous, and when they answered in the affirmative, she told them they were welcome to all she had of that article. They coolly took off what they required, and laid a guinea on the counter as payment; ostentatious to mark that they 'did all in honour.'

PROVOST STEWART'S HOUSE—DONALDSONS THE BOOKSELLERS.

The upper floors of the house which looks down into the Grassmarket formed the mansion of Mr Archibald Stewart, Lord Provost of Edinburgh in 1745. This is an abode of singular structure and arrangements, having its principal access by a close out of another street, and only a postern one into the Bow, and being full of curious little wainscoted rooms, concealed closets, and secret stairs. In one apartment there is a cabinet, or what appears a cabinet, about three feet high: this, when cross-examined, turns out to be the mask of a trap-stair. Only a smuggler, one would think, or a gentleman conducting treasonable negotiations, could have bethought him of building such a house. Whether Provost Stewart, who was a thorough Jacobite, was the designer of these contrivances, I cannot tell; but fireside gossip used to have a strange story as to his putting his trap-stair to use on one important occasion. It was said that, during the occupation of Edinburgh by the Highland army in '45, his lordship was honoured one evening with a secret visit from the Prince and some of his principal officers. The situation was critical, for close by was the line between the Highland guards and the beleaguered environs of the Castle. Intelligence of the Prince's movements being obtained by the governor of the fortress, a party was sent to seize him in the provost's house. They made their approach by the usual access from the Castle-hill Street; but an alarm preceded them, and before they obtained admission, the provost's visitors had vanished through the mysterious cabinet, and made their exit by the back-door. What real foundation there may have been for this somewhat wild-looking story I do not pretend to say.

The house was at a subsequent time the residence of Alexander Donaldson the bookseller, whose practice of reprinting modern English books in Edinburgh, and his consequent litigation with the London booksellers, attracted much attention sixty years since. Printing and publishing were in a low state in Edinburgh before the time of Donaldson. In the frank language of Hugo Arnot: 'The printing of newspapers and of school-books, of the fanatick effusions of Presbyterian clergymen, and the law papers of the Court of Session, joined to the patent Bible printing, gave a scanty employment to four printing-offices.' About the middle of the century, the English law of copyright not extending to Scotland, some of the booksellers began to reprint the productions of the English authors of the day; for example, the *Rambler* was regularly reproduced in this manner in Edinburgh, with no change but the addition of English translations of the Latin mottoes, which were supplied by Mr James Elphinstone. From this and minor causes, it came to pass that, in 1779, there were twenty-seven printing-offices in Edinburgh. The most active man in this trade was Alexander Donaldson, who likewise reprinted in Edinburgh, and sold in London, English books of which the author's fourteen years' copyright had expired, and which were then only protected by a usage of the London trade, rendering it dishonourable as between man and man, among themselves, to reprint a book which had hitherto been the assigned property of one of their number. Disregarding the rule of his fraternity, Donaldson set up a shop in the Strand for the sale of his cheap Edinburgh editions of the books of expired copyright. They met an immense sale, and proved of obvious service to the public, especially to those of limited means; though, as Johnson remarked, this made Donaldson 'no better than Robin Hood, who robbed the rich in order to give to the poor.' In reality, the London booksellers had no right beyond one of class sentiment, and this was fully found when they wrestled with Mr Donaldson at law. Waiving all question on this point, Donaldson may be considered as a sort of morning-star of that reformation which has resulted in the universal cheapening of literary publications. Major Topham, in 1775, speaks of a complete set of the English classics which he was bringing out, 'in a very handsome binding,' at the rate of one and sixpence a volume!

[Donaldson, in 1763, started a twice-a-week newspaper under the name of the *Edinburgh Advertiser*, which was for a long course of years the prominent journal on the Conservative side, and eminently lucrative, chiefly through its multitude of advertisements. All his speculations being of a prosperous nature, he acquired considerable wealth, which he left to his son, the late Mr James Donaldson, by whom the newspaper was conducted for many years. James added largely to his wealth by successful speculations in the funds, where he held so large a sum that the rise of a per cent. made him a thousand pounds richer than he had been the day before. Prompted by the example of Heriot and Watson, and partly, perhaps, by that modification of egotism which makes us love to be kept in the remembrance of future generations, James Donaldson, at his death in 1830, devoted the mass of his fortune—about £240,000—for the foundation of a *hospital* for the maintenance and education of poor children of both sexes; and a structure for the purpose was erected, on a magnificent plan furnished by Mr Playfair, at an expense, it is said, of about £120,000.

The old house in the West Bow—which was possessed by both of these remarkable men in succession, and the scene of their entertainments to the literary men of the last age, with some of whom Alexander Donaldson lived on terms of intimacy—stood unoccupied for several years before 1824, when it was burnt down. New buildings now occupy its site.]

TEMPLARS' LANDS.

We have now arrived at the *Bow-foot*, about which there is nothing remarkable to be told, except that here, and along one side of the Grassmarket, are several houses marked by a cross on some conspicuous part—either an actual iron cross, or one represented in sculpture. This seems a strange circumstance in a country where it was even held doubtful, twenty years ago, whether one could be placed as an ornament on the top of a church tower. The explanation is that these houses were built upon lands originally the property of the Knights Templars, and the cross has ever since been kept up upon them, not from any veneration for that ancient society, neither upon any kind of religious ground; the sole object has been to fix in remembrance certain legal titles and privileges which have been transmitted into secular hands from that source, and which are to this day productive of solid benefits. A hundred years ago, the houses thus marked were held as part of the barony of Drem in Haddingtonshire, the baron of which used to hold courts in them occasionally; and here were harboured many persons not free of the city corporations, to the great annoyance of the adherents of local monopoly. At length, the abolition of heritable jurisdictions in 1747 extinguished this little barony, but not certain other legal rights connected with the *Templar Lands*, which, how-

ever, it might be more troublesome to explain than advantageous
to know.

THE GALLOWS STONE.

In a central situation at the east end of the Grassmarket,
there remained till very lately a massive block of sandstone,
having a quadrangular hole in the middle, being the stone which
served as a socket for the gallows, when this was the common
place of execution. Instead of the stone, there is now only a
St Andrew's cross, indicated by an arrangement of the paving-
stones.

This became the regular scene of executions after the Restoration, and so continued till the year 1784. Hence arises the sense
of the Duke of Rothes's remark when a Covenanting prisoner
proved obdurate: 'Then e'en let him glorify God in the Grassmarket!'—the deaths of that class of victims being always
signalised by psalm-singing on the scaffold. Most of the hundred
persons who suffered for that cause in Edinburgh during the reigns
of Charles II. and James II. breathed their last pious aspirations
at this spot; but several of the most notable, including the Marquis
and Earl of Argyll, were executed at the Cross.

As a matter of course, this was the scene of the Porteous riot
in 1736, and of the subsequent murder of Porteous by the mob.
The rioters, wishing to despatch him as near to the place of his
alleged crime as possible, selected for the purpose a dyer's pole
which stood on the south side of the street, exactly opposite to
the gallows stone.

Some of the Edinburgh executioners have been so far notable
men as to be the subject of traditionary fame. In the reign of
Charles II., Alexander Cockburn, the hangman of Edinburgh, and
who must have officiated at the exits of many of the 'martyrs' in
the Grassmarket, was found guilty of the murder of a bluegown,
or privileged beggar, and accordingly suffered that fate which he
had so often meted out to other men. One Mackenzie, the hangman of Stirling, whom Cockburn had traduced and endeavoured
to thrust out of office, was the triumphant executioner of the
sentence.

Another Edinburgh hangman of this period was a reduced
gentleman, the last of a respectable family who had possessed
an estate in the neighbourhood of Melrose. He had been a
profligate in early life, squandered the whole of his patrimony,
and at length, for the sake of subsistence, was compelled to accept

this wretched office, which in those days must have been unusually obnoxious to popular odium, on account of the frequent executions of innocent and religious men. Notwithstanding his extreme degradation, this unhappy reprobate could not altogether forget his original station and his former tastes and habits. He would occasionally resume the garb of a gentleman, and mingle in the parties of citizens who played at golf in the evenings on Bruntsfield Links. Being at length recognised, he was chased from the ground with shouts of execration and loathing, which affected him so much that he retired to the solitude of the King's Park, and was next day found dead at the bottom of a precipice, over which he was supposed to have thrown himself in despair. This rock was afterwards called the *Hangman's Craig*.

In the year 1700, when the Scottish people were in a state of great excitement on account of the interference of the English government against their expedition to Darien, some persons were apprehended for a riot in the city of Edinburgh, and sentenced to be whipped and put upon the pillory. As these persons had acted under the influence of the general feeling, they excited the sympathy of the people in an extraordinary degree, and even the hangman was found to have scruples about the propriety of punishing them. Upon the pillory they were presented with flowers and wine ; and when arrayed for flagellation, the executioner made a mere mockery of his duty, never once permitting his whip to touch their backs. The magistrates were very indignant at the conduct of their servant, and sentenced him to be scourged in his turn. However, when the Haddington executioner was brought to officiate upon his metropolitan brother, he was so much frightened by the threatening aspect of the mob that he thought it prudent to make his escape through a neighbouring alley. The laugh was thus turned against the magistrates, who, it was said, would require to get a third executioner to punish the Haddington man. They prudently dropped the whole matter.

At a somewhat later period, the Edinburgh official was a man named John Dalgleish. He it was who acted at the execution of Wilson the smuggler in 1736, and who is alluded to so frequently in the tale of the *Heart of Mid-Lothian*. Dalgleish, I have heard, was esteemed, before his taking up this office, as a person in creditable circumstances. He is memorable for one pithy saying. Some one asking him how he contrived in whipping a criminal to adjust the weight of his arm, on which, it is obvious, much must depend : ' Oh,' said he, ' I lay on the lash according to my conscience.' Either Jock, or some later official, was remarked to be a regular *hearer* at the Tolbooth Church. As no other person would sit in the same seat, he always had a pew to himself. He regularly communicated; but here the exclusiveness of his fellow-creatures also marked itself, and the clergyman was obliged to serve a separate table for the hangman, after the rest of the congregation had retired from the church.

The last Edinburgh executioner of whom any particular notice has been taken by the public was John High, commonly called Jock Heich, who acceded to the office in the year 1784, and died so lately as 1817. High had been originally induced to under-take this degrading duty in order to escape the punishment due to a petty offence—that of stealing poultry. I remember him living in his official mansion in a lane adjoining to the Cowgate —a small wretched-looking house, assigned by the magistrates for the residence of this race of officers, and which has only been removed within the last few years, to make way for the extension of the buildings of the Parliament Square. He had then a second wife, whom he used to beat unmercifully. Since Jock's days, no executioner has been so conspicuous as to be known by name. The fame of the occupation seems somehow to have departed.

I have now finished my account of the West Bow; a most antiquated place, yet not without its virtues even as to matters of the present day. Humble as the street appears, many of its shopkeepers and other inhabitants are of a very respectable character. Bankruptcies are said to be very rare in the Bow. Most of the traders are of old standing, and well-to-do in the world; few but what are the proprietors of their own shops and dwellings, which, in such a community, indicates something like wealth. The smarter and more dashing men of Princes Street and the Bridges may smile at their homely externals and dark-some little places of business, or may not even pay them the compliment of thinking of them at all; yet, while they boast not of their 'warerooms,' or their troops of 'young men,' or their plate-glass windows, they at least feel no apprehension from the approach of rent-day, and rarely experience tremulations on the subject of bills. Perhaps, if strict investigation were made, the 'bodies' of the Bow could show more comfortable balances at the New Year than at least a half of the sublime men who pay an income by way of rental in George Street. Not one of them but is respectfully known by a good sum on the creditor side at

Sir William Forbes's; not one but can stand at his shop-door, with his hands in his pockets and his hat on, not unwilling, it may be, to receive custom, yet not liable to be greatly distressed if the customer go by. Such, perhaps, were shopkeepers in the golden age! *

* The narrow, crooked West Bow, descending very steeply from the Lawnmarket to the Grassmarket, has been almost wholly obliterated by Victoria Street, a comparatively wide and gradually sloping street which crosses the line of the old West Bow from George IV. Bridge. Victoria Street was built in 1835-40; and only a few houses on one side of the head of the Bow still stand, and these have been rebuilt.

JAMES'S COURT.

David Hume—James Boswell—Lord Fountainhall.

JAMES'S COURT, a well-known pile of building of great altitude at the head of the Earthen Mound, was erected about 1725–27 by James Brownhill,* a joiner, as a speculation, and was for some years regarded as the *quartier* of greatest dignity and importance in Edinburgh. The inhabitants, who were all persons of consequence in society, although each had but a single floor of four or five rooms and a kitchen, kept a clerk to record their names and proceedings, had a scavenger of their own, clubbed in many public measures, and had balls and parties among themselves exclusively. In those days it must have been quite a step in life when a man was able to fix his family in one of the *flats* of James's Court.

Amongst the many notables who have harboured here, only two or three can be said to have preserved their notability till our day, the chief being David Hume and James Boswell.

Riddel's Land, Lawnmarket.

DAVID HUME.

The first fixed residence of David Hume in Edinburgh appears to have been in *Riddel's Land*, Lawnmarket, near the head of the West Bow. He commenced housekeeping there in 1751, when, according to his own account, he 'removed from the country to the town, the true scene for a man of letters.' It was while in

* From whom it got its name—James's Court.

Riddel's Land that he published his *Political Discourses*, and obtained the situation of librarian to the Faculty of Advocates. In this place also he commenced the writing of his *History of England*. He dates from Riddel's Land in January 1753, but in June we find him removed to *Jack's Land,** a somewhat airier situation in the Canongate, where he remained for nine years. Excepting only the small portion composed in the Lawn-market mansion, the whole of the *History of England* was written in Jack's Land; a fact which will probably raise some interest respecting that locality. It is, in reality, a plain, middle-aged fabric, of no particular appearance, and without a single circumstance of a curious nature connected with it, besides the somewhat odd one that the continuator of the *History*, Smollett, lived, some time after, in his sister's house precisely opposite.

Jack's Land, Canongate.

Hume removed at Whitsunday 1762 to a house which he purchased in James's Court—the eastern portion of the third floor in the west stair (counting from the level of the court). This was such a step as a man would take in those days as a consequence of improvement in his circumstances. The philosopher had lived in James's Court but a short time, when he was taken to France as secretary to the embassy. In his absence, which lasted several years, his house was occupied by Dr Blair, who here had a son of the Duke of Northumberland as a pupil. It is interesting to find Hume, some time after, writing to his friend Dr Ferguson from

---

* A 'land' still standing (1912) as it was when Hume lived there. It was also the residence of the Countess of Eglinton when she left the Stamp Office Close in the High Street. See p. 192.

the midst of the gaieties of Paris: 'I am sensible that I am misplaced, and I wish twice or thrice a day for *my easy-chair and my retreat in James's Court.*' Then he adds a beautiful sentiment: 'Never think, dear Ferguson, that as long as you are master of your own fireside and your own time, you can be unhappy, or that any other circumstance can add to your enjoyment.' * In one of his letters to Blair he speaks minutely of his house: 'Never put a fire in the south room with the red paper. It was so warm of itself that all last winter, which was a very severe one, I lay with a single blanket; and frequently, upon coming in 'at midnight starving with cold, have sat down and read for an hour, as if I had had a stove in the room.' From 1763 till 1766 he lived in high diplomatic situations at Paris; and thinking to settle there for life, for the sake of the agreeable society, gave orders to sell his house in Edinburgh. He informs us, in a letter to the Countess de Boufflers (*General Correspondence*, 4to, 1820, p. 231), that he was prevented by a singular accident from carrying his intention into effect. After writing a letter to Edinburgh for the purpose of disposing of his house, and leaving it with his Parisian landlord, he set out to pass his Christmas with the Countess de Boufflers at L'Isle Adam; but being driven back by a snowstorm, which blocked up the roads, he found on his return that the letter had not been sent to the post-house. More deliberate thoughts then determined him to keep up his Edinburgh mansion, thinking that, if any affairs should call him to his native country, 'it would be very inconvenient not to have a house to retire to.' On his return, therefore, in 1766, he re-entered into possession of his *flat* in James's Court, but was soon again called from it by an invitation from Mr Conway to be an under-secretary of state. At length, in 1769, he returned permanently to his native city, in possession of what he thought opulence—a thousand a year. We find him immediately writing from his retreat in James's Court to his friend Adam Smith, then commencing his great work *On the Wealth of Nations* in the quiet of his mother's house at Kirkcaldy: 'I am glad to have come within sight of you, and to have a view of Kirkcaldy from my windows; but I wish also to be within speaking-terms of you,' &c. To another person he writes: 'I live still, and must for a twelvemonth, in my old house in James's Court, which is very cheerful, and even elegant, but too small to display my great talent for cookery, the science to which I intend to addict the remaining years of my life!'

---

* Burton's *Life of Hume*, ii. 173.

Hume now built a superior house for himself in the New Town, which was then little beyond its commencement, selecting a site adjoining to St Andrew Square. The superintendence of this work was an amusement to him. A story is related in more than one way regarding the manner in which a denomination was conferred upon the street in which this house is situated. Perhaps, if it be premised that a corresponding street at the other angle of St Andrew Square is called *St Andrew Street*—a natural enough circumstance with reference to the square, whose title was determined on in the plan—it will appear likely that the choosing of 'St David Street' for that in which Hume's house stood was not originally designed as a jest at his expense, though a second thought, and the whim of his friends, might quickly give it that application. The story, as told by Mr Burton, is as follows: 'When the house was built and inhabited by Hume, but while yet the street of which it was the commencement had no name, a witty young lady, daughter of Baron Ord, chalked on the wall the words, St David Street. The allusion was very obvious. Hume's "lass," judging that it was not meant in honour or reverence, ran into the house much excited, to tell her master how he was made game of. "Never mind, lassie," he said, "many a better man has been made a saint of before."'

That Hume was a native of Edinburgh is well known. One could wish to know the spot of his birth; but it is not now perhaps possible to ascertain it. The nearest approach made to the fact is from intelligence conveyed by a memorandum in his father's handwriting among the family papers, where he speaks of 'my son David, born in the *Tron Church parish*'—a district comprehending a large square clump of town between the High Street and Cowgate, east of the site of the church itself.

One of Hume's most intimate friends amongst the other sex was Mrs Cockburn, author of one of the beautiful songs called *The Flowers of the Forest*. While he was in France in 1764, she writes to him from *Baird's Close,** Castle-hill:* 'The cloven foot for which thou art worshipped I despise; yet I remember *thee* with affection. I remember that, in spite of vain philosophy, of dark doubts, of toilsome learning, God has stamped his image of benignity so strong upon thy *heart*, that not all the labours of thy head could efface it.' After Hume's return to Edinburgh, he kept

---

* Formerly called Blair's Close (p. 19). The name was altered to Baird's Close when the Gordon property passed into the possession of Baird of Newbyth.

up his acquaintance with this spirited and amiable woman. The late Mr Alexander Young, W.S., had some reminiscences of parties which he attended when a boy at her house, and at which the philosopher was present. Hume came in one evening behind time for her *petit souper*, when, seeing her bustling to get something for him to eat, he called out : ' Now, no trouble, if you please, about quality ; for you know I'm only a glutton, not an epicure.' Mr Young attended at a dinner where, besides Hume, there were present Lord Monboddo and some other learned personages. Mrs Cockburn was then living in the neat first floor of a house at the end of Crighton Street, with windows looking along the Potterrow. She had a son of eccentric habits, in middle life, or rather elderly, who came in during the dinner tipsy, and going into a bedroom, locked himself in, went to bed, and fell asleep. The company in time made a move for departure, when it was discovered that their hats, cloaks, and greatcoats were all locked up in Mr Cockburn's room. The door was knocked at and shaken, but no answer. What was to be done ? At length Mrs Cockburn had no alternative from sending out to her neighbours to borrow a supply of similar integuments, which was soon procured. There was then such fun in fitting the various *savants* with suitable substitutes for their own proper gear ! Hume, for instance, with a dreadnought riding-coat ; Monboddo with a shabby old hat, as unlike his own neat chapeau as possible ! In the highest exaltation of spirits did these two men of genius at length proceed homeward along the Potterrow, Horse Wynd, Assembly Close, &c., making the old echoes merry with their peals of laughter at the strange appearance which they respectively made.*

I lately inspected Hume's *cheerful and elegant* mansion in James's Court, and found it divided amongst three or four tenants in humble life, each possessing little more than a single room. It was amusing to observe that what had been the dining-room and drawing-room towards the north were *each* provided with one of those little side oratories which have been described elsewhere

---

* Mrs Cockburn, writing to Miss Cumming at Balcarres, describes ' a ball ' she gave in this house. ' On Wednesday I gave a ball. How do ye think I contrived to stretch out this house to hold twenty-two people, and had nine couples always dancing ? Yet this is true ; it is also true that we had a table covered with divers eatables all the time, and that everybody ate when they were hungry and drank when they were dry, but nobody ever sat down. . . . Our fiddler sat where the cupboard is, and they danced in both rooms. The table was stuffed into the window and we had plenty of room. It made the bairns all very happy.'—*Mrs Cockburn's Letters*, edited by T. Craig Brown.

as peculiar to a period in Edinburgh house-building, being designed for private devotion. Hume living in a house with two private chapels!

JAMES BOSWELL.

It appears that one of the immediately succeeding leaseholders of Hume's house in James's Court was James Boswell. Mr Burton has made this tolerably clear (*Life of Hume*, ii. 137), and he proceeds to speculate on the fact of Boswell having there entertained his friend Johnson. 'Would Boswell communicate the fact, or tell what manner of man was the landlord of the habitation into which he had, under the guise of hospitality, entrapped the arch-intolerant? Who shall appreciate the mental conflict which Boswell may have experienced on this occasion?' It appears, however, that by the time when Johnson visited Boswell in James's Court, the latter had removed into a better and larger mansion right below and on the level of the court—namely, that now (1846) occupied by Messrs Pillans as a printing-office. This was an extraordinary house in its day; for it consisted of two floors connected by an internal stair. Here it was that the Ursa Major of literature stayed for a few days, in August 1773, while preparing to set out to the Hebrides, and also for some time after his return. Here did he receive the homage of the trembling literati of Edinburgh; here, after handling them in his rough manner, did he relax in play with little Miss Veronica, whom Boswell promised to consider peculiarly in his will for showing a liking to so estimable a man. What makes all this evident is a passage in a letter of Samuel himself to Mrs Thrale (Edinburgh, August 17), where he says: 'Boswell has very handsome and spacious rooms, level with the ground on one side of the house, and on the other four stories high.' Boswell was only tenant of the mansion. It affords a curious idea of the importance which formerly attached to some of these Old Town residences, when we learn that this was part of the entailed estate of the Macdowalls of Logan, one of whom sold it, by permission of an act of parliament, to redeem the land-tax upon his country property.

Boswell ceased to be a citizen of Edinburgh in 1785, when he was pleased to venture before the English bar. He is little remembered amongst the elder inhabitants of our city; but the late Mr William Macfarlane, the well-known small-debt judge, told me that there was *this* peculiarity about him—it was impossible to look in his face without being moved by the comicality which always reigned upon it. He was one of those men whose very look is provocative of mirth. Mr Robert Sym, W.S., who died in 1844, at an advanced age, remembered being at parties in this house in Boswell's time.

LORD FOUNTAINHALL.

Before James's Court was built, its site was occupied by certain closes, in one of which dwelt Lord Fountainhall, so distinguished as an able, liberal, and upright judge, and still more so by his industrious habits as a collector of historical memorabilia, and of the decisions of the Court of Session. Though it is considerably upwards of a century since Lord Fountainhall died,* a traditionary anecdote of his residence in this place has been handed down till the present time by a surprisingly small number of persons. The mother of the late Mr Gilbert Innes of Stow was a daughter of his lordship's son, Sir Andrew Lauder, and she used to describe to her children the visits she used to pay to her venerable grandfather's house, situated, as she said, where James's Court now stands. She and her sister, a little girl like herself, always went with their maid on the Saturday afternoons, and were shown into the room where the aged judge was sitting—a room covered with gilt leather,† and containing many huge presses and cabinets, one of which was ornamented with a death's-head at the top. After amusing themselves for an hour or two with his lordship, they used to get each a shilling from him, and retire to the anteroom, where, as Mrs Innes well recollected, the waiting-maid invariably pounced upon their money, and appropriated it to her own use. It is curious to think that the mother of a gentlewoman living in 1839 (for only then did Miss Innes of Stow leave this earthly scene) should have been familiar with a lawyer who entered at the bar soon after the Restoration (1668), and acted as counsel for the unfortunate Earl of Argyll in 1681 ; a being of an age as different in every respect from the present as the wilds of North America are different from the long-practised lands of Lothian or Devonshire.

The judicial designation of Lord Fountainhall was adopted from a place belonging to him in East Lothian, now the property of his representative, Sir Thomas Dick Lauder. The original name of the place was Woodhead. When the able lawyer came to the

* His lordship died September 20, 1722 (Brunton and Haig's *Historical Account of the Senators of the College of Justice*).

† A stuff brought, I believe, from Spain, and which was at one time much in fashion in Scotland.

bench, and, as usual, thought of a new appellative of a territorial kind—' Woodhead—Lord Woodhead,' thought he ; 'that will never do for a judge!' So the name of the place was changed to Fountainhall, and he became Lord Fountainhall accordingly.

[1868.—The western half of James's Court having been destroyed by accidental fire, the reader will now find a new building on the spot. The houses rendered interesting by the names of Blair, Boswell, Johnson, and Hume are consequently no more.]

Lady Stair's House as Restored.

STORY OF THE COUNTESS OF STAIR.

IN a short alley leading between the Lawnmarket and the Earthen
Mound, and called *Lady Stair's Close*,* there is a substantial

* Lady Stair's Close was originally a *cul de sac*. When the Mound was begun
a thoroughfare was cut through the garden, making the close the principal
communication between the Lawnmarket and Hanover Street, then the western
extremity of the New Town. The name it first bore was 'Lady Gray's Close,'
after the wife of the builder of the house, and that of Lady Stair's Close was
given to it (*The Book of the Old Edinburgh Club*, vol. iii.) early in the eighteenth
century, when the house passed into the possession of the first Lady Stair, a
granddaughter of Sir William Gray of Pittendrum. Lord Rosebery, who represents a branch of the Primroses (other than that to which the second viscount,
mentioned below, belonged), restored the house and presented it to the city in 1907.

old mansion, presenting, in a sculptured stone over the doorway, a small coat-armorial, with the initials W. G. and G. S., the date 1622, and the legend :

FEAR THE LORD, AND DEPART
FROM EVILL.

The letters refer to Sir William Gray of Pittendrum, the original pro- prietor of the house, and his wife. Within there are marks of good style, particularly in the lofty ceiling and an inner stair apart from the common one ; but all has long been turned to common purposes ; while it must be left to the imagination to realise the terraced garden which formerly descended towards the North Loch.

This was the last residence of a lady conspicuous in Scottish society in the early part of the last century—the widow of the celebrated commander and diplomatist, John, Earl of Stair. Lady Eleanor Campbell was, by paternal descent, nearly related to one of the greatest historical figures of the preceding century, being the granddaughter of the Chancellor, Earl of Loudon, whose talents and influence on the Covenanting side were at one time believed to have nearly procured him the honour of a secret death at the command of Charles I. Her ladyship's first adventure in matrimony led to a series of circumstances of a marvellous nature, which I shall set down exactly as they used to be related by friends of the lady in the last century. It was her lot, at an early age, to be united to James, Viscount Primrose, a man of the worst temper and most dissolute manners. Her ladyship, who had no small share of the old chancellor in her constitution, could have managed most men with ease, by dint of superior intellect and force of character ; but the cruelty of Lord Primrose was too much for her. He treated her so barbarously that she had even reason to fear that he would some day put an end to her life. One morning she was dressing herself in her chamber, near an open window, when his lordship entered the room behind her with a drawn sword in his hand. He had opened the door softly, and although his face indicated a resolution of the most horrible nature, he still had the presence of mind to approach her with caution. Had she not caught a glimpse of his face and figure in the glass, he would in all probability have come near enough to execute his bloody purpose before she was aware or could have taken any measures to save herself. Fortunately, she perceived him in time to leap out of the open window into the street. Half-dressed as she was, she immediately, by a very laudable exertion of her natural good sense, went to the house of Lord Primrose's mother, where she told her story, and demanded protection. That protection was at once extended ; and it being now thought vain to attempt a reconciliation, they never afterwards lived together.

Lord Primrose soon afterwards went abroad. During his absence, a foreign conjurer, or fortune-teller, came to Edinburgh, professing, among many other wonderful accomplishments, to be able to inform any person of the present condition or situation of any other person, at whatever distance, in whom the applicant might be interested. Lady Primrose was incited by curiosity to go with a female friend to the lodgings of the wise man in the Canongate, for the purpose of inquiring regarding the motions of her husband, of whom she had not heard for a considerable time. It was at night ; and the two ladies went, with the tartan *screens* or *plaids* of their servants drawn over their faces by way of disguise. Lady Primrose having described the individual in whose fate she was interested, and having expressed a desire to know what he was at present doing, the conjurer led her to a large mirror, in which she distinctly perceived the appearance of the inside of a church, with a marriage-party arranged near the altar. To her astonishment, she recognised in the shadowy bridegroom no other than her husband. The magical scene was not exactly like a picture ; or if so, it was rather like the live pictures of the stage than the dead and immovable delineations of the pencil. It admitted of additions to the persons represented, and of a progress of action. As the lady gazed on it, the ceremonial of the marriage seemed to proceed. The necessary arrangements had at last been made, the priest seemed to have pronounced the preliminary service ; he was just on the point of bidding the bride and bridegroom join hands, when suddenly a gentleman, for whom the rest seemed to have waited a considerable time, and in whom Lady Primrose thought she recognised a brother of her own, then abroad, entered the church, and advanced hurriedly towards the party. The aspect of this person was at first only that of a friend who had been invited to attend the ceremony, and who had come too late ; but as he advanced, the expression of his countenance and figure was altered. He stopped short ; his face assumed a wrathful expression ; he drew his sword, and rushed up to the bridegroom, who prepared to defend himself. The whole scene then became tumultuous and indistinct, and soon after vanished entirely away.*

When Lady Primrose reached home she wrote a minute narrative of the whole transaction, to which she appended the day of the month on which she had seen the mysterious vision. This narrative she sealed up in the presence of a witness, and then deposited it in one of her drawers. Soon afterwards her brother returned from his travels, and came to visit her. She asked if, in the course of his wanderings, he had happened to see or hear anything of Lord Primrose. The young man only answered by saying that he wished he might never again hear the name of that detested personage mentioned. Lady Primrose, however, questioned him so closely that he at last confessed having met his lordship, and that under very strange circumstances. Having spent some time at one of the Dutch cities—it was either Amsterdam or Rotterdam—he had become acquainted with a rich merchant, who had a very beautiful daughter, his only child, and the heiress of his large fortune. One day his friend the merchant informed him that his daughter was about to be married to a Scottish gentleman, who had lately come to reside there. The nuptials were to take place in the course of a few days; and as he was a countryman of the bridegroom, he was invited to the wedding. He went accordingly, was a little too late for the commencement of the ceremony, but fortunately came in time to prevent the sacrifice of an amiable young lady to the greatest monster alive in human shape—his own brother-in-law, Lord Primrose!

The story proceeds to say that although Lady Primrose had proved her willingness to believe in the magical delineations of the mirror by writing down an account of them, yet she was so much surprised by discovering them to be the representation of actual fact that she almost fainted. Something, however, yet remained

* 'Grace, Countess of Aboyne and Moray, in her early youth, had the weakness to consult a celebrated fortune-teller, inhabiting an obscure close in Edinburgh. The sibyl predicted that she would become the wife of two earls, and how many children she was to bear; but withal assured her that when she should see a new coach of a certain colour driven up to her door as belonging to herself, her hearse must speedily follow. Many years afterwards, Lord Moray, who was not aware of this prediction, resolved to surprise his wife with the present of a new equipage; but when Lady Moray beheld from a window a carriage of the ominous colour arrive at the door of Darnaway, and heard that it was to be her own property, she sank down, exclaiming that she was a dead woman, and actually expired in a short time after, November 17, 1738.'—*Notes to Law's Memorials,* p. xcii.

to be ascertained. Did Lord Primrose's attempted marriage take place exactly at the same time with her visit to the conjurer? She asked her brother on what day the circumstance which he related took place. Having been informed, she took out her key, and requested him to go to her chamber, to open a drawer which she described, and to bring her a sealed packet which he would find in that drawer. On the packet being opened, it was discovered that Lady Primrose had seen the shadowy representation of her husband's abortive nuptials on the very evening when they were transacted in reality.*

Lord Primrose died in 1706, leaving a widow who could scarcely be expected to mourn for him. She was still a young and beautiful woman, and might have procured her choice among twenty better matches. Such, however, was the idea she had formed of the marriage state from her first husband that she made a resolution never again to become a wife. She kept her resolution for many years, and probably would have done so till the last but for a singular circumstance. The celebrated Earl of Stair, who resided in Edinburgh during the greater part of twenty years, which he spent in retirement from all official employments, became deeply smitten with her ladyship, and earnestly sued for her hand. If she could have relented in favour of any man, it would have been for one who had acquired so much public honour, and whose private character was also, in general respects, so estimable. But to him also she declared her resolution of remaining unmarried. In his desperation, he resolved upon an expedient which strongly marks the character of the age in respect of delicacy. By dint of bribes to her domestics, he got himself insinuated overnight into a small room in her ladyship's house, where she used to say her prayers every morning, and the window of which looked out upon the principal street of the city. At this window, when the morning was a little advanced, he showed himself, *en déshabillé*, to the people passing along the street; an exhibition which threatened to have such an effect upon her ladyship's reputation that she saw fit to accept of him for a husband.†

---

* Lady Primrose's story forms the groundwork of one of Sir Walter Scott's best short stories, *My Aunt Margaret's Mirror.*

† This story loses its point by the discovery made in St Peter's upon Cornhill, London, of the marriage register of the second Earl of Stair with Lady Primrose, 27th March 1708. Thus they were married persons several years before the presumed date of this story. Miss Rosaline Masson announced the discovery in an article in *Chambers's Journal* for 1912, entitled, 'The Secret

She was more happy as Countess of Stair than she had been as Lady Primrose. Yet her new husband had one failing, which occasioned her no small uneasiness. Like most other gentlemen at that period, he sometimes indulged too much in the bottle. When elevated with liquor, his temper, contrary to the general case, was by no means improved. Thus, on reaching home after a debauch, he generally had a quarrel with his wife, and sometimes even treated her with violence. On one occasion, when quite transported beyond the bounds of reason, he gave her so severe a blow upon the upper part of the face as to occasion the effusion of blood. He immediately after fell asleep, unconscious of what he had done. Lady Stair was so overwhelmed by a tumult of bitter and poignant feeling that she made no attempt to bind up her wound. She sat down on a sofa near her torpid husband, and wept and bled till morning. When his lordship awoke, and perceived her dishevelled and bloody figure, he was surprised to the last degree, and eagerly inquired how she came to be in such an unusual condition. She answered by detailing to him the whole history of his conduct on the preceding evening; which stung him so deeply with regret—for he naturally possessed the most generous feelings—that he instantly vowed to his wife never afterwards to take any species of drink except what was first passed through her hands. This vow he kept most scrupulously till the day of his death. He never afterwards sat in any convivial company where his lady could not attend to sanction his potations. Whenever he gave any entertainment, she always sat next him and filled his wine, till it was necessary for her to retire; after which, he drank only from a certain quantity which she had first laid aside.

With much that was respectable in her character, we must not be too much surprised that Lady Stair was capable of using terms of speech which a subsequent age has learned to look on

Marriage of Lady Primrose and John, Second Earl of Stair.' She makes this comment: 'The testimony of John Waugh, Parson, has lain buried for over two hundred years in the old Register in the city; but the tale, whispered one day, some time about the year 1714, in the High Street of Edinburgh, first among the strutting gallants and loungers at the Cross at noon, and later on, over the delicate tea-cups, in the gossipy gatherings of the fair sex—that tale was nowise buried. It has never died. Did not Kirkpatrick Sharpe repeat it, sixty years after Lady Stair's death, to young Robert Chambers, at that time collecting material for his inimitable book, *Traditions of Edinburgh?* ' The article further tries to answer the question why the Earl of Stair and the young widow made this clandestine marriage, which gave opportunity for the story.

as objectionable, even in the humblest class of society. The
Earl of Dundonald, it appears, had stated to the Duke of
Douglas that Lady Stair had expressed incredulity regarding the
genuineness of the birth of his nephews, the children of Lady
Jane Douglas, and did not consider Lady Jane as entitled to
any allowance from the duke on their account. In support of
what he reported, Dundonald, in a letter to the Lord Justice-
Clerk, gave the world leave to think him 'a damned villain' if
he did not speak the truth. This seems to have involved Lady
Stair unpleasantly with her friends of the house of Douglas, and
she lost little time in making her way to Holyroodhouse, where,
before the duke and duchess and their attendants, she declared
that she had lived to a good old age, and never till now had got
entangled in any *clatters*—that is, scandal. The old dame then
thrice stamped the floor with her staff, each time calling the
Earl of Dundonald 'a damned villain ;' after which she retired
in great wrath. Perhaps this scene was characteristic, for we
learn from letters of Lady M. W. Montagu that Lady Stair
was subject to hysterical ailments, and would be screaming and
fainting in one room, while her daughter, Miss Primrose, and
Lady Mary were dancing in another.

This venerable lady, after being long at the head of society
in Edinburgh, died in November 1759, having survived her
second husband twelve years. It was remembered of her that
she had been the first person in Edinburgh, of her time, to keep
a black domestic servant.*

* Negroes in a servile capacity had been long before known in Scotland.
Dunbar has a droll poem on a female black, whom he calls 'My lady with the
muckle lips.' In *Lady Marie Stuart's Household Book*, referring to the early
part of the seventeenth century, there is mention of 'ane inventorie of the
gudes and geir whilk pertenit to Dame Lilias Ruthven, Lady Drummond,'
which includes as an item, 'the black boy and the papingoe [peacock];' in so
humble an association was it then thought proper to place a human being who
chanced to possess a dark skin.

THE OLD BANK CLOSE.

The Regent Morton—The Old Bank—Sir Thomas Hope—Chiesly of Dalry—Rich Merchants of the Sixteenth Century—Sir William Dick—The Birth of Lord Brougham.

OLD BANK CLOSE.

AMONGST the buildings removed to make way for George IV. Bridge were those of a short blind alley in the Lawnmarket, called the Old Bank Close. Composed wholly of solid goodly structures, this close had an air of dignity that might have almost reconciled a modern gentleman to live in it. One of these, crossing and closing the bottom, had been the Bank of Scotland—the *Auld Bank*, as it used to be half-affectionately called in Edinburgh —previously to the erection of the present handsome edifice in Bank Street. From this establishment the close had taken its name ; but it had previously been called *Hope's Close*, from its being the residence of a son of the cele-brated Sir Thomas Hope, King's Advo-cate in the reign of Charles I.

House of Robert Gourlay.

The house of oldest date in the close was one on the west side, of substantial and even handsome appearance, long and lofty, and presenting some peculiarities of structure nearly unique in our city. There was first a door for the ground-floor, about which there was nothing remarkable. Then there was a door leading by the stair to the *first floor*, and bearing this legend and date upon the architrave :

IN THE IS AL MY TRAIST · 1569.

Close beside this door was another, leading by a longer, but distinct though adjacent stair to the second floor, and presenting on the architrave the initials R. G. From this floor there was an internal stair contained in a projecting turret, which connected it with the higher floor. Thus, it will be observed, there were three houses in this building, each having a distinct access ; a nicety of arrangement which, together with the excellence of the masonry, was calculated to create a more respectful impression regarding the domestic ideas of our ancestors in Queen Mary's time than most persons are prepared for. Finally, in the triangular space surmounting an attic window were the initials of a married couple, D. G., M. S.

Our surprise is naturally somewhat increased when we learn that the builder and first possessor of this house does not appear to have been a man of rank, or one likely to own unusual wealth. His name was Robert Gourlay, and his profession a humble one connected with the law—namely, that of a messenger-at-arms. In the second book of Charters in the Canongate council-house, Adam Bothwell, Bishop of Orkney, and commendator of Holyrood, gave the office of messenger or officer-at-arms to the Abbey to Robert Gourlay, messenger, 'our lovit familiar servitor,' with a salary of forty pounds, and other perquisites. This was the Robert Gourlay who built the noble tenement in the Old Bank Close ; and through his official functions it came into connection with an interesting historical event. In May 1581, when the ex-Regent Morton was brought to Edinburgh to suffer death, he was—as we learn from the memoirs of Moyses, a contemporary—'lodged in Robert Gourlay's house, and there keeped by the waged men.' Gourlay had been able to accommodate in his house those whom it was his professional duty to take in charge as prisoners. Here, then, must have taken place those remarkable conferences between Morton and certain clergymen, in which, with the prospect of death before him, he protested his innocence of Darnley's death, while confessing to a foreknowledge of it. Morton must have resided in the house from May 29, when he arrived in Edinburgh, till June 2, when he fell under the stroke of the 'Maiden.' In the ensuing year, as we learn from the authority just quoted, De la Motte, the French ambassador, was lodged in 'Gourlay's House.'

David Gourlay—probably the individual whose initials appeared on the attic—described as son of John Gourlay, customer, and doubtless grandson of the first man Robert—disposed of the

house in 1637 to Sir Thomas Hope of Craighall in liferent, and
to his second son, Sir Thomas Hope of Kerse.* We may suppose
'the Advocate' to have thus provided a mansion for one of his
children. A grandson in 1696 disposed of the upper floor to
Hugh Blair, merchant in Edinburgh—the grandfather, I presume,
of the celebrated Dr Hugh Blair.

This portion of the house was occupied early in the last
century by Lord Aberuchil, one of King William's judges,
remarkable for the large fortune he accumulated. About 1780
his descendant, Sir James Campbell of Aberuchil, resided in it
while educating his family. It was afterwards occupied by
Robert Stewart, writer, extensively known in Perthshire by the
name of *Rob Uncle*, on account of the immense number of his
nephews and nieces, amongst the former of whom was the late
worthy General Stewart of Garth, author of the work on the
Highland regiments.

The building used by the bank was also a substantial one.
Over the architrave was the legend :

SPES ALTERÆ VITÆ,

with a device emblematising the resurrection—namely, a couple
of cross-bones with wheat-stalks springing from them, and the
date 1588. Latterly it was occupied as the University Printing-
office, and when I visited it in 1824 it contained an old wooden
press, which was believed to be the identical one which Prince
Charles carried with him from Glasgow to Bannockburn to print
his gazettes, but then used as a *proof-press*, like a good hunter
reduced to the sand-cart. This house was removed in 1834,
having been previously sold by the Commissioners of Improvements for £150. The purchaser got a larger sum for a leaden
roof unexpectedly found upon it. When the house was demolished, it was discovered that every window-shutter had a communication by wires with an intricate piece of machinery in the
garret, designed to operate upon a bell hung at a corner on the
outside, so that not a window could have been forced without
giving an alarm.

In the Cowgate, little more than fifty yards from the site of
this building, there is a bulky old mansion, believed to have
been the residence of the celebrated King's Advocate Hope,
himself, the ancestor of all the considerable men of this name
now in Scotland. One can easily see, amidst all the disgrace

---

* Raised to the Bench with the title of Lord Kerse.

into which it has fallen, something remarkable in this house, with two entrances from the street, and two *porte-cochères* leading to other accesses in the rear. Over one door is the legend:

TECUM HABITA : 1616; *

over the other a half-obliterated line, known to have been

AT HOSPES HUMO.

One often finds significant voices proceeding from the builders of these old houses, generally to express humility. Sir Thomas here quotes a well-known passage in Persius, as if to tell the beholder to confine himself to a criticism of his own house; and then, with more certain humility, uses a passage of the Psalms (cxix. 19): 'I am a stranger upon earth,' the latter being an anagram of his own name, thus spelt: THOMAS HOUPE. It is impossible without a passing sensation of melancholy to behold this house, and to think how truly the obscurity of its history, and the wretchedness into which it has fallen, realise the philosophy of the anagram. Verily, the great statesman who once lived here in dignity and the respect of men was but as a stranger who tarried in the place for a night, and was gone.

Courtyard, Hope House.

The *Diary of Sir Thomas Hope*, printed for the Bannatyne Club (1843), is a curious record of the public duties of a great law-officer in the age to which it refers, as well as of the mixture

* The lintel bearing this legend is preserved in a doorway at the top of the staircase of the Free Library, George IV. Bridge. The Cowgate portion of the Library building (1887–89) occupies the site of Sir Thomas Hope's house.

of worldly and spiritual things in which the venerable dignitary was engaged. He is indefatigable in his religious duties and his endeavours to advance the interests of his family; at the same time full of kindly feeling about his sons' wives and their little family matters, never failing, for one thing, to tell how much the midwife got for her attendance on these ladies. There are many passages respecting his prayers, and the 'answers' he obtained to them, especially during the agonies of the opening civil war. He prays, for instance, that the Lord would pity his people, and then hears the words: 'I will preserve and saiff my people'—'but quhither be me or some other, I dar not say.' On another occasion, at the time when the Covenanting army was mustering for Dunse Law to oppose King Charles, Sir Thomas tells that, praying: 'Lord, pitie thy pure [i.e. poor] kirk, for their is no help in man!' he heard a voice saying: 'I will pitie it;' 'for quhilk I blissit the Lord;' immediately after which he goes on: 'Lent to John my *long carabin of rowet wark* all indentit;' &c.*

The Countess of Mar, daughter of Esme, Duke of Lennox, died of a *deadly brash* in Sir Thomas's house in the Cowgate, May 11, 1644.

It is worthy of notice that the Hopes are one of several Scottish families, possessing high rank and great wealth, which trace their descent to merchants in Edinburgh. 'The Hopes are of French extraction, from Picardy. It is said they were originally Houblon, and had their name from the plant [hop], and not from esperance [the virtue in the mind]. The first that came over was a domestic of Magdalene of France, queen of James V.; and of him are descended all the eminent families of Hopes. This John Hope set up as a merchant of Edinburgh, and his son, by Bessie or Elizabeth Cumming, is marked as a member of our first Protestant General Assembly, anno 1560.'†

* While King's Advocate, Sir Thomas Hope had the unique experience of pleading at the Bar before two of his sons who were judges—Lord Craighall and Lord Kerse. There is a tradition that when addressing the Court he remained covered, and that from this circumstance the Lord Advocates still have this privilege, although they do not exercise it. Probably the custom introduced by Sir Thomas Hope originated in his being an officer of state, which entitled him to sit in parliament wearing his hat, and he claimed the same privilege when appearing before the judges.

† See a Memoir by Sir Archibald Steuart Denham in the publications of the Maitland Club.

CHIESLY OF DALRY.

The head of the Old Bank Close was the scene of the assassination of President Lockhart by Chiesly of Dalry,* March 1689. The murderer had no provocation besides a simple judicial act of the president, assigning an aliment or income of £93 out of his estate to his wife and children, from whom it may be presumed he had been separated. He evidently was a man abandoned to the most violent passions—perhaps not quite sane. In London, half a year before the deed, he told Mr Stuart, an advocate, that he was resolved to go to Scotland before Candlemas and kill the president; when, on Stuart remarking that the very imagination of such a thing was a sin before God, he replied : 'Let God and me alone ; we have many things to reckon betwixt us, and we will reckon this too.' The judge was informed of the menaces of Chiesly, but despised them.

On a Sunday afternoon, the last day of March—the town being then under the excitement of the siege of the Castle by the friends of the new government—Lockhart was walking home from church to his house in this alley, when Chiesly came behind, just as he entered the close, and shot him in the back with a pistol. A Dr Hay, coming to visit the president's lady, saw his lordship stagger and fall. The ball had gone through the body, and out at the right breast. He was taken into his house, laid down upon two chairs, and almost immediately was a dead man. Some gentlemen passing seized the murderer, who readily owned he had done the deed, which he said was 'to learn the president to do justice.' When immediately after informed that his victim had expired, he said 'he was not used to do things by halves.' He boasted of the deed as if it had been some grand exploit.

After torture had been inflicted, to discover if he had any accomplices, the wretched man was tried by the magistrates of Edinburgh, and sentenced to be carried on a hurdle to the Cross,† and there hanged, with the fatal pistol hung from his neck, after which his body was to be suspended in chains at the Gallow Lee, and his right hand affixed to the West Port. The body was stolen from the gallows, as was supposed, by his friends,

* The site of Chiesly's house is that occupied by the Episcopal Church Training College in Orwell Place.

† In *The Domestic Annals of Scotland* the place of his execution is given as Drumsheugh, and Sir Walter Scott says he was hanged near his own house of Dalry.

and it was never known what had become of it till more than a century after, when, in removing the hearthstone of a cottage in Dalry Park, near Edinburgh, a human skeleton was found, with the remains of a pistol near the situation of the neck. No doubt was entertained that these were the remains of Chiesly, huddled into this place for concealment, probably in the course of the night in which they had been abstracted from the gallows.

RICH MERCHANTS OF THE SIXTEENTH CENTURY— SIR WILLIAM DICK.

Several houses in the neighbourhood of the Old Bank Close served to give a respectful notion of the wealth and domestic state of certain merchants of an early age. Immediately to the westward, in Brodie's Close, was the mansion of William Little of Liberton, bearing date 1570. This was an eminent merchant, and the founder of a family now represented by Mr Little Gilmour of the Inch, in whose possession this mansion continued under entail, till purchased and taken down by the Commissioners of Improvements in 1836. About 1780 it was the residence of the notorious Deacon Brodie, of whom something may be said elsewhere. Sir William Gray of Pittendrum, mentioned a few pages back as the original owner of the old house in Lady Stair's Close, was another affluent trafficker of that age.

In Riddel's Close, Lawnmarket, there is an enclosed court, evidently intended to be capable of defence. It is the place where John Macmoran, a rich merchant of the time of James VI., lived and carried on his business. In those days even schoolboys trusted to violence for attaining their ends. The youths of the High School,* being malcontent about their holidays, barred themselves up in the school with some provisions, and threatened not to surrender till the magistrates should comply with their demands. John Macmoran, who held the office of one of the bailies, came with a *posse* to deal with the boys, but, finding them obdurate, ordered the door to be prised open with a joist. One within then

---

* This was the first High School, built in 1578 in the grounds of the Blackfriars' Monastery, of which David Malloch, or Mallet, was janitor in 1717. The building faced the Canongate. In 1777 it was replaced by the building now facing Infirmary Street and used in connection with the university. It is this later building that is associated with Sir Walter Scott, Lord Brougham, Lord Jeffrey, Lord Cockburn, and other eminent men of the last quarter of the eighteenth and first quarter of the nineteenth century.

fired a pistol at the bailie, who fell shot through the brain, to the horror of all beholders, including the schoolboys themselves, who with difficulty escaped the vengeance of the crowd assembled on the spot.

It was ascertained that the immediate author of the bailie's death was William Sinclair, son of the chancellor of Caithness. There was a great clamour to have justice done upon him ; but this was a point not easily attained, where a person of gentle blood was concerned, in the reign of James VI. The boy lived to be Sir William Sinclair of Mey, and, as such, was the ancestor of those who have, since 1789, borne the title of Earls of Caithness.

A visit to the fine old mansion of Bailie Macmoran may be recommended. Its masonry is not without elegance. The lower floor of the building is now used as

Bailie Macmoran's House, Riddel's Court.

'The Mechanics' Library.' * Macmoran's house is in the floor above, reached by a stone stair, near the corner of the court. This dwelling offers a fine specimen of the better class of houses at the end of the sixteenth century. The marble jambs of the fireplaces and the carved stucco ceilings are quite entire. The larger room (occupied as a warehouse for articles of saddlery) is that in which took place two memorable royal banquets in 1598—the first on the 24th of April to James VI. with his

* The Mechanics' Library was discontinued when the Free Library was opened. Bailie Macmoran's house is now used as a university settlement.

queen, Anne of Denmark, and her brother the Duke of Holstein; and the second on the 2nd of May, more specially to the Duke of Holstein, but at which their Majesties were present. These banquets, held, as Birrel says, with 'grate solemnitie and mirrines,' were at the expense of the city. It need hardly be said that James VI. was fond of this species of entertainment, and the house of Macmoran was probably selected for the purpose not only because he was treasurer to the corporation and a man of some mark, but because his dwelling offered suitable accommodation. The general aspect of the enclosed court which affords access to Macmoran's house has undergone little or no alteration since these memorable banquets; and in visiting the place, with its quietude and seclusion, one almost feels as if stepping back into the sixteenth century. Considering the destruction all around from city improvements, it is fortunate that this remarkable specimen of an old mansion should have been left so singularly entire. One of the higher windows continues to exemplify an economical arrangement which prevailed about the time of the Restoration—namely, to have the lower half composed of wooden shutters.*

The grandest of all these old Edinburgh merchants was William Dick, ancestor of the Dicks, baronets of Prestonfield. In his youth, and during the lifetime of his father, he had been able to lend £6000 to King James, to defray the expense of his journey to Scotland. The affairs in which he was engaged would even now be considered important. For example, he farmed the customs on wine at £6222, and the crown rents of Orkney at £3000. Afterwards he farmed the excise. His fleets extended from the Baltic to the Mediterranean. The immense wealth he acquired enabled him to purchase large estates. He himself reckoned his property as at one time equal to two hundred thousand pounds sterling.

Strange to say, this great merchant came to poverty, and died in a prison. The reader of the Waverley novels may remember David Deans telling how his father 'saw them toom the sacks of dollars out o' Provost Dick's window intill the carts that carried them to the army at Dunse Law'—'if ye winna believe his testimony, there is the window itsell still standing in the Luckenbooths

* After being the residence for a time of Sir John Clerk of Penicuik and other notable citizens, it was latterly occupied by the widow (the seventh wife) of the Rev. David Williamson—'Dainty Davie'—minister of St Cuthbert's Church at the time of the Revolution.

—I think it's a claith-merchant's buith the day.' This refers
to large advances which Dick made to the Covenanters to enable
them to carry on the war against the king. The house alluded
to is actually now a claith-merchant's booth, having long been
in the possession of Messrs John Clapperton & Company. Two
years after Dunse Law, Dick gave the Covenanters 100,000 merks
in one sum. Subsequently, being after all of royalist tendencies,
he made still larger advances in favour of the Scottish government
during the time when Charles II. was connected with it; and thus
provoking the wrath of the English Commonwealth, his ruin was
completed by the fines to which he was subjected by that party
when triumphant, amounting in all to £65,000.

Poor Sir William Dick—for he had been made a baronet by
Charles I.—went to London to endeavour to recover some part
of his lost means. When he represented the indigence to which
he had been reduced, he was told that he was always able to
procure pie-crust when other men could not get bread. There
was, in fact, a prevalent idea that he possessed some supernatural
means—such as the philosopher's stone—of acquiring money.
(Pie-crust came to be called *Sir William Dick's Necessity*.) The
contrary was shown when the unfortunate man died soon after in
a prison in Westminster. There is a picture in Prestonfield
House, near Edinburgh, the seat of his descendant, representing
him in this last retreat in a mean dress, surrounded by his
numerous hapless family. A rare pamphlet, descriptive of his
case, presents engravings of three such pictures; one exhibiting
him on horseback, attended by guards as Lord Provost of Edinburgh, superintending the unloading of one of his rich ships at
Leith; another as a prisoner in the hands of the bailiffs; the
third as dead in prison. A more memorable example of the
instability of fortune does not occur in our history. It seems
completely to realise the picture in Job (chap. xxvii.): 'The rich
man shall lie down, but he shall not be gathered: he openeth
his eyes, and he is not. Terrors take hold on him as waters, a
tempest stealeth him away in the night. The east wind carrieth
him away, and he departeth: and as a storm, hurleth him out of
his place. For God shall cast upon him, and not spare: he
would fain flee out of his hand. Men shall clap their hands at
him, and shall hiss him out of his place.'

The fortunes of the family were restored by Sir William's
grandson, Sir James, a remarkably shrewd man, who was likewise
a merchant in Edinburgh. There is a traditionary story that

this gentleman, observing the utility of manure, and that the streets of Edinburgh were loaded with it, to the detriment of the comfort of the inhabitants, offered to relieve the town of this nuisance on condition that he should be allowed, for a certain term of years, to carry it away gratis. Consent was given, and the Prestonfield estate became, in consequence, like a garden. The Duke of York had a great affection for Sir James Dick, and used to walk through the Park to visit him at his house very frequently. Hence, according to the report of the family, the way his Royal Highness took came to be called *The Duke's Walk*; afterwards a famous resort for the fighting of duels. Sir James became Catholic, and, while provost in 1681, had his house burned over his head by the collegianers; but it was rebuilt at the public expense. His grandson, Sir Alexander Dick, is referred to in kindly terms in Boswell's *Tour to the Hebrides* as a venerable man of studious habits and a friend of men of letters. The reader will probably learn with some surprise that though Sir William's descendants never recovered any of the money lent by him to the State, a lady of his family, living in 1844, was in the enjoyment of a pension with express reference to that ancient claim.

THE BIRTH OF LORD BROUGHAM.

[1868.—It has been remarked elsewhere that, for a great number of years after the general desertion of the Old Town by persons of condition, there were many denizens of the New who had occasion to look back to the Canongate and Cowgate as the place of their birth. The nativity of one person who achieved extraordinary greatness and distinction, and whose death was an occurrence of yesterday, Henry, Lord Brougham, undoubtedly was connected with the lowly place last mentioned.

The Edinburgh tradition on the subject was that Henry Brougham, younger, of Brougham Hall, in the county of Cumberland, in consequence of a disappointment in love, came to Edinburgh for the diversion of his mind. Principal Robertson, to whom he bore a letter of introduction, recommended the young man to the care of his sister—Mrs Syme, widow of the minister of Alloa —who occupied what was then considered as a good and spacious house at the head of the Cowgate—strictly the third floor of the house now marked No. 8—a house desirable from its having an extraordinary space in front. Here, it would appear, Mr Brougham speedily consoled himself for his former disappointment by falling in love with Eleonora, the daughter of Mrs Syme ; and a marriage, probably a hurried one, soon united the young pair. They set up for themselves (Whitsunday 1778) in an upper floor of a house in the then newly built St Andrew Square, where, in the ensuing September, their eldest son, charged with so illustrious a destiny, first saw the light.*

Mr Brougham conclusively settled in Edinburgh ; he subsequently occupied a handsome house in George Street. He was never supposed to be a man of more than ordinary faculties ; but any deficiency in this respect was amply made up for by his wife, who is represented by all who remember her as a person of uncommon mental gifts. The contrast of the pair drew the attention of society, and was the subject of a gently satiric sketch in Henry Mackenzie's *Lounger*, No. 45, published on the 10th December 1785, which, however, would vainly be looked for in the reprinted copies, as it was immediately suppressed.]

* The house is marked No. 21. Its back windows enjoy a fine view of the Firth of Forth and the Fife hills. The registration of his lordship's birth appears as follows : ' Wednesday, 30th September 1778, Henry Brougham, Esq., parish of St Gilles (*sic*), and Eleonora Syme, his spouse, a son born the 19th current, named Henry Peter. Witnesses, Mr Archibald Hope, Royal Bank, and Principal Robertson.' The parts of the New Town then built belonged to St Giles's parish.

THE OLD TOLBOOTH.

THE genius of Scott has shed a peculiar interest upon this
ancient structure, whose cant name of the *Heart of Mid-
Lothian* has given a title to one of his happiest novels. It stood
in a singular situation, occupying half the width of the High
Street, elbow to elbow, as it were, with St Giles's Church. Antique
in form, gloomy and haggard in aspect, its black stanchioned
windows opening through its dingy walls like the apertures of a
hearse, it was calculated to impress all beholders with a due and
deep sense of what was meant in Scottish law by the *squalor*

carceris. At the west end was a projecting ground-floor, formed of shops, but presenting a platform on which executions took place. The building itself was composed of two parts, one more solid and antique than the other, and much resembling, with its turret staircase, one of those tall, narrow fortalices which are so numerous in the Border counties. Indeed, the probability is that this had been a kind of peel or house of defence, required for public purposes by the citizens of Edinburgh when liable to preda-tory invasions. Doubtless the house or some part of it was of great antiquity, for it was an old and ruinous building in the reign of Mary, and only narrowly saved at that time from destruction. Most likely it was the very *pretorium burgi de Edinburgi* in which a parliament assembled in 1438 to deliberate on the measures rendered necessary by the assassination of the poet-king, James I. In those simple days great and humble things came close together : the house which contained parliaments upstairs, presented shops in the lower story, and thus drew in a little revenue to the magistrates. Here met the Court of Session in its earliest years. Here Mary assembled her parliaments ; and here—on the Tolbooth door—did citizens affix libels by night, charging the Earl of Bothwell with the murder of Darnley. Long, long since all greatness had been taken away from the old building, and it was condemned to be a jail alone, though still with shops underneath. At length, in 1817, the fabric was wholly swept away, in consequence of the erection of a better jail on the Calton Hill. The gateway, with the door and padlock, was transferred to Abbotsford, and, with strange taste on the part of the proprietor, built into a conspicuous part of that mansion.

The principal entrance to the Tolbooth, and the only one used in later days, was at the bottom of the turret next the church. The gateway was of tolerably good carved stone-work, and occupied by a door of ponderous massiness and strength, having, besides the lock, a flap-padlock, which, however, was generally kept unlocked during the day. In front of the door there always paraded, or rather loitered, a private of the town-guard, with his rusty red clothes and Lochaber axe or musket. The door adjacent to the principal gateway was, in the final days of the Tolbooth, ' MICHAEL KETTEN's SHOE-SHOP,' but had formerly been a *thief's hole.* The next door to that, stepping westward, was the residence of the turnkey ; a dismal, unlighted den, where the gray old man was always to be found, when not engaged in unlocking or closing the door. The next door westward was a lock-up house, which

in later times was never used. On the north side, towards the
street, there had once been shops, which were let by the magistrates; but these were converted, about the year 1787, into a
guard-house for the city-guard, on their ancient capitol in the
High Street being destroyed for the levelling of the streets. The
ground-floor, thus occupied for purposes in general remote from
the character of the building, was divided lengthwise by a strong
partition wall; and communication between the rooms above and
these apartments below was effectually interdicted by the strong
arches upon which the superstructure was reared.

On passing the outer door—where the rioters of 1736 thundered
with their sledge-hammers, and finally burnt down all that inter-
posed between them and their prey—the keeper instantly involved
the entrant in darkness by reclosing the gloomy portal. A flight
of about twenty steps then led to an inner door, which, being duly
knocked at, was opened by a bottle-nosed personage, denominated
Peter, who, like his sainted namesake, always carried two or three
large keys. You then entered *the Hall*, which, being free to all
the prisoners except those of the *East End*, was usually filled with
a crowd of shabby-looking but very merry loungers. A small rail
here served as an additional security, no prisoner being permitted
to come within its pale. Here also a sentinel of the city-guard
was always walking, having a bayonet or ramrod in his hand. The
Hall, being also the chapel of the jail, contained an old pulpit of
singular fashion—such a pulpit as one could imagine John Knox
to have preached from; which, indeed, he was traditionally said to
have actually done. At the right-hand side of the pulpit was a
door leading up the large turnpike to the apartments occupied
by the criminals, one of which was of plate-iron. The door was
always shut, except when food was taken up to the prisoners. On
the west end of the hall hung a board, on which were inscribed
the following emphatic lines:

> 'A prison is a house of care,
>   A place where none can thrive,
> A touchstone true to try a friend,
>   A grave for men alive—
>
> Sometimes a place of right,
>   Sometimes a place of wrong,
> Sometimes a place for jades and thieves,
>   And honest men among.'*

---

* These verses are to be found in a curious volume, which appeared in
London in 1618, under the title of *Essayes and Characters of a Prison and*

A part of the hall on the north side was partitioned off into two small rooms, one of which was the captain's pantry, the other his counting-room. In the latter hung an old musket or two, a pair of obsolete bandoleers, and a sheath of a bayonet, intended, as one might suppose, for his defence against a mutiny of the prisoners. Including the space thus occupied, the hall was altogether twenty-seven feet long by about twenty broad. The height of the room was twelve feet. Close to the door, and within the rail, was a large window, thickly stanchioned; and at the other end of the hall, within the captain's two rooms, was a double window of a somewhat extraordinary character. Tradition, supported by the appearance of the place, pointed out this as having formerly been a door by which royalty entered the hall in the days when it was the Parliament House. It is said that a kind of bridge was thrown between this aperture and a house on the other side of the street, and that the sovereign, having prepared himself in that house to enter the hall in his state robes, proceeded at the proper time along the arch—an arrangement by no means improbable in those days of straitened accommodation.

The window on the south side of the hall overlooked the outer gateway. It was therefore employed by the inner turnkey as a channel of communication with his exterior brother when any visitor was going out. He used to cry over this window, in the tone of a military order upon parade: ' Turn your hand,' whereupon the gray-haired man on the pavement below opened the door and permitted the visitor, who by this time had descended the stair, to walk out.

The floor immediately above the hall was occupied by one room for felons, having a bar along part of the floor, to which condemned criminals were chained, and a square box of plate-iron in the centre, called THE CAGE, which was said to have been constructed for the purpose of confining some extraordinary culprit who had broken half the jails in the kingdom. Above this room was another of the same size, also appropriated to felons.

The larger and western part of the edifice, of coarser and apparently more modern construction, contained four floors, all of which were appropriated to the use of debtors, except a part of the lowest one, where a middle-aged woman kept a tavern for the sale of malt liquors. A turnpike stair gave access to the different floors. As it was narrow, steep, and dark, the visitor was assisted in his ascent by a greasy rope, which, some one was sure to inform him afterwards, had been employed in hanging a criminal. In one of the apartments on the second floor was a door leading out to the platform whereon criminals were executed, and in another, on the floor above, was an ill-plastered part of the wall covering the aperture through which the gallows was projected. The fourth flat was a kind of barrack, for the use of the poorest debtors.

There was something about the Old Tolbooth which would have enabled a blindfolded person led into it to say that it was a jail. It was not merely odorous from the ordinary causes of imperfect drainage, but it had poverty's own smell—the odour of human misery. And yet it did not seem at first a downcast scene. The promenaders in the hall were sometimes rather merry, cutting jokes perhaps upon Peter's nose, or chatting with friends on the benches regarding the news of the day. Then Mrs Laing drove a good trade in her little tavern ; and if any messenger were sent out for a bottle of whisky—why, Peter never searched pockets. New men were hailed with :

> ' Welcome, welcome, brother debtor,
>   To this poor but merry place ;
> Here nor bailiff, dun, nor fetter,
>   Dare to show his gloomy face.'

They would be abashed at first, and the first visit of wife or daughter, coming shawled and veiled, and with timorous glances, into the room where the loved object was trying to become at ease with his companions, was always a touching affair. But it was surprising how soon, in general, all became familiar, easy, and even to appearance happy. Each had his story to tell, and sympathy was certain and liberal. The whole management was of a good-natured kind, as far as a regard to regulations would allow. It did not seem at all an impossible thing that a debtor should accommodate some even more desolate friend with a share of his lodging for the night, or for many nights, as is said to have been done in some noted instances, to which we shall presently come.

It was natural for a jail of such old standing to have passed through a great number of odd adventures, and have many strange tales connected with it. One of the most remarkable traits of its character was a sad liability to the failure of its ordinary powers of retention when men of figure were in question. The old house had something like that faculty attributed by Falstaff to the lion and himself—of knowing men who ought not to be too roughly handled. The consequence was that almost every criminal of rank confined in it made his escape. Lord Burleigh, an insane peer, who, about the time of the Union, assassinated a schoolmaster who had married a girl to whom he had paid improper addresses, escaped, while under sentence of death, by changing clothes with his sister. Several of the rebel gentlemen confined there in 1716 were equally fortunate ; a fact on which there was lately thrown a flood of light, when I found, in a manuscript list of subscriptions for the relief of the other rebel gentlemen at Carlisle, the name of the Guidman of the Tolbooth—so the chief-keeper was called— down for a good sum. I am uncertain to which of all these personages the following anecdote, related to me by Sir Walter Scott, refers.

It was contrived that the prisoner should be conveyed out of the Tolbooth in a trunk, and carried by a porter to Leith, where some sailors were to be ready with a boat to take him aboard a vessel about to leave Scotland. The plot succeeded so far as the escape from jail was concerned, but was knocked on the head by an unlucky and most ridiculous accident. It so happened that the porter, in arranging the trunk upon his back, placed the end which corresponded with the feet of the prisoner *uppermost*. The head of the unfortunate man was therefore pressed against the lower end of the box, and had to sustain the weight of the whole body. The posture was the most uneasy imaginable. Yet life was preferable to ease. He permitted himself to be taken away. The porter trudged along with the trunk, quite unconscious of its contents, and soon reached the High Street. On gaining the Netherbow he met an acquaintance, who asked him where he was going with that large burden. To Leith, was the answer. The other inquired if the job was good enough to afford a potation before proceeding farther upon so long a journey. This being replied to in the affirmative, and the carrier of the box feeling in his throat the philosophy of his friend's inquiry, it was agreed that they should adjourn to a neighbouring tavern. Meanwhile, the third party, whose inclinations had not been consulted in this arrangement, was wishing that it were at once well over with him in the Grassmarket. But his agonies were not destined to be of long duration. The porter in depositing him upon the causeway happened to make the end of the trunk come down with such precipitation that, unable to bear it any longer, the prisoner screamed out, and immediately after fainted. The consternation of the porter on hearing a noise from his burden was of course excessive; but he soon recovered presence of mind enough to conceive the occasion. He proceeded to unloose and to burst open the trunk, when the hapless nobleman was discovered in a state of insensibility. As a crowd collected immediately, and the city-guard were not long in coming forward, there was of course no further chance of escape. The prisoner did not recover from his swoon till he had been safely deposited in his old quarters; but, if I recollect rightly, he eventually escaped in another way.

In two very extraordinary instances an escape from justice has, strange as it may appear, been effected by *means* of the Old Tolbooth. At the discovery of the Rye-House Plot, in the reign of Charles II., the notorious Robert Fergusson, usually styled 'The Plotter,' was searched for in Edinburgh, with a view to his being subjected, if possible, to the extreme vengeance of the law. It being known almost certainly that he was in town, the authorities shut the gates, and calculated securely upon having him safe within their toils. The Plotter, however, by an expedient worthy of his ingenious character, escaped by taking refuge in the Old Tolbooth. A friend of his happened to be confined there at the time, and was able to afford protection and concealment to Fergusson, who, at his leisure, came abroad, and betook himself to a place of safer shelter on the Continent. The same device was practised in 1746 by a gentleman who had been concerned in the Rebellion, and for whom a hot search had been carried on in the Highlands.

The case of Katherine Nairne, in 1766, excited in no small degree the attention of the Scottish public. This lady was allied, both by blood and marriage, to some respectable families. Her crime was the double one of poisoning her husband and having an intrigue with his brother, who was her associate in the murder. On her arrival at Leith in an open boat, her whole bearing betrayed so much levity, or was so different from what had been expected, that the mob raised a cry of indignation, and were on the point of pelting her, when she was with some difficulty rescued from their hands by the public authorities. In this case the Old Tolbooth found itself, as usual, incapable of retaining a culprit of condition. Sentence had been delayed by the judges on account of the lady's pregnancy. The midwife employed at her accouchement (who continued to practise in Edinburgh so lately as the year 1805) had the address to achieve a jail-delivery also. For three or four days previous to that concerted for the escape, she pretended to be

ST GILES, WEST WINDOW.

PAGE 105.

7

A SUGGESTION OF THE NORTH LOCH AND ST CUTHBERT'S
from Allan Ramsay's Garden.

PAGE 117.

afflicted with a prodigious toothache, went out and in with her head enveloped in shawls and flannels, and groaned as if she had been about to give up the ghost. At length, when the Peter of that day had become so habituated to her appearance as not very much to heed her exits and her entrances, Katherine Nairne one evening came down in her stead, with her head wrapped all round with the shawls, uttering the usual groans, and holding down her face upon her hands, as with agony, in the precise way customary with the midwife. The inner doorkeeper, not quite unconscious, it is supposed, of the trick, gave her a hearty thump upon the back as she passed out, calling her at the same time a howling old Jezebel, and wishing she would never come back to trouble him any more. There are two reports of the proceedings of Katherine Nairne after leaving the prison. One bears that she immediately left the town in a coach, to which she was handed by a friend stationed on purpose. The coachman, it is said, had orders from her relations, in the event of a pursuit, to drive into the sea, that she might drown herself—a fate which was considered preferable to the ignominy of a public execution. The other story runs that she went up the Lawnmarket to the Castle-hill, where lived Mr ——, a respectable advocate, from whom, as he was her cousin, she expected to receive protection. Being ignorant of the town, she mistook the proper house, and applied at that of the crown agent,* who was assuredly the last man in the world that could have done her any service. As good luck would have it, she was not recognised by the servant, who civilly directed her to her cousin's house, where, it is said, she remained concealed many weeks.† Her future life, it has been reported, was virtuous and fortunate. She was married to a French gentleman, became the mother of a large family, and died at a good old age. Meanwhile, Patrick Ogilvie, her associate in the dark crime which threw a shade over her younger years, suffered in the Grassmarket. He had been a lieutenant in the —— regiment, and was so much beloved by his fellow-soldiers, who happened to be stationed at that time in Edinburgh Castle, that the public authorities judged it necessary

---

* A large white house near the Castle, on the north side of the street, and now (1868) no more.

† Katherine Nairne was the niece of Sir William Nairne, later a judge under the title of Lord Dunsinnane, and it was currently reported that her escape from the Tolbooth was effected through his connivance. Sir William's clerk accompanied the lady to Dover, and had great difficulty in preventing her recognition and arrest through her levity on the journey.

to shut them up in a fortress till the execution was over lest they might have attempted a rescue.

The Old Tolbooth was the scene of the suicide of Mungo Campbell while under sentence of death (1770) for shooting the Earl of Eglintoune. In the district where this memorable event took place, it is somewhat remarkable that the fate of the murderer was more generally lamented than that of the murdered person. Campbell, though what was called 'a graceless man,' was rather popular in his profession of exciseman, on account of his rough, honourable spirit, and his lenity in the matter of smuggling. Lord Eglintoune, on the contrary, was not liked, on account of his improving mania, which had proved a serious grievance to the old-fashioned farmers of Kyle and Cunningham. There was one article, called rye-grass, which he brought in amongst them, and forced them to cultivate; and black prelacy itself had hardly, a century before, been a greater evil. Then, merely to stir them up a little, he would cause them to exchange farms with each other; thus giving their ancient plenishings, what was doubtless much wanted, an airing, but also creating a strong sense that Lord Eglintoune was 'far ower fashious.' His lordship had excited some scandal by his private habits, which helped in no small degree to render unpopular one who was in reality an amiable and upright gentleman. He was likewise somewhat tenacious about matters respecting game—the besetting weakness of British gentlemen in all ages. On the other hand, Campbell, though an austere and unsocial man, acted according to popular ideas both in respect of the game and excise laws. The people felt that he was on their side; they esteemed him for his integrity in the common affairs of life, and even in some degree for his birth and connections, which were far from mean. It was also universally believed, though erroneously, that he had only discharged his gun by accident, on falling backward, while retreating before his lordship, who had determined to take it from him. In reality, Mungo, after his fall, rose on his elbow and wilfully shot the poor earl, who had given him additional provocation by bursting into a laugh at his awkward fall. The Old Tolbooth was supposed by many, at the time, to have had her usual failing in Mungo's case. The interest of the Argyll family was said to have been employed in his favour; and the body which was found suspended over the door, instead of being his, was thought to be that of a dead soldier from the Castle substituted in his place. His relations, however, who were very respectable people in Ayrshire, all acknowledged that he died by his own hand; and this was the general idea of the mob of Edinburgh, who, getting the body into their hands, dragged it down the street to the King's Park, and, inspired by different sentiments from those of the Ayrshire people, were not satisfied till they got it up to the top of Salisbury Crags, from which they precipitated it down the *Cat Nick*.

One of the most remarkable criminals ever confined in the Old Tolbooth was the noted William Brodie. This was a man of respectable connections, and who had moved in good society all his life, unsuspected of any criminal pursuits. It is said that a habit of frequenting cock-pits was the first symptom he exhibited of a decline from rectitude. His ingenuity as a mechanic gave him a fatal facility in the burglarious pursuits to which he afterwards addicted himself. It was then customary for the shopkeepers of Edinburgh to hang their keys upon a nail at the back of their doors, or at least to take no pains in concealing them during the day. Brodie used to take impressions of them in putty or clay, a piece of which he would carry in the palm of his hand. He kept a blacksmith in his pay, who forged exact copies of the keys he wanted, and with these it was his custom to open the shops of his fellow-tradesmen during the night. He thus found opportunities of securely stealing whatever he wished to possess. He carried on his malpractices for many years, and

never was suspected till, having committed a daring robbery upon the Excise Office in Chessels's Court, Canongate, some circumstances transpired which induced him to disappear from Edinburgh. Suspicion then becoming strong, he was pursued to Holland, and taken at Amsterdam, standing upright in a press or cupboard. At his trial, Henry Erskine, his counsel, spoke very eloquently in his behalf, representing, in particular, to the jury how strange and improbable a circumstance it was that a man whom they had themselves known from infancy as a person of good repute should have been guilty of such practices as those with which he was charged. He was, however, found guilty, and sentenced to death, along with his accomplice Smith. At the trial he had appeared in a full-dress suit of black clothes, the greater part of which was of silk, and his deportment throughout the affair was composed and gentlemanlike. He continued during the period which intervened between his sentence

Brodie's
s and
_antern.

and execution to dress well and keep up his spirits. A gentleman of his acquaintance, calling upon him in the condemned room, was surprised to find him singing the song from the *Beggars' Opera*, '' Tis woman seduces all mankind.' Having contrived to cut out the figure of a draughtboard on the stone floor of his dungeon, he amused himself by playing with any one who would join him, and, in default of such, with his right hand against his left. This diagram remained in the room where it was so strangely out of place till the destruction of the jail. His dress and deportment at the gallows (October 1, 1788) displayed a mind at ease, and gave some countenance to the popular notion that he had made certain mechanical arrangements for saving his life. Brodie was the first who proved the excellence of an improvement he had formerly made on the apparatus of the gibbet. This was the substitution of what is called the *drop* for the ancient practice of the double ladder. He inspected the thing with a professional air, and seemed to view the result of his ingenuity with a smile of satisfaction. When placed on that insecure pedestal, and while the rope was adjusted round his neck by the executioner, his courage did not forsake him. On the contrary, even there he exhibited a sort of levity ; he shuffled about, looked gaily around, and finally went out of the world with his hand stuck carelessly into the open front of his vest.

Brodie's Close.

As its infirmities increased with old age, the Tolbooth showed itself incapable of retaining prisoners of even ordinary rank. Within the recollection of people living not long ago, a youth named Hay, the son of a stabler in the Grassmarket, and who was under sentence of death for burglary, effected his escape in a way highly characteristic of the Heart of Mid-Lothian, and of the simple and unprecise system upon which all public affairs were managed before the present age.

A few days before that appointed for the execution, the father went up to the condemned room, apparently to condole with his unhappy son. The irons had been previously got quit of by files. At nightfall, when most visitors had left the jail, old Hay invited the inner turnkey, or man who kept the hall-door, to come into the room and partake of some liquor which he had brought with him. The man took a few glasses, and became mellow just about the time when the bottle was exhausted and when the time of locking up the jail (ten o'clock at that period) was approaching. Hay expressed unwillingness to part at the moment when they were just beginning to enjoy their liquor; a sentiment in which the turnkey heartily sympathised. Hay took a crown from his pocket, and proposed that his friend should go out and purchase a bottle of good rum at a neigh-bouring shop. The man consented, and staggering away down-stairs, neglected to lock the inner door behind him. Young Hay followed close, as had been concerted, and after the man had gone out, and the outer turnkey had closed the outer door, stood in the stair just within that dread portal, ready to spring into the street. Old Hay then put his head to the great window of the hall, and cried : 'Turn your hand ! '—the usual drawling cry which brought the outer turnkey to open the door. The turnkey came mechanically at the cry, and unclosed the outer door, when the young criminal sprang out, and ran as fast as he could down Beth's Wynd, a lane opposite the jail. According to the plan which had been previously concerted, he repaired to a particular part of the wall of the Greyfriars Churchyard, near the lower gate, where it was possible for an agile person to climb up and spring over ; and so well had every stage of the business been planned that a large stone had been thrown down at this place to facilitate the leap.

The youth had been provided with a key which could open Sir George Mackenzie's mausoleum—a place of peculiar horror, as it was supposed to be haunted by the spirit of the bloody persecutor ; but what will not be submitted to for dear life ? Having been brought up in Heriot's Hospital, in the immediate neighbourhood of the churchyard, Hay had many boyish acquaint-ances still residing in that establishment. Some of these he contrived to inform of his situation, enjoining them to be secret, and beseeching them to assist him in his distress. The Herioters of those days had a very clannish spirit—insomuch that to have neglected the interests or safety of any individual of the community, however unworthy he might be of their friendship, would have been looked upon by them as a sin of the deepest dye. Hay's confidants, therefore, considered themselves bound to assist him by all means in their power. They kept his secret faithfully, spared from their own meals as much food as supported him, and ran the risk of severe punishment, as well as of seeing eldritch sights, by visiting him every night in his dismal abode. About six weeks after his escape from jail, when the hue and cry had in a great measure subsided, he ventured to leave the tomb, and it was afterwards known that he escaped abroad.

So ends our gossip respecting a building which has witnessed and contained the meetings of the Scottish parliament in the romantic days of the Jameses—which held the first fixed court of

Sir George Mackenzie's Mausoleum.

law established in the country—which was looked to by the citizens in a rude age as a fortified place for defence against external danger to their lives and goods—which has immured in its gloomy walls persons of all kinds liable to law, from the gallant Montrose and the faithful Guthrie and Argyll down to the humblest malefactor in the modern style of crime—and which, finally, has been embalmed in the imperishable pages of the greatest writer of fiction our country has produced.

SOME MEMORIES OF THE LUCKENBOOTHS.

Lord Coalstoun and his Wig—Commendator Bothwell's House—Lady Anne Bothwell—Mahogany Lands and Fore-stairs—The Krames —Creech's Shop.

A PORTION of the High Street facing St Giles's Church was called the *Luckenbooths*, and the appellation was shared with a middle row of buildings which once burdened the street at that spot. The name is supposed to have been conferred on the shops in that situation as being *close shops*, to distinguish them from the open booths which then lined our great street on both sides; *lucken* signifying closed. This would seem to imply a certain superiority in the ancient

Tolbooth and Luckenbooths—looking East.

merchants of the Luckenbooths; and it is somewhat remarkable that amidst all the changes of the Old Town there is still in this limited locality an unusual proportion of mercers and clothiers of old standing and reputed substantiality.

Previous to 1811, there remained unchanged in this place two tall massive houses, about two centuries old, one of which contained the town mansion of Sir John Byres of Coates, a gentleman of figure in Edinburgh in the reign of James VI., and whose faded tombstone may yet be deciphered in the west wall of the Greyfriars Churchyard. The Byreses of the Coates died out towards the end of the last century, and their estate has since become a site for streets, as our city spread westwards.

The name alone survives in connection with an alley beneath their town mansion—*Byres's Close*.

LORD COALSTOUN AND HIS WIG.

The *fourth floor*, constituting the Byres mansion, after being occupied by such persons as Lord Coupar, Lord Lindores, and Sir James Johnston of Westerhall, fell into the possession of Mr Brown of Coalstoun, a judge under the designation of Lord Coalstoun, and the father of the late Countess of Dalhousie. His lordship lived here in 1757, but then removed to a more spacious mansion on the Castle-hill.

A strange accident one morning befell Lord Coalstoun while residing in this house. It was at that time the custom for advocates, and no less for judges, to dress themselves in gown, wig, and cravat at their own houses, and to walk in a sort of state, thus rigged out, with their cocked hats in their hands, to the Parliament House.* They usually breakfasted early, and when dressed would occasionally lean over their parlour windows, for a few minutes before St Giles's bell sounded the starting peal of a quarter to nine, enjoying the morning air, such as it was, and perhaps discussing the news of the day, or the convivialities of the preceding evening, with a neighbouring advocate on the opposite side of the alley. It so happened that one morning, while Lord Coalstoun was preparing to enjoy his matutinal treat, two girls, who lived in the second floor above, were amusing them-selves with a kitten, which, in thoughtless sport, they had swung over the window by a cord tied round its middle, and hoisted for some time up and down, till the creature was getting rather desperate with its exertions. In this crisis his lordship popped his head out of the window directly below that from which the kitten swung, little suspecting, good easy man, what a danger impended, like the sword of Damocles, over his head, hung, too, by a single—not *hair*, 'tis true, but scarcely more responsible material—*garter*, when down came the exasperated animal at full career directly upon his senatorial wig. No sooner did the girls perceive what sort of a landing-place their kitten had found than, in terror and surprise, they began to draw it up; but this

---

* Up to the year 1830, when George IV. Bridge gave easy access to Parliament House, this quaint custom was followed by Lord Glenlee, who walked from his house in Brown Square, down Crombie's Close, across the Cowgate, and up the Back Stairs.

measure was now too late, for along with the animal up also came the judge's wig, fixed full in its determined talons. His lordship's surprise on finding his wig lifted off his head was much increased when, on looking up, he perceived it dangling its way upwards, without any means visible to him by which its motions might be accounted for. The astonishment, the dread, the almost *awe* of the senator below—the half mirth, half terror of the girls above—together with the fierce and relentless energy of retention on the part of Puss between—altogether formed a scene to which language could not easily do justice. It was a joke soon explained and pardoned ; but assuredly the perpetrators of it did afterwards get many lengthened injunctions from their parents never again to fish over the window, with such a bait, for honest men's wigs.

COMMENDATOR BOTHWELL'S HOUSE.

The eastern of the tenements, which has only been renovated by a new front, formerly was the lodging of Adam Bothwell, Commendator of Holyrood, who is remarkable for having performed the Protestant marriage ceremony for Mary and the Earl of Bothwell. This ecclesiastic, who belonged to an old Edinburgh family of note, and was the uncle of the inventor of logarithms,* is celebrated in his epitaph in Holyrood Chapel as a judge, and the son and father of judges. His son was raised to the peerage in 1607, under the title of Lord Holyroodhouse, the lands of that abbacy, with some others, being erected into a temporal lordship in his favour. The title, however, sunk in the second generation. The circumstance which now gives most interest to the family is one which they themselves would probably have regarded as its greatest disgrace. Among the old Scottish songs is one which breaks upon the ear with the wail of wronged womanhood, mingled with the breathings of its indestructible affections :

> 'Baloo, my boy, lie still and sleep,
> It grieves me sair to see thee weep.
> If thou'lt be silent, I'll be glad ;
> Thy mourning makes my heart full sad. . . .
> Baloo, my boy, weep not for me,
> Whose greatest grief's for wranging thee,
> Nor pity her deserved smart,
> Who can blame none but her fond heart.

* Napier of Merchiston.

Baloo, my boy, thy father's fled,
When he the thriftless son hath played;
Of vows and oaths forgetful, he
Preferred the wars to thee and me:
But now perhaps thy curse and mine
Makes him eat acorns with the swine.

Nay, curse not him; perhaps now he,
Stung with remorse, is blessing thee;
Perhaps at death, for who can tell
But the great Judge of heaven and hell
By some proud foe has struck the blow,
And laid the dear deceiver low,' &c.

Great doubt has long rested on the history of this piteous ditty; but it is now ascertained to have been a contemporary effusion on the sad love-tale of Anne Bothwell, a sister of the first Lord Holyroodhouse. The only error in the setting down of the song was in calling it *Lady* Anne Bothwell's Lament, as the heroine had no pretension to a term implying noble rank. Her lover was a youth of uncommon elegance of person, the Honourable Alexander Erskine, brother of the Earl of Mar, of the first Earl of Buchan, and of Lord Cardross. A portrait of him, which belonged to his mother (the countess mentioned a few pages back), and which is now in the possession of James Erskine, Esq. of Cambo, Lady Mar's descendant, represents him as strikingly handsome, with much vivacity of countenance, dark-blue eyes, a peaked beard, and moustaches. The lovers were cousins. The song is an evidence of the public interest excited by the affair: a fragment of it found its way into an English play of the day, Broom's comedy of *The Northern Lass* (1632). This is somewhat different from any of the stanzas in the common versions of the ballad:

' Peace, wayward bairn. Oh cease thy moan!
Thy far more wayward daddy's gone,
And never will recallèd be,
By cries of either thee or me;
        For should we cry,
        Until we die,
We could not scant his cruelty.
        Baloo, baloo, &c.

He needs might in himself foresee
What thou successively mightst be;
And could he then (though me forego)
His infant leave, ere he did know
        How like the dad
        Would prove the lad,
In time to make fond maidens glad.
        Baloo, baloo,' &c.

Byres's Close, Back of
Commendator Bothwell's House.

The fate of the deceiver proved a remarkable echo of some of the verses of the ballad. Having carried his military experience and the influence of his rank into the party of the Covenanters, he was stationed (1640) with his brother-in-law, the Earl of Haddington, at Dunglass Castle, on the way to Berwick, actively engaged in bringing up levies for the army, then newly advanced across the Tweed; when, by the revenge of an offended page, who applied a hot poker to the powder magazine, the place was blown up. Erskine, with his brother-in-law and many other persons, perished. A branch of the Mar family retained, till no remote time, the awe-mingled feeling which had been produced by this event, which they had been led to regard as a punishment inflicted for the wrongs of Anne Bothwell.

At the back of the Commendator's house there is a projection,* on the top of which is a bartisan or flat roof, faced with three lettered stones. There is a tradition that Oliver Cromwell lived in this house, † and used to come out and sit here to view his navy on the Forth, of which, together with the whole coast, it

* This projection is still a notable architectural feature in the open space at the back of the tenement referred to. The original windows have been built up. One of the lettered stones bearing the words, 'Blessit be God for all his giftis'—a favourite motto with old Edinburgh builders—was removed to Easter Coates house, where it may still be seen in that now old building adjoining St Mary's Cathedral.

† From this tradition it was known as 'The Cromwell Bartizan.' Dunbar's Close did not get its name from its supposed association with Cromwell's soldiers, but from a family that lived in it. At an earlier period it was known as Ireland's Close.

commands a view. As this commander is said to have had his guard-house in the neighbouring alley called Dunbar's Close, there is some reason to give credit to the story, though it is in no shape authenticated by historical record. The same house was, for certain, the residence of Sir William Dick, the hapless son of Crœsus spoken of in a preceding article.

These houses preserved, until their recent renovation, all the characteristics of that ancient mode of architecture which has procured for the edifices constructed upon it the dignified appellative of *Mahogany Lands*. Below were the booths or piazzas, once prevalent throughout the whole town, in which the merchants of the laigh shops, or cellars, were permitted to exhibit their goods to the passengers. The merchant himself took his seat at the head of the stair to attend to the wants of passing customers. By the ancient laws of the burgh, it was required that each should be provided with 'lang wappinis, sick as a spear or a Jeddart staff,' with which he was to sally forth and assist the magistrates in time of need; for example, when a *tulzie* took place between the retainers of rival noblemen meeting in the street.

This house could also boast of that distinguished feature in all ancient wooden structures, a *fore-stair*, an antiquated convenience, or inconvenience, now almost extinct, consisting of a flight of steps, ascending from the pavement to the first floor of the mansion, and protruding a considerable way into the street. Nuisances as they still are, they were once infinitely worse. What will my readers think when they are informed that under these projections our ancestors kept their swine? Yes; *outside stairs* was formerly but a term of outward respect for what were as frequently denominated  *swine's cruives;* and the rude inhabitants of these narrow mansions were permitted, through the day, to stroll about the 'High Gait,' seeking what they might devour among the heaps of filth which then encumbered the street,* as barn-door fowls are at the present

* Edinburgh was not in this respect worse than other European cities. Paris,

day suffered to go abroad in country towns; and, like them (or like the town-geese of Musselburgh, which to this day are privileged to feed upon the race-ground), the sullen porkers were regularly called home in the evening by their respective proprietors.

These circumstances will be held as sufficient evidence, notwithstanding all the enactments for the ' policy of bigginis' and ' decoring the tounes,' that the stranger's constant reproach of the Scots for want of cleanliness was not unmerited. Yet, to show that our countrymen did not lack a taste for decent appearances, let it be recollected that on every occasion of a public procession, entry of a sovereign, or other ceremonial, these forestairs were hung with carpets, tapestry, or arras, and were the principal places for the display of rank and fashion; while the windows, like the galleries of a theatre compared with the boxes, were chiefly occupied by spectators of a lower degree.* The strictest proclamations were always issued, before any such occasion, ordaining the ' middinis' and the ' swine' to be removed, and the stairs to be decorated in the manner mentioned.

Beneath the stair of the house now under review there abode in later times an old man named Bryce, in whose life and circumstances there was something characteristic of a pent-up city like

at least, was equally disgusting. Rigord, who wrote in the twelfth century, tells us that the king, standing one day at the window of his palace near the Seine, and observing that the dirt thrown up by the carriages produced a most offensive stench, resolved to remedy this intolerable nuisance by causing the streets to be paved. For a long time swine were permitted to wallow in them; till the young Philip being killed by a fall from his horse, from a sow running between its legs, an order was issued that no swine should in future run about the street. The monks of the Abbey of St Anthony remonstrated fiercely against this order, alleging that the prevention of the saint's swine from enjoying the liberty of going where they pleased was a want of respect to their patron. It was therefore found necessary to grant them the privilege of wallowing in the dirt without molestation, requiring the monks only to turn them out with bells about their necks.

* 'To recreat hir hie renoun,
 Of curious things thair wes all sort,
 The stairs and houses of the toun
 With tapestries were spread athort:
 Quhair histories men micht behould,
 With images and anticks auld.

THE DESCRIPTION OF THE QVEEN'S MAIESTIES MAIST HONORABLE ENTRY INTO THE TOWN OF EDINBVRGH, VPON THE 19. DAY OF MAII, 1590. BY JOHN BVREL.'—*Watson's Collection of Scots Poems* (1709).

Edinburgh, where every foot of space was valuable. A stock of small hardwares and trinkets was piled up around him, leaving scarcely sufficient room for the accommodation of his own person, which completely filled the vacant space, as a hermit-crab fills its shell. There was not room for the admission of a customer; but he had a *half-door*, over which he sold any article that was demanded; and there he sat from morning till night, with his face turned to this door, looking up the eternal Lawnmarket. The place was so confined that he could not stand upright in it; nor could he stretch out his legs. Even while he sat, there was an uneasy obliquity of the stair, which compelled him to shrink a little aside; and by accustoming himself to this posture for a long series of years, he had insensibly acquired a twist in his shoulders, nearly approaching to a humpback, and his head swung a little to one side. This was *l'air boutiquier* in a most distressing sense.

In the description of this old tenement given in the title-deeds, it is called 'All and haill that Lodging or Timber Land lying in the burgh of Edinburgh, on the north side of the High Street thereof, forgainst the place of the Tolbooth, commonly called the Poor Folks' Purses.' The latter place was a part of the northern wall of the prison, deriving its name from a curious circumstance. It was formerly the custom for the privileged beggars, called *Blue-gowns*, to assemble in the palace yard, where a small donation from the king, consisting of as many pennies as he was years old, was conferred on each of them; after which they moved in procession up the High Street, till they came to this spot, where the magistrates gave each a *leathern purse* and a small sum of money; the ceremony concluding by their proceeding to the High Church to hear a sermon from one of the king's chaplains.[*]

THE KRAMES.

The central row of buildings—the *Luckenbooths proper*—was not wholly taken away till 1817. The narrow passage left between it and the church will ever be memorable to all who knew Edinburgh in those days, on account of the strange scene

[*] In the early times these privileged beggars were called 'Bedesmen,' from telling their beads as they walked from Holyrood to St Giles'. From the erection of the Canongate Church in 1690 the ceremony took place there, until it was discontinued in the first years of Queen Victoria's reign. A well-known worthy of this community was reputed in 1837 to possess property which yielded an annual income of £120.

of traffic which it presented—each recess, angle, and coign of vantage in the wall of the church being occupied by little shops, of the nature of Bryce's, devoted to the sale of gloves, toys, lollipops, &c. These were the *Krames*, so famous at Edinburgh firesides. Singular places of business they assuredly were; often not presenting more space than a good church-pew, yet supporting by their commerce respectable citizenly families, from which would occasionally come men of some consequence in society. At the same spot the constable (Earl of Errol) was wont to sit upon a chair at the ridings of the parliament, when ceremonially receiving the members as they alighted.

I am told that one such place, not more than seven feet by three, had been occupied by a glover named Kennedy, who with his gentle dame stood there retailing their wares for a time sufficient to witness the rise and fall of dynasties, never enjoying all that time the comfort of a fire, even in the coldest weather! This was a specimen of the life led by these patient creatures; many of whom, upon the demolition of their lath and plaster tenements, retired from business with little competencies. Their rents were from £3 to £6 per annum; and it appears that, huddled as the town then was around them, they had no inconsiderable custom. At the end of the row, under the angle of the church, was a brief stair, called *The Lady's Steps*, thought to be a corruption of *Our Lady's Steps*, with reference to a statue of the Virgin, the niche for which was seen in the east wall of the church till the renovation of the building in 1830. Sir George Mackenzie, however, in his *Observations on the Statutes*, states that the Lady's Steps were so called from the infamous Lady March (wife of the Earl of Arran, James VI.'s profligate chancellor), from whom also the nine o'clock evening-bell, being ordered by her to an hour later, came to be called *The Lady's Bell*. When men made bargains at the Cross, it was customary for them to go up to the Lady's Steps, and there consummate the negotiation by wetting thumbs or paying *arles*.

CREECH'S SHOP.

The building at the east end of the Luckenbooths proper had a front facing down the High Street, and commanding not only a view of the busy scene there presented, but a prospect of Aberlady Bay, Gosford House, and other objects in Haddingtonshire. The shop in the east front was that of Mr Creech, a bookseller of facete memory, who had published many books by the principal literary men of his day, to all of whom he was known as a friend and equal. From this place had issued works by Kames, Smith, Hume, Mackenzie, and finally the poems of Burns. It might have been called the Lounger's Observatory, for seldom was the doorway free of some group of idlers, engaged in surveying and commenting on the crowd in front; Creech himself, with his black silk breeches and powdered head, being ever a conspicuous member of the corps. The flat above had been the shop of Allan Ramsay, and the place where, in 1725, he set up the first example of a circulating library known in Scotland.

THE PARLIAMENT HOUSE.

PAGE 128.

UPPER BAXTER'S CLOSE.
Where Burns first resided in Edinburgh.

PAGE 164.

SOME MEMORANDA OF THE OLD KIRK OF ST GILES.

THE central portion or transept of St Giles's Church, opening from the south, formed a distinct place of worship, under the name of the Old Church, and this seems to have been the first arranged for Protestant worship after the Reformation. It was the scene of the prelections of John Knox (who, it will be remembered, was the first minister of the city under the reformed religion), until a month before his death, when it appears that another portion of the building—styled the Tolbooth Kirk—was fitted up for his use.

John Knox's Pulpit.

It also happened to be in the Old Kirk that the celebrated riot of the 23rd of July 1637 took place, when, on the opening of the new Episcopal service - book, Jenny Geddes, of worthy memory, threw her cutty-stool at the dean who read it—the first weapon, and a formidable one it was, employed in the great civil war.*

Jenny Geddes was an herbwoman—*Scottice, a greenwife*—at the Tron Church, where, in former as well as in recent times,

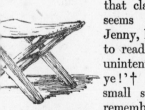

Jenny Geddes's Stool.

that class of merchants kept their stalls. It seems that, in the midst of the hubbub, Jenny, hearing the bishop call upon the dean to read the *collect* of the day, cried out, with unintentional wit: 'Deil colic the wame o' ye!'† and threw at the dean's head the small stool on which she sat; 'a ticket of remembrance,' as a Presbyterian annalist merrily terms it, so well aimed that the

---

* We learn from Crawford's *History of the University* (MS. Adv. Lib.) that the service was read that day in the Old Kirk on account of the more dignified place of worship towards the east being then under the process of alteration or the erection of the altar, 'and other pendicles of that idolatrous worship.'

† *Notes upon the Phœnix edition of the Pastoral Letter*, by S. Johnson, 1694.

clergyman only escaped it by jouking ; * that is, by [ducking or] suddenly bending his person.

Jenny, like the originators of many other insurrections, appears to have afterwards repented of her exertions on this occasion. We learn from the simple diarist, Andrew Nichol, that when Charles II. was known, in June 1650, to have arrived in the north of Scotland, amidst other rejoicings, 'the pure [*q.d.* poor] kaill-wyves at the Trone [Jenny Geddes, no doubt, among the number] war sae overjoyed, that they sacrificed their standis and creellis, yea, the verie *stoollis* they sat on, in ane fyre.' What will give, however, a still more unequivocal proof of the repentance of honest Jenny (after whom, by the way, Burns named a favourite mare), is the conduct expressly attributed to herself on the occasion of the king's coronation in 1661 by the *Mercurius Caledonius:*

'But among all our bontados and caprices,' says that curious register of events, † 'that of the immortal Jenet Geddis, Princesse of the Trone adventurers, was most pleasant ; for she was not only content to assemble all her Creels, Basquets, *Creepies*, ‡ Furmes, and other ingredients that composed the Shope of her Sallets, Radishes, Turnips, Carrots, Spinage, Cabbage, with all other sorts of Pot Merchandise that belongs to the garden, but even her Leather Chair of State, where she used to dispense Justice to the rest of her Langkale Vassals, were all very orderly burned ; she herself countenancing the action with a high-flown flourish and vermilion majesty.'

The Scottish Society of Antiquaries nevertheless exhibit in their museum a clasp-stool, for which there is good evidence that it was the actual stool thrown by Mrs Geddes at the dean.

In the southern aisle of this church, the Regent Murray, three weeks after his assassination at Linlithgow, February 14, 1569-70, was interred : 'his head placed south, contrair the ordour usit ; the sepulchre laid with hewin wark maist curiously, and on the

---

* Wodrow, in his *Diary*, makes a statement apparently at issue with that in the text, both in respect of locality and person :

'It is the constantly believed tradition that it was Mrs Mean, wife to John Mean, merchant in Edinburgh, who threw the first stool when the service-book was read in the New Kirk, Edinburgh, 1637, and that many of the lasses that carried on the fray were preachers in disguise, for they threw stools to a great length.'

† A newspaper commenced after the Restoration, and continued through eleven numbers.

‡ Small stools.

head ane plate of brass.' John Knox preached a funeral-sermon over the remains of his friend, and drew tears from the eyes of all present. In the Tolbooth Church, immediately adjoining to the west, sat the convention which chose the Earl of Lennox as his successor in the regency. Murray's monument was not inelegant for the time; and its inscription, written by Buchanan, is remarkable for emphatic brevity.

This part of the church appears to have formerly been an open lounge. French Paris, Queen Mary's servant, in his confession respecting the murder of Darnley, mentions that, during the communings which took place before that deed was determined on, he one day 'took his mantle and sword, and went to walk (*promener*) in the High Church.' Probably, in consequence of the veneration entertained for the memory of 'the Good Regent,' or else, perhaps, from some simple motive of conveniency, the Earl of Murray's tomb was a place frequently assigned in bills for the payment of the money. It also appears to have been the subject of a similar jest to that respecting the tomb of Duke Humphrey.

Modern Monument to the Marquis of Montrose
(see p. 108).

Robert Sempill, in his *Banishment of Poverty*, a poem referring to the year 1680 or 1681, thus expresses himself:

'Then I knew no way how to fen';
   My guts rumbled like a *hurle-barrow;*
I dined with saints and noblemen,
   Even sweet Saint Giles and Earl of Murray.'

In the immediate neighbourhood of the Earl of Murray's tomb, to the east, is the sepulchre of the Marquis of Montrose, executed in 1650, and here interred most sumptuously, June 1661, after the various parts of his body had been dispersed for eleven years in different directions, according to his sentence.*

* See *St Giles', Edinburgh: Church, College, and Cathedral,* by the Rev. Sir J. Cameron Lees, D.D. ; also *Historical Sketch of St Giles' Cathedral,* by William Chambers, by whom the cathedral was restored in 1872–83. Regarding the reinterment of Montrose, there is a narrative, with some fresh light on the subject, in the paper, 'The Embalming of Montrose,' in the first volume of *The Book of the Old Edinburgh Club.* The monuments to Knox, the Earl of Murray, and the Marquises of Argyll and Montrose are quite modern.

THE PARLIAMENT CLOSE.

Ancient Churchyard—Booths attached to the High Church—Gold-smiths—George Heriot—The Deid-Chack.

PREVIOUS to the seventeenth century, the ground now occupied by the Parliament House, and the buildings adjacent to the south and west, was the churchyard of St Giles's, from the south side of which edifice it extended down a steep declivity to the Cowgate. This might formerly be considered the metropolitan cemetery of Scotland; as, together with the internal space of the church, it contained the ashes of many noble and remarkable personages, John Knox amongst the number. After the Reformation, when Queen Mary conferred the gardens of the Greyfriars upon the town, the churchyard of St Giles's ceased to be much used as a burying-ground; and that extensive and more appropriate place of sepulture succeeded to this in being made *the Westminster Abbey of Scotland.*

The west side of the cemetery of St Giles's was bounded by the house of the provost of the church, who, in 1469, granted part of the same to the citizens for the augmentation of the burying-ground. From the charter accompanying the grant, it appears that the provost's house then also contained the public school of Edinburgh.

In the lower part of the churchyard* there was a small place of worship denominated the *Chapel of Holyrood.* Walter Chapman, the first printer in Edinburgh, in 1528 endowed an altar in this chapel with his tenement in the Cowgate; and, by the tenor of the charter, I am enabled to point out very nearly the residence of this interesting person, who, besides being a printer, was a respectable merchant in Edinburgh, and, it would appear, a very pious man. The tenement is thus described: 'All and haill this tenement of land, back and foir, with houses. biggings, yards, and well † thereof, lying in the Cowgate of Edinburgh, on the south

---

* St Giles' churchyard was divided into two terraces by the old city wall (1450), which was built half-way down the sloping ground on the south side of the High Street. A part of this wall was exposed in 1832 when excavations were made for additional buildings at the Advocates' Library.

† Previous to 1681 the inhabitants of Edinburgh were supplied with water from pump wells in the south side of the Cowgate.

side thereof, near the said chapel, betwixt the lands of James Lamb
on the east, and the lands of John Aber on the west, the arable
lands called Wairam's Croft on the south, and the said street on
the north part.'

BOOTHS.

The precincts of St Giles's being now secularised, the church
itself was, in 1628, degraded by numerous wooden booths being
stuck up around it.   Yet, to show that
some reverence was still paid to the
sanctity of the place, the Town-council
decreed that no tradesmen should be
admitted to these shops except bookbinders, mortmakers (watchmakers),
jewellers, and goldsmiths.   *Bookbinders*
must here be meant to signify booksellers, the latter term not being then
known in Scotland.   Of
mortmakers there could
not be many, for watches
were imported from Ger-
many till about the con-
clusion of the seventeenth
century.   The goldsmiths
were a much more numer-
ous tribe than either of
their companions ; for at
that time there prevailed
in Scotland, amongst the
aristocracy, a sort of rude
magnificence and taste for
show extremely favourable
to these tradesmen.

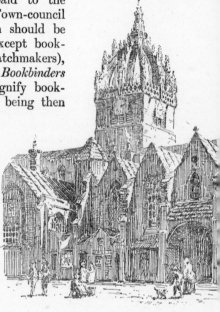

Old St Giles's.

In 1632, the present great hall of the Parliament House was
founded upon the site of the houses formerly occupied by the
ministers of St Giles's.   It was finished in 1639, at an expense of
£11,630 sterling, and devoted to the use of parliament.

It does not appear to have been till after the Restoration
that the Parliament Close was formed, by the erection of a line
of private buildings, forming a square with the church.   These
houses, standing on a declivity, were higher on one side than the
other ; one is said to have been fifteen stories altogether in height.

All, however, were burned down in a great fire which happened in 1700, after which buildings of twelve stories in height were substituted.*

Among the noble inhabitants of the Parliament Close at an early period, the noble family of Wemyss were not the least considerable. At the time of Porteous's affair, when Francis, the fifth earl, was a boy, his sisters persuaded him to act the part of Captain Porteous in a sort of drama which they got up in imitation of that strange scene. The foolish romps actually went the length of tucking up their brother, the heir of the family, by the neck, over a door; and their sports had well-nigh ended in a real tragedy, for the helpless representative of Porteous was black in the face before they saw the necessity of cutting him down.†

The small booths around St Giles's continued, till 1817, to deform the outward appearance of the church. Long before their destruction, the booksellers at least had found the space of six or seven feet too small for the accommodation of their fast-increasing wares, and removed to larger shops in the elegant tenements of the square. One of the largest of the booths, adjacent to the south side of the New or High Church, and having a second story, was occupied, during a great part of the last century, by Messrs Kerr and Dempster, goldsmiths. The first of these gentlemen had been member of parliament for the city, and was the last citizen who ever held that office [in the Scottish parliament]. Such was the humility of people's wishes in those days respecting their houses, that this respectable person actually lived, and had a great number of children, in the small space of the flat over the shop and the cellar under it, which was lighted by a grating in the pavement of the square. The subterraneous part of his house was chiefly devoted to the purposes of a nursery, and proved so insalubrious that all his children died successively at a particular age, with the exception of his son Robert, who, being born much more weakly than the rest, had the good luck to be sent to the country to be nursed, and afterwards grew up to be the author of a work entitled *The Life of Robert Bruce,* and the editor of a large collection of voyages and travels.

GOLDSMITHS.

The goldsmiths of those days were considered a superior class of tradesmen; they appeared in public with scarlet cloak, cocked hat,

* Which also were destroyed in the fires of 1824.

† The Wemysses' footman was one of the few arrested on suspicion of being a ringleader in the Porteous riot.

and cane, as men of some consideration.   Yet in their shops every one of them would have been found working with his own hands at some light labour, in a little recess near the window, generally in a very plain dress, but ready to come forth at a moment's notice to serve a customer.   Perhaps, down to 1780, there was not a goldsmith in Edinburgh who did not condescend to manual labour.

As the whole trade was collected in the Parliament Close, this was of course the place to which country couples resorted, during the last century, in order to make the purchase of silver tea-spoons, which always preceded their nuptials.   It was then as customary a thing in the country for the intending bridegroom to take a journey, a few weeks before his marriage, to the Parliament Close, in order to buy the *silver spoons*, as it was for the bride to have all her clothes and stock of bed-furniture inspected by a committee of matrons upon the wedding eve.   And this important transaction occasioned two journeys : one, in order to select the spoons, and prescribe the initials which were to be marked upon them ; the other, to receive and pay for them.   It must be understood that the goldsmiths of Edinburgh then kept scarcely any goods on hand in their shops, and that the smallest article had to be bespoken from them some time before it was wanted.   A goldsmith, who entered as an apprentice about the beginning of the reign of George III., informed me that they were beginning only at that time to keep a few trifling articles on hand.   Previously another old custom had been abolished.   It had been usual, upon both the occasions above mentioned, for the goldsmith to adjourn with his customer to John's Coffee-house,* or to the Baijen-hole,† and to receive the order or the payment, in a comfortable manner, over a dram and a *caup* of small ale ; which were upon the first occasion paid for by the customer, and upon the second by the trader ; and the goldsmith then was perhaps let into the whole secret counsels of the rustic, including a history of his courtship—in return for which he would take pains to amuse his customer with a sketch of the city news.   In time, as the views and capitals of the Parliament Close goldsmiths became extended, all these pleasant customs were abandoned. ‡

* John's Coffee-house was then situated in the north-east corner of Parliament Close.

† Baijen-hole, see note, p. 155.

‡ In the early times above referred to, £100 was accounted a sufficient capital for a young goldsmith—being just so much as purchased his furnace, tools, &c., served to fit up his shop, and enabled him to enter the Incorporation, which

GEORGE HERIOT.

The shop and workshop of George Heriot existed in this neighbourhood till 1809, when the extension of the Advocates' Library occasioned the destruction of some interesting old *closes* to the west of St Giles's Kirk, and altered all the features of this part of the town. There was a line of three small shops, with wooden superstructures above them, extending between the door of the Old Tolbooth and that of the *Laigh Council-house*, which occupied the site of the present lobby of the Signet Library. A narrow passage led between these shops and the west end of St Giles's ; and George Heriot's shop, being in the centre of the three, was situated exactly opposite to the south window of the Little Kirk. The back windows looked into an alley behind, called Beith's or Bess Wynd. In confirmation of this tradition, George Heriot's name was discovered upon the architrave of the door, being carved in the stone, and apparently having served as his *sign*. Besides this curious memorial, the booth was also found to contain his forge and bellows, with a hollow stone, fitted with a stone cover or lid, which had been used as a receptacle for and a means of extinguishing the living embers of the furnace, upon closing the shop at night. All these curiosities were bought by the late Mr E. Robertson of the Commercial Bank, who had been educated in Heriot's Hospital, and by him presented to the governors, who ordered them to be carefully deposited and preserved in the house, where they now remain. George Heriot's shop was only about seven feet square! Yet his master, King James, is said to have sometimes visited him and been treated by him here. There is a story that one day, when the goldsmith visited His Majesty at Holyrood, he found him sitting beside a fire, which, being composed of perfumed wood, cast an agreeable smell through the room. Upon George Heriot remarking its pleasantness, the king told him that it was quite as costly as it was fine. Heriot said that if His Majesty would come and pay him a visit at his shop, he would show him a still more costly fire.

'Indeed!' said the king; 'and I will.' He accordingly paid the goldsmith a visit, but was surprised to find only an ordinary fire. 'Is this, then, your fine fire?' said he.

alone required £40 out of the £100. The stock with which George Heriot commenced business at a much earlier period (1580)—said to have been about £200—must therefore be considered a proof of the wealth of that celebrated person's family.

'Wait a little,' said George, 'till I get my fuel.' So saying, he took from his bureau a bond for two thousand pounds which he had lent to the king, and laying it in the fire, added : 'Now, whether is your Majesty's fire or mine most expensive ?'

'Yours most certainly, Master Heriot,' said the king.

Adjacent to George Heriot's shop, and contiguous to the Laigh Council-house, there was a tavern, in which a great deal of small legal business used to be transacted in bygone times. Peter Williamson, an original and singular person, who had long been in North America, and therefore designated himself 'from the other world,' kept this house for many years.* It served also as a sort of vestry to the Tolbooth Church, and was the place where the magistrates took what was called the *Deid-chack*—that is, a refreshment or dinner, of which those dignitaries always partook after having attended an execution. The *Deid-chack* is now abjured, like many other of those fashions which formerly rendered the office of a magistrate so much more comfortable than it now is.†

The various kirks which compose St Giles's had all different characters in former times. The High Kirk had a sort of dignified aristocratic character, approaching somewhat to prelacy, and was frequented only by sound church-and-state men, who did not care so much for the sermon as for the gratification of sitting in the same place with His Majesty's Lords of Council and Session and the magistrates of Edinburgh, and who desired to be thought men of sufficient liberality and taste to appreciate the prelections of Blair. The Old Kirk, in the centre of the whole, was frequented

---

* Peter had, in early life, been kidnapped and sold to the plantations. After spending some time among the North American Indians, he came back to Scotland, and began business in Edinburgh as a vintner. Robert Fergusson, in his poem entitled *The Rising of the Session*, thus alludes to a little tavern he kept within the Parliament House :

> 'This vacance is a heavy doom
> On Indian Peter's coffee-room,
> For a' his china pigs are toom ;
>   Nor do we see
> In wine the soukar biskets soom
>   As light's a flee.'

Peter afterwards established a penny-post in Edinburgh, which became so profitable in his hands that the General Post-office gave him a handsome compensation for it. He was also the first to print a street directory in Edinburgh. He died January 19, 1799.

† Provost Creech was the first who had the good taste to abandon the practice.

by people who wished to have a sermon of good divinity, about three-quarters of an hour long, and who did not care for the darkness and dreariness of their temple. The Tolbooth Kirk was the peculiar resort of a set of rigid Calvinists from the Lawnmarket and the head of the Bow, termed the *Towbuith-Whigs*, who loved nothing but *extempore* evangelical sermons, and would have considered it sufficient to bring the house down about their ears if the precentor had ceased, for one verse, the old hillside fashion of reciting the lines of the psalm before singing them. Dr Webster, of convivial memory, was long one of the clergymen of this church, and deservedly admired as a pulpit orator; though his social habits often ran nigh to scandalise his devout and self-denying congregation.

The inhabitants and shopkeepers of the Parliament Square were in former times very sociable and friendly as neighbours, and formed themselves into a sort of society, which was long known by the name of *The Parliament-Close Council.* Of this association there were from fifty to a hundred members, who met once or twice a year at a dinner, when they usually spent the evening, as the newspaper phrase goes, 'in the utmost harmony.' The whim of this club consisted in each person assuming a titular dignity at the dinner, and being so called all the year after by his fellow-members. One was Lord Provost of Edinburgh, another was Dean of Guild, some were bailies, others deacons, and a great proportion state-officers. Sir William Forbes, who, with the kindness of heart which characterised him, condescended to hold a place in this assemblage of mummers, was for a long time *Member for the City.*

Previous to the institution of the police-court, a bailie of Edinburgh used to sit, every Monday, at that part of the Outer Parliament House where the statue of Lord Melville now stands, to hear and decide upon small causes—such as prosecutions for scandals and defamation, or cases of quarrels among the vulgar and the infamous. This judicature, commonly called the *Dirt Court*, was chiefly resorted to by washerwomen from Canonmills and the drunken ale-wives of the Canongate. A list of Dirt-Court processes used always to be hung up on a board every Monday morning at one of the pillars in the piazza at the outside of the Parliament Square; and that part of the piazza, being the lounge of two or three low pettifoggers who managed such pleas, was popularly called the *Scoundrels' Walk.* Early on Monday, it was usual to see one or two threadbare personages, with prodigiously clean linen, bustling about with an air of importance, and occasionally accosted by viragoes with long-eared caps flying behind their heads. These were the agents of the Dirt Court, undergoing conference with their clients.

There was something lofty and august about the Parliament Close, which we shall scarcely ever see revived in any modern part of the town ; so dark and majestic were the buildings all round, and so finely did the whole harmonise with the ancient cathedral which formed one of its sides ! Even the echoes of the Parliament Square had something grand in them. Such, perhaps, were the feelings of William Julius Mickle when he wrote a poem on passing through the Parliament Close of Edinburgh at midnight,* of which the following is one of the best passages :

> ' In the pale air sublime,
> St Giles's column rears its ancient head,
> Whose builders many a century ago
> Were mouldered into dust. Now, O my soul,
> Be filled with sacred awe—I tread
> Above our brave forgotten ancestors. Here lie
> Those who in ancient days the kingdom ruled,
> The counsellors and favourites of kings,
> High lords and courtly dames, and valiant chiefs,
> Mingling their dust with those of lowest rank
> And basest deeds, and now unknown as they.'

* See *Collection of Original Poems by Scotch Gentlemen*, vol. ii. 137 (1762).

MEMORIALS OF THE NOR' LOCH.

HE who now sees the wide hollow space between the Old and New Towns, occupied by beautiful gardens, having their continuity only somewhat curiously broken up by a transverse earthen mound and a line of railway, must be at a loss to realise the idea of the same space presenting in former times a lake, which was regarded as a portion of the physical defences of the city. Yet many, in common with myself, must remember the by no means distant time when the remains of this sheet of water, consisting of a few pools, served as excellent sliding and skating ground in winter, while their neglected grass-green precincts too frequently formed an arena whereon the high and mighty quarrels of Old and New Town *cowlies* * [etymology of the word unknown] were brought to a lapidarian arbitration.

The lake, it after all appears, was artificial, being fed by springs under the Castle Rock, and retained by a dam at the foot of Halkerston's Wynd ; † which dam was a passable way from the city to the fields on the north. Bower, the continuator of Fordun, speaks of a tournament held on the ground, *ubi nunc est lacus*, in 1396, by order of the queen [of Robert III.], at which her eldest son, Prince David, then in his twentieth year, presided. At the beginning of the sixteenth century a ford upon the North Loch is mentioned. Archbishop Beatoun escaped across that ford in 1517, when flying from the unlucky street-skirmish called *Cleanse the Causeway*. In those early times the town corporation kept ducks and swans upon the loch for ornament's sake, and various acts occur in their register for preserving those birds. An act, passed in council between the years 1589 and 1594, ordained ' a boll of oats to be bought for feeding the swans in the North Loch ;' and a person was unlawed at the same time for shooting a swan in the said loch, and obliged to find another in its place. The lake seems to have been a favourite scene for boating. Various houses in the neighbourhood had servitudes of the use of a boat upon it ; and these, in later times, used to be employed to no little purpose in smuggling whisky into the town.

* An Edinburgh term applied to a class of rogues. Probably a corrupt pronunciation of the English word *cully*—to fool, to cheat.

† Where the North Bridge now stands.

The North Loch was the place in which our pious ancestors used to dip and drown offenders against morality, especially of the female sex. The Reformers, therefore, conceived that they had not only done a very proper, but also a very witty thing, when they threw into this lake, in 1558, the statue of St Giles, which formerly adorned their High Church, and which they had contrived to abstract.

It was also the frequent scene of suicide, and on this point one or two droll anecdotes are related. A man was deliberately proceeding to drown himself in the North Loch, when a crowd of the townspeople rushed down to the water-side, venting cries of horror and alarm at the spectacle, yet without actually venturing into the water to prevent him from accomplishing the rash act. Hearing the tumult, the father of the late Lord Henderland threw up his window in James's Court, and leaning out, cried down the brae to the people : ' What 's all the noise about ? Can't ye e'en let the honest man gang to the de'il his ain gate ? ' Whereupon the honest man quietly walked out of the loch, to the no small amusement of his lately appalled neighbours. It is also said that a poor woman, having resolved to put an end to her existence, waded a considerable way into the water, designing to take the fatal plunge when she should reach a place where the lake was sufficiently deep. Before she could satisfy herself on that point, her hoop caught the water, and lifted her off her feet. At the same time the wind caught her figure, and blew her, whether she would or not, into the centre of the pool, as if she had been sailing upon an inverted tub. She now became *alarmed*, screamed for help, and waved her arms distractedly ; all of which signs brought a crowd to the shore she had just left, who were unable, however, to render her any assistance, before she had landed on the other side—fairly cured, it appeared, of all desire of quitting the uneasy coil of mortal life.

THE PARLIAMENT HOUSE.

Old Arrangements of the House—Justice in Bygone Times—Court of Session Garland—Parliament House Worthies.

THE Parliament House, a spacious hall with an oaken arched roof, finished in 1639 for the meetings of the Estates or native parliament, and used for that purpose till the Union, has since then, as is well known, served exclusively as a material portion of the suite of buildings required for the supreme civil judicatory—the Court of Session. This hall, usually styled the *Outer House*, is now a nearly empty space, but it was in a very different state within the recollection of aged practitioners. So lately as 1779, it retained the divisions, furnishings, and other features which it had borne in the days when we had a national legislature—excepting only that the portraits of sovereigns which then adorned the walls had been removed by the Earl of Mar, to whom Queen Anne had given them as a present when the Union was accomplished.

The divisions and furniture, it may be remarked, were understood to be precisely those which had been used for the Court of Session from an early time; but it appears that such changes were made when the parliament was to sit as left the room one free vacant space. The southern portion, separated from the rest by a screen, accommodated the Court of Session. The northern portion, comprising a sub-section used for the Sheriff-court, was chiefly a kind of lobby of irregular form, surrounded by little booths, which were occupied as taverns, booksellers' shops, and toy-shops, all of very flimsy materials.* These *krames*, or boxes, seem to have been established at an early period, the idea being no doubt taken from the former condition of Westminster Hall. John Spottiswoode of Spottiswoode, who, in 1718, published the *Forms of Process before the Court of Session*, mentions that there were 'two keepers of the session-house, who had small salaries to do all the menial offices in the house, and that no small part of their annual perquisites came from the *kramers* in the outer hall.'

---

* A full description of the old Parliament Hall, with a plan showing the divisions and the arrangements of the ' booths,' is given in *Reekiana; or, Minor Antiquities of Edinburgh*. It is not now called the Outer House.

JUSTICE IN BYGONE TIMES.

The memories which have been preserved of the administration of justice by the Court of Session in its earlier days are not such as to increase our love for past times.* This court is described by Buchanan as extremely arbitrary, and by a nearly contemporary historian (Johnston) as infamous for its dishonesty. An advocate or barrister is spoken of by the latter writer as taking money from his clients, and dividing it among the judges for their votes. At this time we find the chancellor (Lord Fyvie) superintending the lawsuits of a friend, and writing to him the way and manner in which he proposed they should be conducted. But the strongest evidence of the corruption of 'the lords' is afforded by an act of 1579, prohibiting them 'be thame selffis or be their wiffis or servandes, to tak in ony time cuming, *buddis*, *brybes*, *gudes*, *or geir*, fra quhatever persone or persons presentlie havand, or that heirefter sall happyne to have, *any actionis or caussis pursewit befoir thame*, aither fra the persewer or defender,' under pain of confiscation. Had not bribery been common amongst the judges, such an act as this could never have been passed.

In the curious history of the family of Somerville there is a very remarkable anecdote illustrative of the course of justice at that period. Lord Somerville and his kinsman, Somerville of Cambusnethan, had long carried on a litigation. The former was at length advised to use certain means for the advancement of his cause with the Regent Morton, it being then customary for the sovereign to preside in the court. Accordingly, having one evening caused his agents to prepare all the required papers, he went next morning to the palace, and being admitted to the regent, informed him of the cause, and entreated him to order it to be called that forenoon. He then took out his purse, as if to give a few pieces to the pages or servants, and slipping it down upon the table, hurriedly left the presence-chamber. The earl cried several times after him: 'My lord, you have left your purse;' but he had no wish to stop. At length, when he was at the outer porch, a servant overtook him with a request that he would go back to breakfast with the regent. He did so, was kindly treated, and soon after was taken by Morton in his coach to the court-room in the city. 'Cambusnethan, by accident, as the coach

---

* Several of the illustrations in the present section are immediately derived from a curious volume, full of entertainment for a denizen of the Parliament House—*The Court of Session Garland*. Edinburgh: Thomas Stevenson. 1839

passed, was standing at Niddry's Wynd head, and having inquired who was in it with the regent, he was answered : " None but Lord Somerville and Lord Boyd ; " upon which he struck his breast, and said : "This day my cause is lost ! " and indeed it proved so.' By twelve o'clock that day, Lord Somerville had gained a cause which had been hanging in suspense for years.

In those days both civil and criminal procedure was conducted in much the same spirit as a suit at war. When a great noble was to be tried for some monstrous murder or treason, he appeared at the bar with as many of his retainers, and as many of his friends and their retainers, as he could muster, and justice only had its course if the government chanced to be the strongest, which often was not the case. It was considered dishonourable not to countenance a friend in troubles of this kind, however black might be his moral guilt. The trial of Bothwell for the assassination of Darnley is a noted example of a criminal outbraving his judges and jury. Relationship, friendly connection, solicitation of friends, and direct bribes were admitted and recognised influences to which the civil judge was expected to give way. If a difficulty were found in inducing a judge to vote against his conscience, he might at least perhaps be induced by some of those considerations to absent himself, so as to allow the case to go in the desired way. The story of the abduction of Gibson of Durie by Christie's Will, and his immurement in a Border tower for some weeks, that his voice might be absent in the decision of a case—as given in the *Border Minstrelsy* by Scott—is only incorrect in some particulars. (As the real case is reported in Pitcairn's *Criminal Trials*, it appears that, in September 1601, Gibson was carried off from the neighbourhood of St Andrews by George Meldrum, younger of Dumbreck, and hastily transported to the castle of Harbottle in Northumberland, and kept there for eight days.) But, after all, Scotland was not singular among European nations in these respects. In Molière's *Misanthrope*, produced in 1666, we find the good-natured Philinte coolly remonstrating with Alceste on his unreasonable resolution to let his lawsuit depend only on right and equity.

'Qui voulez-vous donc, qui pour vous sollicite ? ' says Philinte.
' Aucun juge par vous ne sera visité ? '
'Je ne remuerai point,' returns the misanthrope.
Philinte. Votre partie est forte, et peut par sa cabale entrainer. . . .
Alceste. Il n'importe. . . .
Philinte. Quel homme ! . . . On se riroit de vous, Alceste, si on

vous entendoit parler de la façon.   (*People would laugh at you if
they heard you talk in this manner.*)

It is a general tradition in Scotland that the English judges
whom Cromwell sent down to administer the law in Scotland,
for the first time made the people acquainted with impartiality
of judgment.   It is added that, after the Restoration, when
native lords were again put upon the bench, some one, in presence
of the President Gilmour, lauding the late English judges for the
equity of their proceedings, his lordship angrily remarked : ' De'il
thank them ; a wheen kinless loons ! '   That is, no thanks to
them ; a set of fellows without relations in the country, and who,
consequently, had no one to please by their decisions.

After the Restoration there was no longer direct bribing, but
other abuses still flourished.   The judges were tampered with by
private solicitation.   Decisions went in favour of the man of most
personal or family influence.   The following anecdote of the reign
of Charles II. rests on excellent authority : 'A Scotch gentleman
having entreated the Earl of Rochester to speak to the Duke of
Lauderdale upon the account of a business that seemed to be
supported by a clear and undoubted right, his lordship very
obligingly promised to do his utmost endeavours to engage the
duke to stand his friend in a concern so just and reasonable as
his was ; and accordingly, having conferred with his grace about
the matter, the duke made him this very odd return, that though
he questioned not the right of the gentleman he recommended to
him, yet he could not promise him a helping hand, and far less
success in business, if he knew not first the man, whom perhaps
his lordship had some reason to conceal ; " because," said he to
the earl, " if your lordship were as well acquainted with the
customs of Scotland as I am, you had undoubtedly known this
among others—*Show me the man, and I'll show you the law;*" giving
him to understand that the law in Scotland could protect no man
if either his purse were empty or his adversaries great men, or
supported by great ones.' *

One peculiar means of favouring a particular party was then
in the power of the presiding judge : he could call a cause when
he pleased.   Thus he would watch till one or more judges who
took the opposite view to his own were out of the way—either
in attendance on other duties or from illness—and then calling
the cause, would decide it according to his predilection.   Even

* *A Moral Discourse on the Power of Interest.*   By David Abercromby, M.D.
London, 1691.   P. 60.

the first President Dalrymple, afterwards Viscount Stair, one of the most eminent men whom the Scottish law-courts have ever produced, condescended to favour a party in this way. An act enjoining the calling of causes according to their place in a regular roll was passed in the reign of Charles II.; but the practice was not enforced till the days of President Forbes, sixty years later. We have a remarkable illustration of the partiality of the bench in a circumstance which took place about the time of the Revolution. During the pleadings in a case between Mr Pitilloch, an advocate, and Mr Aytoun of Inchdairnie, the former applied the term *briber* to Lord Harcarse, a judge seated at the moment on the bench, and who was father-in-law to the opposite party. The man was imprisoned for contempt; but this is not the point. Not long after, in this same cause, Lord Harcarse went down to the bar in his gown, and pleaded for his son-in-law Aytoun!

About that period a curious indirect means of influencing the judges began to be notorious. Each lord had a dependant or favourite, generally some young relative, practising in the court, through whom it was understood that he could be prepossessed with a favourable view of any cause. This functionary was called a *Peat* or *Pate*, from a circumstance thus related in Wilkes's *North Briton:* 'One of the former judges of the Court of Session, of the first character, knowledge, and application to business, had a son at the bar whose name was Patrick; and when the suitors came about, soliciting his favour, his question was: "Have you consulted *Pat?*" If the answer was affirmative, the usual reply of his lordship was: "I'll inquire of *Pat* about it; I'll take care of your cause; go home and mind your business." The judge in that case was even as good as his word, for while his brother-judges were robing, he would tell them what pains his son had taken, and what trouble he had put himself to, by his directions, in order to find out the real circumstances of the dispute; and as no one on the bench would be so unmannerly as to question the veracity of the son or the judgment of the father, the decree always went according to the information of *Pat.* At the present era, in case a judge has no son at the bar, his nearest relation (and he is sure to have one there) officiates in that station. But, as it frequently happens, if there are *Pats* employed on each side, the judges differ, and the greatest interest—that is, the longest purse—is sure to carry it.'

I bring the subject to a conclusion by a quotation from the

Court of Session Garland: 'Even so far down as 1737 traces of
the ancient evil may be found. Thus, in some very curious letters
which passed between William Foulis, Esq. of Woodhall, and his
agent, Thomas Gibson of Durie, there is evidence that private
influence could even then be resorted to. The agent writes to his
client, in reference to a pending lawsuit (23rd November 1735):
"I have spoken to Strachan and several of the lords, who are all
surprised Sir F[rancis Kinloch] should stand that plea. By Lord
St Clair's advice, Mrs Kinloch is to wait on Lady Cairnie to-morrow,
to cause her ask the favour of Lady St Clair to solicit Lady Betty
Elphingston and Lady Dun. My lord promises to back his lady,
and to ply both their lords, also Leven and his cousin Murkle.*
He is your good friend, and wishes success; he is jealous Mrs
Mackie will side with her cousin Beatie. St Clair says *Leven* † *has
only once gone wrong upon his hand since he was a Lord of Session.*
Mrs Kinloch has been with Miss Pringle, Newhall. Young Dr
Pringle is *a good agent there,* and discourses Lord Newhall ‡
strongly on the law of nature," &c.

'Again, upon the 23rd of January 1737, he writes: "I can
assure you that when Lord Primrose left this town, he stayed all
that day with Lord J[ustice] C[lerk],§ and went to Andrew
Broomfield at night, and went off post next morning; and what
made him despair of getting anything done was, that it has been
so long delayed, after promising so frankly, when he knew the one
could cause the other trot to him like a penny-dog when he
pleased. But there's another hindrance: I suspect much Penty ‖
has not been in town as yet, and I fancy it's by him the other
must be managed. The Ld. J[ustice] C[lerk] is frank enough, but
the other two are —— clippies. I met with Bavelaw and Mr
William on Tuesday last. I could not persuade the last to go to
a wine-house, so away we went to an aquavity-house, where I told
Mr Wm. what had passed, as I had done before that to Bavelaw.
They seemed to agree nothing could be done just now, but to know

---

* John Sinclair of Murkle, appointed a Lord of Session in 1733.

† Alexander Leslie, advocate, succeeded his nephew as fifth Earl of Leven,
and fourth Earl of Melville, in 1729. He was named a Lord of Session, and
took his seat on the bench on the 11th of July 1734. He died 2nd February
1754.

‡ Sir Walter Pringle of Newhall, raised to the bench in 1718.

§ Andrew Fletcher of Milton was appointed, on the resignation of James
Erskine of Grange, Lord Justice-clerk, and took his seat on the bench 21st June
1735.

‖ Probably Gibson of Pentland.

why Lord Drummore* dissuaded bringing in the plea last winter. *I have desired Lord Haining to speak*, but only expect his answer against Tuesday or Wednesday."

'It is not our intention to pursue these remarks further, although we believe that judicial corruption continued long after the Union. We might adduce Lord President Forbes as a witness on this point, who, one of the most upright lawyers himself, did not take any pains to conceal his contempt for many of his brethren. A favourite toast of his is said to have been : " Here 's to such of the judges as don't deserve the gallows." Latterly, the complaint against the judges was not so much for corrupt dealing, with the view of enriching themselves or their " pet " lawyer, but for weak prejudices and feelings, which but ill accorded with the high office they filled.

'These abuses, the recapitulation of which may amuse and instruct, are now only matter of history—the spots that once sullied the garments of justice are effaced, and the old compend, " Show me the man, and I'll show you the law," is out of date.'

COURT OF SESSION GARLAND.

A curious characteristic view of the Scottish bench about the year 1771 is presented in a doggerel ballad, supposed to have been a joint composition of James Boswell and John Maclaurin,† advocates, and professedly the history of a process regarding a bill containing a clause of penalty in case of failure. This *Court of Session Garland*, as it is called, is here subjoined, with such notes on persons and things as the reader may be supposed to require or care for.

PART FIRST.

The bill charged on was payable at sight,
And decree was craved by Alexander Wight ; ‡
But because it bore a penalty in case of failzie,
It therefore was null, contended Willie Baillie.§

The Ordinary, not choosing to judge it at random,
Did with the minutes make *avisandum ;*
And as the pleadings were vague and windy,
His lordship ordered memorials *hinc inde.*

* Hew Dalrymple of Drummore, appointed a Lord of Session in 1726.
† Afterwards Lord Dreghorn.
‡ Author of a Treatise on Election Laws, and Solicitor-general during the Coalition Ministry in 1783.
§ Afterwards Lord Polkemmet.

We, setting a stout heart to a stay brae,
Took into the cause Mr David Rae.*
Lord Auchinleck,† however, repelled our defence,
And, over and above, decerned for expense.

However, of our cause not being ashamed,
Unto the whole lords we straightway reclaimed ;
And our Petition was appointed to be seen,
Because it was drawn by Robbie Macqueen.‡

The Answer by Lockhart§ himself it was wrote,
And in it no argument nor fact was forgot.
He is the lawyer that from no cause will flinch,
And on this occasion divided the bench.

Alemore‖ the judgment as illegal blames ;
‘’Tis equity, you bitch,’ replies my Lord Kames.¶
‘This cause,’ cries Hailes,** ‘to judge I can't pretend,
For *justice*, I perceive, wants an *e* at the end.’

Lord Coalstoun†† expressed his doubts and his fears ;
And Strichen‡‡ threw in his *weel-weels* and *oh dears*.
‘This cause much resembles the case of Mac-Harg,
And should go the same way,’ says Lordie Barjarg.§§

---

* Afterwards Lord Eskgrove and Lord Justice-clerk.

† Alexander Boswell, Esq., of Auchinleck, the author's father—appointed to the bench in 1754 ; died 1782. This gentleman was a precise old Presbyterian, and therefore the most opposite creature in the world to his son, who was a cavalier in politics and an Episcopalian.

‡ Afterwards Lord Braxfield—appointed 1776 ; died 1800, while holding the office of Lord Justice-clerk. Lord Braxfield is the prototype of Stevenson's *Weir of Hermiston*.

§ Alexander Lockhart, Esq., decidedly the greatest lawyer at the Scottish bar in his day—appointed to the bench in 1774 ; died in 1782.

‖ Andrew Pringle, Esq.—appointed a judge in 1759 ; died 1776. This gentleman was remarkable for his fine oratory, which was praised highly by Sheridan the lecturer (father of R. B. Sheridan) in his *Discourses on English Oratory*.

¶ Henry Home, Esq.—raised to the bench 1752 ; died 1783. This great man, so remarkable for his metaphysical subtlety and literary abilities, was strangely addicted to the use of the coarse word in the text.

** Sir David Dalrymple—appointed a judge in 1766 ; died 1792. A story is told of Lord Hailes once making a serious objection to a law-paper, and, in consequence, to the whole suit to which it belonged, on account of the word *justice* being spelt in the manner mentioned in the text. Perhaps no author ever affected so much critical accuracy as Lord Hailes, and yet there never was a book published with so large an array of *corrigenda et addenda* as the first edition of the *Annals of Scotland*.

†† George Brown, Esq., of Coalstoun—appointed 1756 ; died 1776.

‡‡ Alexander Fraser of Strichen—appointed 1730 ; died 1774.

§§ James Erskine, Esq., subsequently titled Lord Alva—appointed 1761 ; died 1796. He was of exceedingly small stature, and upon that account denominated ‘Lordie.’

'Let me tell you, my lords, this cause is no joke!'
Says, with a horse-laugh, my Lord Elliock.*
'To have read all the papers I pretend not to brag!'
Says my Lord Gardenstone † with a snuff and a wag.

Up rose the President,‡ and an angry man was he—
'To alter the judgment I can never agree!'
The east wing cried 'YES,' and the west wing cried 'NOT;'
And it was carried 'ADHERE'§ by my lord's casting vote.

The cause being somewhat knotty and perplext,
Their lordships did not know how they'd determine next;
And as the session was to rise so soon,
They superseded extract till the 12th of June.‖

PART SECOND.

Having lost it so nigh, we prepare for the summer,
And on the 12th of June presented a reclaimer;
But dreading a refuse, we gave Dundas ¶ a fee,
And though it run nigh, it was carried 'TO SEE.'**

In order to bring aid from usage bygone,
The Answers were drawn by *quondam* Mess John.††
He united with such art our law with the civil,
That the counsel on both sides wished him to the devil.

The cause being called, my Lord Justice-clerk,‡‡
With all due respect, began a loud bark:

* James Veitch, Esq.—appointed 1761; died 1793.

† Francis Garden, Esq.—appointed 1764; died 1793—author of several respectable literary productions.

‡ Robert Dundas, Esq., of Arniston—appointed 1760; died 1787.

§ The bench being semicircular, and the President sitting in the centre, the seven judges on his right hand formed the *east* wing, those on his left formed the *west*. The decisions were generally announced by the words 'Adhere' and 'Alter'—the former meaning an affirmance, the latter a reversal, of the judgment of the Lord Ordinary.

‖ The term of the summer session was then from the 12th of June to the 12th of August.

¶ Henry, first Viscount Melville, then coming forward as an advocate at the Scottish bar. When this great man passed advocate, he was so low in cash that, after going through the necessary forms, he had only one guinea left in his pocket. Upon coming home, he gave this to his sister (who lived with him), in order that she might purchase him a gown; after which he had not a penny. However, his talents soon filled his coffers. The gown is yet preserved by the family.

** 'To See' is to appoint the petition against the judgment pronounced to be answered.

†† John Erskine of Carnock, author of the *Institute of the Law of Scotland.*

‡‡ Thomas Miller, Esq., of Glenlee—appointed to this office in 1766, upon the death of Lord Minto. He filled this situation till the death of Robert

He appealed to his conscience, his heart, and from thence
Concluded—'To ALTER,' but to give no expense.

Lord Stonefield,* unwilling his judgment to pother,
Or to be *anticipate*, agreed with his brother :
But Monboddo † was clear the bill to enforce
Because, he observed, it was the price of a horse.

Says Pitfour,‡ with a wink, and his hat all a-jee,
'I remember a case in the year twenty-three—
The Magistrates of Banff *contra* Robert Carr ;
I remember weel—I was then at the bar.

Likewise, my lords, in the case of Peter Caw,
Superflua non nocent was found to be law.'
Lord Kennet § also quoted the case of one Lithgow,
Where a penalty in a bill was held *pro non scripto*.

The Lord President brought his chair to the plumb,
Laid hold of the bench, and brought forward his bum ;
'In these Answers, my lords, some freedoms are used,
Which I could point out, provided I choosed.

I was for the interlocutor, my lords, I admit,
But am open to conviction as long's I here do sit.
To oppose your precedents, I quote a few cases ;'
And Tait || *à priori*, hurried up the causes.

He proved it as clear as the sun in the sky,
That their maxims of law could not here apply ;
That the writing in question was neither bill nor band,
But something unknown in the law of the land.

The question—'Adhere,' or 'Alter,' being put,
It was carried—'To Alter,' by a casting vote ;
Baillie then moved—'In the bill there's a raze ;'
But by this time their lordships had called a new cause.

A few additions to the notes, in a more liberal space, will
complete what I have to set down regarding the lawyers of the
last age.

Dundas, in 1787, when (January 1788) he was made President of the Court of
Session, and created a baronet, in requital for his long service as a judge.
Being then far advanced in life, he did not live long to enjoy his new accession
of honours, but died in September 1789.

* John Campbell, Esq., of Stonefield.

† James Burnet, Esq.—appointed 1767 ; died 1799.

‡ James Fergusson, Esq.—appointed 1761 ; died 1777.   He always wore his
hat on the bench, on account of sore eyes.

§ Robert Bruce, Esq.—appointed 1764 ; died 1785.

|| Alexander Tait, Clerk of Session.

LOCKHART OF COVINGTON.*

Lockhart used to be spoken of by all old men about the Court of Session as a paragon. He had been at the bar from 1722, and had attained the highest eminence long before going upon the bench, which he did at an unusually late period of life; yet so different were those times from the present that, according to the report of Sir William Macleod Bannatyne to myself in 1833, Lockhart realised only about a thousand a year by his exertions, then thought a magnificent income. The first man at the Scottish bar in our day is believed to gain at least six times this sum annually. Lockhart had an isolated house behind the Parliament Close, which was afterwards used as the Post-office.† It was removed some years ago to make way for the extension of the buildings connected with the court; leaving only its coach-house surviving, now occupied as a broker's shop in the Cowgate.

Mr Lockhart and Mr Fergusson (afterwards Lord Pitfour) were rival barristers—agreeing, however, in their politics, which were of a Jacobite complexion. While the trials of the poor *forty-five* men were going on at Carlisle, these Scottish lawyers heard with indignation of the unscrupulous measures adopted to procure convictions. They immediately set off for Carlisle, arranging with each other that Lockhart should examine evidence, while Fergusson pleaded and addressed the jury; and offering their services, they were gladly accepted as counsel by the unfortunates whose trials were yet to take place. Each exerted his abilities, in his respective duties, with the greatest solicitude, but with very little effect. The jurors of Carlisle had been so frightened by the Highland army that they thought everything in the shape or hue of tartan a damning proof of guilt; and, in truth, there seemed to be no discrimination whatever exerted in inquiring into the merits of any

* He was the grandson of Lord President Lockhart, who was shot by Chiesly of Dalry (see p. 75).

† Within the memory of an old citizen, who was living in 1833, the Post-office was in the first floor of a house near the Cross, above an alley which still bears the name of the Post-office Close. Thence it was removed to a floor in the south side of the Parliament Square, which was fitted up like a shop, and the letters were dealt across an ordinary counter, like other goods. At this time all the out-of-door business of delivery was managed by one letter-carrier. About 1745 the London bag brought on one occasion no more than a single letter, addressed to the British Linen Company. From the Parliament Square the office was removed to Lord Covington's house, above described; thence, after some years, to a house in North Bridge Street; thence to Waterloo Place; and finally, to a new and handsome structure on the North Bridge.

particular criminal ; and it might have been just as fair, and much more convenient, to try them by wholesale or in companies.   At length one of our barristers fell upon an ingenious expedient, which had a better effect than all the eloquence he had expended.   He directed his man-servant to dress himself in some tartan habiliments, to skulk about for a short time in the neighbourhood of the town, and then permit himself to be taken.   The man did so, and was soon brought into court, and accused of the crime of high treason, and would have been condemned to death had not his master stood up, claimed him as his servant, and proved beyond dispute that the supposed criminal had been in immediate attendance upon his person during the whole time of the Rebellion.   This staggered the jury, and, with the aid of a little amplification from the mouth of the young advocate, served to make them more cautious after-wards in the delivery of their important fiat.

To show the estimation in which Lockhart of Covington was held as an advocate, the late Lord Newton, when at the bar, wore his gown till it was in tatters, and at last had a new one made, with a fragment of the neck of the original sewed into it, whereby he could still make it his boast that he wore 'Covington's gown.'

LORD KAMES.

This able judge and philosopher in advance of his time—for such he was—is described by his biographer, Lord Woodhouselee, as indulging in a certain humorous playfulness, which, to those who knew him intimately, detracted nothing from the feeling of respect due to his eminent talents and virtues.   To strangers, his lordship admits, it might convey 'the idea of lightness.'   The simple fact here shadowed forth is that Lord Kames had a roughly playful manner, and used phrases of an ultra-eccentric character. Among these was a word only legitimately applicable to the female of the canine species.   The writer of the *Garland* introduces this characteristic phrase.   When his lordship found his end approaching very near, he took a public farewell of his brethren.   I was in-formed by an ear-and-eye witness, who is certain that he could not be mistaken, that, after addressing them in a solemn speech and shaking their hands all round, in going out at the door of the court-room he turned about, and casting them a last look, cried in his usual familiar tone : 'Fare ye a' weel, ye bitches !' He died eight days after.

It was remarked that a person called *Sinkum the Cawdy*, who had a short and a long leg and was excessively addicted to swearing, used to lie in wait for Lord Kames almost every morning, and walk alongside of him up the street to the Parliament House. The mystery of Sterne's little, flattering Frenchman, who begged so successfully from the ladies, was scarcely more wonderful than this intimacy, which arose entirely from Lord Kames's love of the gossip which Sinkum made it his business to cater for him.

These are not follies of the wise. They are only the tribute which great genius pays to simple nature. The serenity which marked the close of the existence of Kames was most creditable to him, though it appeared, perhaps, in somewhat whimsical forms to his immediate friends. For three or four days before his death, he was in a state of great debility. Some one coming in, and finding him, notwithstanding his weakness, engaged in dictating to an amanuensis, expressed surprise. 'How, man,' said the declining philosopher, 'would you ha'e me stay wi' my tongue in my cheek till death comes to fetch me?'

LORD HAILES.

When Lord Hailes died, it was a long time before any will could be found. The heir-male was about to take possession of his estates, to the exclusion of his eldest daughter. Some months after his lordship's death, when it was thought that all further search was vain, Miss Dalrymple prepared to retire from New Hailes, and also from the mansion-house in New Street, having lost all hope of a will being discovered in her favour. Some of her domestics, however, were sent to lock up the house in New Street, and in closing the window-shutters, Lord Hailes's will dropped out upon the floor from behind a panel, and was found to secure her in the possession of his estates, which she enjoyed for upwards of forty years.

The literary habits of Lord Hailes were hardly those which would have been expected from his extreme nicety of phrase. The late Miss Dalrymple once did me the honour to show me the place where he wrote the most of his works—not the fine room which contained, and still contains, his books—no secluded boudoir, or den, where he could shut out the world, but the parlour fireside, where sat his wife and children.

[1868.—Now that the grave has for thirty years closed over Miss Dalrymple, it may be allowable to tell that she was of dwarfish and deformed figure, while amiable and judicious above the average of her sex. Taking into view her beautiful place of residence and her large wealth, she remarked to a friend one day : ' I can say, for the honour of man, that I never got an offer in my life.']

LORD GARDENSTONE.

This judge had a predilection for pigs. One, in its juvenile years, took a particular fancy for his lordship, and followed him wherever he went, like a dog, reposing in the same bed. When it attained the mature years and size of swinehood, this of course was inconvenient. However, his lordship, unwilling to part with his friend, continued to let it sleep at least in the same room, and, when he undressed, laid his clothes upon the floor as a bed to it. He said that he liked it, for it kept his clothes warm till the morning. In his mode of living he was full of strange, eccentric fancies, which he seemed to adopt chiefly with a view to his health, which was always that of a valetudinarian.*

LORD PRESIDENT DUNDAS.

This distinguished judge was, in his latter years, extremely sub-ject to gout, and used to fall backwards and forwards in his chair— whence the ungracious expression in the *Garland.* He used to characterise his six clerks thus : ' Two of them cannot *read*, two of them cannot *write*, and the other two can neither *read* nor *write !* ' The eccentric Sir James Colquhoun was one of those who could not *read*. In former times it was the practice of the Lord President to have a sand-glass before him on the bench, with which he used to measure out the utmost time that could be allowed to a judge for the delivery of his opinion. Lord President Dundas would never allow a single moment after the expiration of the sand, and he has often been seen to shake his old-fashioned chronometer ominously in the faces of his brethren when their ' ideas upon the subject ' began, in the words of the *Garland*, to get vague and windy.

LORD MONBODDO.

Lord Monboddo's motion for the enforcement of the bill, on account of its representing the value of a horse, is partly an allusion to his Gulliverlike admiration of that animal, but more particularly

* Lord Gardenstone erected the building (in the form of a Grecian temple) which encloses St Bernard's Well, on the Water of Leith, between the Dean Bridge and Stockbridge. He also founded the town of Laurencekirk in Kincardineshire, which he hoped to make a manufacturing centre.

to his having once embroiled himself in an action respecting a horse which belonged to himself. His lordship had committed the animal, when sick, to the charge of a farrier, with directions for the administration of a certain medicine. The farrier gave the medicine, but went beyond his commission, in as far as he mixed it in a liberal *menstruum* of treacle in order to make it palatable. The horse dying next morning, Lord Monboddo raised a prosecution for its value, and actually pleaded his own cause at the bar. He lost the case, however; and is said to have been so enraged in consequence at his brethren that he never afterwards sat with them upon the bench, but underneath amongst the clerks. The report of this action is exceedingly amusing, on account of the great quantity of Roman law quoted by the judges, and the strange circumstances under which the case appeared before them.

Lord Monboddo, with all his oddities, and though generally hated or despised by his brethren, was by far the most learned and not the least upright judge of his time. His attainments in classical learning and in the study of the ancient philosophers were singular in his time in Scotland, and might have qualified him to shine anywhere. He was the earliest patron of one of the best scholars of his age, the late Professor John Hunter of St Andrews, who was for many years his secretary, and who chiefly wrote the first and best volume of his lordship's *Treatise on the Origin of Languages*.

The manners of Lord Monboddo were not more odd than his personal appearance. He looked rather like an old stuffed monkey dressed in a judge's robes than anything else. His face, however, ' sicklied o'er ' with the pale cast of thought, bore traces of high intellect. So convinced is he said to have been of the truth of his fantastic theory of human tails, that whenever a child happened to be born in his house, he would watch at the chamber-door in order to see it in its first state, having a notion that the midwives pinched off the infant tails.

There is a tradition that Lord Monboddo attended and witnessed the catastrophe of Captain Porteous in 1736. He had just that day returned from completing his law education at Leyden, and taken lodgings near the foot of the West Bow, where at that time many of the greatest lawyers resided. When the rioters came down the Bow with their hapless victim, Mr Burnet was roused from bed by the noise, came down in his night-gown with a candle in his hand, and stood in a sort of stupor, looking on, till the tragedy was concluded.

PARLIAMENT HOUSE WORTHIES.

Scott has sketched in *Peter Peebles* the type of a class of crazy and half-crazy litigants who at all times haunt the Parliament House. Usually they are rustic men possessing small properties, such as a house and garden, which they are constantly talking of as their 'subject.' Sometimes a faded shawl and bonnet is associated with the case—objects to be dreaded by every good-natured member of the bar. But most frequently it is simple countrymen who become pests of this kind. That is to say, simple men of difficult and captious tempers, cursed with an overstrong sense of right or an overstrong sense of wrong, under which they would, by many degrees, prefer utter ruin to making the slightest concession to a neighbour. Ruined these men often are ; and yet it seems ruin well bought, since they have all along had the pleasure of seeing themselves and their little affairs the subject of consideration amongst men so much above themselves in rank.

Peebles was, as we are assured by the novelist himself, a real person, who frequented the Edinburgh courts of justice about the year 1792, and 'whose voluminous course of litigation served as a sort of essay piece to most young men who were called to the bar.' * Many persons recollect him as a tall, thin, slouching man, of homely outworn attire, understood to be a native of Linlithgow. Having got into law about a small house, he became deranged by the cause going against him, and then peace was no more for him on earth. He used to tell his friends that he had at present thirteen causes in hand, but was only going to 'move in' seven of them this session. When anxious for a consultation on any of his affairs, he would set out from his native burgh at the time when other people were going to bed, and reaching Edinburgh at four in the morning, would go about the town ringing the bells of the principal advocates, in the vain hope of getting one to rise and listen to him, to the infinite annoyance of many a poor serving-girl, and no less of the Town-guard, into whose hands he generally fell.

Another specimen of the class was Campbell of Laguine, who had perhaps been longer at law than any man of modern times. He was a store-farmer in Caithness, and had immense tracts of land under lease. When he sold his wool, he put the price in his pocket (no petty sum), and came down to waste it in the

* Notes to *Redgauntlet.*

Court of Session. His custom—an amusing example of method in madness—was to pay every meal which he made at the inns on the road *double*, that he might have a *gratis* meal on his return, knowing he would not bring a cross away in his pocket from the courts of justice. Laguine's figure was very extraordinary. His legs were like two circumflexes, both curving outward in the same direction; so that, relative to his body, they took the direction of the blade of a reaping-hook, supposing the trunk of his person to be the handle. These extraordinary legs were always attired in Highland trews, as his body was generally in a gray or tartan jacket, with a bonnet on his head; and duly appeared he at the door of the Parliament House, bearing a tin case, fully as big as himself, containing a plan of his farms. He paid his lawyers highly, but took up a great deal of their time. One gentleman, afterwards high in official situation, observed him coming up to ring his bell, and not wishing that he himself should throw away his time or Laguine his fee, directed that he should be denied. Laguine, however, made his way to the lady of the learned counsel, and sitting down in the drawing-room, went at great length into the merits of his cause, and exhibited his plans; and when he had expatiated for a couple of hours, he departed, but not without leaving a handsome fee, observing that he had as much satisfaction as if he had seen the learned counsel himself. He once told a legal friend of the writer that his laird and he were nearly agreed now—there was only about *ten miles of country* contested betwixt them! When finally this great cause was adjusted, his agent said: 'Well, Laguine, what will ye do now?' rashly judging that one who had, in a manner, lived upon law for a series of years would be at a loss how to dispose of himself now. 'No difficulty there,' answered Laguine; 'I'll dispute your account, and go to law with *you!*' Possessed as he was by a demon of litigation, Campbell is said to have been, apart from his disputes, a shrewd and sensible, and, moreover, an honourable and worthy man. He was one of the first who introduced sheep-farming into Ross-shire and Caithness, where he had farms as large as some whole Lowland or English counties; and but for litigation, he had the opportunity of making much money.

A person usually called, from his trade, the Heckler was another Parliament House worthy. He used to work the whole night at his trade; then put on a black suit, curled his hair behind and powdered it, so as to resemble a clergyman, and came forth to attend to the great business of the day at the Parliament House. He imagined that he was deputed by Divine Providence as a sort of controller of the Court of Session; but as if that had not been sufficient, he thought the charge of the General Assembly was also committed to him; and he used to complain that that venerable body was 'much worse to keep in good order' than the lawyers. He was a little, smart, well-brushed, neat-looking man, and used to talk to himself, smile, and nod with much vivacity. Part of his lunacy was to believe himself a clergyman; and it was chiefly the Teind Court which he haunted, his object there being to obtain an augmentation of his stipend. The appearance and conversation of the man were so plausible that he once succeeded in imposing himself upon Dr Blair as a preacher, and obtained permission to hold forth in the High Church on the ensuing Sunday. He was fortunately recognised when about to mount the pulpit. Some idle boys about the Parliament House, where he was a constant attendant, persuaded him that, as he held two such dignified offices as his imagination shaped out, there must be some salary attached to them, payable, like others upon the Establishment, in the Exchequer. This very nearly brought about a serious catastrophe; for the poor madman, finding his applications slighted at the Exchequer, came there one day with a pistol heavily loaded to shoot Mr Baird, a very worthy man, an officer of that court. This occasioned the Heckler being confined in durance vile for a long time; though, I think, he was at length emancipated.

Other insane fishers in the troubled waters of the law were the following:

Macduff of Ballenloan, who had two cases before the court at once. His success in the one depended upon his showing that he had capacity to manage his own affairs; and in the other, upon his proving himself incapable of doing so. He used to complain, with some apparent reason, that he lost them both!

Andrew Nicol, who was at law thirty years about a *midden-stead—Anglicé*, the situation of a dunghill. This person was a native of Kinross, a sensible-looking countryman, with a large, flat, blue bonnet, in which guise Kay has a very good portrait of him, displaying, with chuckling pride, a plan of his precious midden-stead. He used to frequent the Register House as well as the courts of law, and was encouraged in his foolish pursuits by the roguish clerks of that establishment, by whom he was denominated *Muck Andrew*, in allusion to the object of his litigation. This wretched being, after losing property and credit and his own senses in following a valueless phantom, died at last (1817) in Cupar jail, where he was placed by one of his legal creditors.

CONVIVIALIA.

'Auld Reekie! wale o' ilka toon
That Scotland kens beneath the moon;
Where coothy chields at e'enin' meet,
Their bizzin' craigs and mous to weet,
And blithely gar auld care gae by,
Wi' blinkin' and wi' bleerin' eye.'
ROBERT FERGUSSON.

TAVERN dissipation, now so rare amongst the respectable classes of the community, formerly prevailed in Edinburgh to an incredible extent, and engrossed the leisure hours of all professional men, scarcely excepting even the most stern and dignified. No rank, class, or profession, indeed, formed an exception to this rule. Nothing was so common in the morning as to meet men of high rank and official dignity reeling home from a close in the High Street, where they had spent the night in drinking. Nor was it unusual to find two or three of His Majesty's most honourable Lords of Council and Session mounting the bench in the forenoon in a crapulous state. A gentleman one night stepping

Johnnie Dowie.

into Johnnie Dowie's, opened a side-door, and looking into the room, saw a sort of *agger* or heap of snoring lads upon the floor, illumined by the gleams of an expiring candle. 'Wha may thae be, Mr Dowie?' inquired the visitor. 'Oh,' quoth John in his usual quiet way, 'just twa-three o' Sir Willie's drucken clerks!'—meaning the young gentlemen employed in Sir William Forbes's banking-house, whom of all earthly mortals one would have expected to be observers of the decencies.

To this testimony may be added that of all published works descriptive of Edinburgh during the last century. Even in the preceding century, if we are to believe Taylor the Water-poet, there was no superabundance of sobriety in the town. 'The worst thing,' says that sly humorist in his *Journey* (1623), 'was, that wine and ale were so scarce, and the people such misers of it, that every night, before I went to bed, if any man had asked me a civil question, all the wit in my head could not have made him a sober answer.'

The *diurnal* of a Scottish judge * of the beginning of the last century, which I have perused, presents a striking picture of the habits of men of business in that age. Hardly a night passes without some expense being incurred at taverns, not always of very good fame, where his lordship's associates on the bench were his boon-companions in the debauch. One is at a loss to understand how men who drugged their understandings so habitually could possess any share of vital faculty for the consideration or transaction of business, or how they contrived to make a decent appearance in the hours of duty. But, however difficult to be accounted for, there seems no room to doubt that deep drinking was compatible in many instances with good business talents, and even application. Many living men connected with the Court of Session can yet look back to a juvenile period of their lives when some of the ablest advocates and most esteemed judges were noted for their convivial habits. For example, a famous counsel named Hay, who became a judge under the designation of Lord Newton, was equally remarkable as a bacchanal and as a lawyer.† He considered himself as only the better fitted for business that he had previously imbibed six bottles of claret; and one of his clerks afterwards declared that the best paper he ever knew his lordship dictate was done after a debauch where that amount of liquor had fallen to his share. It was of him that the famous story is told of a client calling for him one day at four o'clock, and being surprised to find him at dinner; when, on the client saying to the servant that he had understood five to be Mr Hay's dinner-hour—'Oh, but, sir,' said the man, 'it is his *yesterday's dinner!*' M. Simond, who, in 1811, published a *Tour in Scotland*, mentions his surprise, on stepping one morning into the Parliament House, to find in the dignified capacity of a judge, and displaying all the gravity suitable to the character, the very gentleman with whom he had spent most of the preceding night in a fierce debauch. This judge was Lord Newton.

Contemporary with this learned lord was another of marvellous powers of drollery, of whom it is told, as a fact too notorious at the time to be concealed, that he was one Sunday morning, not long before church-time, found asleep among the paraphernalia

* Lord Grange, whose *Diary of a Senator of the College of Justice* was published in 1833.

† Lord Newton was known as 'The Mighty.' Lord Cockburn says it was not uncommon for judges on the bench to provide themselves with a bottle of port, which they consumed while listening to the case being tried before them.

of the sweeps, in a shed appropriated to the keeping of these articles at the end of the Town Guard-house in the High Street. His lordship, in staggering homeward alone from a tavern during the night, had tumbled into this place, where consciousness did not revisit him till next day. Of another group of clever but over-convivial lawyers of that age, it is related that, having set to wine and cards on a Saturday evening, they were so cheated out of all sense of time that the night passed before they thought of separating. Unless they are greatly belied, the people passing along Picardy Place next forenoon, on their way to church, were perplexed by seeing a door open, and three gentlemen issue forth, in all the disorder to be expected after a night of drunken vigils, while a fourth, in his dressing-gown, held the door in one hand and a lighted candle in the other, by way of showing them out ! *

The *High Jinks* of Counsellor Pleydell, in *Guy Mannering*, must have prepared many for these curious traits of a bypast age ; and Scott has further illustrated the subject by telling, in his notes to that novel, an anecdote, which he appears to have had upon excellent authority, respecting the elder President Dundas of Arniston, father of Lord Melville. 'It had been thought very desirable, while that distinguished lawyer was king's counsel, that his assistance should be obtained in drawing up an appeal case, which, as occasion for such writings then rarely occurred, was held to be a matter of great nicety. The solicitor employed for the appellant, attended by my informant, acting as his clerk, went to the Lord Advocate's chambers in the Fish-market Close, as I think. It was Saturday at noon, the court was just dismissed, the Lord Advocate had changed his dress and booted himself, and his servant and horses were at the foot of the close to carry him to Arniston. It was scarcely possible to get him to listen to a word respecting business. The wily agent, however, on pretence of asking one or two questions, which would not detain him half-an-hour, drew his lordship, who was no less an eminent *bon-vivant* than a lawyer of unequalled talent, to take a whet at a celebrated tavern, when the learned counsel became gradually involved in a spirited discussion of the law points of the case. At length it occurred to him that he might as well ride to Arniston in the cool of the evening. The horses were directed to be put into the stable, but not to be unsaddled. Dinner was ordered, the law was laid aside for a time, and the bottle circulated

* This story is told of John Clerk, who afterwards sat on the bench as Lord Eldin.

very freely. At nine o'clock at night, after he had been honouring Bacchus for so many hours, the Lord Advocate ordered his horses to be unsaddled—paper, pen, and ink were brought—he began to dictate the appeal case, and continued at his task till four o'clock the next morning. By next day's post the solicitor sent the case to London—a *chef-d'œuvre* of its kind ; and in which, my informant assured me, it was not necessary, on revisal, to correct five words.'

It was not always that business and pleasure were so success-fully united. It is related that an eminent lawyer, who was confined to his room by indisposition, having occasion for the attendance of his clerk at a late hour, in order to draw up a paper required on an emergency next morning, sent for and found him at his usual tavern. The man, though remarkable for the preservation of his faculties under severe application to the bottle, was on this night further gone than usual. He was able, however, to proceed to his master's bedroom, and there take his seat at the desk with the appearance of a sufficiently collected mind, so that the learned counsel, imagining nothing more wrong than usual, began to dictate from his couch. This went on for two or three hours, till, the business being finished, the barrister drew his curtain—to behold *Jamie* lost in a profound sleep upon the table, with the paper still in virgin whiteness before him !

One of the most notable jolly fellows of the last age was James Balfour, an accountant, usually called *Singing Jamie Balfour*, on account of his fascinating qualities as a vocalist. There used to be a portrait of him in the Leith Golf-house, representing him in the act of commencing the favourite song of *When I ha'e a saxpence under my thoom*, with the suitable attitude and a merriness of countenance justifying the traditionary account of the man. Of Jacobite leanings, he is said to have sung *The wee German lairdie, Awa, Whigs, awa,* and *The sow's tail to Geordie* with a degree of zest which there was no resisting.

Report speaks of this person as an amiable, upright, and able man ; so clever in business matters that he could do as much in one hour as another man in three ; always eager to quench and arrest litigation rather than to promote it ; and consequently so much esteemed professionally that he could get business whenever he chose to undertake it, which, however, he only did when he felt himself in need of money. Nature had given him a robust constitution, which enabled him to see out three sets of

boon-companions, but, after all, gave way before he reached
sixty. His custom, when anxious to repair the effects of intemperance, was to wash his head and hands in cold water; this, it
is said, made him quite cool and collected almost immediately.
Pleasure being so predominant an object in his life, it was thought
surprising that at his death he was found in possession of some
little money.

The powers of Balfour as a singer of the Scotch songs of all
kinds, tender and humorous, are declared to have been marvellous;
and he had a happy gift of suiting them to occasions. Being a
great peacemaker, he would often accomplish his purpose by
introducing some ditty pat to the purpose, and thus dissolving
all rancour in a hearty laugh. Like too many of our countrymen,
he had a contempt for foreign music. One evening, in a company
where an Italian vocalist of eminence was present, he professed to
give a song in the manner of that country. Forth came a ridiculous cantata to the tune of *Aiken Drum*, beginning: 'There was
a wife in Peebles,' which the wag executed with all the proper
graces, shakes, and appoggiaturas, making his friends almost expire
with suppressed laughter at the contrast between the style of
singing and the ideas conveyed in the song. At the conclusion,
their mirth was doubled by the foreigner saying very simply:
'De music be very fine, but I no understand de words.' A lady,
who lived in the Parliament Close, told a friend of mine that she
was wakened from her sleep one summer morning by a noise as
of singing, when, going to the window to learn what was the
matter, guess her surprise at seeing Jamie Balfour and some of
his boon-companions (evidently fresh from their wonted orgies),
singing *The king shall enjoy his own again*, on their knees,
around King Charles's statue! One of Balfour's favourite haunts
was a humble kind of tavern called *Jenny Ha's*, opposite to
Queensberry House, where, it is said, Gay had boosed during his
short stay in Edinburgh, and to which it was customary for
gentlemen to adjourn from dinner-parties, in order to indulge in
claret from the butt, free from the usual domestic restraints.
Jamie's potations here were principally of what was called *cappie
ale*—that is, ale in little wooden bowls—with wee thochts of
brandy in it. But, indeed, no one could be less exclusive than
he as to liquors. When he heard a bottle drawn in any house
he happened to be in, and observed the cork to give an unusually
smart report, he would call out: 'Lassie, gi'e me a glass o' *that;*'
as knowing that, whatever it was, it must be good of its kind.

Sir Walter Scott says, in one of his droll little missives to his printer Ballantyne : 'When the press does not follow me, I get on slowly and ill, and put myself in mind of Jamie Balfour, who could run, when he could not stand still.' He here alludes to a matter of fact, which the following anecdote will illustrate : Jamie, in going home late from a debauch, happened to tumble into the pit formed for the foundation of a house in James's Square. A gentle-man passing heard his complaint, and going up to the spot, was entreated by our hero to help him out. 'What would be the use of helping you out,' said the passer-by, 'when you could not stand though you *were* out ?' 'Very true, perhaps ; yet if you help me up, I'll *run* you to the Tron Kirk for a bottle of claret.' Pleased with his humour, the gentleman placed him upon his feet, when instantly he set off for the Tron Church at a pace distanc-ing all ordinary competition ; and accordingly he won the race, though, at the conclusion, he had to sit down on the steps of the church, being quite unable to stand. After taking a minute or two to recover his breath — 'Well, another race to Fortune's for another bottle of claret !' Off he went to the tavern in question, in the Stamp - office Close, and this bet he gained also. The claret, probably with continua-

Stamp-office Close.

tions, was discussed in Fortune's ; and the end of the story is, Balfour sent his new friend home in a chair, utterly done up, at an early hour in the morning.

It is hardly surprising that habits carried to such an extrava-gance amongst gentlemen should have in some small degree affected the fairer and purer part of creation also. It is an old story in Edinburgh that three ladies had one night a merry-meeting in a tavern near the Cross, where they sat till a very late hour. Ascending at length to the street, they scarcely

remembered where they were; but as it was good moonlight,
they found little difficulty in walking along till they came to the
Tron Church. Here, however, an obstacle occurred. The moon,
shining high in the south, threw the shadow of the steeple directly
across the street from the one side to the other; and the ladies,
being no more clear-sighted than they were clear-headed, mistook
this for a broad and rapid river, which they would require to cross
before making further way. In this delusion, they sat down upon
the brink of the imaginary stream, deliberately took off their shoes
and stockings, *kilted* their lower garments, and proceeded to wade
through to the opposite side; after which, resuming their shoes
and stockings, they went on their way rejoicing, as before!
Another anecdote (from an aged nobleman) exhibits the baccha-
nalian powers of our ancestresses in a different light. During the
rising of 1715, the officers of the crown in Edinburgh, having
procured some important intelligence respecting the motions and
intentions of the Jacobites, resolved upon despatching the same
to London by a faithful courier. Of this the party whose interests
would have been so materially affected got notice; and that
evening, as the messenger (a man of rank) was going down the
High Street, with the intention of mounting his horse in the
Canongate and immediately setting off, he met two tall, handsome
ladies, in full dress, and wearing black velvet masks, who accosted
him with a very easy demeanour and a winning sweetness of
voice. Without hesitating as to the quality of these damsels, he
instantly proposed to treat them with a pint of claret at a
neighbouring tavern; but they said that, instead of accepting his
kindness, they were quite willing to treat *him* to his heart's
content. They then adjourned to the tavern, and sitting down,
the whole three drank plenteously, merrily, and long, so that the
courier seemed at last to forget entirely the mission upon which
he was sent, and the danger of the papers which he had about
his person. After a pertinacious debauch of several hours, the
luckless messenger was at length fairly drunk under the table;
and it is needless to add that the fair nymphs then proceeded
to strip him of his papers, decamped, and were no more heard
of; though it is but justice to the Scottish ladies of that period
to say that the robbers were generally believed at the time to
be young men disguised in women's clothes.*

---

* It was very common for Scotch ladies of rank, even till the middle of the
last century, to wear black masks in walking abroad or airing in a carriage;
and for some gentlemen, too, who were vain of their complexion. They were

The custom which prevailed among ladies, as well as gentlemen, of resorting to what were called *oyster-cellars*, is in itself a striking indication of the state of manners during the last century. In winter, when the evening had set in, a party of the most fashionable people in town, collected by appointment, would adjourn in carriages to one of those abysses of darkness and comfort, called in Edinburgh *laigh shops*, where they proceeded to regale themselves with raw oysters and porter, arranged in huge dishes upon a coarse table, in a dingy room, lighted by tallow candles. The rudeness of the feast, and the vulgarity of the circumstances under which it took place, seem to have given a zest to its enjoyment, with which more refined banquets could not have been accompanied. One of the chief features of an oyster-cellar entertainment was that full scope was given to the conversational powers of the company. Both ladies and gentlemen indulged, without restraint, in sallies the merriest and the wittiest ; and a thousand remarks and jokes, which elsewhere would have been suppressed as improper, were here sanctified by the oddity of the scene, and appreciated by the most dignified and refined. After the table was cleared of the oysters and porter, it was customary to introduce brandy or rum-punch—according to the pleasure of the ladies—after which dancing took place ; and when the female part of the assemblage thought proper to retire, the gentlemen again sat down, or adjourned to another tavern to crown the pleasures of the evening with unlimited debauch. It is not (1824) more than thirty years since the late Lord Melville, the Duchess of Gordon, and some other persons of distinction, who happened to meet in town after many years of absence, made up an oyster-cellar party, by way of a frolic, and devoted one winter evening to the revival of this almost forgotten entertainment of their youth.*

kept close to the face by means of a string, having a button of glass or precious stone at the end, which the lady held in her mouth. This practice, I understand, did not in the least interrupt the flow of tittle-tattle and scandal among the fair wearers.

We are told, in a curious paper in the *Edinburgh Magazine* for August 1817, that at the period above mentioned, 'though it was a disgrace for ladies to be seen drunk, yet it was none to be a little intoxicated in good company.'

* The principal oyster-parties, in old times, took place in Lucky Middlemass's tavern in the Cowgate (where the south pier of the [South] bridge now stands), which was the resort of Fergusson and his fellow-wits—as witness his own verse :

'When big as burns the gutters rin,
If ye ha'e catched a droukit skin,

It seems difficult to reconcile all these things with the staid and somewhat square-toed character which our country has obtained amongst her neighbours. The fact seems to be that a kind of Laodicean principle is observable in Scotland, and we oscillate between a rigour of manners on the one hand, and a laxity on the other, which alternately acquire an apparent paramouncy. In the early part of the last century, rigour was in the ascendant; but not to the prevention of a respectable minority of the free-and-easy, who kept alive the flame of conviviality with no small degree of success. In the latter half of the century—a dissolute era all over civilised Europe—the minority became the majority, and the characteristic sobriety of the nation's manners was only traceable in certain portions of society. Now we are in a sober, perhaps tending to a rigorous stage once more. In Edinburgh, seventy years ago (1847), intemperance was the rule to such an degree that exception could hardly be said to exist. Men appeared little in the drawing-room in those days; when they did, not infrequently their company had better have been dispensed with. When a gentleman gave an entertainment, it was thought necessary that he should press the bottle as far as it could be made to go. A particularly good fellow would lock his outer door to prevent any guest of dyspeptic tendencies or sober inclinations from escaping. Some were so considerate as to provide shake-down beds for a general bivouac in a neighbouring apartment. When gentlemen were obliged to appear at assemblies where decency was enforced, they of course wore their best attire. This it was customary to change for something less liable to receive damage, ere going, as they usually did, to conclude the evening by a scene of conviviality. Drinking entered into everything. As Sir Alexander Boswell has observed:

> 'O'er draughts of wine the beau would moan his love,
> O'er draughts of wine the cit his bargain drove,
> O'er draughts of wine the writer penned the will,
> And legal wisdom counselled o'er a gill.'

Then was the time when men, despising and neglecting the com-

> To Luckie Middlemist's loup in,
>   And sit fu' snug,
> Owre oysters and a dram o' gin,
>   Or haddock lug.'

At these fashionable parties, the ladies would sometimes have the oyster-women to dance in the ball-room, though they were known to be of the worst character. This went under the convenient name of *frolic*.

pany of women, always so civilising in its influence, would yet half-kill themselves with bumpers in order, as the phrase went, to *save them*. Drinking to save the ladies is said to have originated with a catch-club, which issued tickets for gratuitous concerts. Many tickets with the names of ladies being prepared, one was taken up and the name announced. Any member present was at liberty to toast the health of this lady in a bumper, and this ensured her ticket being reserved for her use. If no one came forward to honour her name in this manner, the lady was said to be damned, and her ticket was thrown under the table. Whether from this origin or not, the practice is said to have ultimately had the following form. One gentleman would give out the name of some lady as the most beautiful object in creation, and, by way of attesting what he said, drink one bumper. Another champion would then enter the field, and offer to prove that a certain other lady, whom he named, was a great deal more beautiful than she just mentioned—supporting his assertion by drinking two bumpers. Then the other would rise up, declare this to be false, and in proof of his original statement, as well as by way of turning the scale upon his opponent, drink four bumpers. Not deterred or repressed by this, the second man would reiterate, and conclude by drinking as much as the challenger, who would again start up and drink eight bumpers ; and so on, in geometrical progression, till one or other of the heroes fell under the table ; when of course the fair Delia of the survivor was declared the queen supreme of beauty by all present. I have seen a sonnet addressed on the morning after such a scene of contention to the lady concerned by the unsuccessful hero, whose brains appear to have been woefully muddled by the claret he had drunk in her behalf.

It was not merely in the evenings that taverns were then resorted to. There was a petty treat, called a 'meridian,' which no man of that day thought himself able to dispense with ; and this was generally indulged in at a tavern. 'A cauld cock and a feather' was the metaphorical mode of calling for a glass of brandy and a bunch of raisins, which was the favourite regale of many. Others took a glass of whisky, some few a lunch. Scott very amusingly describes, from his own observation, the manner in which the affair of the meridian was gone about by the writers and clerks belonging to the Parliament House. 'If their proceedings were watched, they might be seen to turn fidgety about the hour of noon, and exchange looks with each other from their separate desks, till at length some one of formal and dignified

presence assumed the honour of leading the band ; when away
they went, threading the crowd like a string of wild-fowl, crossed
the square or close, and following each other into the [John's]
coffee-house, drank the meridian, which was placed ready at the
bar. This they did day by day ; and though they did not speak
to each other, they seemed to attach a certain degree of sociability
to performing the ceremony in company.'

It was in the evening, of course, that the tavern debaucheries
assumed their proper character of unpalliated fierceness and
destructive duration. In the words of Robert Fergusson :

> 'Now night, that's cunzied chief for fun,
> Is with her usual rites begun.
>   *   *   *   *
> Some to porter, some to punch,
> Retire ; while noisy ten-hours' drum
> Gars a' the trades gang danderin' hame.
> Now, mony a club, jocose and free,
> Gi'e a' to merriment and glee ;
> Wi' sang and glass they fley the power
> O' care, that wad harass the hour.
>   *   *   *   *
> Chief, O CAPE ! we crave thy aid,
> To get our cares and poortith laid.
> Sincerity and genius true,
> O' knights have ever been the due.
> Mirth, music, porter deepest-dyed,
> Are never here to worth denied.'

All the shops in the town were then shut at eight o'clock ; and
from that hour till ten—when the drum of the Town-guard
announced at once a sort of license for the deluging of the streets
with nuisances,* and a warning of the inhabitants home to their
beds—unrestrained scope was given to the delights of the table.
No tradesman thought of going home to his family till after he
had spent an hour or two at his club. This was universal and
unfailing. So lately as 1824, I knew something of an old-fashioned
tradesman who nightly shut his shop at eight o'clock, and then
adjourned with two old friends, who called upon him at that hour,
to a quiet old public-house on the opposite side of the way,
where they each drank precisely one bottle of Edinburgh ale, ate
precisely one halfpenny roll, and got upon their legs precisely
at the first stroke of ten o'clock.

* The cry of 'Gardy loo !' at this hour was supposed to warn pedestrians ;
but, as Sir Walter Scott says, ' it was sometimes like the shriek of the water-
kelpie, rather the elegy than the warning of the overwhelmed passenger.'

The CAPE CLUB alluded to by Fergusson aspired to a refined and classical character, comprising amongst its numerous members many men of talents, as well as of private worth. Fergusson himself was a member ; as were Mr Thomas Sommers, his friend and biographer ; Mr Woods, a player of eminence on the humble boards of Edinburgh, and an intimate companion of the poet ; and Mr Runciman the painter. The name of the club had its foundation in one of those weak jokes such as 'gentle dullness ever loves.' A person who lived in the Calton was in the custom of spending an hour or two every evening with one or two city friends, and being sometimes detained till after the regular period when the Netherbow Port was shut, it occasionally happened that he had either to remain in the city all night, or was under the necessity of bribing the porter who attended the gate. This difficult *pass*—partly on account of the rectangular corner which he turned immediately on getting out of the Port, as he went homewards down Leith Wynd—the Calton burgher facetiously called *doubling the Cape ;* and as it was customary with his friends every evening when they assembled to inquire 'how he turned the Cape last night,' and indeed to make that circumstance and that phrase, night after night, the subject of their conversation and amusement, 'the Cape' in time became so assimilated with their very existence that they adopted it as a title ; and it was retained as such by the organised club into which shortly after they thought proper to form themselves. The Cape Club owned a regular institution from 1763. It will scarcely be credited in the present day that a jest of the above nature could keep an assemblage of rational citizens, and, we may add, professed wits, merry after a thousand repetitions. Yet it really is true that the patron-jests of many a numerous and enlightened association were no better than this, and the greater part of them worse. As instance the following :

There was the ANTEMANUM CLUB, of which the members used to boast of the state of their hands, *before-hand*, in playing at 'Brag.' The members were all men of respectability, some of them gentlemen of fortune. They met every Saturday and dined. It was at first a purely convivial club ; but latterly, the Whig party gaining a sort of preponderance, it degenerated into a political association.

The PIOUS CLUB was composed of decent, orderly citizens, who met every night, Sundays not excepted, in a *pie-house*, and whose joke was the *équivoque* of these expressions—similar in sound, but different in signification. The agreeable uncertainty as to whether their name arose from their *piety*, or the circumstance of their eating *pies*, kept the club hearty for many years. At their Sunday meetings the conversation usually took a serious turn—perhaps

The Watergate.

upon the sermons which they had respectively heard during the day : this they considered as rendering their title of *Pious* not altogether undeserved. Moreover, they were all, as the saying was, *ten o'clock men*, and of good character. Fifteen persons were considered as constituting a full night. The whole allowable debauch was a gill of toddy to each person, which was drunk, like wine, out of a common decanter. One of the members of the Pious Club was a Mr Lind, a man of at least twenty-five stone weight, immoderately fond of good eating and drinking. It was generally believed of him that were all the oxen he had devoured ranged in a line, they would reach from the Watergate to the Castle-hill, and that the wine he had drunk would swim a seventy-four. His most favourite viand was a very strange one—salmon skins. When dining anywhere, with salmon on the table, he made no scruple of raking all the skins off the plates of the rest of the guests. He had only one toast, from which he never varied : ' Merry days to honest fellows.' A Mr Drummond was esteemed poet-laureate to this club. He was a facetious, clever man. Of his poetical talents, take a specimen in the following lines on Lind :

> 'In going to dinner, he ne'er lost his way,
>   Though often, when done, he was carted away.'

He made the following impromptu on an associate of small figure and equally small understanding, who had been successful in the world :

> 'O thou of genius slow,
>   Weak by nature ;
> A rich fellow,
>   But a poor creature.'

The SPENDTHRIFT CLUB took its name from the extravagance of the members in spending no less a sum than fourpence halfpenny each night! It consisted of respectable citizens of the middle class, and continued in 1824 to exist in a modified state. Its meetings, originally nightly, were then reduced to four a week. The men used to play at whist for a halfpenny—one, two, three—no rubbers; but latterly they had, with their characteristic extravagance, doubled the stake! Supper originally cost no less than twopence; and half a bottle of strong ale, with a dram, stood every member twopence halfpenny; to all which sumptuous profusion might be added still another halfpenny, which was given to the maid-servant—in all, fivepence! Latterly the dram had been disused; but such had been the general increase, either in the cost or the quantity of the indulgences, that the usual nightly expense was ultimately from a shilling to one and fourpence. The winnings at whist were always thrown into the reckoning. A large two-quart bottle or tappit-hen was introduced by the landlady, with a small measure, out of which the company helped themselves; and the members made up their own bill with chalk upon the table. In 1824, in the recollection of the senior members, some of whom were of fifty years' standing, the house was kept by the widow of a Lieutenant Hamilton of the army, who recollected having attended the theatre in the Tennis Court at Holyroodhouse, when the play was the *Spanish Friar*, and when many of the members of the *Union Parliament* were present in the house.

The BOAR CLUB was an association of a different sort, consisting chiefly of wild, fashionable young men; and the place of meeting was not in any of the snug profundities of the Old Town, but in a modern tavern in Shakspeare Square, kept by one Daniel Hogg. The *joke* of this club consisted in the supposition that all the members were *boars*, that their room was a *sty*, that their talk was *grunting*, and in the *double-entendre* of the small piece of stoneware which served as a repository of all the fines being a *pig*. Upon this they lived twenty years. I have, at some expense of eyesight and with no small exertion of patience, perused the soiled and blotted records of the club, which in 1824 were preserved by an old vintner, whose house was their last place of meeting; and the result has been the following memorabilia. The Boar Club commenced its meetings in 1787, and the original members were J. G. C. Schetky, a German musician; David Shaw; Archibald Crawfuird; Patrick Robertson; Robert Ald-

Tappit-hen.

ridge, a famed pantomimist and dancing-master; James Neilson and Luke Cross. Some of these were remarkable men, in particular Mr Schetky. He had come to Edinburgh about the beginning of the reign of George III. He used to tell that on alighting at Ramsay's inn, opposite the Cowgate Port, his first impression of the city was so unfavourable that he was on the point of leaving it again without further acquaintance, and was only prevented from doing so by the solicitations of his fellow-traveller, who was not so much alarmed at the dingy and squalid appearance of this part of Auld Reekie.* He was first employed at St Cecilia's Hall, where the concerts were attended by all the 'rank, beauty, and fashion' of which Edinburgh could then boast, and where, besides the professional performers, many amateurs of great musical skill and enthusiasm, such as Mr Tytler of Woodhouselee,† were pleased to exhibit themselves for the entertainment of their friends, who alone were admitted by tickets. Mr Schetky composed the march of a body of volunteers called the Edinburgh Defensive Band

* This highly appropriate popular *sobriquet* cannot be traced beyond the reign of Charles II. Tradition assigns the following as the origin of the phrase: An old gentleman in Fife, designated Durham of Largo, was in the habit, at the period mentioned, of regulating the time of evening worship by the appearance of the smoke of Edinburgh, which he could easily see, through the clear summer twilight, from his own door. When he observed the smoke increase in density in consequence of the good folk of the city preparing their supper, he would call all the family into the house, saying: 'It's time now, bairns, to tak' the beuks and gang to our beds, for yonder's Auld Reekie, I see, putting on her nicht cap!'

† This gentleman, the 'revered defender of beauteous Stuart,' and the surviving friend of Allan Ramsay, had an unaccountable aversion to cheese, and not only forbade the appearance of that article upon his table, but also its introduction into his house. His family, who did not partake in this antipathy, sometimes smuggled a small quantity of cheese into the house, and ate it in secret; but he almost always discovered it by the *smell*, which was the sense it chiefly offended. Upon scenting the object of his disgust, he would start up and run distractedly through the house in search of it, and not compose himself again to his studies till it was thrown out of doors. Some of his ingenious children, by way of a joke, once got into their possession the coat with which he usually went to the court, and ripping up the sutures of one of its wide, old fashioned skirts, sewed up therein a considerable slice of double Gloster. Mr Tytler was next day surprised when, sitting near the bar, he perceived the smell of cheese rising around him. 'Cheese here too!' cried the querulous old gentleman; 'nay, then, the whole world must be conspiring against me!' So saying, he rose, and ran home to tell his piteous case to Mrs Tytler and the children, who became convinced from this that he really possessed the singular delicacy and fastidiousness in respect of the effluvia arising from cheese which they formerly thought to be fanciful.

which was raised out of the citizens of Edinburgh at the time of the American war, and was commanded by the eminent advocate Crosbie. One of the verses to which the march was set may be given as an admirable specimen of *militia poetry :*

> ' Colonel Crosbie takes the field ;
> To France and Spain he will not yield ;
> But still maintains his high command
> At the head of the noble Defensive Band.'*

Mr Schetky was primarily concerned in the founding of the Boar Club. He was in the habit of meeting every night with Mr Aldridge and one or two other professional men, or gentlemen who affected the society of such persons, in Hogg's tavern ; and it was the host's name that suggested the idea of calling their society the '*Boar* Club.' Their laws were first written down in proper form in 1790. They were to meet every evening at seven o'clock ; each *boar*, on his entry, to contribute a halfpenny to the *pig*. Mr Aldridge was to be perpetual *Grand-boar*, with Mr Schetky for his deputy ; and there were other officers, entitled Secretary, Treasurer, and Procurator-fiscal. A fine of one halfpenny was imposed upon every person who called one of his brother-boars by his proper out-of-club name—the term 'sir' being only allowed. The entry-moneys, fines, and other pecuniary acquisitions were hoarded for a grand annual dinner. The laws were revised in 1799, when some new officials were constituted, such as Poet-laureate, Champion, Archbishop, and Chief-grunter. The fines were then rendered exceedingly severe, and in their exaction no one met with any mercy, as it was the interest of all the rest that the *pig* should bring forth as plenteous a *farrow* as possible at the grand dinner-day. This practice at length occasioning a violent insurrection in the *sty*, the whole fraternity was broken up, and never again returned to 'wallow in the mire.'

The HELL-FIRE CLUB, a terrible and infamous association of wild young men about the beginning of the last century, met in various profound places throughout Edinburgh, where they practised orgies not more fit for seeing the light than the Eleusinian

---

* The dress of the Edinburgh Defensive Band was as follows : a cocked hat, black stock, hair tied and highly powdered ; dark-blue long-tailed coat, with orange facings in honour of the Revolution, and full lapels sloped away to show the white dimity vest ; nankeen small-clothes ; white thread stockings, ribbed or plain ; and short nankeen spatterdashes. Kay has some ingenious caricatures, in miniature, of these redoubted Bruntsfield Links and Heriot's Green warriors. The last two survivors were Mr John M'Niven, stationer, and Robert Stevenson, painter, who died in 1832.

Mysteries. I have conversed with old people who had seen the last worn-out members of the Hell-fire Club, which in the country is to this day believed to have been an association in compact with the Prince of Darkness.

Many years afterwards, a set of persons associated for the purpose of purchasing goods condemned by the Court of Exchequer. For what reason I cannot tell, they called themselves the Hell-fire Club, and their president was named the Devil. My old friend, Henry Mackenzie, whose profession was that of an attorney before the Court of Exchequer, wrote me a note on this subject, in which he says very naïvely : 'In my youngest days, I knew the Devil.'

The SWEATING CLUB flourished about the middle of the last century. They resembled the Mohocks mentioned in the *Spectator*. After intoxicating themselves, it was their custom to sally forth at midnight, and attack whomsoever they met upon the streets. Any luckless wight who happened to fall into their hands was chased, jostled, pinched, and pulled about, till he not only perspired, but was ready to drop down and die with exhaustion. Even so late as the early years of this century, it was unsafe to walk the streets of Edinburgh at night on account of the numerous drunken parties of young men who then reeled about, bent on mischief, at all hours, and from whom the Town-guard were unable to protect the sober citizen.

A club called the INDUSTRIOUS COMPANY may serve to show how far the system of drinking was carried by our fathers. It was a sort of joint-stock company, formed by a numerous set of porter-drinkers, who thought fit to club towards the formation of a stock of that liquor, which they might partly profit by retailing, and partly by the opportunity thus afforded them of drinking their own particular tipple at the wholesale price. Their cellars were in the Royal Bank Close, where they met every night at eight o'clock. Each member paid at his entry £5, and took his turn monthly of the duty of superintending the general business of the company. But the curse of joint-stock companies—negligence on the part of the managers—ultimately occasioned the ruin of the Industrious Company.

About 1790, a club of first-rate citizens used to meet each Saturday afternoon for a *country dinner*, in a tavern which still exists in the village of Canonmills, a place now involved within the limits of the New Town. To quote a brief memoir on the subject, handed to me many years ago by a veteran friend, who was a good deal of the *laudator temporis acti*: 'The club was pointedly attended ; it was too good a thing to miss being present at. They kept their own claret, and managed all matters as to living perfectly well.' Originally the fraternity were contented with a very humble room ; but in time they got an addition built to the house for their accommodation, comprehending one good-sized room with two windows, in one of which is a pane containing an olive-dove ; in the other, one containing a wheat-sheaf, both engraved with a diamond. 'This,' continues Mr Johnston, 'was the doing of William Ramsay [banker], then residing at Warriston —the tongue of the trump to the club. Here he took great delight to drink claret on the Saturdays, though he had such a paradise near at hand to retire to ; but then there were Jamie Torry, Jamie Dickson, Gilbert Laurie, and other good old council friends with whom to crack [that is, chat] ; and the said cracks were of more value in this dark, unseemly place than the enjoyments of home. I never pass these two engraved panes of glass but I venerate them, and wonder that, in the course of fifty years, they have not been destroyed, either from drunkenness within or from misrule without.' *

Edinburgh boasted of many other associations of the like nature, which it were perhaps best merely to enumerate in a tabular form, with the appropriate joke opposite each, as

THE DIRTY CLUB................No gentleman to appear in clean linen.
THE BLACK WIGS...............Members wore black wigs.
THE ODD FELLOWS............Members wrote their names upside down.
THE BONNET LAIRDS..........Members wore blue bonnets.
THE DOCTORS OF FACULTY{Members regarded as physicians, and so
    CLUB ....{ styled ; wearing, moreover, gowns and
                              { wigs.

And so forth. There were the CALEDONIAN CLUB and the UNION CLUB, of whose foundation history speaketh not. There was the WIG CLUB, the president of which wore a wig of extraordinary materials, which had belonged to the Moray family for three generations, and each new *entrant* of which drank to the fraternity in a quart of claret without pulling bit. The Wigs usually drank twopenny ale, on which it was possible to get satisfactorily drunk for a groat ; and with this they ate souters' clods,† a coarse,

---

* One of the panes is now (1847) destroyed, the other cracked. [The tavern is now out of existence.]

† Souters' clods and other forms of bread fascinating to youngsters, as well as penny pies of high reputation, were to be had at a shop which all old Edinburgh people speak of with extreme regard and affection—the *Baijen Hole*—situated immediately to the east of Forrester's Wynd and opposite to

lumpish kind of loaf.* There was also the Brownonian System Club, which, oddly enough, bore no reference to the license which that system had given for a phlogistic regimen—for it was a douce citizenly fraternity, venerating ten o'clock as a sacred principle— but in honour of the founder of that system, who had been a constituent member.

The Lawnmarket Club was composed chiefly of the woollen-traders of that street, a set of whom met every morning about seven o'clock, and walked down to the Post-office, where they made themselves acquainted with the news of the morning. After a plentiful discussion of the news, they adjourned to a public-house and got a dram of brandy. As a sort of ironical and self-inflicted satire upon the strength of their potations, they sometimes called themselves the *Whey Club*. They were always the first persons in the town to have a thorough knowledge of the foreign news; and on Wednesday mornings, when there was no post from London, it was their wont to meet as usual, and, in the absence of real news, amuse themselves by the invention of what was imaginary; and this they made it their business to circulate among their uninitiated acquaintances in the course of the fore-noon. Any such unfounded articles of intelligence, on being suspected or discovered, were usually called *Lawnmarket Gazettes*, in allusion to their roguish originators.

In the year 1705, when the Duke of Argyll was commissioner in the Scottish parliament, a singular kind of fashionable club, or coterie of ladies and gentlemen, was instituted, chiefly by the exertions of the Earl of Selkirk, who was the distinguished beau of that age. This was called the Horn Order, a name which, as usual, had its origin in the whim of a moment. A horn-spoon having been used at some merry-meeting, it occurred to the club, which was then in embryo, that this homely implement would be a good badge for the projected society; and this being proposed, it was instantly agreed by all the party that the 'Order of the Horn' would be a good caricature of the more ancient and better-

the Old Tolbooth. The name—a mystery to later generations—seems to bear reference to the Baijens or Baijen Class, a term bestowed in former days upon the junior students in the college. *Bajan* or *bejan* is the French *bejaune*, '*bec jaune*,' 'greenbill,' 'greenhorn,' 'freshman.'

* The fullest account yet published of this extraordinary coterie is that of Mr H. A. Cockburn in *The Book of the Old Edinburgh Club*, vol. iii. Creech refers to it in ironical terms as 'the virtuous, the venerable and dignified Wig who so much to their own honour and kind attention always inform the public of their meetings.' The reputation of the club was very different.

sanctioned honorary dignities. The phrase was adopted; and the members of the *Horn Order* met and caroused for many a day under this strange designation, which, however, the common people believed to mean more than met the ear. Indeed, if all accounts of it be true, it must have been a species of masquerade, in which the sexes were mixed and all ranks confounded.*

* The following were other eighteenth century Edinburgh clubs :

THE POKER CLUB originated in a combination of gentlemen favourable to the establishment of militia in Scotland, and its name, happily hit on by Professor Adam Ferguson, was selected to avoid giving offence to the Government. A history of the club is given in Dugald Stewart's Life, and also in Carlyle's *Autobiography*, where he says : 'Dinner was on the table soon after two o'clock, at one shilling a head, the wine to be confined to sherry and claret, and the reckoning called at six o'clock.' The minutes of this interesting club are preserved in the University Library.

THE MIRROR CLUB, formed by the contributors to the periodical of that name. It had really existed before under the name of 'The Tabernacle.' 'The Tabernacle,' or 'The Feast of Tabernacles,' as Ramsay of Ochtertyre calls it, was a company of friends and admirers of Henry Dundas, first Viscount Melville.

THE EASY CLUB, founded by Allan Ramsay the poet, consisted of twelve members, each of whom was required to assume the name of some Scottish poet. Ramsay took that of Gawin Douglas.

THE CAPILLAIRE CLUB was 'composed of all who were inclined to be witty and joyous.'

THE FACER CLUB, which met in Lucky Wood's tavern in the Canongate, was perhaps not of a high order. If a member did not drain his measure of liquor, he had to throw it at his own face.

THE GRISKIN CLUB also met in the Canongate. Dr Carlyle and those who took part with him in the production of Home's *Douglas* at the Canongate playhouse formed this club, and gave it its name from the pork griskins which was their favourite supper dish.

THE RUFFIAN CLUB, 'composed of men whose hearts were milder than their manners, and their principles more correct than their habits of life.'

THE WAGERING CLUB, instituted in 1775, still meets annually. An account of this club is given in *The Book of the Old Edinburgh Club*, vol. ii.

Others may be mentioned by name only : THE DIVERSORIUM, THE HAVERAL, THE WHIN BUSH, THE SKULL, THE SIX FOOT, THE ASSEMBLY OF BIRDS, THE CARD, THE BORACHED, THE HUMDRUM, THE APICIAN, THE BLAST AND QUAFF, THE OCEAN, THE PIPE, THE KNIGHTS OF THE CAP AND FEATHER, THE REVOLUTIONARY, THE STOIC, and THE CLUB, referred to in Lockhart's *Life of Scott*.

Of a later period than those mentioned above were THE GOWKS CLUB; THE RIGHT AND WRONG, of which James Hogg gives a short account; and THE FRIDAY CLUB, instituted by Lord Cockburn, who also wrote an interesting history of it, recently printed by Mr H. A. Cockburn, in vol. iii. of *The Book of the Old Edinburyh Club*.

TAVERNS OF OLD TIMES.

WHEN the worship of Bacchus held such sway in our city, his peculiar temples—the taverns—must, one would suppose, have been places of some importance. And so they were, comparatively speaking; and yet, absolutely, an Edinburgh tavern of the last century was no very fine or inviting place. Usually these receptacles were situated in obscure places—in courts or closes, away from the public thoroughfares; and often they presented such narrow and stifling accommodations as might have been expected to repel rather than attract visitors. The truth was, however, that a coarse and darksome snugness was courted by the worshippers. Large, well-lighted rooms, with a look-out to a street, would not have suited them. But allow them to dive through some Erebean alley, into a cavern-like house, and there settle themselves in a cell unvisited of Phœbus, with some dingy flamen of either sex to act as minister, and their views as to circumstances and properties were fulfilled.

The city traditions do not go far back into the eighteenth century with respect to taverns; but we obtain some notion of the principal houses in Queen Anne's time from the Latin lyrics of Dr Pitcairn, which Ruddiman published, in order to prove that the Italian muse had not become extinct in our land since the days of Buchanan. In an address *To Strangers*, the wit tells those who would acquire some notion of our national manners to avoid the triple church of St Giles's:

'Tres ubi Cyclopes fanda nefanda boant'—

where three horrible monsters bellow forth sacred and profane discourse—and seek the requisite knowledge in the sanctuaries of the rosy god, whose worship is conducted by night and by day. 'At one time,' says he, 'you may be delighted with the bowls of Steil of the *Cross Keys;* then other heroes, at the *Ship,* will show you the huge cups which belonged to mighty bibbers of yore. Or you may seek out the sweet-spoken Katy at *Buchanan's,* or *Tennant's* commodious house, where scalloped oysters will be brought in with your wine. But *Hay* calls us, than whom no woman of milder disposition or better-stored cellar can be named in the whole town. Now it will gratify you to make your way into the Avernian

grottoes and caves never seen of the sun ; but remember to make
friends with the dog which guards the threshold. Straightway
Mistress Anne will bring the native liquor. Seek the innermost
rooms and the snug seats : these know the sun, at least, when
Anne enters. What souls joying in the Lethæan flood you may
there see ! what frolics, God willing, you may partake of ! Mind-
less of all that goes on in the outer world, joys not to be
told to mortal do they there imbibe. But perhaps you may
wish by-and-by to get back into the world—which is indeed no
easy matter. I recommend you, when about to descend, to take
with you a trusty Achates [a caddy] : say to Anne, " Be sure you
give him no drink." By such means it was that Castor and Pollux
were able to issue forth from Pluto's domain into the heavenly
spaces. Here you may be both merry and wise ; but beware how
you toast kings and their French retreats,' &c. The sites of
these merry places of yore are not handed down to us ; but
respecting another, which Pitcairn shadows forth under the
mysterious appellation of *Greppa*, it chances that we possess some
knowledge. It was a suite of dark underground apartments in
the Parliament Close, opening by a descending stair opposite the
oriel of St Giles's, in a mass of building called the Pillars. By the
wits who frequented it, it was called the *Greping-office*, because
one could only make way through its dark passages by groping.
It is curious to see how Pitcairn works this homely Scottish idea
into his Sapphics, talking, for example, by way of a good case of
bane and antidote, of

' Fraudes Egidii, venena Greppæ.'

A venerable person has given me an anecdote of this singular
mixture of learning, wit, and professional skill in connection with
the Greping-office. Here, it seems, according to a custom which
lasted even in London till a later day, the clever physician used
to receive visits from his patients. On one occasion a woman
from the country called to consult him respecting the health of
her daughter, when he gave a shrewd hygienic advice in a pithy
metaphor not be mentioned to ears polite. When, in consequence
of following the prescription, the young woman had recovered her
health, the mother came back to the Greping-office to thank Dr
Pitcairn and give him a small present. Seeing him in precisely
the same place and circumstances, and surrounded by the same
companions as on the former occasion, she lingered with an
expression of surprise. On interrogation, she said she had only

one thing to speer at him (ask after), and she hoped he would not be angry.

'Oh no, my good woman.'

'Well, sir, have you been sitting here ever since I saw you last?'

According to the same authority, small claret was then sold at twentypence the Scottish pint, equivalent to tenpence a bottle. Pitcairn once or twice sent his servant for a regale of this liquor on the Sunday forenoon, and suffered the disappointment of having it intercepted by the *seizers*, whose duty it was to make capture of all persons found abroad in time of service, and appropriate whatever they were engaged in carrying that smelled of the common enjoyments of life. To secure his claret for the future from this interference, the wit caused the wine on one occasion to be drugged in such a manner as to produce consequences more ludicrous than dangerous to those drinking it. The triumph he thus attained over a power which there was no reaching by any appeal to common-sense or justice must have been deeply relished in the Greping-office.

Pitcairn was professedly an Episcopalian, but he allowed himself a latitude in wit which his contemporaries found some difficulty in reconciling with any form of religion. Among the popular charges against him was that he did not believe in the existence of such a place as hell; a point of heterodoxy likely to be sadly disrelished in Scotland. Being at a book-sale, where a copy of Philostratus sold at a good price and a copy of the Bible was not bidden for, Pitcairn said to some one who remarked the circumstance: 'Not at all wonderful; for is it not written, " *Verbum Dei manet in eternum* "?' For this, one of the *Cyclopes*, a famous Mr Webster, called him publicly an atheist. The story goes on to state that Pitcairn prosecuted Webster for defamation in consequence, but failed in the action from the following circumstance: The defender, much puzzled what to do in the case, consulted a shrewd-witted friend of his, a Mr Pettigrew, minister of Govan, near Glasgow. Pettigrew came to Edinburgh to endeavour to get him out of the scrape. 'Strange,' he said, ' since he has caught so much at your mouth, if we can catch nothing at his.' Having laid his plan, he came bustling up to the physician at the Cross, and tapping him on the shoulder, said: 'Are you Dr Pitcairn the atheist?'

The doctor, in his haste, overlooking the latter part of the query, answered: 'Yes,'

' Very good,' said Pettigrew ; ' I take you all to witness that he has confessed it himself.'

Pitcairn, seeing how he had been outwitted, said bitterly to the minister of Govan, whom he well knew : ' Oh, Pettigrew, that skull of yours is as deep as hell.'

' Oh, man,' replied Pettigrew, ' I 'm glad to find you have come to believe there is a hell.' The prosecutor's counsel, who stood by at the time, recommended a compromise, which accordingly took place.

A son of Pitcairn was minister of Dysart ; a very good kind of man, who was sometimes consulted in a medical way by his parishioners. He seems to have had a little of the paternal humour, if we may judge from the following circumstance : A lady came to ask what her maid-servant should do for sore or tender eyes. The minister, seeing that no active treatment could be recommended, said : ' She must do naething wi' them, but just rub them wi' her elbucks [elbows].'

Allan Ramsay mentions, of Edinburgh taverns in his day,

' Cumin's, Don's, and Steil's,'

as places where one may be as well served as at *The Devil* in London.

"'Tis strange, though true, he who would shun all evil,
Cannot do better than go to the Devil.'

JOHN MACLAURIN.

One is disposed to pause a moment on Steil's name, as it is honourably connected with the history of music in Scotland. Being a zealous lover of the divine science and a good singer of the native melodies, he had rendered his house a favourite resort of all who possessed a similar taste, and here actually was formed (1728) the first regular society of amateur musicians known in our country. It numbered seventy persons, and met once a week, the usual entertainments consisting in playing on the harpsichord and violin the concertos and sonatas of Handel, then newly published. Apparently, however, this fraternity did not long continue to use Steil's house, if I am right in supposing his retirement from business as announced in an advertisement of February 1729, regarding ' a sale by auction, of the haill pictures, prints, music-books, and musical instruments, belonging to Mr John Steill ' (*Caledonian Mercury*).

Coming down to a later time—1760–1770—we find the tavern in highest vogue to have been *Fortune's*, in the house which the

Earl of Eglintoune had once occupied in the Stamp-office Close
The gay men of rank, the scholarly and philosophical, the common
citizens, all flocked hither; and the royal commissioner for the
General Assembly held his levees here, and hence proceeded to
church with his cortège, then additionally splendid from having
ladies walking in it in their court-dresses as well as gentlemen.*
Perhaps the most remarkable set of men who met here was the
POKER CLUB,† consisting of Hume, Robertson, Blair, Fergusson, and
many others of that brilliant galaxy, but whose potations were
comparatively of a moderate kind.

The *Star and Garter*, in Writers' Court, kept by one Clerihugh
(the *Clerihugh's* alluded to in *Guy Mannering*), was another
tavern of good consideration, the favourite haunt of the magistrates and Town-council, who in those days mixed much more
of private enjoyments with public duties than would now be
considered fitting.‡   Here the Rev. Dr Webster used to meet them
at dinner, in order to give them the benefit of his extensive knowledge and great powers of calculation when they were scheming
out the New Town.

A favourite house for many of the last years of the bygone
century was *Douglas's*, in the Anchor Close, near the Cross, a
good specimen of those profound retreats which have been spoken
of as valued in the inverse ratio of the amount of daylight which
visited them.   You went a few yards down the dark, narrow alley,
passing on the left hand the entry to a scale stair, decorated with
'THE LORD IS ONLY MY SVPORT;' then passed another door,
bearing the still more antique legend: 'O LORD, IN THE IS AL MY
TRAIST;' immediately beyond, under an architrave calling out
'BE MERCIFVL TO ME,' you entered the hospitable mansion of
Dawney Douglas, the scene of the daily and nightly orgies of the
Pleydells and Fairfords, the Hays, Erskines, and Crosbies, of the
time of our fathers.   Alas! how fallen off is now that temple

---

* The Scottish peers on occasions of election of representatives to the House
of Lords frequently brought their meetings to a close by dining at Fortune's
Tavern.

† See note, p. 157.

‡ 'The wags of the eighteenth century used to tell of a certain city treasurer
who, on being applied to for a new rope to the Tron Kirk bell, summoned the
Council to deliberate on the demand; an adjournment to Clerihugh's Tavern,
it was hoped, might facilitate the settlement of so weighty a matter, but one
dinner proved insufficient, and it was not till their third banquet that the
application was referred to a committee, who spliced the old rope, and settled
the bill!'—Wilson's *Memorials of Old Edinburgh*.

of Momus and the Bacchanals! You find it divided into a multitude of small lodgings, where, instead of the merry party, vociferous with toasts and catches, you are most likely to be struck by the spectacle of some poor lone female, pining under a parochial allowance, or a poverty-struck family group, one-half of whom are disposed on sick-beds of straw mingled with rags—the terrible exponents of our peculiar phasis of civilisation.

The frequenter of Douglas's, after ascending a few steps, found himself in a pretty large kitchen—a dark, fiery Pandemonium, through which numerous ineffable ministers of flame were continually flying about, while beside the door sat the landlady, a large, fat woman, in a towering head-dress and large-flowered silk gown, who bowed to every one passing. Most likely on emerging from this igneous region, the party would fall into the hands of Dawney himself, and so be conducted to an apartment. A perfect contrast was he to his wife : a thin, weak, submissive man, who spoke in a whisper, never but in the way of answer, and then, if possible, only in monosyllables. He had a habit of using the word 'quietly' very frequently, without much regard to its being appropriate to the sense ; and it is told that he one day made the remark that ' the Castle had been firing to-day—*quietly ;* ' which, it may well be believed, was not soon forgotten by his customers. Another trait of Dawney was that some one lent him a volume of Clarendon's history to read, and daily frequenting the room where it lay, used regularly, for some time, to put back the reader's mark to the same place ; whereupon, being by-and-by asked how he liked the book, Dawney answered : ' Oh, very weel ; but dinna ye think it's gay mickle the same thing o'er again ? ' The house was noted for suppers of tripe, rizzared haddocks, mince collops, and *hashes,* which never cost more than sixpence a head. On charges of this moderate kind the honest couple grew extremely rich before they died.

The principal room in this house was a handsome one of good size, having a separate access by the second of the entries which have been described, and only used for large companies, or for guests of the first importance. It was called *the Crown Room,* or *the Crown*—so did the guests find it distinguished on the tops of their bills—and this name it was said to have acquired in consequence of its having once been used by Queen Mary as a councilroom, on which occasions the emblem of sovereignty was disposed in a niche in the wall, still existing. How the queen should have had any occasion to hold councils in this place tradition does not undertake to explain; but assuredly, when we consider the nature of all public accommodations in that time, we cannot say there is any decided improbability in the matter. The house appears of sufficient age for the hypothesis. Perhaps we catch a hint on the general possibility from a very ancient house farther down the close, of whose original purpose or owners we know nothing, but which is adumbrated by this legend:

ANGVSTA AD VSVM AVGVSTA[M]
W F   B G

The Crown Room, however, is elegant enough to have graced even the presence of Queen Mary, so that she only had not had to reach it by the Anchor Close. It is handsomely panelled, with a decorated fireplace, and two tall windows towards the alley. At present this supposed seat of royal councils, and certain seat of the social enjoyments of many men of noted talents, forms a back-shop to Mr Ford, grocer, High Street, and, all dingy and out of countenance, serves only to store hams, firkins of butter, packages of groceries, and bundles of dried cod.*

The gentle Dawney had an old Gaelic song called Crochallan, which he occasionally sang to his customers. This led to the establishment of a club at his house, which, with a reference to the militia regiments then raising, was called the Crochallan Corps, or Crochallan Fencibles, and to which belonged, amongst other men of original character and talent, the well-known William Smellie, author of the *Philosophy of Natural History*. Each member bore a military title, and some were endowed with ideal offices of a ludicrous character: for example, a lately surviving associate had been *depute-hangman* to the corps. Individuals committing a fault were subjected to a mock trial, in which such members as were barristers could display their forensic talents to the infinite amusement of the brethren. Much mirth and not a little horse-play prevailed. Smellie, while engaged professionally in printing the Edinburgh edition of the poems of Burns, introduced that genius to the Crochallans, when a scene of rough banter took place between him and certain privileged old hands, and the bard declared at the conclusion that he had 'never been so abominably thrashed in his life.' There was one predominant wit, Willie Dunbar by name, of whom the poet has left a characteristic picture:

* Since this was written, the whole group of buildings has been taken down, and new ones substituted (1868).

> 'As I came by Crochallan,
>   I cannily keekit ben—
> Rattling roaring Willie
>   Was sitting at yon board en'—
> Sitting at yon board en',
>   Amang gude companie;
> Rattling roaring Willie,
>   Ye're welcome hame to me!'

He has also described Smellie as coming to Crochallan with his old cocked hat, gray surtout, and beard rising in its might:

> 'Yet though his caustic wit was biting, rude,
>   His heart was warm, benevolent, and good.'

The printing-office of this strange genius being at the bottom of the close, the transition from the correction of proofs to the roaring scenes at Crochallan must have been sufficiently easy for Burns.

I am indebted to a privately printed memoir on the Anchor Close for the following anecdote of Crochallan: 'A comical gentleman, one of the members of the corps [old Williamson of Cardrona, in Peeblesshire], got rather tipsy one evening after a severe *field-day*. When he came to the head of the Anchor Close, it occurred to him that it was necessary that he should take possession of the Castle. He accordingly set off for this purpose. When he got to the outer gate, he demanded immediate possession of the garrison, to which he said he was entitled. The sentinel, for a considerable time, laughed at him; he, however, became so extremely clamorous that the man found it necessary to apprise the commanding officer, who immediately came down to inquire into the meaning of such impertinent conduct. He at once recognised his friend Cardrona, whom he had left at the festive board of the Crochallan Corps only a few hours before. Accordingly, humouring him in the conceit, he said: 'Certainly you have every right to the command of this garrison; if you please, I will conduct you to your proper apartment.' He accordingly conveyed him to a bedroom in his house. Cardrona took formal possession of the place, and immediately afterwards went to bed. His feelings were indescribable when he looked out of his bedroom window next morning, and found himself surrounded with soldiers and great guns. Some time afterwards this story came to the ears of the Crochallans; and Cardrona said he never afterwards had the life of a dog, so much did they tease and harass him about his strange adventure.'

There is a story connected with the air and song of Crochallan which will tell strangely after these anecdotes. The title is properly *Cro Chalien*—that is, 'Colin's Cattle.' According to Highland tradition, Colin's wife, dying at an early age, *came back*, some months after she had been buried, and was seen occasionally in the evenings milking her cow as formerly, and singing this plaintive air. It is curious thus to find Highland superstition associated with a snug tavern in the Anchor Close and the convivialities of such men as Burns and Smellie.

John Dowie's, in Liberton's Wynd, a still more perfect specimen of those taverns which Pitcairn eulogises—

'Antraque Cocyto penè propinqua'—

enjoyed the highest celebrity during the latter years of the past and early years of the present century. A great portion of this house was literally without light, consisting of a series of windowless chambers, decreasing in size till the last was a mere box, of irregular oblong figure, jocularly, but not inappropriately, designated *the Coffin.* Besides these, there were but two rooms possessing light, and as that came from a deep, narrow alley, it was light little more than in name. Hither, nevertheless, did many of the Parliament House men come daily for their meridian. Here nightly assembled companies of cits, as well as of men of wit and of fashion, to spend hours in what may, by comparison, be de-

Dowie's Tavern.

cribed as gentle conviviality. The place is said to have been howff of Fergusson and Burns in succession. Christopher North somewhere alludes to meetings of his own with Tom Campbell in that couthy mansion. David Herd, the editor of he Scottish songs, Mr Cumming of the Lyon Office, and George Paton the antiquary were regular customers, each seldom allowing a night to pass without a symposium at Johnie Dowie's. Now, these men are all gone; their very habits are becoming matters of history; while, as for their evening haunt, the place which knew it once knows it no more, the new access to the Lawnmarket, by George IV. Bridge, passing over the area where it stood.

Johnie Dowie's was chiefly celebrated for ale — *Younger's Edinburgh ale*—a potent fluid which almost glued the lips of he drinker together, and of which few, therefore, could despatch more than a bottle. John, a sleek, quiet-looking man, in a last-century style of attire, always brought in the liquor himself. decanted it carefully, drank a glass to the health of the company, and then retired. His neat, careful management of the bottle must have entirely met the views of old William Coke, the Leith bookseller, of whom it is told that if he saw a green-horn of a waiter acting in a different manner, he would rush indignantly up to him, take the ale out of his hands, caress it tenderly, as if to soothe and put it to rights again, and then proceed to the business of decanting it himself, saying: 'You rascal, is that the way you attend to your business? Sirrah, you ought to handle a bottle of ale as you would do a new-born babe!'

Dowie's was also famed for its *petits soupers*, as one of its customers has recorded ·

> ''Deed, gif ye please,
> Ye may get a bit toasted cheese,
> A crumb o' tripe, ham, dish o' peas,
>   The season fitting ;
> An egg, or, cauler frae the seas,
>   A fleuk or whiting.'

When the reckoning came to be paid, John's duty usually consisted simply in counting the empty bottles which stood on a little shelf where he had placed them above the heads of his customers, and multiplying these by the price of the liquor— usually threepence. Studious of decency, he was rigorous as to hours, and, when pressed for additional supplies of liquor at a particular time, would say : 'No, no, gentlemen ; it's past twelve o'clock, and time to go home.'

Of John's conscientiousness as to money matters there is some illustration in the following otherwise trivial anecdote. David Herd, being one night prevented by slight indisposition from joining in the malt potations of his friends, called for first one and then another glass of spirits, which he dissolved, *more Scotico*, in warm water and sugar. When the reckoning came to be paid, the antiquary was surprised to find the second glass charged a fraction higher than the first—as if John had been resolved to impose a tax upon excess. On inquiring the reason, however, honest John explained it thus : 'Whe, sir, ye see, the first glass was out o' the auld barrel, and the second was out o the new ; and as the whisky in the new barrel cost me mair than the other, whe, sir, I've just charged a wee mair for't.' An ordinary host would have doubtless equalised the price by raising that of the first glass to a level with the second. It is gratifying, but, after this anecdote, not surprising, that John eventually retired with a fortune said to have amounted to six thousand pounds. He had a son in the army, who attained the rank of major, and was a respectable officer.

We get an idea of a class of taverns, humbler in their appointments, but equally comfortable perhaps in their entertainments, from the description which has been preserved of *Mrs Flockhart's* —otherwise *Lucky Fykie's*—in the Potterrow. This was a remarkably small, as well as obscure mansion, bearing externally the appearance of a huckstry shop. The lady was a neat, little, thin, elderly woman, usually habited in a plain striped blue gown, and apron of the same stuff, with a black ribbon round her head and lappets tied under her chin. She was far from being poor in circumstances, as her husband, the umquhile John Flucker, or Flockhart, had left her some ready money, together with his whole stock-in-trade, consisting of a multifarious variety of articles—as ropes, tea, sugar, whip-shafts, porter, ale, beer, yellow sand, *calm-stane*, herrings, nails, cottonwicks, stationery, thread, needles, tapes, potatoes, lollipops, onions, matches, &c., constituting her a very respectable *merchant*, as the phrase was understood in Scotland. On Sundays, too, Mrs Flockhart's little visage might have been seen in a frontgallery seat in Mr Pattieson's chapel in the Potterrow. Her abode, situated opposite to Chalmers's Entry in that suburban

horoughfare, was a square of about fifteen feet each way, divided
agreeably to the following diagram :

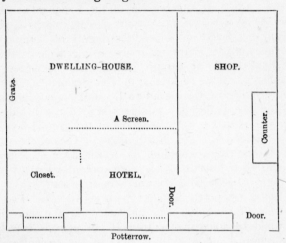

Potterrow.

Each forenoon was this place, or at least all in front of the
screen, put into the neatest order ; at the same time three
bottles, severally containing brandy, rum, and whisky, were
placed on a bunker-seat in the window of the 'hotel,' flanked
by a few glasses and a salver of gingerbread biscuits. About
noon any one watching the place from an opposite window
would have observed an elderly gentleman entering the humble
shop, where he saluted the lady with a 'Hoo d'ye do, mem ? '
and then passed into the side space to indulge himself with a
glass from one or other of the bottles. After him came another,
who went through the same ceremonial ; after him another
again ; and so on. Strange to say, these were men of importance
in society—some of them lawyers in good employment, some
bankers, and so forth, and all of them inhabitants of good houses
in George Square. It was in passing to or from forenoon
business in town that they thus regaled themselves. On special
occasions Lucky could furnish forth a *soss*—that is, stew—which
the votary might partake of upon a clean napkin in the closet,
a place which only admitted of one chair being placed in it.
Such were amongst the habits of the fathers of some of our
present (1824) most distinguished citizens !

This may be the proper place for introducing the few notices
which I have collected respecting Edinburgh inns of a past date.

The oldest house known to have been used in the character of an inn is one situated in what is called Davidson's or the White Horse Close, at the bottom of the Canongate. A sort of *porte-cochère* gives access to a court having mean buildings on either hand, but facing us a goodly structure of antique fashion having two outside stairs curiously arranged, and the whole reminding us much of certain houses still numerous in the Netherlands. A date, deficient in the decimal figure (16–3), gives us assurance of the seventeenth century, and, judging from the style of the building, I would say the house belongs to an early portion of that age. The whole of the ground-floor, accessible from the street called North Back of Canongate, has been used as stables, thus reminding us of the absence of nicety in a former age, when human beings were content to sit with only a wooden floor between themselves and their horses.

This house, supposed to have been styled *The White Horse Inn* or *White Horse Stables* (for the latter was the more common word), would be conveniently situated for persons travelling to or arriving from London, as it is close to the ancient exit of the town in that direction. The adjacent Water-gate took its name from a horse-pond, which probably was an appendage of this mansion. The manner of procedure for a gentleman going to London in the days of the *White Horse* was to come booted to this house with saddle-bags, and here engage and mount a suitable roadster, which was to serve all the way. In 1639, when Charles I. had made his first pacification with the Covenanters, and had come temporarily to Berwick, he sent messages to the chief lords of that party, desiring some conversation with them. They were unsuspectingly mounting their horses at this inn, in order to ride to Berwick, when a mob, taught by the clergy to suspect that the king wished only to wile over the nobles to his side, came and forcibly prevented them from commencing their designed journey. Montrose alone broke through this restraint; and assuredly the result in his instance was such as to give some countenance to the suspicion, as thenceforward he was a royalist in his heart.

The *White Horse* has ceased to be an inn from a time which no 'oldest inhabitant' of my era could pretend to have any recollection of. The only remaining fact of interest connected with it is one concerning Dr Alexander Rose, the last Bishop of Edinburgh, and the last survivor of the established Episcopacy of Scotland. Bishop Keith, who had been one of his presbyters, and describes him as a sweet-natured man, of a venerable aspect, states that he died March 20, 1720, 'in his own sister's house in the Canongate, in which street he also lived.' Tradition points to the floor immediately above the *porte-cochère* by which the stable-yard is entered from the street as the humble mansion in which the bishop breathed his last. I know at least one person who never goes past the place without an emotion of respect, remembering the self-abandoning devotion of the Scottish prelates to their engagements at the Revolution : *

> 'Amongst the faithless, faithful only found.'

To the elegant accommodations of the best New Town establishments of the present day, the inns of the last century present a contrast which it is difficult by the greatest stretch of imagination to realise. For the west road, there was the *White Hart* in the Grassmarket ; for the east, the *White Horse Inn* in Boyd's Close, Canongate ; for the south, and partly also the east, Peter Ramsay's, at the bottom of St Mary's Wynd. Arnot, writing in 1779, describes them as 'mean buildings ; their apartments dirty and dismal ; and if the waiters happen to be out of the way, a stranger will perhaps be shocked with the novelty of being shown into a room by a dirty, sunburnt wench, without shoes or stockings.' The fact is, however, these houses were mainly used as places for keeping horses. Guests, unless of a very temporary character, were usually relegated to lodging-houses, of which there were several on a considerable scale—as Mrs Thomson's at the Cross, who advertises, in 1754, that persons not bringing 'their silver plate, tea china, table china, and tea linen, can be served in them all ; ' also in wines and spirits ; likewise that persons boarding with her 'may expect everything in a very genteel manner.' But hear the unflattering Arnot on these houses. 'He [the stranger] is probably conducted to the third or fourth floor, up dark and dirty stairs, and there shown into apartments meanly fitted up and poorly furnished. . . . In Edinburgh, letting of lodgings is a business by itself, and thereby the prices are very extravagant ; and every article of furniture, far from wearing the appearance of having been purchased for a happy owner, seems to be scraped together with a penurious hand, to pass muster before a stranger who will never wish to return ! '

---

* The 'White Horse' is introduced in *The Abbot*—it was the scene of Roland Græme's encounter with young Seton.

Ramsay's was almost solely a place of stables. General Paoli,* on visiting Edinburgh in 1771, came to this house, but was immediately taken home by his friend Boswell to James's Court, where he lived during his stay in our city; his companion, the Polish ambassador, being accommodated with a bed by Dr John Gregory, in a neighbouring floor. An old gentleman of my acquaintance used to talk of having seen the Duke of Hamilton one day lounging in front of Ramsay's inn, occasionally chatting with any gay or noble friend who passed. To one knowing the Edinburgh of the present day, nothing could seem more extravagant than the idea of such company at such places. I nevertheless find Ramsay, in 1776, advertising that, exclusive of some part of his premises recently offered for sale, he is 'possessed of a good house of entertainment, good stables for above one hundred horses, and sheds for above twenty carriages.' He retired from business about 1790 with £10,000.†

The modern *White Horse* was a place of larger and somewhat better accommodations, though still far from an equality with even the second-rate houses of the present day. Here also the rooms were directly over the stables.

It was almost a matter of course that Dr Johnson, on arriving in Edinburgh, August 17, 1773, should have come to the *White Horse*, which was then kept by a person of the name of Boyd. His note to Boswell informing him of this fact was as follows:

'Saturday night.
'Mr Johnson sends his compliments to Mr Boswell, being just arrived at Boyd's.'

When Boswell came, he found his illustrious friend in a violent passion at the waiter for having sweetened his lemonade without the ceremony of a pair of sugar-tongs. Mr William Scott, afterwards Lord Stowell, accompanied Johnson on this occasion; and he informs us, in a note to Croker's edition of Boswell, that when he heard the mistress of the house styled, in Scotch fashion, *Lucky*, which he did not then understand, he thought she should rather have been styled *Unlucky*, for the doctor seemed as if he would destroy the house.‡

* The Corsican patriot whose acquaintance Boswell made on his tour abroad. Johnson characterised him as having 'the loftiest port of any man he had ever seen.'

† Peter Ramsay was a brother of William Ramsay of Barnton, the well known sporting character of the early part of the nineteenth century.

‡ A punning friend, remarking on the old Scottish practice of styling elderly landladies by the term *Lucky*, said: 'Why not?—*Felix qui pot——*'

James Boyd, the keeper of this inn, was addicted to horse-racing, and his victories on the turf, or rather on Leith sands, are frequently chronicled in the journals of that day. It is said that he was at one time on the brink of ruin, when he was saved by a lucky run with a white horse, which, in gratitude, he kept idle all the rest of its days, besides setting up its portrait as his sign. He eventually retired from this 'dirty and dismal' inn with a fortune of several thousand pounds; and, as a curious note upon the impression which its slovenliness conveyed to Dr Johnson, it may be stated as a fact, well authenticated, that at the time of his giving up the house he possessed *napery* to the value of five hundred pounds!

A large room in the *White Horse* was the frequent scene of the marriages of runaway English couples, at a time when these irregularities were permitted in Edinburgh. On one of the windows were scratched the words:

'JEREMIAH AND SARAH BENTHAM, 1768.'

Could this be the distinguished jurist and codificator, on a journey to Scotland in company with a female relation? *

* The following curious advertisement, connected with an inn in the Canongate, appeared in the *Edinburgh Evening Courant* for July 1, 1754. The advertisement is surmounted by a woodcut representing the stage-coach, a towering vehicle, protruding at top—the coachman a stiff-looking, antique little figure, who holds the reins with both hands, as if he were afraid of the horses running away—a long whip streaming over his head and over the top of the coach, and falling down behind—six horses, like starved rats in appearance—a postillion upon one of the leaders, with a whip:

'The Edinburgh Stage-Coach, for the better accommodation of Passengers, will be altered to a new genteel two-end Glass Machine, hung on Steel Springs, exceeding light and easy, to go in ten days in summer and twelve in winter; to set out the first Tuesday in March, and continue it from Hosea Eastgate's, the *Coach and Horses* in Dean Street, Soho, London, and from John Somerville's in the Canongate, Edinburgh, every other Tuesday, and meet at Burrowbridge on Saturday night, and set out from thence on Monday morning, and get to London and Edinburgh on Friday. In the winter to set out from London and Edinburgh every other [alternate] Monday morning, and to go to Burrowbridge on Saturday night; and to set out from thence on Monday morning, and get to London and Edinburgh on Saturday night. Passengers to pay as usual. Performed, if God permits, by your dutiful servant,

HOSEA EASTGATE.

'Care is taken of small parcels *according to their value*.'

THE CROSS—CADDIES

THE Cross, a handsome octagonal building in the High Street, surmounted by a pillar bearing the Scottish unicorn, was the great centre of gossip in former days. The principal coffee-houses and booksellers' shops were close to this spot. The chief merchants, the leading official persons, the men of learning and talents, the laird, the noble, the clergyman, were constantly clustering hereabouts during certain hours of the day. It was the very centre and cynosure of the old city.

During the reigns of the first and second Georges, it was customary for the magistrates of Edinburgh to drink the king's health on his birthday on a stage erected at the Cross—loyalty being a virtue which always becomes peculiarly ostentatious when it is under any suspicion of weakness. On one of these occasions the ceremony was interrupted by a shower of rain, so heavy that the company, with one consent, suddenly dispersed, leaving their entertainment half-finished. When they returned, the glasses were found full of water, which gave a Jacobite lady occasion for the following epigram, reported to me by a venerable bishop of the Scottish Episcopal Church :

> ' In Cana once Heaven's king was pleased
>   With some gay bridal folks to dine,
> And then, in honour of the feast,
>   He changed the water into wine.
>
> But when, to honour Brunswick's birth,
>   Our tribunes mounted the Theâtre,
> He would not countenance their mirth,
>   But turned their claret into water !'

As the place where state proclamations were always made, where the execution of noted state criminals took place, and where many important public ceremonials were enacted, the Cross of Edinburgh is invested with numberless associations of a most interesting kind, extending over several centuries. Here took place the mysterious midnight proclamation, summoning the Flodden lords to the domains of Pluto, as described so strikingly in *Marmion ;* the witness being ' Mr Richard Lawson, ll-disposed, ganging in his gallery fore-stair.' Here did King James VI. bring together his barbarous nobles, and make them shake hands over a feast partaken of before the eyes of the people. Here did the Covenanting lords read their protests against Charles's feeble proclamations. Here fell Montrose, Huntly, the Argylls, Warriston, and many others of note, victims of political dissension. Here were fountains set a-flowing with the blood-red wine, to celebrate the passing of kings along the causeway. And here, as a last notable fact, were Prince Charles and his father proclaimed by their devoted Highlanders, amidst screams of pipe and blare of trumpet, while the beautiful Mrs Murray of Broughton sat beside the party on horseback, adorned with white ribbons, and with a drawn sword in her hand! How strange it seems that a time should at length have come when a set of magistrates thought this structure an encumbrance to the street, and had it removed. This event took place in 1756— the ornamental stones dispersed, the pillar taken to the park at Drum.*

The Cross was the peculiar citadel and rallying-point of a species of lazzaroni called *Caddies* or *Cawdies*, which formerly existed in Edinburgh, employing themselves chiefly as street-messengers and *valets de place*. A ragged, half-blackguard-looking set they were, but allowed to be amazingly acute and intelligent, and also faithful to any duty entrusted to them. A stranger coming to reside temporarily in Edinburgh got a caddy attached to his service to conduct him from one part of the town to another, to run errands for him; in short, to be wholly at his bidding.

> 'Omnia novit,
> Græculus esuriens, in cœlum, jusseris, ibit.'

A caddy *did* literally know everything—of Edinburgh; even to that kind of knowledge which we now only expect in a street directory. And it was equally true that he could hardly be asked to go anywhere, or upon any mission, that he would not go. On the other hand, the stranger would probably be astonished to find that, in a few hours, his caddy was acquainted with every par-

---

* The pillar was restored to Edinburgh, and for some years stood within an enclosed recess on the north side of St Giles'. When Mr W. E. Gladstone rebuilt the Cross in 1885, a little to the south of its former site, between St Giles' Church and the Police Office, the original pillar was replaced in its old position.

ticular regarding himself, where he was from, what was his purpose in Edinburgh, his family connections, and his own tastes and dispositions. Of course for every particle of scandal floating about Edinburgh, the caddy was a ready book of reference. We sometimes wonder how our ancestors did without newspapers. We do not reflect on the living vehicles of news which then existed : the privileged beggar for the country people ; for townsfolk, the caddies.

The caddy is alluded to as a useful kind of blackguard in Burt's *Letters from the North of Scotland*, written about 1740. He says that although they are mere wretches in rags, lying upon stairs and in the streets at night, they are often considerably trusted, and seldom or never prove unfaithful. The story told by tradition is that they formed a society under a chief called their constable, with a common fund or box ; that when they committed any misdemeanour, such as incivility or lying, they were punished by this officer by fines, or sometimes corporeally ; and if by any chance money entrusted to them should not be forthcoming, it was made up out of the common treasury. Mr Burt says : 'Whether it be true or not I cannot say, but I have been told by several that one of the judges formerly abandoned two of his sons for a time to this way of life, as believing it would create in them a sharpness which might be of use to them in the future course of their lives.' Major Topham, describing Edinburgh in 1774, says of the caddies : ' In short, they are the tutelary guardians of the city ; and it is entirely owing to them that there are fewer robberies and less housebreaking in Edinburgh than anywhere else.'

Another conspicuous set of public servants characteristic of Edinburgh in past times were the *Chairmen*, or carriers of sedans, who also formed a society among themselves, but were of superior respectability, in as far as none but steady, considerate persons of so humble an order could become possessed of the means to buy the vehicle by which they made their bread. In former times, when Edinburgh was so much more limited than now, and rather an assemblage of alleys than of streets, sedans were in comparatively great request. They were especially in requisition amongst the ladies—indeed, almost exclusively so. From time immemorial the sons of the Gael have monopolised this branch of service ; and as far as the business of a sedan-carrier can yet be said to exist amongst us, it is in the possession of Highlanders.

The reader must not be in too great haste to smile when I

claim his regard for an historical person among the chairmen of Edinburgh. This was Edward Burke, the immediate attendant of Prince Charles Edward during the earlier portion of his wanderings in the Highlands. Honest Ned had been a chairman in our city, but attaching himself as a servant to Mr Alexander Macleod of Muiravonside, aide-de-camp to the Prince, it was his fortune to be present at the battle of Culloden, and to fly from the field in his Royal Highness's company. He attended the Prince for several weeks, sharing cheerfully in all his hardships, and doing his best to promote his escape. Thus has his name been inseparably associated with this remarkable chapter of history. After parting with Charles, this poor man underwent some dreadful hardships while under hiding, his fears of being taken having reference chiefly to the Prince, as he was apprehensive that the enemy might torture him to gain intelligence of his late master's movements. At length the Act of Indemnity placed him at his ease; and the humble creature who, by a word of his mouth, might have gained thirty thousand pounds, quietly returned to his duty as a chairman on the streets of Edinburgh! Which of the venal train of Walpole, which even of the admirers of Pulteney, is more entitled to admiration than Ned Burke? A man, too, who could neither read nor write—for such was actually his case.*

One cannot but feel it to be in some small degree a consolatory circumstance, and not without a certain air of the romance of an earlier day, that a bacchanal company came with a bowl of punch, the night before the demolition, and in that mood of mind when men shed 'smiles that might as well be tears,' drank the Dredgie of the Cross upon its doomed battlements.

---

* Bishop Forbes inserts in his manuscript (which I possess) a panegyrical epitaph for Ned Burke, stating that he died in Edinburgh in November 1751. He also gives the following particulars from Burke's conversation :

'One of the soles of Ned's shoes happening to come off, Ned cursed the day upon which he should be forced to go without shoes. The Prince, hearing him, called to him and said : "Ned, look at me"—when (said Ned) I saw him holding up one of his feet at me, where there was de'il a sole upon the shoe; and then I said : "Oh, my dear ! I have nothing more to say. You have stopped my mouth indeed."

'When Ned was talking of seeing the Prince again, he spoke these words : "If the Prince do not come and see me soon, good faith I will go and see my daughter [Charles having taken the name of Betty Burke when in a female disguise], and crave her; for she has not yet paid her christening money, and as little has she paid the coat I ga'e her in her greatest need."'

'Oh! be his tomb as lead to lead,
Upon its dull destroyer's head!
A minstrel's malison is said.'*

* 'Upon the 26th of February [1617], the Cross of Edinburgh was taken down. The old long stone, about forty footes or thereby in length, was to be translated, by the devise of certain mariners in Leith, from the place where it had stood past the memory of man, to a place beneath in the High Street, without any harm to the stone; and the body of the old Cross was demolished, and another builded, whereupon the long stone or obelisk was erected and set up, on the 25th day of March.'—Calderwood's *Church History*.

THE TOWN-GUARD.

ONE of the characteristic features of Edinburgh in old times was its Town-guard, a body of military in the service of the magistrates for the purposes of a police, but dressed and armed in all respects as soldiers. Composed for the most part of old Highlanders, of uncouth aspect and speech, dressed in a dingy red uniform with cocked hats, and often exchanging the musket for an antique native weapon called the Lochaber axe, these men were (at least in latter times) an unfailing subject of mirth to the citizens, particularly the younger ones. In my recollection they had a sort of Patmos in the ground-floor of the Old Tolbooth, where a few of them might constantly be seen on duty, endeavouring to look as formidable as possible to the little boys who might be passing by. On such occasions as executions, or races at Leith, or the meeting of the General Assembly, they rose into a certain degree of consequence; but in general they could hardly be considered as of any practical utility. Their numbers were at that time much reduced—only twenty-five privates, two sergeants, two corporals, and a couple of drummers. Every night did their drum beat through the Old Town at eight o'clock, as a kind of curfew. No other drum, it seems, was allowed to sound on the High Street between the Luckenbooths and Netherbow. They also had an old practice of giving a *charivari* on the drum on the night of a marriage before the lodgings of the bridegroom; of course not without the expectation of something wherewithal to drink the health of the young couple. A strange remnant of old times altogether were the *Town Rats*, as the poor old fellows were disrespectfully called by the boys, in allusion to the hue of their uniform.

Previous to 1805, when an unarmed police was established for the protection of the streets, the Town-guard had consisted of three equally large companies, each with a lieutenant (complimentarily called captain) at its head. Then it was a somewhat more respectable body, not only as being larger, but invested with a really useful purpose. The unruly and the vicious stood in some awe of a troop of men bearing lethal weapons, and generally somewhat frank in the use of them. If sometimes roughly handled on kings' birthdays and other exciting occasions, they in their turn did not fail to treat cavalierly enough any unfortunate roisterer whom they might find breaking the peace. They had, previous to 1785, a guard-house in the middle of the High Street, the 'black hole' of which had rather a bad character among the bucks and the frail ladies. One of their sergeants in those days, by name John Dhu, is commemorated by Scott as the fiercest-looking fellow he ever saw. If we might judge from poor Robert Fergusson, they were truly formidable in his time. He says :

> 'And thou, great god o' aquavitæ,
>   Wha sway'st the empire o' this city ; . . .
>   Be thou prepared
>   To hedge us frae that *black banditti*,
>   The City-guard.'

He adds, apostrophising the irascible veterans :

> 'Oh, soldiers, for your ain dear sakes,
>   For Scotland's love—the land o' cakes—
>   Gi'e not her bairns sae deadly paiks,
>   Nor be sae rude,
>   Wi' firelock and Lochaber axe,
>   As spill their blude !'

The affair at the execution of Wilson the smuggler in 1736, when, under command of Porteous, they fired upon and killed many of the mob, may be regarded as a peculiarly impressive example of the stern relation in which they stood to the populace of a former age.

The great bulk of the corps was drawn either from the Highlands directly or from the Highland regiments. A humble Highlander considered it as getting a *berth* when he was enlisted into the Edinburgh Guard. Of this feeling we have a remarkable illustration in an anecdote which I was told by the late Mr Alexander Campbell regarding the Highland bard, Duncan Macintyre, usually called *Donacha Bhan*. This man, really an exquisite poet to those understanding his language, became the object of a kind interest to many educated persons in Perthshire, his native county. The Earl of Breadalbane sent to let him know that he wished to befriend him, and was anxious to procure him some situation that might put him comparatively at his ease. Poor Duncan returned his thanks, and asked his lordship's interest—to get him into the Edinburgh Town-guard—pay, sixpence a day ! What sort of material these men would have proved in the hands of the magis-

trates if Provost Stewart had attempted by their means and the
other forces at his command to hold out the city against Prince
Charlie seems hardly to be matter of doubt. I was told the
following anecdote of a member of the corps, on good authority.
Robert Stewart, a descendant of the Stewarts of Bonskeid in
Athole, was then a private in the City-guard. When General
Hawley left Edinburgh to meet the Highland army in the west
country, Stewart had just been relieved from duty for the customary period of two days. Instantly forming his plan of action,
he set off with his gun, passed through the English troops on
their march, and joined those of the Prince. Stewart fought next
day like a hero in the battle of Falkirk, where the Prince had the
best of it; and next morning our Town-guardsman was back to
Edinburgh in time to go upon duty at the proper hour. The
captain of his company suspected what business Robert and his
gun had been engaged in, but preserved a friendly silence.

The *Gutter-blood* people of Edinburgh had an extravagant idea
of the antiquity of the Guard, led probably by a fallacy arising
from the antiquity of the individual men. They used to have a
strange story—too ridiculous, one would have thought, for a
moment's credence anywhere—that the Town-guard existed before
the Christian era. When the Romans invaded Britain, some of
the Town-guard joined them; and three were actually present in
Pilate's guard at the Crucifixion! In reality, the corps took its
rise in the difficulties brought on by bad government in 1682,
when, at the instigation of the Duke of York, it was found
necessary to raise a body of 108 armed men, under a trusty
commander, simply to keep the people in check.*

Fifty years ago (1824) the so-called captaincies of the Guard
were snug appointments, in great request among respectable old
citizens who had not succeeded in business. Kay has given us
some illustrations of these extraordinary specimens of soldier-
craft, one of whom was nineteen stone. Captain Gordon of
Gordonstown, representative of one of the oldest families in
Scotland, found himself obliged by fortune to accept of one of
these situations.

Scott, writing his *Heart of Mid-Lothian* in 1817, says: 'Of
late, the gradual diminution of these civic soldiers reminds one
of the abatement of King Lear's hundred knights. The edicts of
each set of succeeding magistrates have, like those of Goneril
and Regan, diminished this venerable band with similar question

* See *Domestic Annals of Scotland*, ii. 436.

—" What need have we of five-and-twenty ?—ten ?—five ? " and now it is nearly come to : " What need we one ? " A spectre may indeed here and there still be seen of an old gray-headed and gray-bearded Highlander, with war-worn features, but bent double by age ; dressed in an old-fashioned cocked-hat, bound with white tape instead of silver lace, and in coat, waistcoat, and breeches of a muddy-coloured red ; bearing in his withered hand an ancient weapon, called a Lochaber axe—a long pole, namely, with an axe at the extremity, and a hook at the back of the hatchet. Such a phantom of former days still creeps, I have been informed, round the statue of Charles II. in the Parliament Square, as if the image of a Stuart were the last refuge for any memorial of our ancient manners,' &c. At the close of this very year, the ' What need we one ? ' was asked, and answered in the negative ; and the corps was accordingly dissolved. ' Their last march to do duty at Hallow Fair had something in it affecting. Their drums and fifes had been wont, in better days, to play on this joyous occasion the lively tune of

"Jockey to the fair ;"

but on this final occasion the afflicted veterans moved slowly to the dirge of

"The last time I came owre the muir."'*

The half-serious pathos of Scott regarding this corps becomes wholly so when we learn that a couple of members survived to make an actual last public appearance in the procession which consecrated his richly deserved monument, August 15, 1846.

* *Waverley Annotations*, i. 435.

EDINBURGH MOBS.

The Blue Blanket—Mobs of the Seventeenth Century—Bowed Joseph.

THE Edinburgh populace was noted, during many ages, for its readiness to rise in tumultuary fashion, whether under the prompting of religious zeal or from inferior motives. At an early time they became an impromptu army, each citizen possessing weapons which he was ready and willing to use. Thus they are understood to have risen in 1482 to redeem James III. from restraint in the Castle; for which service, besides certain privileges, 'he granted them,' says Maitland, 'a banner or standard, with a power to display the same in defence of their king, country, and their own right.' The historian adds: 'This flag, at present denominated the BLUE BLANKET, is kept by the Convener of the Trades; at whose appearance therewith, 'tis said that not only the artificers of Edinburgh are obliged to repair to it, but all the artisans or craftsmen within Scotland are bound to follow it, and fight under the Convener of Edinburgh, as aforesaid.' The Blue Blanket, I may mention, has become a sort of myth in Edinburgh, being magnified by the popular imagination into a banner which the citizens carried with them to the Holy Land in one of the Crusades—expeditions which took place before Edinburgh had become a town fit to furnish any distinct corps of armed men.[*]

When the Protestant faith came to stir up men's minds, the lower order of citizens became a formidable body indeed. James VI., who had more than once experienced their violence, and consequently knew them well, says very naïvely in his *Basilicon Doron*, or 'Book of Instruction' to his son: 'They think we should be content with their work, how bad and dear soever it be; and if they be in anything controuled, up goeth the *Blue Blanket!*'

The tumults at the introduction of the Service-book, in 1637, need only be alluded to. So late as the Revolution there appears a military spirit of great boldness in the Edinburgh populace, reminding us of that of Paris in our own times: witness the bloody contests which took place in accomplishing the destruction of the

[*] What is said to be the original Blue Blanket is still preserved in the National Museum of Antiquities of Scotland.

papistical arrangements at the Abbey, December 1688. The Union mobs were of unexampled violence; and Edinburgh was only kept in some degree of quiet, during the greater part of that crisis, by a great assemblage of troops. Finally, in the Porteous mob we have a singular example of popular vengeance, wreaked out in the most cool but determined manner. Men seem to have been habitually under an impression in those days that the law was at once an imperfect and a partial power. They seem to have felt themselves constantly liable to be called upon to supplement its energy, or control or compensate for its errors. The mob had at that time a part in the state.

In this 'fierce democracy' there once arose a mighty Pyrrhus, who contrived, by dint of popular qualifications, to subject the rabble to his command, and to get himself elected, by acclamation, dictator of all its motions and exploits. How he acquired his wonderful power is not recorded; but it is to be supposed that his activity on occasions of mobbing, his boldness and sagacity, his strong voice and uncommonly powerful whistle, together with the mere whim or humour of the thing, conspired to his promotion.

'General' Joe Smith
laying down the Law
to the Magistrates.

His trade was that of a cobbler, and he resided in some obscure den in the Cowgate. His person was low and deformed, with the sole good property of great muscular strength in the arms. Yet this wretch, miserable and contemptible as he appeared, might be said to have had at one time the command of the Scottish metropolis. The magistrates, it is true, assembled every Wednesday forenoon to manage the affairs and deliberate upon the improvements of the city; but their power was merely that of a viceroyalty. *Bowed Joseph*, otherwise called General Joseph Smith, was the only true potentate; and their resolutions could only be carried into effect when not inconsistent with his views of policy.

In exercising the functions of his perilous office, it does not appear that he ever drew down the vengeance of the more lawfully constituted authorities of the land. On the contrary, he was in some degree countenanced by the magistracy, who, however, patronised him rather from fear than respect. They

THE CASTLE
from Princes Street.

PAGE 214.

BLACKFRIARS' WYND.

PAGE 228.

frequently sent for him in emergencies, in order to consult with him regarding the best means of appeasing and dispersing the mob. On such occasions nothing could equal the consequential air which he assumed. With one hand stuck carelessly into his side, and another slapped resolutely down upon the table—with a majestic toss of the head, and as much fierceness in his little gray eye as if he were himself a mob—he would stand before the anxious and feeble council, pleading the cause of his compeers, and suggesting the best means of assuaging their just fury. He was generally despatched with a promise of amendment and a hogshead of good ale, with which he could easily succeed in appeasing his men, whose dismissal, after a speech from himself and a libation from the barrel, was usually accomplished by the simple words: '*Now disperse, my lads!*'

Joseph was not only employed in directing and managing the mobs, but frequently performed exploits without the co-operation of his greasy friends, though always for their amusement and in their behalf. Thus, for instance, when Wilkes by his celebrated Number 45 incensed the Scottish nation so generally and so bitterly, Joseph got a cart, fitted up with a high gallows, from which depended a straw-stuffed effigy of North Britain's arch-enemy, with the devil perched upon his shoulder; and this he paraded through the streets, followed by the multitude, till he came to the Gallow Lee in Leith Walk, where two criminals were then hanging in chains, beside whom he exposed the figures of Wilkes and his companion. Thus also, when the Douglas cause was decided against the popular opinion in the Court of Session, Joseph went up to the chair of the Lord President as he was going home to his house, and called him to account for the injustice of his decision. After the said decision was reversed by the House of Lords, Joseph, by way of triumph over the Scottish court, dressed up fifteen figures in rags and wigs, resembling the judicial attire, mounted them on asses, and led them through the streets, telling the populace that they saw the fifteen senators of the College of Justice!

When the craft of shoemakers used, in former times, to parade the High Street, West Bow, and Grassmarket, with inverted tin kettles on their heads and schoolboys' rulers in their hands, Joseph—who, though a leader and commander on every other public occasion, was not admitted into this procession on account of his being only a cobbler—dressed himself in his best clothes. with a royal crown painted and gilt and a wooden truncheon, and marched pompously through the city till he came to the Nether-bow, where he planted himself in the middle of the street to await the approach of the procession, which he, as a citizen of Edinburgh, proposed to welcome into the town. When the royal shoemaker came to the Netherbow Port, Joseph stood forth, removed the truncheon from his haunch, flourished it in the air, and pointing it to the ground, with much dignity of manner, addressed his paste-work majesty in these words: 'O great King Crispianus! what are we in thy sight but a parcel of puir slaister-kytes—creeshy cobblers—sons of bitches?' And I have been assured that this ceremony was performed in a style of burlesque exhibiting no small artistic power.

Joseph had a wife, whom he would never permit to walk beside him, it being his opinion that women are inferior to the male part of creation, and not entitled to the same privileges. He compelled his spouse to walk a few paces behind him; and when he turned, she was obliged to make a circuit so as to maintain the precise distance from his person which he assigned to her. When he wished to say anything to her, he whistled as upon a dog, upon which she came up to him submissively and heard what he had to say; after which she respectfully resumed her station in the rear.

After he had figured for a few years as an active partisan of the people, his name waxed of such account with them that it is said he could in the course of an hour collect a crowd of not fewer than ten thousand persons, all ready to obey his high behests, or to disperse at his bidding. In collecting his troops he employed a drum, which, though a general, he did not disdain to beat with his own hands; and never, surely, had the fiery cross of the Highland chief such an effect upon the warlike devotion of his clan as Bowed Joseph's drum had upon the spirit of the Edinburgh rabble. As he strode along, the street was cleared of its loungers, every close pouring forth an addition to his train, like the populous glens adjacent to a large Highland strath giving forth their accessions to the general force collected by the aforesaid cross. The Town Rats, who might peep forth like old cautious snails on hearing his drum, would draw in their horns with a Gaelic execration, and shut their door, as he approached; while the *Lazy Corner* was, at sight of him, a lazy corner no longer; and the West Bow ceased to resound as he descended.

It would appear, after all, that there was a moral foundation for Joseph's power, as there must be for that of all governments of a more regular nature that would wish to thrive or be lasting

The little man was never known to act in a bad cause, or in any way to go against the principles of natural justice. He employed his power in the redress of such grievances as the law of the land does not or cannot easily reach ; and it was apparent that almost everything he did was for the sake of what he himself designated *fair-play*. Fair-play, indeed, was his constant object, whether in clearing room with his brawny arms for a boxing-match, insulting the constituted authorities, sacking the granary of a monopolist, or besieging the Town-council in their chamber.

An anecdote which proves this strong love of fair-play deserves to be recorded. A poor man in the Pleasance having been a little deficient in his rent, and in the country on business, his landlord seized and rouped his household furniture, turning out the family to the street. On the poor man's return, finding the house desolate and his family in misery, he went to a neighbouring stable and hanged himself.* Bowed Joseph did not long remain ignorant of the case ; and as soon as it was generally known in the city, he shouldered on his drum, and after beating it through the streets for half-an-hour, found himself followed by several thousand persons, inflamed with resentment at the landlord's cruelty. With this army he marched to an open space of ground now covered by Adam Street, Roxburgh Street, &c., named in former times Thomson's Park, where, mounted upon the shoulders of six of his lieutenant-generals, he proceeded to harangue them, in Cambyses's vein, concerning the flagrant oppression which they were about to revenge. He concluded by directing his men to sack the premises of the cruel landlord, who by this time had wisely made his escape ; and this order was instantly obeyed. Every article which the house contained was brought out to the street, where, being piled up in a heap, the general set fire to them with his own hand, while the crowd rent the air with their acclamations. Some money and bank-notes perished in the blaze, besides an eight-day clock, which, sensible to the last, calmly struck ten just as it was consigned to the flames.

On another occasion, during a scarcity, the mob, headed by Joseph, had compelled all the meal-dealers to sell their meal at a certain price per peck, under penalty of being obliged to shut up their shops. One of them, whose place of business was in the Grassmarket, agreed to sell his meal at the price fixed by the general, for the good of the poor, as he said ; and he did so under the superintendence of Joseph, who stationed a party at the shop-

* *Scots Magazine*, June 1767.

door to preserve peace and good order till the whole stock was disposed of, when, by their leader's command, the mob gave three hearty cheers, and quietly dispersed. Next day, the unlucky victualler let his friends know that he had not suffered so much by this compulsory trade as might be supposed ; because, though the price was below that of the market, he had taken care to use a measure which gave only about three-fourths instead of the whole. It was not long ere this intelligence came to the ears of our tribune, who, immediately collecting a party of his troops, beset the meal-dealer before he was aware, and compelled him to pay back a fourth of the price of every peck of meal sold ; then giving their victim a hearty drubbing, they sacked his shop, and quietly dispersed as before.

Some foreign princes happening to visit Edinburgh during Joseph's administration, at a period of the year when the mob of Edinburgh was wont to amuse itself with an annual burning of the pope, the magistrates felt anxious that this ceremony should for once be dispensed with, as it might hurt the feelings of their distinguished visitors. The provost, in this emergency, resolved not to employ his own authority, but that of Joseph, to whom, accordingly, he despatched his compliments, with half a guinea, begging his kind offices in dissuading the mob from the performance of their accustomed sport. Joseph received the message with the respect due to the commission of 'his friend the Lord Provost,' and pocketed the half-guinea with a complacent smile ; but standing up to his full height, and resolutely shaking his rough head, he gave for answer that 'he was highly gratified by his lordship's message ; but, everything considered, the pope *must be burnt!*' And so the pope, honest man, *was* burnt with all the honours accordingly.

Joseph was at last killed by a fall from the top of a Leith stage-coach, in returning from the races, while in a state of intoxication, about the year 1780. It is to be hoped, for the good of society, that 'we ne'er shall look upon his like again.' *

* The skeleton of this singular being exists entire in the class-room of the professor of anatomy in the College.

BICKERS.

AMONGST the social features of a bygone age in Edinburgh
were the *bickers* in which the boys were wont to indulge—
that is, street conflicts, conducted chiefly with stones, though
occasionally with sticks also, and even more formidable weapons.
One cannot but wonder that, so lately as the period when elderly
men now living were boys, the powers for preserving peace in the
city should have been so weak as to allow of such battles taking
place once or twice almost every week. The practice was, however, only of a piece with the general rudeness of those old days;
and, after all, there was more appearance than reality of danger
attending it. It was truly, as one who had borne a part in it has
remarked, 'only a rough kind of play.' *

The most likely time for a bicker was Saturday afternoon, when
the schools and hospitals held no restraint over their tenants.
Then it was almost certain that either the Old Town and New
Town boys, the George Square and Potterrow boys, the Herioters
and the Watsoners, or some other parties accustomed to regard
themselves as natural enemies, would meet on some common
ground, and fall a-pelting each other. There were hardly anywhere two adjoining streets but the boys respectively belonging
to them would occasionally hold encounters of this kind; and the
animosity assumed a darker tinge if there was any discrepancy of
rank or condition between the parties, as was apt to be the case
when, for instance, the Old Town lads met the children of the
aristocratic streets to the north. Older people looked on with
anxiety, and wondered what the Town-guard was about, and
occasionally reports were heard that such a boy had got a wound
in the head, while another had lost a couple of his front teeth; it
was even said that fatal cases had occurred in the memory of aged
citizens. Yet, to the best of my recollection—for I do remember
something of bickers—there was little likelihood of severe damage.
The parties somehow always kept at a good distance from each
other, and there was a perpetual running in one direction or
another; certainly nothing like hand-to-hand fighting. Occasionally attempts were made to put down the riot, but seldom with

* Notes to *Waverley.*

much success; for it was one of the most ludicrous features of
these contests that whenever the Town-guard made its appearance
on the ground, the belligerent powers instantly coalesced against
the common foe. Besides, they could quickly make their way to
other ground, and there continue the war.

Bickers must have had a foundation in human nature : from no
temporary effervescence of the boy-mind did they spring; pleasant,
though wrong, had they been from all time. Witness the following act of the Town-council so long ago as 1529 : ' *Bikkyrringis
betwix Barnis.*—It is statut and ordainit be the prouest ballies
and counsall Forsamekle as ther has bene gret bikkyrringis betwix
barnis and followis in tymes past and diuerse thar throw hurt in
perell of ther lyffis and gif sik thingis be usit thar man diuerse
barnis and innocentis be slane and diuisione ryse amangis
nychtbouris theirfor we charge straitlie and commandis in our
Souerane Lord the Kingis name the prouest and ballies of this
burgh that na sic bykkyrringis be usit in tymes to cum. Certifing
that and ony persone be fund bykkyrrand that faderis and moderis
sall ansuer and be accusit for thar deidis and gif thai be vaga-
bondis thai to be scurgit and bannist the toune.'

An anecdote which Scott has told of his share in the bickers
which took place in his youth between the George Square youth
and the plebeian fry of the neighbouring streets is so pat to this
occasion that its reproduction may be excusable. ' It followed,'
he says, ' from our frequent opposition to each other, that, though
not knowing the names of our enemies, we were yet well acquainted
with their appearance, and had nicknames for the most remarkable
of them. One very active and spirited boy might be considered
as the principal leader in the cohort of the suburbs. He was, I
suppose, thirteen or fourteen years old, finely made, tall, blue-
eyed, with long fair hair, the very picture of a youthful Goth.
This lad was always first in the charge and last in the retreat—
the Achilles, at once, and Ajax, of the Crosscauseway. He was
too formidable to us not to have a cognomen, and, like that of
a knight of old, it was taken from the most remarkable part of his
dress, being a pair of old green livery breeches, which was the
principal part of his clothing; for, like Pentapolin, according to
Don Quixote's account, Green Breeks, as we called him, always
entered the battle with bare arms, legs, and feet.

' It fell that, once upon a time, when the combat was at the
thickest, this plebeian champion headed a sudden charge, so rapid
and furious that all fled before him. He was several paces before

his comrades, and had actually laid his hands on the patrician
standard, when one of our party, whom some misjudging friend
had entrusted with a *couteau de chasse*, or hanger, inspired with a
zeal for the honour of the corps worthy of Major Sturgeon himself,
struck poor Green Breeks over the head with strength sufficient
to cut him down. When this was seen, the casualty was so far
beyond what had ever taken place before that both parties fled
different ways, leaving poor Green Breeks, with his bright hair
plentifully dabbled in blood, to the care of the watchman, who
(honest man) took care not to know who had done the mischief.
The bloody hanger was flung into one of the Meadow ditches,
and solemn secrecy was sworn on all hands; but the remorse and
terror of the actor were beyond all bounds, and his apprehensions
of the most dreadful character. The wounded hero was for a few
days in the Infirmary, the case being only a trifling one. But
though inquiry was strongly pressed on him, no argument could
make him indicate the person from whom he had received the
wound, though he must have been perfectly well known to him.
When he recovered, and was dismissed, the author and his brother
opened a communication with him, through the medium of a
popular gingerbread baker, of whom both parties were customers,
in order to tender a subsidy in name of smart-money. The sum
would excite ridicule were I to name it; but sure I am that the
pockets of the noted Green Breeks never held as much money of
his own. He declined the remittance, saying that he would not
sell his blood; but at the same time reprobated the idea of being
an informer, which he said was *clam*—that is, base or mean.
With much urgency he accepted a pound of snuff for the use of
some old woman—aunt, grandmother, or the like—with whom he
lived. We did not become friends, for the bickers were more
agreeable to both parties than any more pacific amusement; but
we conducted them ever after under mutual assurances of the
highest consideration for each other.' *

* *Waverley Annotations*, 1. 70.

SUSANNA, COUNTESS OF EGLINTOUNE.

THE house on the west side of the Old Stamp-office Close, High Street, formerly Fortune's Tavern, was, in the early part of the last century, the family mansion of Alexander, Earl of Eglintoune. It is a building of considerable height and extent, accessible by a broad scale stair. The alley in which it is situated bears great marks of former respectability, and contained, till the year 1821, the Stamp-office, then removed to the Waterloo Buildings.*

The ninth Earl of Eglintoune † was one of those patriarchal peers who live to an advanced age—indefatigable in the frequency of their marriages and the number of their children—who linger on and on, with an unfailing succession of young countesses, and die at last leaving a progeny interspersed throughout the whole of Douglas's *Peerage*, two volumes, folio, re-edited by Wood. His lordship, in early life, married a sister of Lady Dundee, who brought him a large family, and died just about that happy period when she could not have greatly increased it. His next wife was a daughter of Chancellor Aberdeen, who only added one daughter to his stock, and then paused, in a fit of ill-health, to the great vexation of his lordship, who, on account of his two sons by the first countess having died young, was anxious for an heir. This was a consummation to his nuptial happiness which Countess Anne did not seem at all likely to bring about, and the chagrin of his lordship must have been increased by the longevity which her very ill-health seemed to confer upon her ; for her ladyship was one of those valetudinarians who are too well acquainted with death, being always just at his door, ever to come to closer quarters with him. At this juncture the blooming Miss Kennedy was brought to Edinburgh by her father, Sir Archibald, the rough old cavalier,

* The buildings in this alley are now demolished.

† He is said to have been a nobleman of considerable talent, and a great underhand supporter of the exiled family ; see the *Lockhart Papers*. George Lockhart had married his daughter Euphemia, or *Lady Effie*, as she was commonly called. In the *Edinburgh Annual Register* there is preserved a letter from Lord Eglintoune to his son, replete with good sense as well as paternal affection.

who made himself so conspicuous in *the Persecution* and in Dundee's wars.

Susanna Kennedy, though the daughter of a lady considerably under the middle size—one of the three co-heiresses of the Covenanting general, David Leslie (Lord Newark), whom Cromwell overthrew at Dunbar—was six feet high, extremely handsome, elegant in her carriage, and had a face and complexion of most bewitching loveliness. Her relations and nurses always anticipated that she was to marry the Earl of Eglintoune, in spite of their disparity of age; * for, while walking one day in her father's garden at Culzean, there alighted upon her shoulder a hawk, with his lordship's name upon its bells, which was considered an infallible omen of her fate. Her appearance in Edinburgh, which took place about the time of the Union, gained her a vast accession of lovers among the nobility and gentry, and set all the rhyming fancies of the period agog. Among her swains was Sir John Clerk of Penicuik, a man of learning and talent in days when such qualities were not common. As Miss Kennedy was understood to be fond of music, he sent her a flute as a love-gift; from which it may be surmised that this instrument was played by females in that age, while as yet the pianoforte was not. When the young lady attempted to blow the instrument, something was found to interrupt the sound, which turned out to be a copy of verses in her praise :

> ' Harmonious pipe, I languish for thy bliss,
> When pressed to Silvia's lips with gentle kiss !
> And when her tender fingers round thee move
> In soft embrace, I listen and approve
> Those melting notes which soothe my soul in love.
> Embalmed with odours from her breath that flow,
> You yield your music when she's pleased to blow ;
> And thus at once the charming lovely fair
> Delights with sounds, with sweets perfumes the air.
> Go, happy pipe, and ever mindful be
> To court bewitching Silvia for me ;
> Tell all I feel—you cannot tell too much—
> Repeat my love at each soft melting touch—
> Since I to her my liberty resign,
> Take thou the care to tune her heart to mine.'

Unhappily for this accomplished and poetical lover, Lord Eglintoune's sickly wife happened just about this time to die, and set his lordship again at large among the spinsters of Scotland. Admirers of a youthful, impassioned, and sonnet-making cast might have trembled at his approach to the shrine of their

* The earl was forty-nine and Miss Kennedy twenty.

divinity; for his lordship was one of those titled suitors who
however old and horrible, are never rejected, except in novels and
romances. It appears that poor Clerk had actually made a
declaration of his passion for Miss Kennedy, which her father was
taking into consideration, a short while before the death of Lady
Eglintoune. As an old friend and neighbour, Sir Archibald
thought he would consult the earl upon the subject, and he
accordingly proceeded to do so. Short but decisive was the
conference. 'Bide a wee, Sir Archy,' said his lordship; 'my
wife's very sickly.' With Sir Archibald, as with Mrs Slipslop
the least hint sufficed: the case was at once settled against the
elegant baronet of Penicuik. The lovely Susanna accordingly
became in due time the Countess of Eglintoune.

Even after this attainment of one of the greatest blessings
that life has to bestow,* the old peer's happiness was like to
have been destroyed by another untoward circumstance. It was
true that he had the handsomest wife in the kingdom, and she
brought him as many children as he could desire. One after
another came no fewer than seven daughters. But then his
lordship wanted a male heir; and every one knows how poor a
consolation a train of daughters, however long, proves in such a
case. He was so grieved at the want of a son that he threatened
to divorce his lady. The countess replied that he need not do
that, for she would readily agree to a separation, provided he
would give back what he had with her. His lordship, supposing
she alluded only to pecuniary matters, assured her she should have
her fortune to the last penny. 'Na, na, my lord,' said she, 'that
winna do: return me my youth, beauty, and virginity, and dismiss
me when you please.' His lordship, not being able to comply
with this demand, willingly let the matter drop; and before the
year was out her ladyship brought him a son, who established
the affection of his parents on an enduring basis. Two other
male children succeeded. The countess was remarkable for a
manner quite peculiar to herself, and which was remembered as
the *Eglintoune air*, or the *Eglintoune manner*, long after her
death. A Scottish gentleman, writing from London in 1730,
says: 'Lady Eglintoune has set out for Scotland, much satisfied
with the honour and civilities shown her ladyship by the queen
and all the royal family: she has done her country more honour
than any lady I have seen here, both by a genteel and a prudent

* The anecdote which follows is chiefly taken from *The Tell-tale*, a rare
collection, published in 1762.

behaviour.' *   Her daughters were also handsome women.   It was
a goodly sight, a century ago, to see the long procession of sedans,
containing Lady Eglintoune and her daughters, devolve from the
close and proceed to the Assembly Rooms, where there was sure
to be a crowd of plebeian admirers congregated to behold their
lofty and graceful figures step from the chairs on the pavement.
It could not fail to be a remarkable sight—eight beautiful women,
conspicuous for their stature and carriage, all dressed in the
splendid though formal fashions of that period, and inspired at
once with dignity of birth and consciousness of beauty!   Alas!
such *visions* no longer illuminate the dark tortuosities of Auld
Reekie!

Many of the young ladies found good matches, and were the
mothers of men more or less distinguished for intellectual attainments.   Sir James Macdonald, the Marcellus of the Hebrides,
and his two more fortunate brothers, were the progeny of Lady
Margaret; and in various other branches of the family talent
seems to be hereditary.

The countess was herself a blue-stocking—at that time a sort
of prodigy—and gave encouragement to the humble literati of
her time.   The unfortunate Boyse dedicated a volume of poems
to her; and I need scarcely remind the Scottish reader that the
Gentle Shepherd was laid at her ladyship's feet.   The dedication
prefixed to that pastoral drama contains what appears the usual
amount of extravagant praise; yet it was perhaps little beyond
the truth.   For the 'penetration, superior wit, and profound
judgment' which Allan attributes to her ladyship, she was perhaps
indebted in some degree to the lucky accident of her having
exercised it in the bard's favour; but he assuredly overstrained
his conscience very little when he said she was 'possessed of every
outward charm in the most perfect degree.'   Neither was it too
much to speak of 'the unfading beauties of wisdom and piety'
which adorned her ladyship's mind.' †   Hamilton of Bangour's

* Notes by C. K. Sharpe in Stenhouse's edition of the *Scots Musical
Museum,* ii. 200.

† As a specimen of the complimentary intercourse of the poet with Lady
Eglintoune, an ancedote is told of her having once sent him a basket of fine
fruit; to which he returned this stanza:

> 'Now, Priam's son, ye may be mute,
>   For I can bauldly brag wi' thee;
> Thou to the fairest gave the fruit—
>   The fairest gave the fruit to me.'

The love of raillery has recorded that on this being communicated by

prefatory verses, which are equally laudatory and well bestowed,
contain the following beautiful character of the lady, with a just
compliment to her daughters :

> ' In virtues rich, in goodness unconfined,
>   Thou shin'st a fair example to thy kind ;
>   Sincere, and equal to thy neighbours' fame,
>   How swift to praise, how obstinate to blame !
>   Bold in thy presence bashfulness appears,
>   And backward merit loses all its fears.
>   Supremely blest by Heaven, Heaven's richest grace
>   Confest is thine—an early blooming race ;
>   Whose pleasing smiles shall guardian wisdom arm—
>   Divine instruction !—taught of thee to charm,
>   What transports shall they to thy soul impart
>   (The conscious transports of a parent's heart),
>   When thou behold'st them of each grace possessed,
>   And sighing youths imploring to be blest
>   After thy image formed, with charms like thine,
>   Or in the visit or the dance * to shine :
>   Thrice happy who succeed their mother's praise,
>   The lovely Eglintounes of other days ! '

It may be remarked that her ladyship's thorough-paced Jacobitism,
which she had inherited from her father, tended much to make
her the friend of Ramsay, Hamilton, and other Cavalier bards.
She was, it is believed, little given to patronising Whig poets.

The patriarchal peer who made Susanna so happy a mother
died in 1729, leaving her a dowager of forty, with a good jointure.
Retiring to the country, she employed her widowhood in the
education of her children, and was considered a perfect example to
all mothers in this useful employment.   In our days of freer
manners, her conduct might appear too reserved.   The young
were taught to address her by the phrase ' Your ladyship ; ' and she
spoke to them in the same ceremonious style.   Though her eldest
son was a mere boy when he succeeded to the title, she constantly
called him Lord Eglintoune ; and she enjoined all the rest of the
children to address him in the same manner.   When the earl grew

Ramsay to his friend Eustace Budgell, the following comment was soon after
received from the English wit :

> ' As Juno fair, as Venus kind,
>   She may have been who gave the fruit ;
>   But had she had Minerva's mind,
>   She 'd ne'er have given 't to such a brute.'

* An old gentleman told our informant that he never saw so beautiful a
figure in his life as Lady Eglintoune at a Hunters' Ball in Holyrood House,
dancing a minuet in a large hoop, and a suit of black velvet, trimmed with
gold.

up, they were upon no less formal terms; and every day in the world he took his mother by the hand at the dinner-hour, and led her downstairs to her chair at the head of his table, where she sat in state, a perfect specimen of the stately and ostentatious politeness of the last age.

All this ceremony was accompanied with so much affection that the countess was never known to refuse her son a request but one—to walk as a peeress at the coronation of King George III. Lord Eglintoune, then a gentleman of the bedchamber, was proud of his mother, and wished to display her noble figure on that occasion. But she jestingly excused herself by saying that it was not worth while for so old a woman to buy new robes.

The unhappy fate of her eldest and favourite son—shot by a man of violent passions, whom he was rashly treating as a poacher (1769)—gave her ladyship a dreadful shock in her old age. The earl, after receiving the fatal wound, was brought to Eglintoune Castle, when his mother was immediately sent for from Auchans. What her feelings must have been when she saw one so dear to her thus suddenly struck down in the prime of his days may be imagined. The tenderness he displayed towards her and others in his last hours is said to have been to the last degree noble and affecting.

When Johnson and Boswell returned from their tour to the Hebrides, they visited Lady Eglintoune at Auchans. She was so well pleased with the doctor, his politics, and his conversation that she embraced and kissed him at parting, an honour of which the gifted tourist was ever afterwards extremely proud. Boswell's account of the interview is interesting. 'Lady Eglintoune,' says he, 'though she was now in her eighty-fifth year, and had lived in the country almost half a century, was still a very agreeable woman. Her figure was majestic, her manners high-bred, her reading extensive, and her conversation elegant. She had been the admiration of the gay circles, and the patroness of poets. Dr Johnson was delighted with his reception here. Her principles in church and state were congenial with his. In the course of conversation, it came out that Lady Eglintoune was married the year before Dr Johnson was born; upon which she graciously said to him that she might have been his mother, and she now adopted him.'

This venerable woman amused herself latterly in taming and patronising rats. She kept a vast number of these animals in her pay at Auchans, and they succeeded in her affections to the poets and artists whom she had loved in early life. It does not reflect much credit upon the latter that her ladyship used to complain of never having met with true gratitude except from four-footed animals.   She had a panel in the oak wainscot of her dining-room, which she tapped upon and opened at meal-times, when ten or twelve jolly rats came tripping forth and joined her at table. At the word of command, or a signal from her ladyship, they retired again obediently to their native obscurity—a trait of good sense in the character and habits of the animals which, it is hardly necessary to remark, patrons do not always find in two-legged protégés.

Her ladyship died in 1780, at the age of ninety-one, having preserved her stately mien and beautiful complexion to the last.   The latter was a mystery of fineness to many ladies not the third of her age.   As her secret may be of service to modern beauties, I shall, in kindness to the sex, divulge it.   *She never used paint, but washed her face periodically with* sow's MILK!   I have seen a portrait, taken in her eighty-first year, in which it is observable that her skin is of exquisite delicacy and tint.   Altogether, the countess was a woman of ten thousand!

The joiture-house of this fine old country-gentlewoman—Auchans Castle, a capital specimen of the Scottish manor-house of the seventeenth century, situated near Irvine—is now uninhabited, and the handsome wainscoted rooms in which she entertained Johnson and Boswell are fast hastening to decay.   One last trait may now be recorded; in her ladyship's bedroom at this place was hung a portrait of her sovereign *de jure*, the ill-starred Charles Edward, so situated as to be *the first object which met her sight on awaking in the morning.*

FEMALE DRESSES OF LAST CENTURY.

LADIES in the last century wore dresses and decorations many of which were of an inconvenient nature ; yet no one can deny them the merit of a certain dignity and grace. How fine it must have been to see, as an old gentleman told me he had seen, two hooped ladies moving along the Lawnmarket in a summer evening, and filling up the whole footway with their stately and voluminous persons !

Amongst female articles of attire in those days were calashes, bongraces, capuchins, negligées, stomachers, stays, hoops, lappets, pinners, plaids, fans, busks, rumple-knots, &c., all of them now forgotten.

The calash was a species of hood, constructed of silk upon a framework of cane, and was used as a protection to a cap or head-dress in walking out or riding in a carriage. It could be folded back like the hood of a carriage, so as to lie gathered together behind the neck.

The bongrace was a bonnet of silk and cane, in shape somewhat like a modern bonnet.

The capuchin was a short cloak, reaching not below the elbows. It was of silk, edged with lace, or of velvet. Gentlemen also wore capuchins. The first Sir William Forbes frequently appeared at the Cross in one. A lady's *mode tippet* was nearly the same piece of dress.

The negligée was a gown, projecting in loose and ample folds from the back. It could only be worn with stays. It was entirely open in front, so as to show the stomacher, across which it was laced with flat silk cords, while below it opened more widely and showed the petticoat. This latter, though shorter, was sometimes more splendid than the gown, and had a deep flounce. Ladies in walking generally carried the skirt of the gown over the arm, and exhibited the petticoat ; but when they entered a room, they always came sailing in, with the train sweeping full and majestically behind them.

The stomacher was a triangular piece of rich silk, one corner pointing downwards and joining the fine black lace-bordered apron, while the other two angles pointed to the shoulders. Great pains were usually discovered in the adornment of this beautiful and most attractive piece of dress.   Many wore jewels upon it ; and a lady would have thought herself poor indeed if she could not bedizen it with strings of bugles or tinsel.

Stays were made so long as to touch the chair, both in front and rear, when a lady sat.   They were calculated to fit so tightly that the wearers had to hold by the bedpost while the maid was lacing them.   There is a story told of a lady of high rank in Scotland, about 1720, which gives us a strange idea of the rigours and inconvenience of this fashion.   She stinted her daughters as to diet, with a view to the improvement of their shapes ; but the young ladies, having the cook in their interest, used to unlace their stays at night, after her ladyship went to bed, and make a hearty meal. They were at last discovered, by the smell of a roast goose, carried upstairs to their bedchamber ; as unluckily their lady-mother did not take snuff,* and was not asleep.

The hoop was contemporary with, and a necessary appendage of, the stays.   There were different species of hoops, being of various shapes and uses.   The pocket-hoop, worn in the morning, was like a pair of small panniers, such as one sees on an ass.   The bell-hoop was a sort of petticoat, shaped like a bell and made with cane or rope for framework.   This was not quite full-dress.   There was also a straw petticoat, a species of hoop such as is so common in French prints.   The full-sized evening hoop was so monstrous that people saw one-half of it enter the room before the wearer. This was very inconvenient in the Old Town, where doorways and closes were narrow.   In going down a close or a turnpike stair, ladies tilted them up and carried them under their arms.   In case of this happening, there was a *show petticoat* below ; and such care was taken of appearances that even the *garters* were worn fine, being either embroidered or having gold and silver fringes and tassels.

The French silks worn during the last century were beautiful, the patterns were so well drawn and the stuff of such excellent quality.   The dearest common brocade was about a guinea a yard ; if with gold or silver, considerably more.

* Snuff-taking was prevalent among young women in our grandmothers' time.   Their flirts used to present them with pretty snuff-boxes.   In one of the monthly numbers of the *Scots Magazine* for the year 1745 there is a satirical poem by a swain upon the practice of snuff-taking ; to which a lady replies next month, defending the fashion as elegant and of some account in coquetry. Almost all the old ladies who survived the commencement of this century took snuff.   Some kept it in pouches, and abandoned, for its sake, the wearing of white ruffles and handkerchiefs.

THE COWGATE.

'Nothing is humble or homely, but everything magnificent!'

PAGE 240.

JOHN KNOX'S MANSE.

PAGE 274

The lappet was a piece of Brussels or point lace, hanging in two pieces from the crown of the head and streaming gracefully behind.

Pinners, such as the celebrated Egyptian Sphinx wears, were pinned down the stomacher.

Plaids were worn by ladies to cover their heads and muffle their faces when they went into the street. The council records of Edinburgh abound in edicts against the use of this piece of dress, which, they said, confounded decent women with those who were the contrary.

Fans were large, the sticks curiously carved, and if of leather, generally very well painted—being imported from Italy or Holland. In later times these have been sometimes framed like pictures and hung on the walls.

All women, high and low, wore enormous busks, generally with a heart carved at the upper end. In low life this was a common present to sweethearts; if from carpenters, they were artificially veneered.

The rumple-knot was a large bunch of ribbons worn at the peak of the waist behind. Knots of ribbons were then numerous over the whole body. There were the breast-knots, two hainch-knots (at which there were also buttons for looping up the gown behind), a knot at the tying of the beads behind the neck, one in front and another at the back of the head-gear, and knots upon the shoes. It took about twelve yards or upwards to make a full suit of ribbons.*

Other minor articles of dress and adornment were the *befong* handkerchief (spelt at random), of a stuff similar to what is now called *net*, crossed upon the breast; paste ear-rings and necklace; broad black bracelets at the wrists; a *pong pong*—a jewel fixed to a wire with a long pin at the end, worn in front of the cap, and which shook as the wearer moved. It was generally stuck in the cushion over which the hair was turned in front. Several were frequently worn at once. A song in the *Charmer*, 1751, alludes to this bijou:

'Come all ye young ladies whose business and care
Is contriving new dresses, and curling your hair;
Who flirt and coquet with each coxcomb who comes
To toy at your toilets, and strut in your rooms;
While you're placing a patch, *or adjusting pong pong*,
Ye may listen and learn by the truth of my song.'

* A gown then required ten yards of stuff.

Fly-caps, encircling the head, worn by young matrons, and mob-caps, falling down over the ears, used only by old ones; pockets of silk or satin, of which young girls wore one above their other attire; silk or linen stockings—never of cotton, which is a modern stuff—slashed with pieces of a colour in strong contrast with the rest, or gold or silver clocks, wove in. The silk stockings were very thick, and could not be washed on account of the gold or silver. They were frequently of scarlet silk, and (1733) worn both by ladies and gentlemen. High-heeled shoes, set off with fine lace or sewed work, and sharply pointed in front.

To give the reader a more picturesque idea of the former dresses of the ladies of Edinburgh, I cite a couple of songs, the first wholly old, the second a revivification:

' I 'll gar our guidman trow that I 'll sell the ladle,
If he winna buy to me a new side-saddle—
To ride to the kirk, and frae the kirk, and round about the toun—
Stand about, ye fisher jades, and gi'e my goun room!

I 'll gar our guidman trow that I 'll tak the fling-strings,
If he winna buy to me twelve bonnie goud rings,
Ane for ilka finger, and twa for ilka thumb—
Stand about, ye fisher jades, and gi'e my goun room!

I 'll gar our guidman trow that I 'm gaun to dee,
If he winna fee to me twa valets or three,
To beir my tail up frae the dirt and ush me through the toun—
Stand about, ye fisher jades, and gi'e my goun room!'

' As Mally Lee cam' down the street, her *capuchin* did flee;
She coost a look behind her, to see her *negligee*.
    And we 're a' gaun east and wast, we 're a' gaun agee,
    We 're a' gaun east and wast, courtin' Mally Lee.*

She had twa *lappets* at her head, that flaunted gallantlie,
And *ribbon knots* at back and breast of bonnie Mally Lee.
    And we 're a' gaun, &c.

A' down alang the Canongate were beaux o' ilk degree;
And mony ane turned round to look at bonnie Mally Lee.
    And we 're a' gaun, &c.

And ilka bab her *pong pong* gi'ed, ilk lad thought that 's to me;
But feint a ane was in the thought of bonnie Mally Lee.
    And we 're a' gaun, &c.

* This verse appears in a manuscript subsequent to 1760. The name, how-ever, is Sleigh, not Lee. Mrs Mally Sleigh was married in 1725 to the Lord Lyon Brodie of Brodie. Allan Ramsay celebrates her.

Frae Seton's Land a countess fair looked owre a window hie,
And pined to see the genty shape of bonnie Mally Lee.
   And we're a' gaun, &c.

And when she reached the palace porch, there lounged erls three ;
And ilk ane thought his Kate or Meg a drab to Mally Lee.
   And we're a' gaun, &c.

The dance gaed through the palace ha', a comely sight to see ;
But nane was there sae bright or braw as bonnie Mally Lee.
   And we're a' gaun, &c.

Though some had jewels in their hair, like stars 'mang cluds did shine,
Yet Mally did surpass them a' wi' but her glancin' eyne.
   And we're a' gaun, &c.

A prince cam' out frae 'mang them a', wi' garter at his knee,
And danced a stately minuet wi' bonnie Mally Lee.
   And we're a' gaun, &c.'

THE LORD JUSTICE-CLERK ALVA.*

Ladies Sutherland and Glenorchy—The Pin or Risp.

THIS eminent person—a cadet of
the ancient house of Mar
(born 1680, died 1763)—had
his town mansion in an
obscure recess of the
High Street called
Mylne Square,† the
first place bearing such
a designation in our
northern capital : it
was, I may remark,
built by one of a
family of Mylnes, who
are said to have been
master-masons to the
Scottish monarchs for
eight generations, and
some of whom are at this
day architects by profession.‡
Lord Alva's residence was in the
second and third floors of the large
building on the west side of the
square. Of the same structure, an Earl
of Northesk occupied another *flat*. And,
to mark the character of Lord Alva's abode,
part of it was afterwards, in the hands of a Mrs Reynolds,
used as a lodging-house of the highest grade. The Earl of

Mylne's Court,
where some of the Mylne family resided.

* James Erskine on ascending the bench first took the title of Lord Tinwald,
from his estate in Dumfriesshire. That of Lord Alva he assumed when he
purchased the family estate of Alva, in Clackmannanshire, from his eldest
brother, Sir Charles Erskine.

† The site of Mylne Square is now occupied by the block of buildings directly
opposite the north front of the Tron Church.

‡ The first of this name was made 'master-mason' to the king in 1481,
and the position descended in regular succession in the family till 1710, when
they adopted the style of architect.

Hopetoun, while acting as Commissioner to the General Assembly, there held viceregal state. But to return to Lord Alva: it gives a curious idea of the habits of such a dignitary before the rise of the New Town that we should find him content with this dwelling while in immediate attendance upon the court, and happy during the summer vacation to withdraw to the shades of his little villa at Drumsheugh, standing on a spot now surrounded by *town*. Lord Lovat, who, on account of his numerous law-pleas, was a great intimate of Lord Alva's, frequently visited him here; and Mrs Campbell of Monzie, Lord Alva's daughter, used to tell that when she met Lord Lovat on the stair he always took her up in his arms and kissed her, to her great annoyance and horror—*he was so ugly*. During one of his law-pleas, he went to a dancing-school ball, which Misses Jean and Susanna, Lord Alva's daughters, attended. He had his pocket full of *sweeties*, as Mrs Campbell expressed it; and so far did he carry his exquisitely refined system of cunning, that—in order no doubt to find favour with their father—he devoted the greater share of his attentions and the whole of his comfits to them alone. Those who knew this singular man used to say that, with all his duplicity, faithlessness, and cruelty, his character exhibited no redeeming trait whatever: nobody ever knew any good of him.

In his Mylne Square mansion Lord Alva's two step-daughters were married; one to become Countess of Sutherland, the other Lady Glenorchy. There was something very striking in the fate of Lady Sutherland and of the earl, her husband—a couple distinguished as much by personal elegance and amiable character as by lofty rank. Lady Sutherland was blessed with a temper of extraordinary sweetness, which shone in a face of so much beauty as to have occasioned admiration where many were beautiful—the coronation of George III. and his queen. The happiness of the young pair had been increased by the birth of a daughter. One unlucky day his lordship, coming after dinner into the drawing-room at Dunrobin a little flushed with wine, lifted up the infant above his head by way of frolic, when, sad to tell, he dropped her by accident on the floor, and she received injuries from which she never recovered. This incident had such an effect upon his lordship's spirits that his health became seriously affected, so as finally to require a journey to Bath, where he was seized with an infectious fever. For twenty-one successive days and nights he was attended by his wife, then pregnant, till she herself caught the fatal distemper. The countess's death was concealed from his lordship;

nevertheless, when his delirium left him, the day before he died, he frequently said : ' I am going to join my dear wife ; ' appearing to know that she had ' already reached the goal with mended pace ! ' Can it be that we are sometimes able to penetrate the veil which hangs, in thick and gloomy folds, between this world and the next ; or does the ' mortal coil ' in which the light of mind is enveloped become thinner and more transparent by the wearing of deadly sickness ? The bodies of the earl and countess were brought to Holyrood House, where they had usually resided when in town, and lay in state for some time previous to their interment in one grave in the Abbey Chapel. The death of a pair so young, so good, and who had stood in so distinguished a position in society—leaving one female infant to a disputed title—made a deep impression on the public, and was sincerely lamented in their own immediate circle. Of much poetry written on the occasion, a specimen may be seen in Evans's *Old Ballads*. Another appears in Brydges's *Censura Literaria*, being the composition of Sir Gilbert Elliot of Minto :

> ' In pity, Heaven bestowed
> An early doom : lo, on the self-same bier,
> A fairer form, cold by her husband's side,
> And faded every charm. She died for thee,
> For thee, her only love. In beauty's prime,
> In youth's triumphant hour, she died for thee.
>
> Bring water from the brook, and roses spread
> O'er their pale limbs ; for ne'er did wedded love
> To one sad grave consign a lovelier pair,
> Of manners gentler, or of purer heart ! '

Lady Glenorchy, the younger sister of Lady Sutherland, was remarkable for her pious disposition. Exceedingly unfortunate in her marriage, she was early taught to seek consolation from things ' not of this world.' I have been told that nothing could have been more striking than to hear this young and beautiful creature pouring forth her melodious notes and hymns, while most of her sex and age at that time exercised their voices only upon the wretched lyrics imported from Vauxhall and Ranelagh, or the questionable verses of Ramsay and his contemporaries. She met with her rich reward, even in this world ; for she enjoyed the applause of the wealthy and the blessings of the poor, with that supreme of all pleasures—the conviction that the eternal welfare of those in whose fate she was chiefly interested was forwarded, if not perfected, by her precepts and example.*

* Lady Glenorchy built a chapel, which was named after her, on the low ground to the south of the Calton Hill. The chapel was swept away, along

It is not unworthy of notice, in this record of all that is old and quaint in our city, that the Lord Justice-clerk's house was provided with a *pin* or *risp*, instead of the more modern convenience—a knocker. The Scottish ballads, in numberless passages, make reference to this article : no hero in those compositions ever comes to his mistress's door but he *tirles at the pin*. What, then, was a pin ? It was a small slip or bar of iron, starting out from the door vertically, serrated on the side towards the door, and provided with a small ring, which, being drawn roughly along the serrations or nicks, produced a harsh and grating sound, to summon the servant to open. Another term for the article was a *crow*. In the fourth eclogue of Edward Fairfax, a production of the reign of James VI. and I., quoted in the *Muses' Library*, is this passage :

> 'Now, farewell Eglon ! for the sun stoops low,
> And calling guests before my sheep-cot's door ;
> Now *clad in white, I see my porter-crow;*
> Great kings oft want these blessings of the poor ;'

with the following note : 'The ring of the door, called a *crow*, and when covered with white linen, denoted the mistress of the house was in travel.' It is quite appropriate

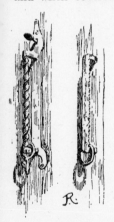

Old Risps.

to this explanation that a small Latin vocabulary, published by Andrew Simpson in 1702, places among the parts of a house, '*Corvex— a clapper or ringle.*' Hardly one specimen of the pin, crow, or ringle now survives in the Old Town. They were almost all disused many years ago, when knockers were generally substituted as more stylish. Knockers at that time did not long remain in repute, though they have never been altogether superseded, even by bells, in the Old Town. The comparative merit of knockers and pins was for a long time a controversial point, and many knockers got their heads twisted off in the course of the dispute. Pins were, upon the whole, considered very inoffensive, decent, old-fashioned things, being made of a modest metal, and making little

with that of the fine Gothic building Trinity College Church, for the convenience of the North British Railway. The lady's name is still preserved in Lady Glenorchy's Established Church in Roxburgh Place and Lady Glenorchy's United Free Church in Greenside.

show upon a door; knockers were thought upstart, prominent, brazen-faced articles, and received the full share of odium always conferred by Scotsmen of the old school upon tasteful improvements. Every drunken fellow, in reeling home at night, thought it good sport to carry off all the knockers that came in his way; and as drunken gentlemen were very numerous, many acts of violence were committed, and sometimes a whole stair was found stripped of its knockers in the morning; when the voice of lamentation raised by the servants of the sufferers might have reminded one of the wailings of the Lennox dairy-women after a *creagh* in the days of old. Knockers were frequently used as missile weapons by the bucks of that day against the Town-guard; and the morning sun sometimes saw the High Street strewed with them. The aforesaid Mrs Campbell remembered residing in an Old Town house, which was one night disturbed in the most intolerable manner by a drunken party at the knocker. In the morning the greater part of it was found to be gone; and it was besides discovered, to the horror of the inmates, that part of a finger was left sticking in the fragments, with the appearance of having been forcibly wrenched from the hand.

MARLIN'S AND NIDDRY'S WYNDS.

Tradition of Marlin the Pavier—House of Provost Edward— Story of Lady Grange.

WHERE South Bridge Street now stands, there formerly existed two wynds, or alleys, of the better class, named Marlin's and Niddry's Wynds. Many persons of importance lived in these obscurities. Marlin's Wynd, which extended from behind the Tron Church, and contained several bookshops and stalls, the favourite lounge of the lovers of old literature, was connected with a curious tradition, which existed at the time when Maitland wrote his *History of Edinburgh* (1753). It was said that the High Street was first paved or *causewayed* by one Marlin, a Frenchman, who, thinking that specimen of his ingenuity the best monument he could have, desired to be buried under it, and was accordingly interred at the head of this wynd, which derived its name from him. The tradition is so far countenanced by there having formerly been a space in the pavement at this spot, marked by six flat stones, in the shape of a grave. According, however, to more authentic information, the High Street was first paved in 1532 * by John and Bartoulme Foliot, who appear to have had nothing in common with this legendary Marlin, except country. The grave of at least Bartoulme Foliot is distinctly marked by a flat monument in the Chapel-Royal at Holyrood House. It is possible, nevertheless, that Marlin may have been the more immediate executor or superintendent of the work.

Niddry's Wynd abounded in curious antique houses, many of which had been the residences of remarkable persons. The most interesting *bit* was a paved court, about half-way down, on the west side, called Lockhart's Court, from its having latterly been the residence of the family of Lockhart of Carnwath.† This was,

---

* The Canongate seems to have been paved about the same time. In 1535 the king granted to the Abbot of Holyrood a duty of one penny upon every loaded cart, and a halfpenny upon every empty one, to repair and maintain the causeway.

† George Lockhart of Carnwath lived here in 1753. Afterwards he resided in Ross House, a suburban mansion, which afterwards was used as a lying-in hospital. The park connected with this house is now occupied by George

in reality, a quadrangular palace, the whole being of elegant old architecture in one design, and accessible by a deep arched gateway. It was built by Nicol Edward, or Udward, who was provost of Edinburgh in 1591; a wealthy citizen, and styled in his *writts*, 'of old descent in the burgh.' On a mantelpiece within the house his arms were carved, along with an anagram upon his name:

VA D'UN VOL À CHRIST—

Go with one flight to Christ; which, the reader will find, can only be made out by Latinising his name into NICHOLAUS EDUARTUS. We learn from Moyses's *Memoirs* that, in January 1591, this house was the temporary residence of James VI. and his queen, then recently arrived from Denmark; and that, on the 7th of February, the Earl of Huntly passed hence, out of the immediate royal presence, when he went to murder the Bonny Earl of Moray at Donibrissle; which caused a suspicion that His Majesty was concerned in that horrid outburst of feudal hate. Lockhart's Court was latterly divided into several distinct habitations, one of which, on the north side of the quadrangle, was occupied by the family of Bruce of Kinnaird, the celebrated traveller. In the part on the south side, occupied by the Carnwath family, there was a mantelpiece in the drawing-room of magnificent workmanship, and reaching to the ceiling. The whole mansion, even in its reduced state, bore an appearance of security and strength which spoke of other times; and there was, moreover, a profound dungeon underground, which was only accessible by a secret trap-door, opening through the floor of a small closet, the most remote of a suite of rooms extending along the south and west sides of the court. Perhaps, at a time when to be rich was neither so

Square. While in Mr Lockhart's possession Ross House was the scene of many gay routs and balls.

The Lords Ross, the original proprietors of this mansion, died out in 1754. One of the last persons in Scotland supposed to be possessed by an evil spirit was a daughter of George, the second last lord. A correspondent says : ' A person alive in 1824 told me that, when a child, he saw her clamber up to the top of an old-fashioned four-post bed like a cat. In her fits it was almost impossible to hold her. About the same time, a daughter of Lord Kinnaird was supposed to have the second-sight. One day, during divine worship in the High Church, she fainted away; on her recovery, she declared that when Lady Janet Dundas (a daughter of Lord Lauderdale) entered the pew with Miss Dundas, who was a beautiful young girl, she saw the latter as it were in a shroud gathered round her neck, and upon her head. Miss Dundas died a short time after.'

common nor so safe as now, Provost Edward might conceal his hoards in this *massy more.*

Alexander Black of Balbirney, who was provost of Edinburgh from 1579 to 1583, had a house at the head of the wynd. King James lodged in this house on the 18th of August 1584, and walked from it in state next day to hold a parliament in the Tolbooth. Here also lodged the Chancellor Thirlstain, in January 1591, while the king and queen were the guests of Nicol Edward.* It must be understood that these visits of royalty were less considered in the light of an honour than of a tax. The king in those times went to live at the board of a wealthy subject when his own table happened to be scantily furnished ; which was too often the case with poor King James.

On the east side of the wynd, nearly opposite to Lockhart's Court, was a good house,† which, early in the last century, was possessed by James Erskine of Grange, best known by his judicial title of Lord Grange, and the brother of John, Earl of Mar. This gentleman has acquired an unhappy notoriety in consequence of his treatment of his wife. He was externally a professor of ultra-evangelical views of religion, and a patron of the clergy on that side, yet in his private life is understood to have been far from exemplary. The story of Lady Grange, as Mrs Erskine was called, had a character of romance about it which has prevented it from being forgotten. It also reflects a curious light upon the state of manners in Scotland in the early part of the eighteenth century. The lady was a daughter of that Chiesly of Dalry whom we have already seen led by an insane violence of temper to commit one of the most atrocious of murders.

STORY OF LADY GRANGE. ‡

Lord and Lady Grange had been married upwards of twenty years, and had had several children, when, in 1730, a separation

* Both facts from Moyses's *Memoirs.*

† In the house to the north of this was a shop kept by an eccentric personage, who exhibited a sign bearing this singular inscription :

ORRA THINGS BOUGHT AND SOLD—

which signified that he dealt in odd articles, such as a single shoe-buckle, one of a pair of skates, a teapot wanting a lid, or perhaps, as often, a lid *minus* a teapot ; in short, any unpaired article which was not to be got in the shops where only new things were sold, and which, nevertheless, was now and then as indispensably wanted by householders as anything else.

‡ The present article is almost wholly from original sources, a fact probably unknown to a contemporary novelist, who has made it the groundwork of a

was determined on between them. It is usually difficult in such cases to say in what degree the parties are respectively blamable; how far there have been positive faults on one side, and want of forbearance on the other, and so forth. If we were to believe the lady in this instance, there had been love and peace for twenty years, when at length Lord Grange took a sudden dislike to his wife, and would no longer live with her. He, on the other hand, speaks of having suffered long from her 'unsubduable rage and madness,' and of having failed in all his efforts to bring her to a reasonable conduct. There is too much reason to believe that the latter statement is in the main true; although, were it more so, it would still leave Lord Grange unjustifiable in the measures which he took with respect to his wife. It is tradition-ally stated that in their unhappy quarrels the lady did not scruple to remind her husband whose daughter she was—thus hinting at what she was capable of doing if she thought herself deeply aggrieved. However all this might be, in the year 1730 a separation was agreed to (with great reluctance on the part of the lady), his lordship consenting to give her a hundred a year for her maintenance so long as she should continue to live apart from him.

After spending some months in the country, Lady Grange returned to Edinburgh, and took a lodging near her husband's house, for the purpose, as she tells us, of endeavouring to induce him to take her back, and that she might occasionally see her children. According to Lord Grange, she began to torment him by following him and the children on the street 'in a scandalous and shameful manner,' and coming to his house, and calling re-proaches to him through the windows,* especially when there was company with him. He thus writes: 'In his house, at the bottom of Niddry's Wynd, where there is a court through which one enters the house, one time among others, when it was full of chairs, chairmen, and footmen, who attended the company that were with himself, or his sister Lady Jane Paterson, then keeping house together, she came into this court, and among that mob shame-

<hr>

fiction without any acknowledgment. Some additional particulars may be found in *Tales of the Century*, by John Sobieski Stuart (Edinburgh, 1846). In the *Spalding Miscellany*, vol. iii., are several letters of Lord Grange, containing allusions to his wife; and a production of his, which has been printed under the title of *Diary of a Senator of the College of Justice* (Stevenson, Edinburgh, 1833), is worthy of perusal.

* Here and elsewhere a paper in Lord Grange's own hand is quoted.

lessly cried up to the windows injurious reproaches, and would not go away, though entreated, till, hearing the late Lord Lovat's voice, who was visiting Mr E——, and seeing two of his servants among the other footmen, " Oh," said she, " is your master here ? " and instantly ran off.' He speaks of her having attacked him one day in church ; at another time she forced him to take refuge with his son in a tavern for two hours. She even threatened to assault him on the bench, ' which he every day expected ; for she professed that she had no shame.'

The traditionary account of Lady Grange represents her fate as having been at last decided by her threatening to expose her husband to the government for certain treasonable practices. It would now appear that this was partially true. In his statement, Lord Grange tells us that he had some time before gone to London to arrange the private affairs of the Countess of Mar, then become unable to conduct them herself, and he had sent an account of his procedure to his wife, including some reflections on a certain great minister (doubtless Walpole), who had thwarted him much, and been of serious detriment to the interests of his family in this matter. This document she retained, and she now threatened to take it to London and use it for her husband's disadvantage, being supported in the design by several persons with whom she associated. While denying that he had been concerned in anything treasonable, Lord Grange says, ' he had already too great a load of that great minister's wrath on his back to stand still and see more of it fall upon him by the treachery and madness of such a wife and such worthy confederates.' The lady had taken a seat in a stage-coach for London.* Lord Grange caused a friend to go and make interest to get her money returned, and the seat let to another person ; in which odd proceeding he was successful. Thus was the journey stayed for the meantime ; but the lady declared her resolution to go as soon as possible. ' What,' says Lord Grange, ' could a man do with such a wife ? There was great reason to think she would daily go on to do mischief to her family, and to affront and bring a blot on her children, especially her daughters. There were things that could not be redressed in a court of justice, and we had not then a madhouse to lock such unhappy people up in.'

---

* ' Then, and some time before and after, there was a stage-coach from hence to England.' So says his lordship ; implying that in 1751, when he was writing, there was no such public conveniency ! It had been tried, and had failed.

The result of his lordship's deliberations was a plan for what he calls 'sequestrating' his wife. It appears to have been concerted between himself and a number of Highland chiefs, including, above all, the notorious Lord Lovat.* We now turn to the lady's narrative, which proceeds to tell that, on the evening of the 22nd of January 1732, a party of Highlandmen, wearing the livery of Lord Lovat, made their way into her lodgings, and forcibly seized her, throwing her down and gagging her, then tying a cloth over her head, and carrying her off as if she had been a corpse. At the bottom of the stair was a chair containing a man, who took the hapless lady upon his knees, and held her fast in his arms till they had got to a place in the outskirts of the town. Then they took her from the chair, removed the cloth from her head, and mounted her upon a horse behind a man, to whom she was tied; after which the party rode off 'by the lee light of the moon,' to quote the language of the old ballads, whose incidents the present resembles in character.

The treatment of the lady by the way was, if we can believe her own account, by no means gentle. The leader, although a gentleman (Mr Forster of Corsebonny), disregarded her entreaties to be allowed to stop on account of cramp in her side, and only answered by ordering a servant to renew the bandages over her mouth. She observed that they rode along the Long Way (where Princes Street now stands), past the Castle, and so to the Linlithgow road. After a ride of nearly twenty miles, they stopped at Muiravonside, the house of Mr John Macleod, advocate, where servants appeared waiting to receive the lady—and thus showed that the master of the house had been engaged to aid in her abduction. She was taken upstairs to a comfortable bedroom; but a man being posted in the room as a guard, she could not go to bed nor take any repose. Thus she spent the ensuing day, and when it was night, she was taken out and remounted in the same fashion as before; and the party then rode along through the Torwood, and so to the place called Wester Polmaise, belonging to a gentleman of the

* If we could believe Lord Lovat, however, he personally was innocent, and regretted he was innocent, of any association with the abduction of Lady Grange. 'They said it was all my contrivance, and that it was my servants that took her away; but I defyed them then, as I do now, and do declare to you upon honour, that I do not know what has become of that woman, where she is or who takes care of her, but if I had contrived and assisted, and saved my Lord Grange from that devil, who threatened every day to murder him and his children, I would not think shame of it before God or man.'—Letter of Lord Lovat's quoted in *Genealogie of the Hayes of Tweeddale.*

name of Stewart, whose steward or factor was one of the cavalcade.
Here was an old tower, having one little room on each floor, as is
usually the case in such buildings; and into one of these rooms,
the window of which was boarded over, the lady was conducted.
She continued here for thirteen or fourteen weeks, supplied with a
sufficiency of the comforts of life, but never allowed to go into the
open air; till at length her health gave way, and the factor began
to fear being concerned in her death.   By his intercession with
Mr Forster, she was then permitted to go into the court, under a
guard; but such was the rigour of her keepers that the garden
was still denied to her.

Thus time passed drearily on until the month of August, during
all which time the prisoner had no communication with the
external world.   At length, by an arrangement made between Lord
Lovat and Mr Forster, at the house of the latter, near Stirling,
Lady Grange was one night forcibly brought out, and mounted
again as formerly, and carried off amidst a guard of horsemen.
She recognised several of Lovat's people in this troop, and found
Forster once more in command.   They passed by Stirling Bridge,
and thence onward to the Highlands; but she no longer knew the
way they were going.   Before daylight they stopped at a house,
where she was lodged during the day, and at night the march
was resumed.   Thus they journeyed for several days into the
Highlands, never allowing the unfortunate lady to speak, and
taking the most rigid care to prevent any one from becoming
aware of her situation.   During this time she never had off her
clothes: one day she slept in a barn, another in an open enclosure.
Regard to delicacy in such a case was impossible.   After a
fortnight spent at a house on Lord Lovat's ground (probably in
Stratherrick, Inverness-shire), the journey was renewed in the
same style as before; only Mr Forster had retired from the party,
and the lady found herself entirely in the hands of Frasers.

They now crossed a loch into Glengarry's land, where they
lodged several nights in cow-houses or in the open air, making
progress all the time to the westward, where the country becomes
extremely wild.   At Lochourn, an arm of the sea on the west
coast, the unfortunate lady was transferred to a small vessel which
was in waiting for her.   Bitterly did she weep, and pitifully
implore compassion; but the Highlanders understood not her
language; and though they had done so, a departure from the
orders which had been given them was not to be expected from
men of their character.   In the vessel, she found that she was in

the custody of one Alexander Macdonald, a tenant of one o
the Western Islands named Heskir, belonging to Sir Alexande
Macdonald of Sleat ; and here we have a curious indication of the
spirit in which the Highlanders conducted such transactions. ' I
told him,' says the lady, ' that I was stolen at Edinburgh, and
brought there by force, and that it was contrary to the laws what
they were doing. He answered that he would not keep me, or
any other, against their will, *except Sir Alexander Macdonald were
in the affair.*' While they lay in Lochourn, waiting for a wind,
the brother and son of Macdonald of Scothouse came to see but
not to relieve her. Other persons visited the sloop, and among
these one William Tolmy, a tenant of the chief of Macleod, and
who had once been a merchant at Inverness. This was the first
person she had seen who expressed any sympathy with her. He
undertook to bear information of her retreat to her friend and
' man of business,' Mr Hope of Rankeillor, in Edinburgh ; but it
does not appear that he fulfilled his promise.

Lady Grange remained in Macdonald's charge at Heskir nearly
two years—during the first year without once seeing bread, and
with no supply of clothing ; obliged, in fact, to live in the same
miserable way as the rest of the family ; afterwards some little
indulgence was shown to her. This island was of desolate aspect,
and had no inhabitant besides Macdonald and his wife. The
wretchedness of such a situation for a lady who had been all her
life accustomed to the refined society of a capital may of course
be imagined. Macdonald would never allow her to write to any
one ; but he went to his landlord, Sir Alexander, to plead for the
indulgences she required. On one of these occasions, Sir Alexander
expressed his regret at having been concerned in such an affair,
and wished he were quit of it. The wonder is how Erskine should
have induced all these men to interest themselves in the ' sequestration' of his wife. One thing is here remarkable : they were all of
them friends of the Stuart family, as was Macleod of Macleod,
into whose hands the lady subsequently fell. It therefore becomes
probable that Erskine had at least convinced them that her
seclusion from the world was necessary in some way for the
preservation of political secrets important to them.

In June 1734 a sloop came to Heskir to take away the lady ;
it was commanded by a Macleod, and in it she was conveyed to
the remotest spot of ground connected with the British Islands—
namely, the isle of St Kilda, the property of the chief of Macleod,
and remarkable for the simple character of the poor peasantry

ho occupy it. There cannot, of course, be a doubt that those
ho had an interest in the seclusion of Lady Grange regarded
is as a more eligible place than Heskir, in as far as it was more
ut of the way, and promised better for her complete and per-
anent confinement. In some respects it was an advantageous
hange for the lady : the place was not uninhabited, as Heskir
ery nearly was ; and her domestic accommodation was better.
n St Kilda, she was placed in a house or cottage of two small
partments, tolerably well furnished, with a girl to wait upon
er, and provided with a sufficiency of good food and clothing.
Of educated persons the island contained not one, except for a
hort time a Highland Presbyterian clergyman, named Roderick
Maclennan. There was hardly even a person capable of speaking
or understanding the English language within reach. No books,
no intelligence from the world in which she had once lived. Only
once a year did a steward come to collect the rent paid in kind by
the poor people ; and by him was the lady regularly furnished
with a store of such articles, foreign to the place, as she needed—
usually a stone of sugar, a pound of tea, six pecks of wheat, and an
anker of spirits.* Thus she had no lack of the common necessaries
of life ; she only wanted society and freedom. In this way she
spent seven dreary years in St Kilda. How she contrived to pass
her time is not known. We learn, however, some particulars of
her history during this period from the testimony of those who
had a charge over her. If this is to be believed, she made
incessant efforts, though without effect, to bribe the islanders to
assist in liberating her. Once a stray vessel sent a boat ashore
for water ; she no sooner heard of it than she despatched the
minister's wife to apprise the sailors of her situation, and entreat
them to rescue her ; but Mrs Maclennan did not reach the spot
till after they had departed. She was kind to the peasantry,
giving them from her own stores, and sometimes had the women
to come and dance before her ; but her temper and habits were
not such as to gain their esteem. Often she drank too much; and
whenever any one near her committed the slightest mistake, she
would fly into a furious passion, and even resort to violence.
Once she was detected in an attempt, during the night, to obtain
a pistol from above the steward's bed, in the room next to her
own. On his awaking and seeing her, she ran off to her own bed.
One is disposed, of course, to make all possible allowances for a
person in her wretched circumstances ; yet there can be little

* About four gallons.

doubt, from the evidence before us, that it was a natural and habitual violence of temper which displayed itself during her residence in St Kilda.

Meanwhile it was known in Edinburgh that Lady Grange had been forcibly carried away and placed in seclusion by orders of her husband; but her whereabouts was a mystery to all besides a few who were concerned to keep it secret. During the years which had elapsed since her abduction, Mr Erskine had given up his seat on the bench, and entered into political life as a friend of the Prince of Wales and opponent of Sir Robert Walpole. The world had wondered at the events of his domestic life, and several persons denounced the singular means he had adopted for obtaining domestic peace. But, in the main, he stood as well with society as he had ever done. At length, in the winter of 1740–41, a communication from Lady Grange for the first time reached her friends. It was brought by the minister Maclennan and his wife, who had left the island in discontent, after quarrelling with Macleod's steward. The idea of a lady by birth and education being immured for a series of years in an outlandish place where only the most illiterate peasantry resided, and this by the command of a husband who could only complain of her irritable temper, struck forcibly upon public feeling, and particularly upon the mind of Lady Grange's legal agent, Mr Hope of Rankeillor, who had all along felt a keen interest in her fate. Of Mr Hope it may be remarked that he was also a zealous Jacobite; yet, though all the persons engaged in the lady's abduction were of that party, he hesitated not to take active measures on the contrary side. He immediately applied to the Lord Justice-clerk (supreme criminal judge) for a warrant to search for and liberate Lady Grange. This application was opposed by the friends of Mr Erskine, and eventually it was defeated; yet he was not on that account deterred from hiring a vessel, and sending it with armed men to secure the freedom of the lady—a step which, as it was illegal and dangerous, obviously implied no small risk on his own part. This ship proceeded no farther than the harbour called the Horse-shoe, in Lorn (opposite to the modern town of Oban), where the master quarrelled with and set on shore Mrs Maclennan, his guide. Apparently the voyage was not prosecuted in consequence of intelligence being received that the lady had been removed to another place, where she was kept in more humane circumstances. If so, its object might be considered as in part at least, though indirectly, accomplished.

I have seen a warrant, signed in the holograph of Normand
Macleod—the same insular chief who, a few years after, lost
public respect in consequence of his desertion of the Jacobite
cause, and showing an active hostility to Prince Charles when in
hiding. The document is dated at Dunvegan, February 17,
1741, and proceeds upon a rumour which has reached the writer
that a certain gentlewoman, called Lady Grange, was carried to
his isle of St Kilda in 1734, and has ever since been confined
there under cruel circumstances. Regarding this as a scandal
which he is bound to inquire into (as if it could have hitherto
been a secret to him), he orders his baron-bailie of Harris,
Donald Macleod of Bernera (this was a gallant fellow who went
out in the 'Forty-five), to proceed to that island and make the
necessary investigations. I have also seen the original precognition taken by honest Donald six days thereafter, when the
various persons who had been about Lady Grange gave evidence
respecting her. The general bearing of this testimony, besides
establishing the fact of her confinement as a prisoner, is to the
effect that she was treated well in all other respects, having a
house forty feet long, with an inner room and a chimney to it,
a curtained bed, arm-chair, table, and other articles; ample store
of good provisions, including spirits; and plenty of good
clothes; but that she was addicted to liquor, and liable to
dreadful outbreaks of anger. Evidence was at the same time
taken regarding the character of the Maclennans, upon whose
reports Mr Hope had proceeded. It was Mr Erskine's interest
to establish that they were worthless persons, and to this effect
strong testimony was given by several of the islanders, though
it would be difficult to say with what degree of verity. The
whole purpose of these precognitions was to meet the clamours
raised by Mr Hope as to the barbarities to which Lady Grange
had been subjected. They had the effect of stopping for a
time the legal proceedings threatened by that gentleman; but
he afterwards raised an action in the Court of Session for payment of the arrears of aliment or allowance due to the lady,
amounting to £1150, and obtained decreet or judgment in the
year 1743 against the defender in absence, though he did not
choose to put it in force.

The unfortunate cause of all these proceedings ceased to be a
trouble to any one in May 1745. Erskine, writing from Westminster, June 1, in answer to an intimation of her death, says:
'I most heartily thank you, my dear friend, for the timely notice

you gave me of the death of *that person*. It would be
ridiculous untruth to pretend grief for it ; but as it brings to m
mind a train of various things for many years back, it gives m
concern. Her retaining wit and facetiousness to the last sur
prises me. These qualities none found in her, no more tha
common-sense or good-nature, before she went to these parts
and of the reverse of all which, if she had not been irrecoverabl
possest, in an extraordinary and insufferable degree, after man
years' fruitless endeavours to reclaim her, she had never see
these parts. I long for the particulars of her death, which, you
are pleased to tell me, I am to have by next post.'

Mr Hope's wife and daughters being left as heirs of Lady
Grange, an action was raised in their name for the £1150
formerly awarded, and for three years additional of her annuity ;
and for this compound sum decreet was obtained, which was
followed by steps for forcing payment. The Hopes were aware,
however, of the dubious character of this claim, seeing that Mr
Erskine, from whatever causes, had substituted an actual subsistence since 1732. They accordingly intimated that they aimed
at no personal benefit from Lady Grange's bequest ; and the
affair terminated in Mr Erskine reimbursing Mr Hope for all
the expenses he had incurred on behalf of the lady, including
that for the sloop which he had hired to proceed to St Kilda for
her rescue.

It is humbly thought that this story casts a curious and faithful
light upon the age of our grandfathers, showing things in a kind
of transition from the sanguinary violence of an earlier age to the
humanity of the present times. Erskine, not to speak of his
office of a judge in Scotland, moved in English society of the
highest character. He must have been the friend of Lyttelton,
Pope, Thomson, and other ornaments of Frederick's court ; and
as the brother-in-law of the Countess of Mar, who was sister of
Lady Mary Wortley Montagu, he would figure in the brilliant circle
which surrounded that star of the age of the second George. Yet
he does not appear to have ever felt a moment's compunction at
leaving the mother of his children to pine and fret herself to
death in a half-savage wilderness—

'Placed far amidst the melancholy main ;'

for in a paper which expresses his feelings on the subject pretty
freely, he justifies the 'sequestration' as a step required by
prudence and decency ; and in showing that the gross neces-

aries of life were afforded to his wife, seems to have considered
that his whole duty towards her was discharged. Such an insensibility could not be peculiar to one man: it indicates the
temper of a class and of an age. While congratulating ourselves
on the improved humanity of our own times, we may glance with
satisfaction to the means which it places in our power for the
proper treatment of patients like Mrs Erskine. Such a woman
would now be regarded as the unfortunate victim of disease,
and instead of being forcibly carried off under cloud of night by
a band of Highlanders, and committed to confinement on the
outskirts of the world, she would, with proper precautions, be
remitted to an asylum, where, by gentle and rational management, it might be hoped that she would be restored to mental
health, or, at the worst, enabled to spend the remainder of her
days in the utmost comfort which her state admitted of.

[1868.—About the middle of Cant's Close,* on the west side,
there exists a remarkable edifice, different from all others in the
neighbourhood. It is two
stories in height, the second
story being reached by an
outside stone stair within
a small courtyard, which
had originally been shut in
by a gate. The stone pillars
of the gateway are decorated
with balls at the top, as
was the fashion of entrances
to the grounds of a country
mansion. The building is
picturesque in character, in
the style of the sixteenth
century in Scotland. As
it resembles a neat, old-
fashioned country-house, one
wonders to find it jammed

Old Mansion, Cant's Close.

up amidst tall edifices in this confined alley. Ascending the stair,
we find that the interior consists of three or four apartments,

* Named after John Cant, a pious citizen of the sixteenth century, who, with
his wife, Agnes Kerkettle, was a contributor to the foundation of the Convent
of St Catherine of Siena on the south side of the Meadows. The district is
now known as Sciennes—pronounced *Sheens*.

with handsome panelled walls and elaborately carved stucc
ceilings. The principal room has a double window on the wes
to Dickson's Close.*

Daniel Wilson, in his *Memorials of Edinburgh*, speaks of th
building in reference to Dickson's Close. He says : ' A littl
lower down the close on the same side, an old and curious ston
tenement bears on its lower crow-step the Haliburton arms
impaled with another coat, on one shield. It is a singularl
antique and time-worn edifice, evidently of considerable antiquity
A curious double window projects on a corbelled base into th
close, while the whole stone-work is so much decayed as greatl
to add to its picturesque character. In the earliest deed which
exists, bearing date 1582, its first proprietor, Master Jame.
Halyburton—a title then of some meaning—is spoken of in
indefinite terms as *umq^le*, or deceased ; so that it is a building
probably of the early part of the sixteenth century.' It is known
that the adjoining properties on the north once pertained to
the collegiate church of Crichton ; while those on the east, in
Strichen's Close, comprehended the town residence of the Abbot
of Melrose, 1526.

The adjoining woodcut [p. 221] will give some idea of this
strange old mansion in Cant's Close, with its gateway and flight of
steps. In looking over the titles, we find that the tenement was
conveyed in 1735 from Robert Geddes of Scotstoun, Peeblesshire,
to George Wight, a burgess of Edinburgh, since which period it
has gradually deteriorated ; every apartment, from the ground to
the garret, is now a dwelling for a separate family ; and the
whole surroundings are most wretched. The edifice formed one
of the properties removed under the Improvement Act of 1867.]

* Only fragments of the ancient buildings remain in Cant's and Dickson's
Closes.

ABBOT OF MELROSE'S LODGING.

Sir George Mackenzie—Lady Anne Dick.

IN Catholic times several of the great dignitaries of the Church had houses in Edinburgh, as the Archbishop of St Andrews at the foot of Blackfriars Wynd, the Bishop of Dunkeld in the Cowgate, and the Abbot of Cambuskenneth in the Lawnmarket.* The Abbot of Melrose's 'lodging' appears from public documents to have been in what is now called Strichen's Close, in the High Street, immediately to the west of Blackfriars Wynd. It had a garden extending down to the Cowgate and up part of the opposite slope.

A successor of the abbot in this possession was Sir George Mackenzie of Rosehaugh, king's advocate in the reigns of Charles II. and James II., and author of several able works in Scottish law, as well as a successful cultivator of miscellaneous literature. He got a charter of the property from the magistrates in 1677. The house occupied by Sir George still exists,† and appears to have been a goodly enough mansion for its time. It is now, however, possessed by a brass-

Strichen's Close.

* At the head of the Old Bank Close, to the westward; burned down in 1771.

† Only a small portion of this building now remains.

founder as a place of business. From Sir George the alley wa
called Rosehaugh's Close, till, this house falling by marriage con

nection into the posses-
sion of Lord Strichen,
it got the name of
Strichen's Close, which
it still bears. Lord
Strichen was a judge of
the Court of Session for
forty-five years subse-
quent to 1730. He was
the direct ancestor of the
present Lord Lovat of
the British peerage.

Mackenzie has still a
place in the popular
imagination in Edin-
burgh as the *Bluidy
Mackingie*, his office having been to prosecute the
unruly Covenanters. It
therefore happens that
the founder of our

Back of Mackenzie's House, looking into
Cant's House.

greatest national library,* one whom Dryden regarded as a
friend, and who was the very first writer of classic English
prose in Scotland, is a sort of Raw-head and Bloody-bones
by the firesides of his native capital. He lies in a beautiful
mausoleum, which forms a conspicuous object in the Greyfriars
Churchyard, and which describes him as an ornament to his age,
and a man who was kind to all, 'except a rebellious crew, from
whose violence, with tongue and pen, he defended his country and
king, whose virulence he stayed by the sword of justice, and whose
ferocity he, by the force of reason, blunted, and only did not
subdue.' This monument was an object of horror to the good
people of Edinburgh, as it was almost universally believed that
the spirit of the persecutor could get no rest in its superb but
gloomy tenement. It used to be 'a feat' for a set of boys, in a
still summer evening, to march up to the ponderous doors, bedropt
with white tears upon a black ground, and cry in at the keyhole:

'Bluidy Mackingie, come out if ye daur,
Lift the sneck, and draw the bar!'

* The Advocates' Library.

after which they would run away as if some hobgoblin were in chase of them, probably not looking round till they were out of the churchyard.

Sir George Mackenzie had a country-house called Shank, about ten miles to the south of Edinburgh,* now a ruin. One day the Marquis of Tweeddale, having occasion to consult him about some law business, rode across the country, and arrived at so early an hour in the morning that the lawyer was not yet out of bed. Soliciting an immediate audience, he was admitted to the bed-room, where he sat down and detailed the case to Sir George, who gave him all necessary counsel from behind the curtains. When the marquis advanced to present a fee, he was startled at the apparition of a female hand through the curtains, in an attitude expressive of a readiness to receive, while no hand appeared on the part of Sir George. The explanation was that Sir George's lady, as has been the case with many a weaker man, took entire charge of his purse.†

Several of the descendants of this great lawyer have been remarkable for their talents. None, perhaps, possessed more of the *vivida vis animi* than his granddaughter, Lady Anne Dick of Corstorphine (also granddaughter, by the father's side, to the clever but unscrupulous 'Tarbat Register,' the first Earl of Cromarty).‡ This lady excited much attention in Edinburgh society by her eccentric manners and her droll pasquinade verses : one of those beings she was who astonish, perplex, and fidget their fellow-creatures, till at last the world feels a sort of relief when they are removed from the stage. She made many enemies by her lampoons ; and her personal conduct only afforded them too good room for revenge. Sometimes she would dress herself in men's clothes, and go about the town in search of adventures. One of her frolics ended rather disgracefully, for she and her maid, being apprehended in their disguise, were lodged all night in the Town Guard-house. It may be readily imagined that by those whom her wit had exasperated such

---

* In the parish of Borthwick.

† This anecdote was related to me by the first Lord Wharncliffe, grandson's grandson to Sir George, about 1828.

‡ Cromarty, at seventy, contrived to marry 'a young and beautiful countess in her own right, a widow, wealthy, and in universal estimation. The following distich was composed on the occasion :

Thou sonsie auld carl, the world has not thy like,
For ladies fa' in love with thee, though thou be ane auld tyke.'

C. K. Sharpe, Notes to *Law's Memorials*, p. xlvii.

follies would be deeply relished and made the most of. We must not, therefore, be surprised at Scandal telling that Lady Anne had at one period lain a whole year in bed, in a vain endeavour—to baffle *himself*.

Through private channels have oozed out at this late day a few specimens of Lady Anne's poetical abilities; less brilliant than might be expected from the above character of her, yet having a certain air of dash and *espièglerie* which looks appropriate. They are partly devoted to bewailing the coldness of a certain Sir Peter Murray of Balmanno, towards whom she chose to act as a sort of she-Petrarch, but apparently in the mere pursuit of whim. One runs in the following tender strain:

> 'Oh, when he dances at a ball,
>   He's rarely worth the seeing;
> So light he trips, you would him take
>   For some aërial being!
> While pinky-winky go his een,
>   How blest is each bystander!
> How gracefully he leads the fair,
>   When to her seat he hands her!
>
> But when in accents saft and sweet,
>   He chants forth *Lizzie Baillie*,
> His dying looks and attitude
>   Enchant, they cannot fail ye.
> The loveliest widow in the land,
>   When she could scarce disarm him,
> Alas! the belles in Roxburghshire
>   Must never hope to charm him!
>
> O happy, happy, happy she,
>   Could make him change his plan, sir,
> And of this rigid bachelor,
>   Convert the married man, sir:
> O happy, and thrice happy she,
>   Could make him change his plan, sir,
> And to the gentle Benedick
>   Convert the single man, sir,' &c.

In another, tired, apparently, of the apathy of this sweet youth, she breaks out as follows:

> 'Oh, wherefore did I cross the Forth,
>   And leave my love behind me?
> Why did I venture to the north,
>   With one that did not mind me?
>
> Had I but visited Carin!
>   It would have been much better,
> Than pique the prudes, and make a din
>   For careless, cold Sir Peter!

I'm sure I've seen a better limb,
  And twenty better faces;
But still my mind it ran on him,
  When I was at the races.

At night, when we went to the ball,
  Were many there discreeter;
The well-bred duke, and lively Maule,
  Panmure behaved much better.

They kindly showed their courtesy,
  And looked on me much sweeter;
Yet easy could I never be,
  For thinking on Sir Peter.

I fain would wear an easy air,
  But, oh, it looked affected,
And e'en the fine ambassador
  Could see he was neglected.

Though Powrie left for me the spleen,
  My temper grew no sweeter;
I think I'm mad—what do I mean,
  To follow cold Sir Peter!'

Her ladyship died, without issue, in 1741.

BLACKFRIARS WYND.

Palace of Archbishop Bethune—Boarding-Schools of the Last Century—The Last of the Lorimers—Lady Lovat.

THOSE who now look into Blackfriars Wynd—passing through it is out of the question—will be surprised to learn that, all dismal and wretched as it is in all respects, it was once a place of some respectability and even dignity. On several of its tall old *lands* may be seen inscriptions implying piety on the part of the founder—one, for example :

PAX INTRANTIBUS,
SALUS EXEUNTIBUS ;

another :

MISERERE MEI, DEUS ;

this last containing in its *upper floor* all that the adherents of Rome had forty years ago as a place of worship in Edinburgh— the chapel to which, therefore, as a matter of course, the late Charles X. resorted with his suite, when residing as Comte d'Artois in Holyrood House. The alley gets its name from having been the access to the Blackfriars' Monastery on the opposite slope, and being built on their land.

PALACE OF ARCHBISHOP BETHUNE [OR BEATON].

At the foot of the wynd, on the east side, is a large mansion of antique appearance, forming two sides of a quadrangle, with a *porte-cochère* giving access to a court behind, and a picturesque overhanging turret at the exterior angle.* This house was built by James Bethune, Archbishop of Glasgow (1508–1524), chancellor of the kingdom, and one of the Lords Regent under the Duke of Albany during the minority of James V. Lyndsay, in his *Chronicles*, speaks of it as 'his owen ludging quhilk he biggit in the Freiris Wynd.' Keith, at a later period, says : 'Over the entry of which the arms of the family of Bethune are to be seen to this day.' Common report represents it as the house of Cardinal Bethune, who was the nephew of the Archbishop of

---

* This historic building was demolished many years ago. Its main front faced the Cowgate, and to the north and east were extensive gardens.

Glasgow ; and it is not improbable that the one prelate bequeathed it to the other, and that it thus became what Maitland calls it, ' the archiepiscopal palace belonging to the see of St Andrews.'

Cardinal Bethune's House.

The ground-floor of this extensive building is arched over with strong stone-work, after the fashion of those houses of defence of the same period which are still scattered over the country. Some years ago, when one of the arches was removed to make way for a common ceiling, a thick layer of sand, firmly beaten down, was found between the surface of the vault and the floor above. Ground-floors thus formed were applied in former times to inferior domestic uses, and to the storing of articles of value. The chief apartments for living in were on the floor above—that is, the so-called *first floor*. And such is the case in all the best houses of an old fashion in the city of St Andrews at this day.

I shall afterwards have something to say of an event of the year 1517, with which Archbishop Bethune's house was connected. It appears to have been occupied by James V. in 1528, while he was deliberating on the propriety of calling a parliament.*

The Bethune palace is now, like its confrères, abandoned to the humblest class of tenants. Eighty years ago, however, it must still have been a tolerably good house, as it was then the residence of Bishop Abernethy Drummond, of the Scottish Episcopal communion, the husband of the heiress of Hawthornden. This worthy

* In this house, too, Queen Mary was entertained at a banquet given by the citizens. ' Upon the nynt day of Februar at evin the Queen's grace come up in ane honourable manner fra the palice of Holyrudhouse to the Cardinal's ludging in Blackfriars Wynd, . . . and efter supper the honest young men in the town come with ane convoy to her,' and escorted her back to Holyrood.— *Diurnal of Occurrents.*

Before the opening of the original High School in the grounds of the Blackfriars' Monastery the pupils were temporarily accommodated in Beaton's palace.

divine occupied some space in the public eye in his day, and was
particularly active in obtaining the repeal of the penal statutes
against his church.　Some wag, figuring the surprise in high places
at a stir arising from a quarter so obscure, penned this epigram:

> 'Lord Sydney, to the privy-council summoned,
> 　By testy majesty was questioned quick:
> "Eh, eh! who, who's this Abernethy Drummond,
> 　And where, in Heaven's name, is his bishopric?"'

BOARDING-SCHOOLS OF THE LAST CENTURY.

When the reader hears such things of the Freir Wynd, he must
not be surprised overmuch on perusing the following advertisement
from the *Edinburgh Gazette* of April 19, 1703: 'There is a
Boarding-school to be set up in Blackfriars Wynd, in Robinson's
Land, upon the west side of the wynd, near the middle thereof, in
the first door of the stair leading to the said land, against the
latter end of May, or first of June next, where young Ladies and
Gentlewomen may have all sorts of breeding that is to be had in
any part of Britain, and great care taken of their conversation.'

I know not whether this was the same seminary which, towards
the middle of the century, was kept by a distinguished lady named
Mrs Euphame or Effie Sinclair, who was descended from the ancient
family of Longformacus, in Berwickshire, being the granddaughter
of Sir Robert Sinclair, first baronet of Longformacus, upon whom
that dignity was conferred by King Charles II., in consideration
of his services and losses during the civil war.　Mrs Effie was
allied to many of the best families in Scotland, who made it a
duty to place their children under her charge; and her school was
thus one of the most respectable in Edinburgh.　By her were
educated the beautiful Miss Duff, afterwards Countess of Dumfries
and Stair, and, by a second marriage, lady of the Honourable
Alexander Gordon (Lord Rockville); the late amiable and excel-
lently well informed Mrs Keith, sister of Sir Robert Keith,
commonly called, from his diplomatic services, *Ambassador Keith;* *

---

* The title 'Ambassador Keith' is usually applied to Sir Robert's father, who,
after several minor diplomatic appointments on the Continent, was the representative of Great Britain at the court of St Petersburg.　An interesting
sketch of him, under the title of 'Felix,' by Mrs Cockburn, is appended to the
volume of that lady's *Letters*, edited by Mr T. Craig Brown.　Miss Keith,
known to Edinburgh society as 'Sister Anne,' was Scott's 'Mrs Bethune
Balliol' of the *Chronicles of the Canongate*.　This gentleman was absent from
Edinburgh about twenty-two years, and returned at a time when it was sup-

the two Misses Hume of Linthill; and Miss Rutherford, the mother of Sir Walter Scott. All these ladies were Scottish cousins to Mrs Effie. To judge by the proficiency of her scholars, although much of what is called accomplishment might be then left untaught, she must have been possessed of uncommon talents for education; for all the ladies before mentioned had well-cultivated minds, were fond of reading, wrote and spelled admirably, were well acquainted with history and with *belles-lettres*, without neglecting the more homely duties of the needle and the account-book; and, while two of them were women of extraordinary talents, all of them were perfectly well-bred in society.

It may be added that many of these young ladies were sent to reside with and be *finished off* by the Honourable Mrs Ogilvie, lady of the Honourable Patrick Ogilvie of Longmay and Inch-martin, who was supposed to be the *best-bred* woman of her time in Scotland (ob. 1753). Her system was very rigorous, according to the spirit of the times. The young ladies were taught to sit quite upright; and the mother of my informant (Sir Walter Scott), even when advanced to nearly her eightieth year, never permitted her back to touch the chair in sitting. There is a remarkably good and characteristic anecdote told of the husband of this rigorous preceptress, a younger brother of the Earl of Find-later, whose exertions, while Lord High-chancellor of Scotland, in favour of the Union were so conspicuous. The younger brother, it appears, had condescended to trade a little in cattle, which was not considered derogatory to the dignity of a Scottish gentleman at that time, and was by no means an uncommon practice among them.

However, the earl was offended at the measure, and upbraided his brother for it. 'Haud your tongue, man!' said the cattle-

posed that manners were beginning to exhibit symptoms of great improvement. He, however, complained that they were degenerated. In his early time, he said, every Scottish gentleman of £300 a year travelled abroad when young, and brought home to the bosom of domestic life, and to the profession in which it might be his fate to engage, a vast fund of literary information, knowledge of the world, and genuine good manners, which dignified his character through life. But towards the year 1770 this practice had been entirely given up, and in consequence a sensible change was discoverable upon the face of good society. (See the *Life of John Home*, by Henry Mackenzie, Esq.).

dealer; 'better sell nowte than sell nations,' pronouncing the last word with peculiar and emphatic breadth.

I am tempted, by the curious and valuable document appended, to suspect that the female accomplishments of the last century were little behind those of the present in point of useless elaboration.

'*Thursday, December* 9, 1703.—Near Dundee, at Dudhope, there is to be taught, by a gentlewoman from London, the following works, viz.—1. Wax-work of all sorts, as any one's picture to the life, figures in shadow glasses, fruits upon trees or in dishes, all manner of confections, fish, flesh, fowl, or anything that can be made of wax.—2. Philligrim-work of any sort, whether hollow or flat.—3. Japan-work upon timber or glass.—4. Painting upon glass.—5. Sashes for windows, upon sarsnet or transparent paper.—6. Straw-work of any sort, as houses, birds, or beasts.—7. Shell-work, in sconces, rocks, or flowers.—8. Quill-work.—9. Gum-work.—10. Transparent-work.—11. Puff-work.—12. Paper-work.—13. Plate-work on timber, brass, or glass.—14. Tortoise-shell-work.—15. Mould-work, boxes and baskets.—16. Silver landskips.—17. Gimp-work.—18. Bugle-work.—19. A sort of work in imitation of japan, very cheap.—20. Embroidering, stitching, and quilting.—21. True point or tape lace.—22. Cutting glass.—23. Washing gauzes, or Flanders lace and point.—24. Pastry of all sorts, with the finest cuts and shapes that's now used in London.—25. Boning fowls, without cutting the back.—26. Butter-work.—27. Preserving, conserving, and candying.—28. Pickling and colouring.—29. All sorts of English wines.—30. Writing and arithmetic.—31. Music, and the great end of dancing, which is a good carriage; and several other things too tedious here to be mentioned. Any who are desirous to learn the above works may board with herself at a reasonable rate, or may board themselves in Dundee, and may come to her quarterly.'—Advertisement in *Edinburgh Gazette*, 1703.

'The g
end
danci

Another distinguished Edinburgh boarding-school of the last century was kept by two ladies, of Jacobite predilections, named the Misses Ged, in Paterson's Court, Lawnmarket. They were remarkable at least for their family connections, for it was a brother of theirs who, under the name of Don Patricio Ged, rendered such kindly and effective service to Commodore Byron, as gratefully recorded in the well-known *Narrative*, and gracefully touched on by Campbell in the *Pleasures of Hope*:

'He found a warmer world, a milder clime,
   A home to rest, a shelter to defend,
   Peace and repose, *a Briton and a friend.*'

Another member of the family, William Ged, originally a goldsmith in Edinburgh, was the inventor of stereotype printing. The Misses Ged were described by their friends as of the Geds of Baldridge, near Dunfermline ; thorough Fife Jacobites every one of them. The old ladies kept a portrait of the Chevalier in their parlour, and looked chiefly to partisans of the Stuarts for support. They had another relative of less dignity, who, accepting a situation in the Town-guard, became liable to satiric reference from Robert Fergusson :

'Nunc est bibendum, et bendere bickerum magnum,
   Cavete Town-guardum, *Dougal Geddum,* atque Campbellum.'

Dougal had been a silversmith, but in his own conceit his red coat as a Town-guard officer made him completely military. Seeing a lady without a beau at the door of the Assembly Room, he offered his services, 'if the arm of an old soldier could be of any use.' 'Hoot awa, Dougal,' said the lady, accepting his assistance, however ; 'an auld tinkler, you mean.'

THE LAST OF THE LORIMERS.

To return for a moment to the archiepiscopal palace. It contained, about eighty years ago, a person calling himself a LORIMER—an appellative once familiar in Edinburgh, being applied to those who deal in the ironwork used in saddlery.*

* It is curious to observe how, in correspondence with the change in our manners and customs, one trade has become extinct, while another succeeded in its place. At the end of the sixteenth century the manufacture of offensive weapons predominated over all other trades in Edinburgh. We had then cutlers, whose *essay-piece,* on being admitted of the corporation, was 'ane plain finished quhanzear' or sword ; gaird-makers, whose business consisted in fashioning sword-handles ; Dalmascars, who gilded the said weapon ; and belt-makers, who wrought the girdles that bound it to the wearer's body. There were also dag-makers, who made hackbuts (short-guns) and dags (pistols). These various professions all became associated in the general one of armourers, or gunsmiths, when the wearing of weapons went into desuetude—there being then no further necessity for the expedition and expediency of the modern political economist's boasted ' division of labour.' As the above arts gave way, those which tended to provide the comforts and luxuries of civilised life gradually arose. About 1586 we find the first notice of locksmiths in Edinburgh, and there was then only one of the trade, whose essay was simply 'a kist lock.' In 1609, however, as the security of property increased, the essay was 'a kist

LADY LOVAT.

The widow of the rebel Lord Lovat spent a great portion of a long widowhood and died (1796) in a house at the head of Blackfriars Wynd.

Her ladyship was a niece of the first Duke of Argyll, and born as she herself expressed it, in the year *Ten*—that is, 1710. The politic *Mac Shemus** marked her out as a suitable second wife in consideration of the value of the Argyll connection. As he was above thirty years her senior, and not famed for the tenderest treatment of his former spouse, or for any other amiable trait of disposition, she endeavoured, by all gentle means, to avoid the match; but it was at length effected through the intervention of her relations, and she was carried north to take her place in the semi-barbarous state which her husband held at Castle Downie.

Nothing but misery could have been expected from such an alliance. The poor young lady, while treated with external decorum, was in private subjected to such usage as might have tried the spirit of a Griselda. She was occasionally kept confined in a room by herself, from which she was not allowed to come forth even at meals, only a scanty supply of coarse food being sent to her from his lordship's table. When pregnant, her husband coolly told her that if she brought forth a girl he would put it on the back of the fire. His eldest son by the former marriage was a sickly child. Lovat therefore deemed it necessary to raise a strong motive in the step-mother for the child being taken due care of during his absence in the Lowlands. On going from home, he would calmly inform her that any harm

lock and a hingand bois lock, with an double plate lock;' and in 1644 'a key and sprent band' were added to the essay. In 1682 'a cruik and cruik band' were further added; and in 1728, for the safety of the lieges, the locksmith's essay was appointed to be 'a cruik and cruik band, a pass lock with a round filled bridge, not cut or broke in the backside, with nobs and jamb bound.' In 1595 we find the first notice of shearsmiths. In 1609 a heckle-maker was admitted into the Corporation of Hammermen. In 1613 a tinkler makes his appearance; Thomas Duncan, the first tinkler, was then admitted. Pewterers are mentioned so far back as 1588. In 1647 we find the first knock-maker (*clock-maker*), but so limited was his business that he was also a locksmith. In 1664 the first white-iron man was admitted; also the first harness-maker, though lorimers had previously existed. Paul Martin, a distressed French Protestant, in 1691, was the first manufacturer of surgical instruments in Edinburgh. In 1720 we find the first pin-maker; in 1764, the first edge-tool maker and first fish-hook maker.

* The Highland appellative of **Lord Lovat**, expressing *the son of Simon*.

befalling *the boys* in his absence would be attended with the penalty of her own death, for in that event he would undoubtedly shoot her through the head. It is added that she did, from this in addition to other motives, take an unusual degree of care of her step-son, who ever after felt towards her the tenderest love and gratitude. One is disposed to believe that there must be some exaggeration in these stories; and yet when we consider that it is an historical fact that Lovat applied to Prince Charles for a warrant to take President Forbes *dead or alive* (Forbes being his friend and daily intimate), it seems no extravagance that he should have acted in this manner to his wife. Sir Walter Scott tells an additional story, which helps out the picture. ' A lady, the intimate friend of her youth, was instructed to visit Lady Lovat, as if by accident, to ascertain the truth of those rumours concerning her husband's conduct which had reached the ears of her family. She was received by Lord Lovat with an extravagant affectation of welcome, and with many assurances of the happiness his lady would receive from seeing her. The chief then went to the lonely tower in which Lady Lovat was secluded, without decent clothes, and even without sufficient nourishment. He laid a dress before her becoming her rank, commanded her to put it on, to appear, and to receive her friend as if she were the mistress of the house; in which she was, in fact, a naked and half-starved prisoner. And such was the strict watch which he maintained, and the terror which his character inspired, that the visitor durst not ask, nor Lady Lovat communicate, anything respecting her real situation.' * Afterwards, by a letter rolled up in a clew of yarn and dropped over a window to a confidential person, she was enabled to let her friends know how matters actually stood; and steps were then taken to obtain her separation from her husband. When, some years later, his political perfidy had brought him to the Tower—forgetting all past injuries, and thinking only of her duty as a wife, Lady Lovat offered to come to London to attend him. He returned an answer, declining the proposal, and containing the only expressions of kindness and regard which she had ever received from him since her marriage.

The singular character of Lord Lovat makes almost every particular regarding him worth collecting.

Previous to 1745, when the late Mr Alexander Baillie of Dochfour was a student at the grammar-school of Inverness,

* *Quarterly Review*, vol. xiv. p. 326.

cock-fights were very common among the boys. This detestable sport, by the way, was encouraged by the schoolmasters of those days, who derived a profit from the beaten cocks, or, as they were called, *fugies*, which became, at the end of every game, their appropriated perquisite. In pursuit of cocks, Mr Baillie went to visit his friends in the Aird, and in the course of his researches was introduced to Lord Lovat, whose policy it was, on all occasions, to show great attentions to his neighbours and their children. The situation in which his lordship was found by the schoolboy was, if not quite unprecedented, nevertheless rather surprising. He was stretched out in bed between two Highland lasses, who, on being seen, affected out of modesty to hide their faces under the bedclothes. The old lord accounted for this strange scene by saying that his blood had become cold, and he was obliged to supply the want of heat by the application of animal warmth.

It is said that he lay in bed for the most part of the two years preceding the Rebellion; till, hearing of Prince Charles's arrival in Arisaig, he roused himself with sudden vehemence, crying to an attendant : 'Lassie, bring me my brogues—I 'll rise *noo !* '

One of his odd fancies was to send a retainer every day to Loch Ness, a distance of eight miles, for the water he drank.

His intimacy with his neighbour President Forbes is an amusing affair, for the men must have secretly known full well what each other was, and yet policy made them keep on decent terms for a long course of years. Lovat's son by the subject of this notice—the Honourable Archibald Campbell Fraser—was a boy at Petty school in 1745. The President sometimes invited him to dinner. One day, pulling a handful of foreign gold pieces out of his pocket, he carelessly asked the boy if he had ever seen such coins before. Here was a stroke worthy of Lovat himself, for undoubtedly he meant thus to be informed whether the lord of Castle Downie was accustomed to get remittances for the Chevalier's cause from abroad.

After the death of Lord Lovat, there arose some demur about his lady's jointure, which was only £190 per annum. It was not paid to her for several years, during which, being destitute of other resources, she lived with one of her sisters. Some of her numerous friends—among the rest, Lord Strichen—offered her the loan of money to purchase a house and suffice for present main-tenance. But she did not choose to encumber herself with debts which she had no certain prospect of repaying. At length the dispute about her jointure was settled in a favourable manner, and her ladyship received in a lump the amount of past dues, but of which she expended £500 in purchasing a house at the head of Blackfriars Wynd,* and a further sum upon a suite of plain substantial furniture.

It would surprise a modern dowager to know how much good Lady Lovat contrived to do amongst her fellow-creatures with this small allowance. It is said that the succeeding Lady of Lovat, with a jointure of £4000, was less distinguished for her benefactions. In Lady Lovat's dusky mansion, with a waiting-maid, cook, and footboy, she not only maintained herself in the style of a gentlewoman, but could welcome every kind of Highland cousin to a plain but hospitable board, and even afford permanent shelter to several unfortunate friends. A certain Lady Dorothy Primrose, who was her niece, lived with her for several years, using the best portion of her house, namely, the rooms fronting the High Street, while she herself was contented with the duller apartments towards the *wynd*. There was another desolate old person, styled Mistress of Elphinstone, whom Lady Lovat supported as a friend and equal for many years. Not by habit a card-player herself, she would make up a whist-party every week for the benefit of *the Mistress*. At length the poor Mistress came to a sad fate. A wicked, perhaps half-crazy boy, grandson to her ladyship, having taken an antipathy to his venerable relative, put poison into the oatmeal porridge which she was accustomed to take at supper. Feeling unwell that night, she did not eat any, and the Mistress took the porridge instead, of which she died. The boy was sent away, and died in obscurity.

An unostentatious but sincere piety marked the character of Lady Lovat. Perhaps her notions of Providence were carried to the verge of a kind of fatalism ; for not merely did she receive all crosses and troubles as trials arranged for her benefit by a Higher Hand, but when a neighbouring house on one occasion took fire, she sat unmoved in her own mansion, notwithstanding the entreaties of the magistrates, who ordered a sedan to be brought for her removal. She said if her hour was come, it would be vain to try to elude her fate ; and if it was not come, she would be safe where she was. She had a conscientiousness almost ludicrously nice. If detained from church on any occasion, she always doubled her usual oblation at the *plate* next time. When her

---

* First door up the stair at the head of the wynd, on the west side. The house was burnt down in 1824, but rebuilt in its former arrangement.

chimney took fire, she sent her fine to the Town-guard before they knew the circumstance. Even the tax-collector experienced her ultra-rectitude. When he came to examine her windows, she took him to a closet lighted by a single pane, looking into a narrow passage between two houses. He hesitated about charging for such a small modicum of light, but her ladyship insisted on his taking note of it.*

Lady Lovat was of small stature, had been thought a beauty, and retained in advanced old age much of her youthful delicacy of features and complexion. Her countenance bore a remarkably sweet and pleasing expression. When at home, her dress was a red silk gown, with ruffled cuffs, and sleeves puckered like a man's shirt; a fly-cap, encircling the head, with a mob-cap laid across it, falling down over the cheeks, and tied under the chin; her hair dressed and powdered; a double muslin handkerchief round the neck and bosom; *lammer-beads;* a white lawn apron, edged with lace; black stockings with red gushets; high-heeled shoes.† She usually went abroad in a chair, as I have been informed by the daughter of a lady who was one of the first inhabitants of the New Town, and whom Lady Lovat regularly visited there once every three months. As her chair emerged from the head of Blackfriars Wynd, any one who saw her sitting in it, so neat and fresh and clean, would have taken her for a queen in waxwork, pasted up in a glass-case.

Lady Lovat was intimate with Lady Jane Douglas; and one of the strongest evidences in favour of Lord Douglas being the son of that lady‡ was the following remarkable circumstance: Lady Lovat, passing by a house in the High Street, saw a child at a window, and remarked to a friend who was with her: 'If I thought Lady Jane Douglas could be in Edinburgh, I would say that was her child—he is so like her!' Upon returning home, she found a note from Lady Jane, informing her that she had just arrived in Edinburgh, and had taken lodgings in ——— Land, which proved to be the house in which Lady Lovat had observed the child, and that child was young Archibald Douglas. Lady Lovat was a person of such strict integrity that no consideration could have tempted her to say what she did not think; and at

* [The window-tax was first imposed in 1695, and repealed in 1851.]

† An old domestic of her ladyship's preserved one of her shoes as a relic for many years. The heel was three inches deep.

‡ [The view of the famous 'Douglas Cause,' affirmed in the House of Lords in 1771.]

he time she saw the child, she had no reason to suppose that
Lady Jane was in Scotland.

Such was the generosity of her disposition that when her
grandson Simon was studying law, she at various times presented
him with £50, and when he was to pass as an advocate she sent
him £100. It was wonderful how she could spare such sums
from her small jointure. Whole tribes of grand-nephews and
grand-nieces experienced the goodness of her heart, and loved
her with almost filial affection. She frequently spoke to them of
her misfortunes, and was accustomed to say : ' I dare say, bairns,
he events of my life would make a good *novelle ;* but they have
been of so strange a nature that nobody would believe them '—
meaning that they wanted the *vraisemblance* necessary in fiction.
She contemplated the approach of death with fortitude, and in
anticipation of her obsequies, had her grave-clothes ready and
he stair whitewashed. Yet the disposal of her poor remains
little troubled her. When asked by her son if she wished to be
placed in the burial-vault at Beaufort, she said : ' 'Deed, Archie,
e needna put yoursel' to ony fash about me, for I dinna care
hough ye lay me aneath that hearthstane ! ' After all, it chanced,
from some misarrangements, that her funeral was not very promptly
executed ; whereupon a Miss Hepburn of Humbie, living in a
floor above, remarked, ' she wondered what they were keeping her
sae lang for—stinkin' a' the stair.' This gives some idea of circumstances connected with Old Town life.

The conduct of her ladyship's son in life was distinguished by
a degree of eccentricity which, in connection with that of his son
already stated, tends to raise a question as to the character of
Lord Lovat, and make us suspect that wickedness so great as his
could only result from a certain unsoundness of mind. It is
admitted, however, that the eldest son, Simon, who rose to be a
major-general in the army, was a man of respectable character.
He retained nothing of his father but a genius for making fine
speeches.[*] The late Mrs Murray of Henderland told me she was
present at a supper-party given by some gentleman in the Horse
Wynd, where General Fraser, eating his egg, said to the hostess :
Mrs ——, other people's eggs overflow with *milk ;* but yours
run over with *cream !* '

* Mrs Grant of Laggan held another opinion of General Simon Fraser. A
pleasing exterior covered a large share of the paternal character—' No heart
was ever harder, no hands more rapacious than his.'

THE COWGATE.

LOOKING at the present state of this ancient street, it is impossible to hear without a smile the description of it given by Alexander Alesse about the year 1530—*Ubi nihil est humile aut rusticum, sed omnia magnifica!* ('Where nothing is humble or homely, but everything magnificent!') The street was, he tells us, that in which the nobles and judges resided, and where the palaces of princes were situated. The idea usually entertained of its early history is that it rose as an elegant suburb after the year 1460, when the existing city, consisting of the High Street alone, was enclosed in a wall. It would appear, however, that some part of it was built before that time, and that it was in an advanced, if not complete, state as a street not long after. It was to enclose this esteemed suburb that the city wall was extended after the battle of Flodden.

HOUSE OF GAVIN DOUGLAS THE POET—SKIRMISH OF CLEANSE-THE-CAUSEWAY.

So early as 1449, Thomas Lauder, canon of Aberdeen, granted an endowment of 40s. annually to a chaplain in St Giles's Church, 'out of his own house lying in the Cowgaite, betwixt the land of the Abbot of Melrose on the east, and of George Cochrane on the west.' This appears to have been the same Thomas Lauder who was preceptor to James II., and who ultimately became Bishop of Dunkeld. We are told that, besides many other munificent acts, he purchased a lodging in Edinburgh *for himself and his successors.** That its situation was the same as that above described appears from a charter of Thomas Cameron, in 1498, referring to a house on the south side of the Cowgate, 'betwixt *the Bishop of Dunkeld's land on the east*, and William Rappilowe's on the west, the common street on the north, and the gait that leads to the Kirk-of-Field on the south.'

* Myln's *Lives of the Bishops of Dunkeld.* Edinburgh, 1831.

From these descriptions we attain a tolerably distinct idea of the site of the house of the bishops of Dunkeld in Edinburgh, including, of course, one who is endeared to us from a peculiar cause—Gavin Douglas, who succeeded to the see in 1516. This house must have stood nearly opposite to the bottom of Niddry Street, but somewhat to the eastward. It would have gardens behind, extending up to the line of the present Infirmary Street.

We thus not only have the pleasure of ascertaining the Edinburgh whereabouts of one of our most distinguished national poets, but we can now read, with a somewhat clearer intelligence, a remarkable chapter in the national history.

It was in April 1520 that the Hamiltons (the party of the Earl of Arran), with Bethune, Archbishop of Glasgow, called an assembly of the nobility in Edinburgh, in order to secure the government for the earl. The rival magnate, the Earl of Angus, soon saw danger to himself in the great crowds of the Hamilton party which flocked into town. Indeed warlike courses seem to have been determined on by that side. Angus sent his uncle, the Bishop of Dunkeld, to caution them against any violence, and to offer that he should submit to the laws if any offence were laid to his charge. The reverend prelate, proceeding to the place of assembly, which was in the archbishop's house, at the foot of Blackfriars Wynd, found the Hamilton party obstinate. Thinking an archbishop could not or ought not to allow strife to take place if he could help it, he appealed to Bethune, who, however, had actually prepared for battle by putting on armour under his rochet. 'Upon my conscience, my lord,' said Bethune, 'I know nothing of the matter,' at the same time striking his hand upon his breast, which caused the armour to return a rattling sound. Douglas's remark was simply, 'Your conscience clatters;' a happy pun for the occasion, clatter being a Scotch word signifying to tell tales. Gavin then returned to his lodging, and told his nephew that he must do his best to defend himself with arms. 'For me,' he said, 'I will go to my chamber and pray for you.' With our new light as to the locality of the Bishop of Dunkeld's lodging, we now know that Angus and his uncle held their consultations on this occasion within fifty yards of the house in which the Hamiltons were assembled. The houses, in fact, nearly faced each other in the same narrow street.

Angus now put himself at the head of his followers, who, though not numerous, stood in a compact body in the High Street. They were, moreover, the favourites of the Edinburgh citizens, who handed spears from their windows to such as were not armed with that useful weapon. Presently the Hamiltons came thronging up from the Cowgate, through narrow lanes, and entering the High Street in separate streams, armed with swords only, were at a great disadvantage. In a short time the Douglases had cleared the streets of them, killing many, and obliging Arran himself and his son to make their escape through the North Loch, mounted on a coal-horse. Archbishop Bethune, with others, took refuge in the Blackfriars' Monastery, where he was seized behind the altar and in danger of his life, when Gavin Douglas, learning his perilous situation, flew to save him, and with difficulty succeeded in his object. Here, too, local knowledge is important. The Blackfriars' Monastery stood where the High School latterly was, a spot not more than a hundred yards from the houses of both Bethune and Gavin Douglas. It would not necessarily require more than five minutes to apprise Douglas of Bethune's situation, and bring him to the rescue.

The popular name given to this street battle is characteristic —*Cleanse-the-Causeway*.

COLLEGE WYND—BIRTHPLACE OF SIR WALTER SCOTT.

The old buildings of the College of Edinburgh, themselves mean, had for their main access, in former times, only that narrow dismal alley called the College Wynd,* leading up from the Cowgate. Facing down this humble lane was the gateway, displaying a richly ornamented architrave. The wynd itself, strange as the averment may now appear, was the abode of many of the professors. The illustrious Joseph Black lived at one time in a house adjacent to the College gate, on the east side, afterwards removed to make way for North College Street.† Another floor of the same building was occupied by Mr Keith, father of the late Sir Alexander Keith of Ravelston, Bart. ; and there did the late Lord Keith reside in his student days. There was a tradition, but of a vague nature, that Goldsmith, when studying at the Edinburgh University, lived in the College Wynd.

The one peculiar glory of this humble place remains to be mentioned—its being the birthplace of Sir Walter Scott. In the third floor of the house just described, accessible by an entry

---

* Originally the name was the 'Wynd of the Blessed Virgin Mary in the Fields,' as being the approach to the collegiate church so named which stood on the site of the University—the 'Kirk o' Field' of the Darnley tragedy.

† Now Chambers Street.

25 George Square.

leading to a common stair behind, did this distinguished person first see the light, August 15, 1771. It was a house of plain aspect, like many of its old neighbours yet surviving; its truest disadvantage, however, being in the unhealthiness of the situation, to which Sir Walter himself used to attribute the early deaths of several brothers and sisters born before him. When the house was required to give way for the public conveniency, the elder Scott received a fair price for his portion of it; he had previously removed to an airier mansion, No. 25 George Square, where Sir Walter spent his boyhood and youth.

In the course of a walk through this part of the town in 1825, Sir Walter did me the honour to point out the site of the house in which he had been born. On his mentioning that his father had got a good price for his share of it, in order that it might be taken down for the public convenience, I took the liberty of jocularly expressing my belief that more money might have been made of it, and the public certainly *much more* gratified, if it had remained to be shown as the birthplace of a man who had written so many popular books. ‘Ay, ay,’ said Sir Walter, ‘that is very well; but I am afraid I should have required to be dead first, and that would not have been so comfortable, you know.’

In the transition state of the College, from old to new buildings, the gate at the head of the wynd was shut up by Principal Robertson, who, however, living within the walls, found this passage convenient as an access to the town, and used it accordingly. It became the joke of a day, that from being the principal gate it had become only a gate for the Principal.*

* A small ‘bit’ of College Wynd, ending in a *cul de sac*, is all that remains of this once leading thoroughfare between the city and the ‘Oure Tounis Colledge.’

THE HORSE WYND.

This alley, connecting the Cowgate with the grounds on the south side of the town within the walls, and broad enough for a carriage, is understood to have derived its name from an inn which long ago existed at its head, where the Gaelic Church long after stood. Although the name is at least as old as the middle of the seventeenth century, none of the buildings appear older than the middle of the eighteenth. They had all been renewed by people desirous of the benefit of such air as was to be had in an alley double the usual breadth. Very respectable members of the bar were glad to have a flat in some of the tall *lands* on the east side of the wynd.*

On the west side of the wynd, about the middle, the Earl of Galloway had built a distinct mansion, ornamented with vases at top. They kept a coach and six, and it was alleged that when the countess made calls, the leaders were sometimes at the door she was going to, when she was stepping into the carriage at her own door. This may be called a *tour de force* illustration of the nearness of friends to each other in Old Edinburgh.

TAM O' THE COWGATE.

A court of old buildings, in a massive style of architecture, existed, previous to 1829, on a spot in the Cowgate now occupied by the southern piers of George IV. Bridge. In the middle of the last century it was used as the Excise-office; but even this was a kind of declension from its original character. It is certain that the celebrated Thomas Hamilton, first Earl of Haddington, President of the Court of Session, and Secretary of State for Scotland, lived here at the end of the sixteenth century, renting the house from Macgill of Rankeillour.† This distinguished person, from the circumstance of his living here, was endowed by his master, King James, with the nickname of TAM O' THE COWGATE, under which title he is now better remembered than by any other.

The earl, who had risen through high legal offices to the peerage, and who was equally noted for his penetration as a

* When it became an unfashionable place of residence it was dubbed by the fops of the town 'Cavalry Wynd.' The northern end of Guthrie Street is the site of the old Horse Wynd.

† Macgill was King's Advocate to James VI., and is said to have died of grief when his rival, Thomas Hamilton, was preferred for the presidentship.

judge, his industry as a collector of decisions, and his talent for amassing wealth, was one evening, after a day's hard labour in the public service, solacing himself with a friend over a flask of wine in his house in the Cowgate *—attired, for his better ease, in a nightgown, cap, and slippers—when he was suddenly disturbed by a great hubbub which arose under his window in the street. This soon turned out to be a *bicker* between the High School youths and those of the College; and it also appeared that the latter, fully victorious, were, notwithstanding a valiant defence, in the act of driving their antagonists before them. The Earl of Haddington's sympathies were awakened in favour of the retiring party, for he had been brought up at the High School, and going thence to complete his education at Paris, had no similar reason to affect the College. He therefore sprang up, dashed into the street, sided with and rallied the fugitives, and took a most animated share in the combat that ensued, so that finally the High School youths, acquiring fresh strength and valour at seeing themselves befriended by the prime judge and privy-councillor of their country (though not in his most formidable habiliments), succeeded in turning the scale of victory upon the College youths, in spite of their superior individual ages and strength. The earl, who assumed the command of the party, and excited their spirits by word as well as action, was not content till he had pursued the Collegianers through the Grassmarket, and out at the West Port, the gate of which he locked against their return, thus compelling them to spend the night in the suburbs and the fields. He then returned home in triumph to his castle of comfort in the Cowgate, and resumed the enjoyment of his friend and flask. We can easily imagine what a rare jest this must have been for King Jamie.

A Court of Old Buildings.

* Most of the traditionary anecdotes in this article were communicated by Charles, eighth Earl of Haddington, through conversation with Sir Walter Scott, by whom they were directly imparted to the author.

When this monarch visited Scotland in 1617, he found the old statesman very rich, and was informed that the people believed him to be in possession of the Philosopher's Stone there being no other feasible mode of accounting for his immense wealth, which rather seemed the effect of supernatural agency than of worldly prudence or talent. King James, quite tickled with the idea of the Philosopher's Stone, and of so enviable a talisman having fallen into the hands of a Scottish judge, was not long in letting his friend and gossip know of the story which he had heard respecting him. The Lord President immediately invited the king, and the rest of the company present, to come to his house next day, when he would both do his best to give them a good dinner and lay open to them the mystery of the Philosopher's Stone. This agreeable invitation was of course accepted; and the next day saw his Cowgate *palazzo* thronged with king and courtiers, all of whom the President feasted to their hearts' content. After dinner the king reminded him of his Philosopher's Stone, and expressed his anxiety to be speedily made acquainted with so rare a treasure, when the pawky lord addressed His Majesty and the company in a short speech, concluding with this information, that his whole secret lay in two simple and familiar maxims— 'Never put off till to-morrow what can be done to-day; nor ever trust to another's hand what your own can execute.' He might have added, from the works of an illustrious contemporary :

'This is the only witchcraft I have used ;'

and none could have been more effectual.

A ludicrous idea is obtained from the following anecdote of the estimation in which the wisdom of the Earl of Haddington was held by the king, and at the same time, perhaps, of that singular monarch's usual mode of speech. It must be understood, by way of prefatory illustration, that King James, who was the author of the earl's popular appellation, ' *Tam o' the Cowgate*,' had a custom of bestowing such ridiculous *sobriquets* on his principal councillors and courtiers. Thus he conferred upon that grave and sagacious statesman, John, Earl of Mar, the nickname *Jock o' Sklates*—probably in allusion to some circumstance which occurred in their young days when they were the fellow-pupils of Buchanan. On hearing of a meditated alliance between the Haddington and Mar families, His Majesty exclaimed, betwixt jest and earnest : 'The Lord haud a grup o' me! If Tam o' the Cowgate's son marry Jock o' Sklates's daughter, what's to come o' *me?*' The good-natured monarch probably apprehended that so close a union betwixt two of his most subtle statesmen might make them too much for their master—as hounds are most dangerous when they hunt in couples.

The Earl of Haddington died in 1637, full of years and honours. At Tyningham, the seat of his family, there are two portraits of his lordship, one a half-length, the other a head; as also his state-dress; and it is a circumstance too characteristic to be overlooked that in the crimson-velvet breeches there are no fewer than *nine pockets!* Among many of the earl's papers which remain in Tyningham House, one contains a memorandum conveying a curious idea of the way in which public and political affairs were then managed in Scotland. The paper details the heads of a petition in his own handwriting to the Privy Council, and at the end is a note 'to *gar* [that is, make] the chancellor' do something else in his behalf.

A younger son of Tam o' the Cowgate was a person of much ingenuity, and was popularly known, for what reason I cannot tell, by the nickname of 'Dear Sandie Hamilton.' He had a foundry in the Potterrow, where he fabricated the cannon employed in the first Covenanting war in 1639. This artillery, be it remarked, was not formed exclusively of metal. The greater part of the composition was leather; and yet, we are informed, they did some considerable execution at the battle of Newburnford, above Newcastle (August 28, 1640), where the Scots drove a large advanced party of Charles I.'s troops before them, thereby causing the king to enter into a new treaty. The cannon, which were commonly called 'Dear Sandie's Stoups,' were carried in swivel fashion between two horses.

The Excise-office had been removed, about 1730, from the Parliament Square to the house occupied many years before by Tam o' the Cowgate. It afforded excellent accommodations for this important public office. The principal room on the second floor, towards the Cowgate, was a very superb one, having a stucco ceiling divided into square compartments, each of which contained some elegant device. To the rear of the house was a bowling-green, which the Commissioners of Excise let on lease to a person of the name of Thomson. In those days bowling was a much more prevalent amusement than now, being chiefly a favourite with the graver order of the citizens. There were then no fewer than three bowling-greens in the grounds around Heriot's Hospital; one in the Canongate, near the Tolbooth; another on the opposite side of the street; another immediately behind the palace of Holyrood House, where the Duke of York used to play when in Scotland; and perhaps several others scattered about the outskirts of the town. The arena behind the Excise-office was called Thomson's Green, from the name of the man who kept it; and it may be worth while to remind the reader that it is alluded to in that pleasant-spirited poem by Allan Ramsay, in imitation of the *Vides ut alta* of Horace:

> ' Driving their ba's frae whins or tee,
> There 's no ae gouffer to be seen,
> Nor doucer folk wysing a-jee
> The byas bowls on Tamson's green.'

The green was latterly occupied by the relict of this Thomson; and among the bad debts on the Excise books, all of which are yearly brought forward and enumerated, there still stands a sum of something more than six pounds against Widow Thomson, being the last half-year's rent of *the green*, which the poor woman had been unable to pay. The north side of Brown's Square was built upon part of this space of ground; the rest remained a vacant area for the recreation of the people dwelling in Merchant Street, until the erection of the bridge, which has overrun that, as well as every other part of the scene of this article.*

* Near by is the Magdalen Chapel, a curious relic of the sixteenth century, belonging to the Corporation of Hammermen. It was erected immediately before the Reformation by a pious citizen, Michael Macquhan, and Jonet Rhynd, his widow, whose tomb is shown in the floor. The windows towards the south were anciently filled with stained glass; and there still remain some specimens of that kind of ornament, which, by some strange chance, had survived the Reformation. In a large department at the top of one window are the arms of Mary of Guise, who was queen-regent at the time the chapel was built. The arms of Macquhan and his wife are also to be seen. In the lower panes, which have been filled with small figures of saints, only one remains—a St Bartholomew—who, by a rare chance, has survived the general massacre. The whole is now very carefully preserved. When the distinguished Reformer, John Craig, returned to Scotland at the Reformation, after an absence of twenty-four years, he preached for some time in this chapel, in the Latin language, to a select congregation of the learned, being unable, by long disuse, to hold forth in his vernacular tongue. This divine subsequently was appointed a colleague to John Knox, and is distinguished in history for having refused to publish the banns between Queen Mary and Bothwell, and also for having written the National Covenant in 1589. Another circumstance in the history of this chapel is worthy of notice. The body of the Earl of Argyll, after his execution, June 30, 1685, was brought down and deposited in this place, to wait till it should be conveyed to the family burying-place at Kilmun.

ST CECILIA'S HALL.

FEW persons now living (1847) recollect the elegant concerts that were given many years ago in what is now an obscure part of our ancient city, known by the name of St Cecilia's Hall. They did such honour to Edinburgh, nearly for half a century, that I feel myself called on to make a brief record of them, and am glad to be enabled to do so by a living authority, one of the most fervent worshippers in the temple of the goddess. Hear, then, his last *aria parlante* on this interesting theme.

'The concerts of St Cecilia's Hall formed one of the most liberal and attractive amusements that any city in Europe could boast of. The hall was built on purpose at the foot of Niddry's Wynd, by a number of public-spirited noblemen and gentlemen ; and the expense of the concerts was defrayed by about two hundred subscribers paying two or three guineas each annually ; and so respectable was the institution considered, that upon the death of a member there were generally several applications for the vacancy, as is now the case with the Caledonian Hunt. The concerts were managed by a governor and a set of six or more directors, who engaged the performers—the principal ones from Italy, one or two from Germany, and the rest of the orchestra was made up of English and native artists. The concerts were given weekly during most of the time that I attended ; the instrumental music consisting chiefly of the concertos of Corelli and Handel, and the overtures of Bach, Abel, Stamitz, Vanhall, and latterly of Haydn and Pleyel ; for at that time, and till a good many years after, the magnificent symphonies of Haydn, Mozart, and Beethoven, which now form the most

St Cecilia's Hall.

attractive portions of all public concerts, had not reached this country. Those truly grand symphonies do not seem likely to be superseded by any similar compositions for a century to come, transcending so immensely, as they do, all the orchestral compositions that ever before appeared; yet I must not venture to prophesy, when I bear in mind what a powerful influence fashion and folly exercise upon music, as well as upon other objects of taste. When the overtures and quartettes of Haydn first found their way into this country, I well remember with what coldness the former were received by most of the grave Handelians, while at the theatres they gave delight. The old concert gentlemen said that his compositions wanted the solidity and full harmony of Handel and Corelli; and when the celebrated leader—the elder Cramer—visited St Cecilia's Hall, and played a spirited charming overture of Haydn's, an old amateur next to whom I was seated asked me: "Whase music is that, now?" "Haydn's, sir," said I. "Poor new-fangled stuff," he replied; "I hope I shall never hear it again!" Many years have since rolled away, and mark what some among us now say: A friend, calling lately on an old lady much in the fashionable circle of society, heard her give directions to the pianist who was teaching her nieces to bring them some new and fashionable pieces of music, but no more of the *unfashionable* compositions of Haydn! Alas for those ladies whose taste in music is regulated by fashion, and who do not know that the music of Haydn is the admiration and delight of all the real lovers and judges of the art in Europe!

'The vocal department of our concerts consisted chiefly of the songs of Handel, Arne, Gluck, Sarti, Jornelli, Guglielmi, Paisiello, Scottish songs, &c.; and every year, generally, we had an oratorio of Handel performed, with the assistance of a principal bass and a tenor singer, and a few chorus-singers from the English cathedrals; together with some Edinburgh amateurs,* who cultivated that sacred and sublime music; Signor and Signora Domenico Corri, the latter our *prima donna*, singing most of the principal songs, or most interesting portions of the music. On such occasions the hall was always crowded to excess by a splendid

* The amateurs who took the lead as choristers were Gilbert Innes, Esq. of Stow; Alexander Wight, Esq., advocate; Mr John Hutton, papermaker; Mr John Russel, W.S.; and Mr George Thomson. As an instrumentalist, we could boast of our countryman the Earl of Kelly, who also composed six overtures for an orchestra, one of which I heard played in the hall, himself leading the band.

assemblage, including all the beauty and fashion of our city. A supper to the directors and their friends at Fortune's Tavern generally followed the oratorio, where the names of the chief beauties who had graced the hall were honoured by their healths being drunk : the champion of the lady whom he proposed as his toast being sometimes challenged to maintain the pre-eminence of her personal charms by the admirer of another lady filling a glass of double depth to her health, and thus forcing the champion of the first lady to *say more* by drinking a still deeper bumper in honour of her beauty ; and if this produced a rejoinder from the other, by his seizing and quaffing the cup of *largest* calibre, there the contest generally ended, and the deepest drinker *saved* his lady, as it was phrased, although he might have had some difficulty in saving himself from a flooring while endeavouring to regain his seat.* Miss Burnet of Monboddo and Miss Betsy Home, reigning beauties of the time, were said more than once to have been the innocent cause of the fall of man in this way. The former was gifted with a countenance of heavenly sweetness and expression, which Guido, had he beheld it, would have sought to perpetuate upon canvas as that of an angel ; while the other lady, quite piquant and brilliant, might have sat to Titian for a Hebe or one of the Graces. Miss Burnet died in the bloom of youth, universally regretted both for her personal charms and the rare endowments of her mind. Miss Home was happily married to Captain Brown, her ardent admirer, who had made her his *toast* for years, and vowed he would continue to do so till he toasted her *Brown*. This sort of exuberant loyalty to beauty was by no means uncommon at the convivial meetings of those days, when " time had not thinned our flowing hair, nor bent us with his iron hand."

'Let me call to mind a few of those whose lovely faces at the concerts gave us the sweetest zest for the music. Miss Cleghorn of Edinburgh, still living in single-blessedness ; Miss Chalmers of Pittencrief, who married Sir William Miller of Glenlee, Bart. ; Miss Jessie Chalmers of Edinburgh, who was married to Mr Pringle of Haining ; Miss Hay of Hayston, who married Sir William Forbes of Pitsligo, Bart. ; Miss Murray of Lintrose, who was called the *Flower of Strathmore*, and upon whom Burns wrote the song :

> " Blithe, blithe, and merry was she,
> Blithe was she but and ben ;
> Blithe by the banks of the Earn,
> And blithe in Glenturit Glen."

* See a different account of this custom, p. 147.

She married David Smith, Esq. of Methven, one of the Lords of Session; Miss Jardine of Edinburgh, who married Mr Home Drummond of Blairdrummond—their daughter, if I mistake not, is now the Duchess of Athole; Miss Kinloch of Gilmerton, who married Sir Foster Cunliffe of Acton, Bart.; Miss Lucy Johnston of East Lothian, who married Mr Oswald of Auchincruive; Miss Halket of Pitferran, who became the wife of the celebrated Count Lally-Tollendal; and Jane, Duchess of Gordon, celebrated for her wit and spirit, as well as for her beauty. These, with Miss Burnet and Miss Home, and many others whose names I do not distinctly recollect, were indisputably worthy of all the honours conferred upon them. But beauty has tempted me to digress too long from my details relative to the hall and its concerts, to which I return.

'The hall [built in 1762 from a design of Mr Robert Mylne, after the model of the great opera theatre of Parma] was an exact oval, having a concave elliptical ceiling, and was remarkable for the clear and perfect conveyance of sounds, without responding echoes, as well as for the judicious manner in which the seating was arranged. In this last respect, I have seen no concert-room equal to it either in London or Paris. The orchestra was erected at the upper end of the hall, opposite to the door of entrance; a portion of the area, in the centre or widest part, was without any seats, and served as a small promenade, where friends could chat together during the intervals of performance. The seats were all *fixed* down on both sides of the hall, and each side was raised by a gradual elevation from the level area, backward, the rows of seats behind each other, till they reached a passage a few feet broad, that was carried quite round the hall behind the last of the elevated seats; so that when the audience was seated, each half of it fronted the other—an arrangement much preferable to that commonly adopted, of placing all the seats upon a *level* behind each other, for thus the whole company must look one way, and see each other's *backs*. A private staircase at the upper end of the hall, not seen by the company, admitted the musicians into the orchestra; in the front of which stood a harpsichord, with the singers, and the principal violoncellist; and behind these, on a platform a little elevated, were the violins, and other stringed and wind instruments, just behind which stood a noble organ. The hall, when filled, contained an audience of about four hundred. No money was taken for admission, tickets being given gratis to the lovers of music, and to strangers. What a pity that such a liberal and gratifying institution should have ceased to exist!

But after the New Town arose, the Old was deserted by the upper classes: the hall was too small for the increased population, and concerts were got up at the Assembly Rooms and Corri's Rooms by the professional musicians, and by Corri himself. Now a capacious Music Hall is erected behind the Assembly Rooms, where a pretty good subscription concert is carried on; and from the increased facility of intercourse between Paris, London, and Edinburgh, it seems probable that concerts by artists of the highest talents will ere long be set on foot in Edinburgh in this fine hall, diversified sometimes by oratorios or Italian operas.

'Before concluding this brief memoir of St Cecilia's Hall Concerts, I shall mention the chief performers who gave attractions to them. These were Signor and Signora Domenico Corri, from Rome; he with a falsetto voice, which he managed with much skill and taste; the signora with a fine, full-toned, flexible soprano voice. Tenducci, though not one of the band, nor resident among us, made his appearance occasionally when he came to visit the Hopetoun family, his liberal and steady patrons; and while he remained he generally gave some concerts at the hall, which made quite a sensation among the musicals. I considered it a jubilee year whenever Tenducci arrived, as no singer I ever heard sang with more expressive simplicity, or was more efficient, whether he sang the classical songs of Metastasio, or those of Arne's *Artaxerxes*, or the simple melodies of Scotland. To the latter he gave such intensity of interest by his impassioned manner, and by his clear enunciation of the words, as equally surprised and delighted us. I never can forget the pathos and touching effect of his *Gilderoy*, *Lochaber no more*, *The Braes of Ballenden*, *I'll never leave thee*, *Roslin Castle*, &c. These, with the *Verdi prati* of Handel, *Fair Aurora* from Arne's *Artaxerxes*, and Gluck's *Che faro*, were above all praise. Miss Poole, Mr Smeaton, Mr Gilson, and Mr Urbani were also for a time singers at the hall—chiefly of English and Scottish songs.

'In the instrumental department we had Signor Puppo, from Rome or Naples, as leader and violin concerto player, a most capital artist; Mr Schetky, from Germany, the principal violon-cellist, and a fine solo concerto player; Joseph Reinagle, a very clever violoncello and viola player; Mr Barnard, a very elegant violinist; Stephen Clarke, an excellent organist and harpsichord player; and twelve or fifteen violins, basses, flutes, violas, horns, and clarionets, with extra performers often from London. Upon the resignation of Puppo, who charmed all hearers, Stabilini succeeded him, and held the situation till the institution was at an end : he had a good round tone, though, to my apprehension, he did not exceed mediocrity as a performer.

'But I should be unpardonable if I omitted to mention the most accomplished violin-player I ever heard, Paganini only excepted—I mean Giornovicki, who possessed in a most extraordinary degree the various requisites of his beautiful art : execution peculiarly brilliant, and finely articulated as possible ; a tone of the richest and most exquisite quality ; expression of the utmost delicacy, grace, and tenderness ; and an animation that commanded your most intense and eager attention. Paganini did not appear in Edinburgh till [thirty years] after the hall was closed. There, as well as at private parties, I heard Giornovicki often, and always with no less delight than I listened to Paganini.* Both, if I may use the expression, threw their whole hearts and souls into their Cremonas, bows, and fingers.

"Hall of sweet sounds, adieu, with all thy fascinations of langsyne,
 My dearest reminiscences of music all are thine."'

G. T. Octogenarius Edinburgensis, Feb. 1847.†

Stabilini, to whom our dear G. T. refers, and who died in 1815, much broken down by dissipation, was obliged, against his will, to give frequent attendance at the private concerts of one of these gentlemen performers, where Corelli's trios were in great vogue. There was always a capital supper afterwards, at which Stab (so he was familiarly called) ate and drank for any two. A waggish

---

* ['John M. Giornovicki, commonly known in Britain under the name of Jarnowick, was a native of Palermo. About 1770 he went to Paris, where he performed a concerto of his famous master Lolli, but did not succeed. He then played one of his own concertos, that in A major, and became quite the fashion. The style of Giornovicki was highly elegant and finished, his intonation perfect, and his taste pure. The late Domenico Dragonetti, one of the best judges in Europe, told me that Giornovicki was the most elegant and graceful violin-player he had ever heard before Paganini, but that he wanted power. He seems to have been a dissipated and passionate man ; a good swordsman too, as was common in those days. One day, in a dispute, he struck the Chevalier St George, then one of the greatest violin-players and best swordsmen in Europe. St George said coolly : "I have too much regard for his musical talent to fight him." A noble speech, showing St George in all respects the better man. Giornovicki died suddenly at St Petersburg in 1804.'—G. F. G.]

† G. T., it may now be explained, was George Thomson, the well-known and generally loved editor of the *Melodies of Scotland*. He might rather have described himself as *Nonogenarius*, for at his death, in 1851, he had reached the age of ninety-four, his violin, as he believed, having prolonged his life much beyond the usual term.

friend, who knew his opinion of Edinburgh amateurs, meeting him next day, would ask : ' Well, Mr Stabilini, what sort of music had you the other night at —— ——'s ? '

' Vera good soaper, sir ; vera good soaper ! '

' But tell us the verse you made about one of these parties.'

Stabilini, twitching up his shirt-collar, a common trick of his, would say :

> ' A piece ov toarkey for a hungree bellee
> Is moatch sup*eer*ior to Corelli ! '

The accent, the manner, the look with which this was delivered, is said to have been beyond expression rich.

It is quite remarkable, when we consider the high character of the popular melodies, how late and slow has been the introduction of a taste for the higher class of musical compositions into Scotland. The Earl of Kelly, a man of yesterday, was the first Scotsman who ever composed music for an orchestra.* This fact seems sufficient. It is to be feared that the beauty of the melodies is itself partly to be blamed for the indifference to higher music. There is too great a disposition to rest with the distinction thus conferred upon the nation ; too many are content to go no further for the enjoyments which music has to give. It would be well if, while not forgetting those beautiful simple airs, we were more generally to open our minds to the still richer charms of the German and the Italian muses.

---

* The earl was the leader of the amateur orchestra of St Cecilia's Hall, which included Lord Colville, Sir John Pringle, Mr Seton of Pitmedden, General Middleton, Lord Elcho, Sir Gilbert Elliot, Mrs Forbes of Newhall, and others of the aristocracy. General Middleton was credited with 'singing a song with much humour,' which he sometimes accompanied with a key and tongs. Sir Gilbert Elliot, who played the German flute, was the first to introduce that instrument to a Scottish audience. St Cecilia's Hall has passed through many vicissitudes since then, and is now a bookbinder's warehouse, but its fine ceiling and the orchestral balcony at the southern end are still preserved as memorials of its early days.

THE MURDER OF DARNLEY.

WHILE this event is connected with one of the most problematical points in our own history, or that of any other nation, it chances that the whole topography of the affair is very distinctly recorded. We know not only the exact spot where the deed was perpetrated, but almost every foot of the ground over which the perpetrators walked on their way to execute it. It is chiefly by reason of the depositions and confessions brought out by the legal proceedings against the inferior instruments that this minute knowledge is attained.

The house in which the unfortunate victim resided at the time was one called the Prebendaries' Chamber, being part of the suite of domestic buildings connected with the collegiate church of St-Mary-in-the-Fields (usually called the *Kirk o' Field*). Darnley was brought to lodge here on the 30th of January 1566-7. He had contracted the smallpox at Glasgow, and it was thought necessary, or pretended to be thought necessary, to lodge him in this place for air, as also to guard against infecting the infant prince, his son, who was lodged in Holyrood House. The house, which then belonged, by gift, to a creature of the Earl of Bothwell, has been described as so very mean as to excite general surprise. Yet, speaking by comparison, it does not appear to have been a bad temporary lodging for a person in Darnley's circumstances. It consisted of two stories, with a *turnpike* or spiral staircase behind. The gable adjoined to the town-wall, which there ran in a line east and west, and the cellar had a postern opening through that wall. In the upper floor were a chamber and closet, with a little gallery having a window also through the town-wall.* Here

---

* About seventy paces to the east of the site of the Prebendaries' Chamber, and exactly opposite to the opening of Roxburgh Place, was a projection in the wall, which has been long demolished and the wall altered. Close, however, to the west of the place, and near the ground, are some remains of an arch in the wall, which Malcolm Laing supposes to have been a gun-port connected with the projection at this spot. It certainly has no connection, as Arnot and (after him) Whitaker have supposed, with the story of Darnley's murder. [This relic of the Flodden wall is now removed, but a portion of the wall itself still stands behind the houses at the north-east junction of Drummond Street and the Pleasance. Another portion was recently discovered at the

Darnley was deposited in an old purple travelling-bed. Underneath his room was an apartment in which the queen slept for one or two nights before the murder took place. On the night of Sunday, February 9, she was attending upon her husband in his sick-room, when the servants of the Earl of Bothwell deposited the powder in her room, immediately under the king's bed. The queen afterwards took her leave, in order to attend the wedding of two of her servants at the palace.

It appears, from the confessions of the wretches executed for this foul deed, that as they returned from depositing the powder they saw ' the Queenes grace gangand before thame with licht torches up the Black Frier Wynd.' On their returning to Bothwell's lodging at the palace, that nobleman prepared himself for the deed by changing his gay suit of ' hose, stockit with black velvet, passemented with silver, and doublett of black satin of the same maner,' for ' ane uther pair of black hose,* and ane canvas doublet white, and tuke his syde [long] riding-cloak about him, of sad English claith, callit the new colour.' He then went, attended by Paris, the queen's servant, Powry, his own porter, Pate Wilson, and George Dalgleish, ' downe the turnepike altogedder, and along the bak of the Queene's garden, till you come to the bak of the cunyie-house [mint], and the bak of the stabbillis, till you come to the Canongate fornent the Abbey zett.' After passing up the Canongate, and gaining entry with some difficulty by the Netherbow Port, ' thai gaid up abone Bassentyne's hous on the south side of the gait,† and knockit at ane door beneath the sword slippers, and callit for the laird of Ormistounes, and one within answerit he was not thair ; and thai passit down a cloiss beneath the Frier Wynd [*apparently Toddrick's Wynd*], and enterit in at the zett of the Black Friers, till thay came to the back wall and dyke of the town-wall, whair my lord and Paris past in over the wall.' The explosion took place soon after, about two in the morning. The earl then came back to his attendants at this spot, and ' thai past all away togidder out at the Frier zett, and sinderit in the Cowgait.' It is here evident that the alley now called the High School Wynd was the avenue by which the conspirators approached

east end of Lothian Street, between that street and the Royal Scottish Museum. Another part forms the north side of a *cul de sac* at Lindsay Place, and at the Vennel is the largest part of this old wall, with one of its few towers, forming the western boundary of the grounds of Heriot's Hospital.]

* Hose in those days covered the whole of the lower part of the person.

† This indicates pretty nearly the site of the house of Bassendyne, the early printer. It must have been opposite, or nearly opposite, to the Fountain Well.

the scene of their atrocity. Bothwell himself, with part of his attendants, went up the same wynd 'be east the Frier Wynd,' and crossing the High Street, endeavoured to get out of the city by leaping a broken part of the town-wall in Leith Wynd, but finding

High School Wynd.

it too high, was obliged to rouse once more the porter at the Netherbow. They then passed—for every motion of the villains has a strange interest—down St Mary's Wynd, and along the south back of the Canongate to the earl's lodgings in the palace.

The house itself, by this explosion, was destroyed, '*even*,' as the queen tells in a letter to her ambassador in France, '*to the very grund-stane.*' The bodies of the king and his servant were found next morning in a garden or field on the outside of the town-wall. The buildings connected with the Kirk o' Field were afterwards converted into the College of King James, now our Edinburgh University. The hall of the Senatus in the new buildings occupies nearly the exact site of the Prebendaries' Chamber, the ruins of which are laid down in De Witt's map of 1648.

MINT CLOSE.

The Mint—Robert Cullen—Lord Chancellor Loughborough.

THE *Cunyie House*, as the Scottish Mint used to be called, was near Holyrood Palace in the days of Queen Mary. In the regency of Morton a large house was erected for it in the Cowgate, where it may still be seen,* with the following inscription over the door :

BE. MERCYFULL. TO. ME. O. GOD.   1574.

In the reign of Charles II. other buildings were added behind, forming a neat quadrangle ; and here was the Scottish coin produced till the Union, when a separate coinage was given up and this establishment abandoned ; though, to gratify prejudice, the offices were still kept up as sinecures. This court with its buildings was a sanctuary for persons prosecuted for debt, as was the King's Stables, a mean place at the west end of the Grassmarket. There was, however, a small den near the top of the oldest building, lighted by a small window looking up the Cowgate, which was used as a jail for debtors or other delinquents condemned by the Mint's own officers.

In the western portion of the old building, accessible by a stair from the court, is a handsome room with an alcove ceiling, and lighted by two handsomely proportioned windows, which is known to have been the council-room of the Mint, being a portion of the private mansion of the master. Here, in May 1590, on a Sunday evening, the town of Edinburgh entertained the Danish lords who accompanied James VI. and his queen from her native court— namely, Peter Monk, the admiral of Denmark ; Stephen Brahe, captain of Eslinburg [perhaps a relative of Tycho ?] ; Braid Ransome Maugaret ; Nicholaus Theophilus, Doctor of Laws ; Henry Goolister, captain of Bocastle ; William Vanderwent ; and some others. For this banquet, 'maid in Thomas Aitchinsoune, master of the cunyie-house lugeing,' it was ordered 'that the thesaurer caus by and lay in foure punsheouns wyne ; John Borthuik baxter

* Now removed and the site built over. There was also a Cunyie House in Candlemaker Row, which was used as the Mint during the regency of Mary of Guise.

to get four bunnis of beir, with foure gang of aill, and to furneis breid ; Henry Charteris and Roger Macnacht to caus hing the hous with tapestrie, set the burdis, furmis, chandleris [*candlesticks*], and get flowris ; George Carketill and Rychert Doby to provyde the cupbuirds and men to keep thame ; and my Lord Provest was content to provyde naprie and twa dozen greit veschell, and to avance ane hunder pund or mair, as thai sall haif a do.'

In the latter days of the Mint as an active establishment, the coining-house was in the ground-floor of the building, on the north side of the court ; in the adjoining house, on the east side, was the finishing-house, where the money was polished and fitted for circulation. The chief instruments used in coining were a hammer and steel dies, upon which the device was engraved. The metal, being previously prepared of the proper fineness and thickness, was cut into longitudinal slips, and a square piece being cut from the slip, it was afterwards rounded and adjusted to the weight of the money to be made. The blank pieces of metal were then placed between two dies, and the upper one was struck with a hammer. After the Restoration another method was introduced—that of the mill and screw, which, modified by many improvements, is still in use. At the Union, the ceremony of destroying the dies of the Scottish coinage took place in the Mint. After being heated red-hot in a furnace, they were defaced by three impressions of a broad-faced *punch*, which were of course visible on the dies as long as they existed ; but it must be recorded that all these implements, which would now have been great curiosities, are lost, and none of the machinery remains but the press, which, weighing about half a ton, was rather too large to be readily appropriated, or perhaps it would have followed the rest.

The floors over the coining-house—bearing the letters, c. r. ii., surmounting a crown, and the legend, GOD SAVE THE KING, 1674, originally the mansion of the master—were latterly occupied by the eminent Dr Cullen, whose family were all born here, and who died here himself in 1792.

ROBERT CULLEN.

Robert Cullen, the son of the physician, made a great impression on Edinburgh society by his many delightful social qualities, and particularly his powers as a mimic of the Mathews genus. He manifested this gift in his earliest years, to the no small discomposure of his grave old father. One evening, when Dr Cullen was going to the theatre, Robert entreated to be taken along with him, but for some reason was condemned to remain at home. Some time after the departure of the doctor, Mrs Cullen heard him come along the passage, as if from his own room, and say at her door : 'Well, after all, you may let Robert go.' Robert was accordingly allowed to depart for the theatre, where his appearance gave no small surprise to his father. On the old gentleman coming home and remonstrating with his lady for allowing the boy to go, it was discovered that the voice which seemed to give the permission had proceeded from the young wag himself.

In maturer years, Cullen could not only mimic any voice or mode of speech, but enter so thoroughly into the nature of any man that he could supply exactly the ideas which he was likely to use. His imitations were therefore something much above mimicries—they were artistic representations of human character. He has been known in a social company, where another individual was expected, to stand up, in the character of that person, and return thanks for the proposal of his health ; and this was done so happily that when the individual did arrive and got upon his legs to speak for himself, the company was convulsed with an almost exact repetition of what Cullen had previously uttered, the manner also and every inflection of the voice being precisely alike. In relating anecdotes, of which he possessed a vast store, he usually prefaced them with a sketch of the character of the person referred to, which greatly increased the effect, as the story then told characteristically. These sketches were remarked to be extremely graphic and most elegantly expressed.

When a young man, residing with his father, he was very intimate with Dr Robertson, the Principal of the university. To show that Robertson was not likely to be easily imitated, it may be mentioned, from the report of a gentleman who has often heard him making public orations, that when the students observed him pause for a word, and would themselves mentally supply it, they invariably found that the word which he did use was different from that which they had hit upon. Cullen, however, could imitate him to the life, either in his more formal speeches or in his ordinary discourse. He would often, in entering a house which the Principal was in the habit of visiting, assume his voice in the lobby and stair, and when arrived at the drawing-room door, astonish the family by turning out to be—Bob Cullen. Lord Greville, a pupil of the Principal's, having been one night detained at a protracted debauch, where Cullen was also present, the latter gentleman next morning got admission to the bedroom of the young nobleman, where, personating Dr Robertson, he sat down by the bedside, and with all the manner of the reverend Principal, gave him a sound lecture for having been out so late last night. Greville, who had fully expected this visit, lay in remorseful silence, and allowed his supposed monitor to depart without saying a word. In the course of a quarter of an hour, however, when the real Dr Robertson entered, and commenced a harangue exactly duplicating that just concluded, he could not help exclaiming that it was *too bad* to give it him twice over. 'Oh, I see how it is,' said Robertson, rising to depart; 'that rogue Bob Cullen must have been with you.' The Principal became at length accustomed to Bob's tricks, which he would seem, from the following anecdote, to have regarded in a friendly spirit. Being attended during an illness by Dr Cullen, it was found necessary to administer a liberal dose of laudanum. The physician, however, asked him, in the first place, in what manner laudanum affected him. Having received his answer, Cullen remarked, with surprise, that he had never known any one affected in the same way by laudanum besides his son Bob. 'Ah,' said Robertson, '*does the rascal take me off there too?*'

Mr Cullen entered at the Scottish bar in 1764, and, distinguishing himself highly as a lawyer, was raised to the bench in 1796, when he took the designation of Lord Cullen. He cultivated elegant literature, and contributed some papers of acknowledged merit to the *Mirror* and *Lounger;* but it was in conversation that he chiefly shone.

The close adjoining to the Mint contains several old-fashioned houses of a dignified appearance. In a floor of one bearing the date 1679, and having a little court in front, Alexander Wedderburn, Earl of Rosslyn and Lord Chancellor of England, resided while at the Scottish bar. This, as is well known, was a very brief interval ; for a veteran barrister having one day used the term 'presumptuous boy' with reference to him, and his own caustic reply having drawn upon him a rebuke from the bench, he took off his gown, and making a bow, said he would never more plead where he was subjected to insult, but would seek a wider field for his exertions. His subsequent rapid rise at the English bar is matter of history. It is told that, returning to Edinburgh at the end of his life, after an absence of many years, he wished to see the house where he had lived while a Scotch advocate. Too infirm to walk, he was borne in a chair to the foot of the Mint Close to see this building. One thing he was particularly anxious about. While residing here, he had had five holes made in the little court to play at some bowling game of which he was fond. He wished, above all things, to see these holes once more, and when he found they were still there, he expressed much satisfaction. Churchill himself might have melted at such an anecdote of the old days of him who was

> 'Pert at the bar, and in the senate loud.'

About midway up the close is a turreted mansion, accessible from Hyndford's Close, and having a tolerably good garden connected with it. This was, in 1742, the residence of the Earl of Selkirk; subsequently it was occupied by Dr Daniel Rutherford, professor of botany. Sir Walter Scott, who, being a nephew of that gentleman, was often in the house in his young days, communicated to me a curious circumstance connected with it. It appears that the house immediately adjacent was not furnished with a stair wide enough to allow of a coffin being carried down in decent fashion. It had, therefore, what the Scottish law calls a *servitude* upon Dr Rutherford's house, conferring the perpetual liberty of bringing the deceased inmates through a passage into that house and down *its* stair into the lane.

GREYFRIARS' CHURCHYARD.

PAGE 288.

ST JOHN'S CLOSE.
Entrance to Canongate Kilwinning Mason Lodge.

MISS NICKY MURRAY.

THE dancing assemblies of Edinburgh were for many years, about the middle of the last century, under the direction and dictatorship of the Honourable Miss Nicky Murray, one of the sisters of the Earl of Mansfield. Much good sense, firmness, knowledge of the world and of the histories of individuals, as well as a due share of patience and benevolence, were required for this office of unrecognised though real power; and it was generally admitted that Miss Murray possessed the needful qualifications in a remarkable degree, though rather more marked by good manners than good-nature. She and her sisters lived for many years in a floor of a large building at the head of Bailie Fife's Close—a now unhallowed locality, where, I believe, Francis Jeffrey attended his first school. In their narrow mansion, the Miss Murrays received flights of young lady-cousins from the country, to be finished in their manners and introduced into society. No light task must theirs have been, all things considered. I find a highly significant note on the subject inserted by an old gentleman in an interleaved copy of my first edition: 'It was from Miss Nicky Murray's—a relation of the Gray family—that my father ran off with my mother, then not sixteen years old.'

The Assembly Room of that time was in the *close* where the Commercial Bank was afterwards established.* First there was a lobby, where chairs were disburdened of their company, and where a reduced gentleman, with pretensions to the title of Lord Kirkcudbright—descendant of the once great Maclellans of Galloway—might have been seen selling gloves; this being the person alluded to in a letter written by Goldsmith while a student in Edinburgh: ' One day, happening to slip into Lord Kilcobry's—don't be surprised, his lordship is only a glover!' The dancing-room opened directly from the lobby, and above stairs was a tea-room. The

---

* The Assembly Room, afterwards occupied by the Commercial Bank, was in Bell's Wynd, to which place it was removed in 1756 from the older room in Assembly Close. A scallop-shell above the entrance to Bell's Wynd long commemorated the site of the Clamshell Turnpike, the lodging of the Earl of Home, to which Queen Mary, accompanied by Darnley, retreated on their return from Dunbar in 1566, rather than enter Holyrood so soon after the murder of Rizzio.

former had a railed space in the centre, within which the dancers were arranged, while the spectators sat round on the outside ; and no communication was allowed between the different sides of this sacred pale. The lady-directress had a high chair or throne at one end. Before Miss Nicky Murray, Lady Elliot of Minto and Mrs Brown of Coalstoun, wives of judges, had exercised this lofty authority, which was thought honourable on account of the charitable object of the assemblies. The arrangements were of a rigid character, and certainly tending to dullness. There being but one set allowed to dance at a time, it was seldom that any person was twice on the floor in one night. The most of the time was spent in acting the part of lookers-on, which threw great duties in the way of conversation upon the gentlemen. These had to settle with a partner for the year, and were upon no account permitted to change, even for a single night. The appointment took place at the beginning of the season, usually at some private party or ball given by a person of distinction, where the fans of the ladies were all put into a gentleman's cocked hat : the gentlemen put in their hands and took a fan, and to whomsoever the fan belonged, that was to be his partner for the season. In the general rigours of this system, which sometimes produced ludicrous combinations, there was, however, one palliative—namely, the fans being all distinguishable from each other, and the gentleman being in general as well acquainted with the fan as the face of his mistress, and the hat being open, it was possible to peep in, and exercise, to a certain extent, a principle of selection whereby he was perhaps successful in procuring an appointment to his mind. All this is spiritedly given in a poem of Sir Alexander Boswell :

> 'Then were the days of modesty of mien !
> Stays for the fat, and quilting for the lean ;
> The ribboned stomacher, in many a plait,
> Upheld the chest, and dignified the gait ;
> Some Venus, brightest planet of the train,
> Moved in a lustering *halo*, propped with cane.
> Then the *Assembly Close* received the fair—
> Order and elegance presided there—
> Each gay Right Honourable had her place,
> To walk a minuet with becoming grace.
> No racing to the dance, with rival hurry—
> Such was thy sway, O famed Miss Nicky Murray !
> Each lady's fan a chosen Damon bore,
> With care selected many a day before ;
> For, unprovided with a favourite beau,
> The nymph, chagrined, the ball must needs forego ;

But, previous matters to her taste arranged,
Certes, the constant couple never changed ;
Through a long night, to watch fair Delia's will,
The same dull swain was at her elbow still.'

A little before Miss Nicky's time, it was customary for gentlemen to walk alongside the chairs of their partners, with their
swords by their sides, and so escort them home. They called
next afternoon upon their Dulcineas to inquire how they were
and drink tea. The fashionable time for seeing company in those
days was the evening, when people were all abroad upon the street,
as in the forenoon now, making calls and *shopping*. The people
who attended the assemblies were very *select*. Moreover, they
were all known to each other ; and the introduction of a stranger
required nice preliminaries. It is said that Miss Murray, on
hearing a young lady's name pronounced for the first time, would
say : ' Miss ——, of what ? ' If no territorial addition could be
made, she manifestly cooled. Upon one occasion, seeing a man at
the assembly who was born in a low situation and raised to wealth
in some humble trade, she went up to him, and, without the least
deference to his fine-laced coat, taxed him with presumption in
coming there, and turned him out of the room.

Major Topham praises the regularity and propriety observed at
the assemblies, though gently insinuating their heaviness. He says :
' I was never at an assembly where the authority of the manager
was so observed or respected. With the utmost politeness, affa-
bility, and good-humour, Miss Murray attends to every one. All
petitions are heard, and demands granted, which appear reasonable.
The company is so much the more obliged to Miss Murray, as the
task is by no means to be envied. The crowd which immediately
surrounds her on entering the room, the impetuous applications
of *chaperons*, maiden-aunts, and the earnest entreaties of lovers to
obtain a ticket in one of the first sets for the dear object, render
the fatigue of the office of lady-directress almost intolerable.' *

* It must have been after Miss Nicky Murray's day that an Edinburgh
Writer to the Signet, describing the unruliness of an assembly, writes : ' I saw
an English lady stand up at the head of a sett with a ticket No. 1 of that sett.
By-and-bye my namesake, Miss Mary ——, came up, hauling after her a
foolish-looking young man, who did as he was bid, and with all the ease in the
world placed herself above the stranger, No. 1. The lady politely said there
must be some mistake, for she had that place. "No," said Miss Mary, "I can't
help your ticket, for I have the Lady Directress's permission to lead down the
sett !' The lady had spunk, and scolded, for which I liked her the better ;
only she dealt her sarcasms about Scotch politeness, Edinburgh manners, and
so forth, rather too liberally and too loudly.'

Early hours were kept in those days, and the stinted time was never exceeded. When the proper hour arrived for dissolving the party, and the young people would crowd round the throne to petition for one other set, up rose Miss Nicky in unrelenting rigidity of figure, and with one wave of her hand silenced the musicians :

> 'Quick from the summit of the grove they fell,
> And left it inharmonious.'

[THE BISHOP'S LAND.

ON the north side of the High Street, a hundred yards or so below the North Bridge, there existed previous to 1813 an unusually large and handsome old *land* or building named the *Bishop's Land.* It rested upon an arcade or *piazza*, as it is called, and the entry in the first floor bore the ordinary legend:

BLISSIT BE ZE LORD FOR ALL HIS GIFTIS,

together with the date 1578, and a shield impaled with two coats of arms. Along the front of this floor was a balcony composed of brass, a thing unique in the ancient city. The house had been the Edinburgh residence of Archbishop John Spottiswood. Most unfortunately the whole line of building towards the street was burned down in the year 1813.

In the latter part of the last century the Bishop's Land was regarded as a very handsome residence, and it was occupied accordingly by persons of consideration. The dictum of an old citizen to me many years ago was: 'Nobody without livery-servants lived in the Bishop's Land.' Sir Stuart Threipland of Fingask occupied the first floor. His estate, forfeited by his father in 1716, was purchased back by him, with money obtained through his wife, in 1784; and the title, which was always given to him by courtesy, was restored as a reality to his descendants by George IV. He had himself been engaged in the affair of 1745-6, and had accompanied 'the Prince' in some part of his wanderings. In the hands of this 'fine old *Scottish* gentleman,' for such he was, his house in the Bishop's Land was elegantly furnished, there being in particular some well-painted portraits of royal personages—*not of the reigning house.* These had all been sent to his father and himself by the persons represented in them, who thus showed their gratitude for efforts made and sufferings incurred in their behalf. There were five windows to the street, three of them lighting the drawing-room; the remaining two lighted the eldest son's room. A dining-room, Sir Stuart's bedroom, his sister Janet's (who kept house for him) room, and other apartments were in the rear, some lighted from the adjacent close—and these still exist, having been spared by the fire. The kitchen and servants' rooms were below.

In the next floor above lived the Hamiltons of Pencaitland ; in the next again, the Aytouns of Inchdairnie. Mrs Aytoun, who was a daughter of Lord Rollo, would sometimes come down the stair in a winter evening, lighting herself with a little wax-taper, to drink tea with *Mrs* Janet Threipland, for so she called herself, though unmarried. In the uppermost floor of all lived a reputable tailor and his family. All the various tenants, including the tailor, were on good neighbourly terms with each other ; a pleasant thing to tell of this bit of the old world, which has left nothing of the same kind behind it in these later days, when we all live at a greater distance, physical and moral, from each other.]

JOHN KNOX'S MANSE.

THE lower portion of the High Street, including *the Netherbow*, was, till a recent time, remarkable for the antiquity of the greater number of the buildings, insomuch that no equal portion of the city was more distinctly a memorial of the general appearance of the whole as it was in the sixteenth and seventeenth centuries. On the north side of the High Street, immediately adjacent to the Netherbow, there was a nest of tall wooden-fronted houses of one character, and the age of which generally might be guessed from the date existing upon one—1562. This formed a perfect example of the *High Gait* as it appeared to Queen Mary, excepting that the open booths below had been converted into close shops. The *fore-stairs*—that is, outside stairs ascending to the *first floor* (technically so called), from which the women of Edinburgh reviled the hapless queen as she rode along the street after her surrender at Carberry — were unchanged in this little district.

The popular story regarding houses of this kind is that they took their origin in an inconvenience which was felt in having the Boroughmoor covered with wood, as it proved from that circumstance a harbour for robbers. To banish the robbers, it was necessary to extirpate the wood. To get this done, the magistrates granted leave to the citizens to project their house-fronts seven feet into the street, provided they should execute the work with timber cut from the Boroughmoor. Robert Fergusson follows up this story in a burlesque poem by relating how, consequently,

> ' Edina's mansions with lignarian art
> Were piled and fronted. Like an ark she seemed
> To lie on mountain's top, with shapes replete,
> Clean and unclean——
> To Jove the Dryads prayed, nor prayed in vain,
> For vengeance on her sons. At midnight drear
> Black showers descend, and teeming myriads rise
> Of bugs abhorrent '——

The only authentic information to be obtained on the point is presented by Maitland, when he tells us that the clearing of the Boroughmoor of timber took place in consequence of a charter from James IV. in 1508. He says nothing of robbers, but attributes the permission granted by the magistrates for the making of wooden projections merely to their desire of getting sale for their timber. After all, I am inclined to trace this fashion to taste. The wooden fronts appear to have originated in open galleries—an arrangement often spoken of in early writings. These, being closed up or formed into a range of windows, would produce the wooden-fronted house. It is remarkable that the wooden fronts do not in many instances bear the appearance of afterthoughts, as the stone structure within often shows such an arrangement of the fore wall as seems designed to connect the projecting part with the chambers within, or to give these chambers as much as possible of the borrowed light. At the same time, it is somewhat puzzling to find, in the closes below the buildings, gateways with hooks for hinges seven feet or so from the present street-front—an arrangement which does not appear necessary on the supposition that the houses were built designedly with a stone interior and a wooden projection.

In the Netherbow the street receives a contraction from the advance of the houses on the north side, thus closing a species of parallelogram, of which the Luckenbooths formed the upper extremity—the market-place of our ancient city. The uppermost of the prominent houses — having of course two fronts meeting in a right angle, one fronting to the line of street, the other looking up the High Street—is pointed to by tradition as the residence or manse of John Knox during his incumbency as minister of Edinburgh, from 1560 till (with few interruptions) his death in 1572. It is a picturesque building of three aboveground floors, constructed of substantial ashlar masonry, but on a somewhat small scale, and terminating in curious gables and masses of chimneys. A narrow door, right in the angle, gives access to a small room, lighted by one long window presented to the westward, and apparently the *hall* of the mansion in former times. Over the window and door is this legend, in an unusually old kind of lettering :

LVFE · GOD · ABVFE · AL · AND · YI · NYCHTBOVR · [AS ·] YI · SELF·

The word 'as' is obliterated. The words are, in modern English, simply the well-known scriptural command : 'Love God above all, and thy neighbour as thyself.' Perched upon the corner above the door is a small effigy of the Reformer, preaching in a pulpit, and pointing with his right hand to a stone above his head in that direction, which presents in rude sculpture the sun bursting from clouds, with the name of the Deity inscribed on his disc in three languages :

ΘΕΟΣ
DEUS
GOD

Dr M'Crie, in his *Life of John Knox*, states that the Reformer, on commencing duty in Edinburgh at the conclusion of the struggles with the queen-regent, 'lodged in the house of David Forrest, a burgess of Edinburgh, from which he removed to the lodging which had belonged to Durie, Abbot of Dunfermline.' The magistrates acted liberally towards their minister, giving him a salary of two hundred pounds Scottish money, and paying his house-rent for him, at the rate of fifteen merks yearly. In October 1561 they ordained the Dean of Guild, ' with al diligence, to mak ane warm studye of dailles to the minister, Johne Knox, within his hous, aboue the hall of the same, with lyht and wyndokis thereunto, and all uther necessaris.' This study is generally supposed to have been a very small wooden projection, of the kind described a few pages back, still seen on the front of the *first floor*. Close to it is a window in the angle of the building, from which Knox is said by tradition to have occasionally held forth to multitudes below.

The second floor, which is accessible by two narrow spiral stairs, one to the south, another to the west, contains a tolerably spacious room, with a ceiling ornamented by stucco mouldings, and a window presented to the westward. A partition has at one time divided this room from a narrow one towards the north, the ceiling of which is composed of the beams and flooring of the attic flat, all curiously painted with flower-work in an ancient taste. Two inferior rooms extend still farther to the northward. It is to be remarked that the wooden projection already spoken of extends up to this floor, so that there is here likewise a small room in front; it contains a fireplace, and a recess which might have been a cupboard or a library, besides two small windows. That this fireplace, this recess, and also the door by which the wooden chamber is entered from the decorated room should all be formed in the front wall of the house, and with a necessary relation to the wooden projection, strikes one as difficult to reconcile with the idea of that projection being an afterthought; the appearances rather indicate the whole having been formed at once, as parts of one design.

The attic floor exhibits strong oaken beams, but the flooring is in bad order.

In the lower part of the house there is a small room, said by tradition to have been used in times of difficulty for the purpose of baptising children ; there is also a well to supply the house with water, besides a secret stair, represented as communicating subterraneously with a neighbouring alley.

From the size of this house, and the variety of accesses to it, it becomes tolerably certain that Knox could have occupied only a portion of it. The question arises, which part did he occupy? Probability seems decidedly in favour of the *first floor*—that containing the window from which he is traditionally said to have preached, and where his effigy appears. An authentic fact in the Reformer's life favours this supposition. When under danger from the hostility of the queen's party in the castle—in the spring of 1571—'one evening a musket-ball was fired in at his window, and lodged in the roof of the apartment in which he was sitting. It happened that he sat at the time in a different part of the room from that which he had been accustomed to occupy, otherwise the ball, from the direction it took, must have struck him' (M'Crie). The second floor is too high to have admitted of a musket being fired in at one of the windows. A ball fired in at the ground-floor would not have struck the ceiling. The only feasible supposition in the case is that the Reformer dwelt in the *first floor*, which was not beyond an assassin's aim, and yet at such a height that a ball fired from the street would hit the ceiling.*

* [The right of this house to be called 'John Knox's House' has been strenuously disputed ; several other houses in which Knox actually lived have been identified by Robert Miller, F.S.A.Scot., Lord Dean of Guild of Edinburgh, in *John Knox and the Town Council of Edinburgh, with a Chapter on the so-called 'John Knox's House'* (1898). For the genuineness of the tradition, said not to be older than 1806, see Lord Guthrie's *John Knox and John Knox's House* (1898).]

HYNDFORD'S CLOSE.

AT the bottom of the High Street, on the south side, there is an uncommonly huge and dense mass of stone buildings or *lands*, penetrated only by a few narrow closes. One of these is Hyndford's Close, a name indicating the noble family which once had lodgment in it. This was a Scotch peerage not without its glories—witness particularly the third earl, who acted as ambassador in succession to Prussia, to Russia, and to Vienna. It is now extinct: its *bijouterie*, its pictures, including portraits of Maria Theresa, and other royal and imperial personages, which had been presented as friendly memorials to the ambassador, have all been dispersed by the salesman's hammer, and Hyndford's Close, on my trying to get into it lately (1868), was inaccessible (literally) from filth.

Hyndford's Close.

The entry and stair at the head of the close on the west side was a favourite residence, on account of the ready access to it from the street. In the second floor of this house lived, about the beginning of the reign of George III., Lady Maxwell of Monreith, and there brought up her beautiful daughters, one of whom became Duchess of Gordon. The house had a dark passage, and the kitchen door was passed in going to the dining-room, according to an agreeable old practice in Scotch houses, which lets the guests know on entering what they have to expect. The fineries of Lady Maxwell's daughters were usually hung up, after washing, on a screen in this passage to dry ; while the coarser articles of dress, such as shifts and petticoats, were slung decently out of sight at the window, upon a projecting contrivance similar to a dyer's pole, of which numerous specimens still exist at windows in the Old Town for the convenience of the poorer inhabitants.

So easy and familiar were the manners of the great in those times, fabled to be so stiff and decorous, that Miss Eglintoune, afterwards Lady Wallace, used to be sent with the tea-kettle across the street to the Fountain Well for water to make tea. Lady Maxwell's daughters were the wildest romps imaginable. An old gentleman, who was their relation, told me that the first time he saw these beautiful girls was in the High Street, where Miss Jane, afterwards Duchess of Gordon, was riding upon a sow, which Miss Eglintoune thumped lustily behind with a stick. It must be understood that in the middle of the eighteenth century vagrant swine went as commonly about the streets of Edinburgh as dogs do in our own day, and were more generally fondled as pets by the children of the last generation.* It may, however, be remarked that the sows upon which the Duchess of Gordon and her witty sister rode, when children, were not the common vagrants of the High Street, but belonged to Peter Ramsay, of the inn in St Mary's Wynd, and were among the last that were permitted to roam abroad. The two romps used to watch the animals as they were let loose in the forenoon from the stable-yard (where they lived among the horse-litter), and get upon their backs the moment they issued from the close.

The extraordinary cleverness, the genuine wit, and the delightful *abandon* of Lady Wallace made an extraordinary impression on Scottish society in her day. It almost seemed as if some faculty divine had inspired her. A milliner bringing home a cap to her when she was just about to set off to the Leith races was so unlucky as to tear it against the buckle of a porter's knee in the street. 'No matter,' said her ladyship; and instantly putting it on, restored all to grace by a single pin. The cap thus misarranged was found so perfectly exquisite that ladies tore their caps on nails, and pinned them on in the hope of imitating it. It was, however, a grace beyond the reach of art.

Of the many *bon mots* attributed to her, one alone seems

* The following advertisement, inserted in the *Edinburgh Courant* of August 1, 1754, illustrates the above in a striking manner: 'If any person has lost a LARGE SOW, let them call at the house of Robert Fiddes, gardener to Lord Minto, over against the Earl of Galloway's, in the Horse Wynd, where, upon proving the property, paying expenses and damages done by the said sow, they may have the same restored.'

worthy, from its being unhackneyed, of appearing here. The son of Mr Kincaid, king's printer—a great Macaroni, as the phrase went; that is, dandy—was nicknamed, from his father's lucrative patent, *Young Bibles*. This beau entering a ballroom one evening, some of the company asked who was that extraordinary-looking young man. 'Only Young Bibles,' quoth Lady Wallace, 'bound in calf, and gilt, but not lettered!'

[In the same stair in Hyndford's Close lived another lady of rank, and one who, for several reasons, filled in her time a broad space in society. This was Anne, Countess of Balcarres, the progenitrix of perhaps as many persons as ever any woman was in the same space of time. Her eldest daughter, Anne, authoress of the ballad of *Auld Robin Gray*, was, of all her eleven children, the one whose name is most likely to continue in remembrance —yea, though another of them put down the Maroon war in the West Indies. When in Hyndford's Close, Lady Balcarres had for a neighbour in the same alley Dr Rutherford, the uncle of Sir Walter Scott; and young Walter, often at his uncle's, occasionally accompanied his aunt 'Jeanie' to Lady Balcarres's. Forty years after, having occasion to correspond with Lady Anne Barnard, *née* Lindsay, he told her: 'I remember all the *locale* of Hyndford's Close perfectly, even to the Indian screen with Harlequin and Columbine, and the harpsichord, though I never had the pleasure of hearing Lady Anne play upon it. I suppose the close, once too clean to soil the hem of your ladyship's garment, is now a resort for the lowest mechanics— and so wears the world away. . . . It is, to be sure, more picturesque to lament the desolation of towers on hills and haughs, than the degradation of an Edinburgh close; but I cannot help thinking on the simple and cosie retreats where worth and talent, and elegance to boot, were often nestled, and which now are the resort of misery, filth, poverty, and vice.'*

The late Mrs Meetham, a younger sister of Miss Spence Yeaman, of Murie, in the Carse of Gowrie, had often heard her grand-aunt, Miss Molly Yeaman, describe, from her own recollection, the tea-drinkings of the Countess of Balcarres in Hyndford's Close. The family was not rich, and it still retained something of its ancient Jacobitism. The tea-drinkings, as was not uncommon, took place in my lady's bedroom. At the foot of a four-posted bed, exhibiting a finely worked coverlet, stood John, an elderly man-servant, and a *character*, in full Balcarres

* Lord Lindsay's *Lives of the Lindsays*, iii. 190.

livery, an immense quantity of worsted lace on his coat. Resting with his arm round a bedpost, he was ready to hand the kettle when required. As the ladies went chattering on, there would sometimes occur a difficulty about a date or a point in genealogy, and then John was appealed to to settle the question. For example, it came to be debated how many of the Scotch baronetcies were real; for, as is still the case, many of them were known to be fictitious, or assumed without legal grounds. Here John was known to be not only learned, but eloquent. He began : 'Sir James Kinloch, Sir Stuart Threipland, Sir John Wedderburn, Sir —— Ogilvy, Sir James Steuart of Coltness' [all of them forfeited baronets, be it observed] : 'these, leddies, are the only *real* baronets. For the rest, I do believe, the Deil'—— then a figurative declaration not fit for modern print, but which made the Balcarres party only laugh, and declare to John that they thought him not far wrong.]

HOUSE OF THE MARQUISES OF TWEEDDALE—
THE BEGBIE TRAGEDY.

THE town mansion of the Marquises of Tweeddale was one of
large extent and dimensions, in a
court which still bears the title of
that family, nearly opposite to the
mansion of John
Knox.* When
John, the fourth
marquis, was Sec-
retary of State for
Scotland, in the
reign of George
II., this must have
been a dwelling of
considerable import-
ance in the eyes of
his countrymen. It
had a good garden
in the rear, with a

Tweeddale Court.

* 'During this peace-
able time [1668-1675], he
[John, Earl of Tweeddale]
built the park of Yester
of stone and lime, near
seven miles about, in
seven years' time, at the
expense of 20,000 pound ;
bought a house in Edin-
burgh from Sir William
Bruce for 1000 pound
sterling, and ane other
house within the same
court, which, being re-
built from the foundation,
the price of it and repara-
tions of both stood him
1000 sterling.' — Father
Hay's *Genealogie of the Hayes of Tweeddale* (Edinburgh, 1835), p. 32.

yard and coach entry from the Cowgate. Now all the buildings and 'pertinents' are in the occupation of Messrs Oliver & Boyd, the well-known publishers.

The passage from the street into Tweeddale Court is narrow and dark, and about fifteen yards in length. Here, in 1806, when the mansion was possessed as a banking-house by the British Linen Company, there took place an extraordinary tragedy. About five

Scene of the Begbie Murder.

o'clock of the evening of the 13th of November, when the short midwinter day had just closed, a child, who lived in a house accessible from the close, was sent by her mother with a kettle to obtain a supply of water for tea from the neighbouring well. The little girl, stepping with the kettle in her hand out of the public stair into the close, stumbled in the dark over something which lay there, and which proved to be the body of a man just expiring. On an alarm being given, it was discovered that this was William Begbie, a porter connected with the bank, in whose heart a knife was stuck up to the haft, so that he bled to death before uttering a word which might tend to explain the dismal transaction. He was at the same time found to have been robbed of a package of notes to the value of above four thousand pounds, which he had been entrusted, in the course of his ordinary duty, to carry from the branch of the bank at Leith to the head-office.[*]

* The notes are thus described in the *Hue and Cry*: £1300 in twenty-pound notes of Sir W. Forbes and Company; £1000 in twenty-pound notes of the

BAKEHOUSE CLOSE.

Back of 'Speaking House.'

PAGE 313.

GOLFERS ON LEITH LINKS.

PAGE 320.

The blow had been given with an accuracy and a calculation of consequences showing the most appalling deliberation in the assassin; for not only was the knife directed straight into the most vital part, but its handle had been muffled in a bunch of soft paper, so as to prevent, as was thought, any sprinkling of blood from reaching the person of the murderer, by which he might have been by some chance detected. The knife was one of those with broad thin blades and wooden handles which are used for cutting bread, and its rounded front had been ground to a point, apparently for the execution of this horrible deed. The unfortunate man left a wife and four children to bewail his loss.

The singular nature and circumstances of Begbie's murder occasioned much excitement in the public mind, and every effort was of course made to discover the guilty party. No house of a suspicious character in the city was left unsearched, and parties were despatched to watch and patrol all the various roads leading out into the country. The bank offered a reward of five hundred pounds for such information as might lead to the conviction of the offender or offenders; and the government further promised the king's pardon to any except the actual murderer who, having been concerned in the deed, might discover their accomplices. The sheriff of Edinburgh, Mr Clerk Rattray, displayed the greatest zeal in his endeavours to ascertain the circumstances of the murder, and to detect and seize the murderer, but with surprisingly little success. All that could be ascertained was that Begbie, in proceeding up Leith Walk on his fatal mission, had been accompanied by 'a man;' and that about the supposed time of the murder 'a man' had been seen by some children to run out of the close into the street and down Leith Wynd, a lane leading off from the Netherbow at a point nearly opposite to the close. There was also reason to believe that the knife had been bought in a shop about two o'clock on the day of the murder, and that it had been afterwards ground upon a grinding-stone and smoothed on a hone. A number of suspicious characters were apprehended and examined; but all, with one exception, produced satisfactory proofs of their innocence. The exception was a carrier between Perth and Edinburgh, a man of dissolute and irregular habits, of great bodily strength, and known to be a

Leith Banking Company; £1400 in twenty, ten, and five pound notes of different banks; 240 guinea and 440 pound notes of different banks—in all, £4392.

dangerous and desperate character. He was kept in custody fo
a considerable time on suspicion, having been seen in the Canon
gate, near the scene of the murder, a very short time after it wa
committed. It has since been ascertained that he was then goin
about a different business, the disclosure of which would hav
subjected him to a capital punishment. It was in consequenc
of the mystery he felt himself impelled to preserve on this subjec
that he was kept so long in custody; but at length facts an
circumstances came out to warrant his discharge, and he wa
discharged accordingly.

Months rolled on without eliciting any evidence respecting th
murder, and, like other wonders, it had ceased in a great measur
to engage public attention, when, on the 10th of August 1807
a journeyman mason, in company with two other men, passin
through the Bellevue grounds in the neighbourhood of the city
found, in a hole in a stone enclosure by the side of a hedge, a
parcel containing a large quantity of bank-notes, bearing th
appearance of having been a good while exposed to the weather
After consulting a little, the men carried the package to th
sheriff's office, where it was found to contain about £3000 in larg
notes, being those which had been taken from Begbie. Th
British Linen Company rewarded the men with two hundre
pounds for their honesty; but the circumstance passed withou
throwing any light on the murder itself.

Up to the present day the murderer of Begbie has not bee
discovered; nor is it probable, after the space of time which ha
elapsed, that he will ever be so. It is most likely that the grav
has long closed upon him. The only person on whom publi
suspicion alighted with any force during the sixteen years ensuin
upon the transaction was a medical practitioner in Leith, a dis
solute man and a gambler, who put an end to his own existenc
not long after the murder. But I am not acquainted with an
particular circumstances on which this suspicion was grounde
beyond the suicide, which might spring from other causes. It wa
not till 1822 that any further light was thrown on this mysteriou
case. In a work then published under the title of *The Life an
Trial of James Mackoull*, there was included a paper by M
Denovan, the Bow Street officer, the object of which was to prov
that Mackoull was the murderer, and which contained at least on
very curious statement.

Mr Denovan had discovered in Leith a man, then acting a
a teacher, but who in 1806 was a sailor-boy, and who ha

witnessed some circumstances immediately connected with the murder. The man's statement was as follows: 'I was at that time (November 1806) a boy of fourteen years of age. The vessel to which I belonged had made a voyage to Lisbon, and was then lying in Leith harbour. I had brought a small present from Portugal for my mother and sister, who resided in the Netherbow, Edinburgh, immediately opposite to Tweeddale's Close, leading to the British Linen Company's Bank. I left the vessel late in the afternoon, and as the articles I had brought were contraband, I put them under my jacket, and was proceeding up Leith Walk, when I perceived a tall man carrying a yellow-coloured parcel under his arm, and a genteel man, dressed in a black coat, dogging him. I was a little afraid: I conceived the man who carried the parcel to be a smuggler, and the gentleman who followed him to be a custom-house or excise officer. In dogging the man, the supposed officer went from one side of the Walk to the other [the Walk is a broad street], as if afraid of being noticed, but still kept about the same distance behind him. I was afraid of losing what I carried, and shortened sail a little, keeping my eyes fixed on the person I supposed to be an officer, until I came to the head of Leith Street, when I saw the smuggler take the North Bridge, and the custom-house officer go in front of the Register Office; here he looked round him, and imagining he was looking for me, I hove to, and watched him. He then looked up the North Bridge, and, as I conceive, followed the smuggler, for he went the same way. I stood a minute or two where I was, and then went forward, walking slowly up the North Bridge. I did not, however, see either of the men before me; and when I came to the south end or head of the Bridge, supposing that they might have gone up the High Street or along the South Bridge, I turned to the left, and reached the Netherbow, without again seeing either the smuggler or the officer. Just, however, as I came opposite to Tweeddale's Close, *I saw the custom-house officer come running out of it with something under his coat:* I think he ran down the street. Being much alarmed, and supposing that the officer had also seen me and knew what I carried, I deposited my little present in my mother's with all possible speed, and made the best of my way to Leith, without hearing anything of the murder of Begbie until next day. On coming on board the vessel, I told the mate what a narrow escape I conceived I had made: he seemed somewhat alarmed (having probably, like myself, smuggled some trifling article from

Portugal), and told me in a peremptory tone that I should not go ashore again without first acquainting him. I certainly heard of the murder before I left Leith, and concluded that the man I saw was the murderer; but the idea of waiting on a magistrate and communicating what I had seen never struck me. We sailed in a few days thereafter from Leith; and the vessel to which I belonged having been captured by a privateer, I was carried to a French prison, and only regained my liberty at the last peace. I can now recollect distinctly the figure of the man I saw; he was well dressed, had a genteel appearance, and wore a black coat. I never saw his face properly, for he was before me the whole way up the Walk; I think, however, he was a stout big man, but not so tall as the man I then conceived to be a smuggler.'

This description of the supposed custom-house officer coincides exactly with that of the appearance of Mackoull; and other circumstances are given which almost make it certain that he was the murderer. This Mackoull was a London rogue of unparalleled effrontery and dexterity, who for years haunted Scotland, and effected some daring robberies. He resided in Edinburgh from September 1805 till the close of 1806, and during that time frequented a coffee-house in the *Ship Tavern* at Leith. He professed to be a merchant expelled by the threats of the French from Hamburg, and to live by a new mode of dyeing skins, but in reality he practised the arts of a gambler and a pickpocket. He had a mean lodging at the bottom of New Street in the Canongate, near the scene of the murder of Begbie, to which it is remarkable that *Leith Wynd* was the readiest as well as most private access from that spot. No suspicion, however, fell upon Mackoull at this period, and he left the country for a number of years, at the end of which time he visited Glasgow, and there effected a robbery of one of the banks. For this crime he did not escape the law. He was brought to trial at Edinburgh in 1820, was condemned to be executed, but died in jail while under reprieve from his sentence.

The most striking part of the evidence which Mr Denovan adduces against Mackoull is the report of a conversation which he had with that person in the condemned cell of the Edinburgh jail in July 1820, when Mackoull was very doubtful of being reprieved. To pursue his own narrative, which is in the third person: 'He told Captain Sibbald [the superior of the prison] that he intended to ask Mackoull a single question relative to the murder of Begbie, but would first humour him by a few jokes, so as to throw him off his guard, and prevent him from thinking he had called for any particular purpose [it is to be observed that Mr Denovan had a professional acquaintance with the condemned man]; but desired Captain Sibbald to watch the features of the prisoner when he (Denovan) put his hand to his chin, for he would then put the question he meant. After talking some time on different topics, Mr Denovan put this very simple question to the prisoner: "By the way, Mackoull, if I am correct, you resided at the foot of New Street, Canongate, in November 1806—did you not?" He stared—he rolled his eyes, and, as if falling into a convulsion, threw himself back upon his bed. In this condition he continued for a few moments, when, as if recollecting himself, he started up, exclaiming wildly: "No, —— ——! I was then in the East Indies—in the West Indies. What do you mean?" "I mean no harm, Mackoull," he replied; "I merely asked the question for my own curiosity; for I think when you left these lodgings you went to Dublin. Is it not so?" "Yes, yes, I went to Dublin," he replied; "and I wish I had remained there still. I won £10,000 there at the tables, and never knew what it was to want cash, although you wished the folks here to believe that they locked me up in Old Start (Newgate), and brought down your friend Adkins to swear he saw me there: this was more than your duty." He now seemed to rave, and lose all temper, and his visitor bade him good-night, and left him.'

It appears extremely probable, from the strong circumstantial evidence which has been offered by Mr Denovan, that Mackoull was the murderer of Begbie.

One remaining fact regarding the Netherbow will be listened to with some interest. It was the home—perhaps the native spot—of William Falconer, the author of *The Shipwreck*, whose father was a wigmaker in this street.*

* It was in this part of the High Street also that Robert Lekprevick, the Scottish printer, lived before he removed to St Andrews in 1571.

[THE LADIES OF TRAQUAIR.

LADY LOVAT was at the head of a genus of old ladies of quality, who, during the last century, resided in third and fourth *flats* of Old Town houses, wore pattens when they went abroad, had miniatures of the Pretender next their hearts, and gave tea and card parties regularly every fortnight. Almost every generation of a Scottish family of rank, besides throwing off its swarm of male cadets, who went abroad in quest of fortune, used to produce a corresponding number of daughters, who stayed at home, and for the most part became old maids. These gentlewomen, after the death of their parents, when, of course, a brother or nephew succeeded to the family seat and estate, were compelled to leave home, and make room for the new laird to bring up a new generation, destined in time to experience the same fate. Many of these ladies, who in Catholic countries would have found protection in nunneries, resorted to Edinburgh, where, with the moderate family provision assigned them, they passed inoffensive and sometimes useful lives, the peace of which was seldom broken otherwise than by irruptions of their grand-nephews, who came with the hunger of High School boys, or by the more stately calls of their landed cousins and brothers, who rendered their visits the more auspicious by a pound of hyson for the caddy, or a replenishment of rappee for the snuff-box. The *leddies*, as they were called, were at once the terror and the admiration of their neighbours in the stair, who looked up to them as the patronesses of the *land*, and as shedding a light of gentility over the flats below.

In the best days of the Old Town, people of all ranks lived very closely and cordially together, and the whole world were in a manner next-door neighbours. The population being dense, and the town small, the distance between the houses of friends was seldom considerable. When a hundred friends lived within the space of so many yards, the company was easily collected, and consequently meetings took place more frequently, and upon more trivial occasions, than in these latter days of stately dinners and fantastic balls. Tea—simple tea—was then almost the only meal to which invitations were given. Tea-parties, assembling at four o'clock, were resorted to by all who wished for elegant social intercourse. There was much careful ceremonial in the dispensaion of those pretty, small china cups, individualised by the numbers marked on each of the miniature spoons which circulated with them, and of which four or five returns were not uncommon. The spoon in the saucer indicated a wish for more—in the cup the reverse. A few tunes on the spinnet, a Scotch song from some young lady (solo), and the unfailing whist-table furnished the entertainment. At eight o'clock to a minute would arrive the sedan, or the lass with the lantern and pattens, and the whole company would be at home before the eight o'clock drum of the Town-guard had ceased to beat.

In a house at the head of the Canongate, but having its entrance from St Mary's Wynd, and several stairs up, lived two old maiden ladies of the house of Traquair—the Ladies Barbara and Margaret Stuart. They were twins, the children of Charles, the fourth earl, and their birth on the 3rd of September, the anniversary of the death of Cromwell, brought a Latin epigram from Dr Pitcairn—of course previous to 1713, which was the year of his own death. The learned doctor anticipated for them 'timid wooers,' but they nevertheless came to old age unmarried. They drew out their innocent, retired lives in this place, where, latterly, one of their favourite amusements was to make dolls, and little beds for them to lie on—a practice not quite uncommon in days long gone by, being to some degree followed by Queen Mary.*

I may give, in the words of a long-deceased correspondent, an anecdote of the ladies of Traquair, referring to the days when potatoes had as yet an equivocal reputation, and illustrative of the frugal scale by which our 'leddies' were in use to measure the luxuries of their table. 'Upon the return one day of their weekly ambassador to the market, and the anxious investigation by the old ladies of the contents of Jenny's basket, the little morsel of mutton, with a portion of accompanying off-falls, was duly approved of. "But, Jenny, what's this in the bottom of the basket?" "Oo, mem, just a dozen o' 'taties that Lucky, the green-wife, wad ha'e me to tak'—they wad eat sae fine wi' the mutton." "Na, na, Jenny; tak' back the 'taties—we need nae provocatives in this house."'

The latest survivor of these Traquair ladies died in 1794.]

---

* '—— deliure a Jacques le tailleur deux chanteaux de damas gris broches dor pour faire vne robbe a vne poupine;' also 'trois quartz et demi de toille dargent et de soze blanche pour faire vne cotte et aultre chose a des poupines.' —*Catalogues of the Jewels, Dresses, Furniture, &c. of Mary Queen of Scots,* edited by Joseph Robertson. Edinburgh, 1863, p. 139.

GREYFRIARS CHURCHYARD.

Signing of the Covenant—Henderson's Monument—Bothwell Bridge Prisoners—A Romance.

THIS old cemetery—the burial-place of Buchanan,* George Jameson the painter, Principal Robertson, Dr Blair, Allan Ramsay, Henry Mackenzie, and many other men of note—whose walls are a circle of aristocratic sepulchres, will ever be memorable as the scene of the Signing of the Covenant; the document having first been produced in the church, after a sermon by Alexander Henderson, and signed by all the congregation from the Earl of Sutherland downward, after which it was handed out to the multitudes assembled in the kirkyard, and signed on the flat monuments, amidst tears, prayers, and aspirations which could find no words; some writing with their blood! Near by, resting well from all these struggles, lies the preacher under a square obelisk-like monument; near also rests, in equal peace, the Covenant's enemy, Sir George Mackenzie. The inscriptions on Henderson's stone were ordered by Parliament to be erased at the Restoration; and small depressions are pointed out in it as having

Henderson's Monument
Greyfriars.

* A skull represented as Buchanan's has long been shown in the College of Edinburgh. It is extremely thin, and being long ago shown in company with that of a known idiot, which was, on the contrary, very thick, it seemed to form a commentary upon the popular expression which sets forth density of bone as an invariable accompaniment of paucity of brain. The author of a diatribe called *Scotland Characterised*, which was published in 1701, and may be found in the *Harleian Miscellany*, tells us that he had seen the skull in question, and that it bore 'a very pretty distich upon it [the composition of Principal Adamson, who had caused the skull to be lifted]—the first line I have forgot, but the second was :

"Et decus es tumulo jam, Buchanane, tuo." '

been inflicted by bullets from the soldiery when executing this order. With the '88 came a new order of things, and the inscriptions were then quietly reinstated.

BOTHWELL BRIDGE PRISONERS.

As if there had been some destiny in the matter, the Greyfriars Churchyard became connected with another remarkable event in the religious troubles of the seventeenth century. At the south-west angle, accessible by an old gateway bearing emblems of mortality, and which is fitted with an iron-rail gate of very old workmanship, is a kind of supplement to the burying-ground—an oblong space, now having a line of sepulchral enclosures on each side, but formerly empty. On these enclosures the visitor may remark, as he passes, certain names venerable in the history of science and of letters; as, for instance, Joseph Black and Alexander Tytler. On one he sees the name of Gilbert Innes of Stow, who left a million, to take six feet of earth here. These, however, do not form the matter in point. Every lesser particular becomes trivial beside the extraordinary use to which the place was put by the Government in the year 1679. Several hundred of the prisoners taken at Bothwell Bridge were confined here in the open air, under circumstances of privation now scarcely credible. They had hardly anything either to lie upon or to cover them; their allowance of provision was four ounces of bread per day, with water derived from one of the city pipes, which passed near the place. They were guarded by day by eight and through the night by twenty-four men; and the soldiers were told that if any prisoner escaped, they should answer it life for life by cast of dice. If any prisoner rose from the ground by night, he was shot at. Women alone were permitted to commune with them, and bring them food or clothes; but these had often to stand at the entrance from morning till night without getting access, and were frequently insulted and maltreated by the soldiers, without the prisoners being able to protect them, although in many cases related by the most endearing ties. In the course of several weeks a considerable number of the prisoners had been liberated upon signing a bond, in which they promised never again to take up arms against the king or without his authority; but it appears that about four hundred, refusing mercy on such terms, were kept in this frightful bivouac for five months, being only allowed at the approach of winter to have shingle huts erected over them, which was boasted of as a great mercy. Finally, on the 15th of November, a remnant, numbering two hundred and fifty-seven, were put on board a ship to be sent to Barbadoes. The vessel was wrecked on one of the Orkney Islands, when only about forty came ashore alive.

From the gloom of this sad history there is shed one ray of romance. Amongst the charitable women of Edinburgh who came to minister to the prisoners, there was one attended by a daughter —a young and, at least by right of romance, a fair girl. Every few days they approached this iron gate with food and clothes, either from their own stores or collected among neighbours. Between the young lady and one of the juvenile prisoners an attachment sprang up. Doubtless she loved him for the dangers he had passed in so good a cause, and he loved her because she pitied them. In happier days, long after, when their constancy had been well tried by an exile which he suffered in the planta- tions, this pair were married, and settled in Edinburgh, where they had sons and daughters. A respectable elderly citizen tells me he is descended from them.*

* [Dr David Hay Fleming has shown that the contemporary evidence is all in favour of the Covenant's having been signed *in* the Greyfriars' Church, and not in the churchyard ; see a chapter by him in Mr Moir Bryce's *Old Greyfriars' Church, Edinburgh* (1912). And in the same book Mr Moir Bryce has proved that the small strip of ground long erroneously believed to be the Covenanters' prison was not separated off till 1703–4, and that the Covenanters were interned on a much larger area to the east, now built over.]

STORY OF MRS MACFARLANE.

'Let them say I am romantic; so is every one said to be that either admires a fine thing or does one. On my conscience, as the world goes, 'tis hardly worth anybody's while to do one for the honour of it. Glory, the only pay of generous actions, is now as ill paid as other just debts; and neither Mrs Macfarlane for immolating her lover, nor you for constancy to your lord, must ever hope to be compared to Lucretia or Portia.'—*Pope to Lady Mary W. Montagu.*

POPE here alludes to a tragical incident which took place in Edinburgh on the 2nd of October 1716. The victim was a young Englishman, who had been sent down to Scotland as a Commissioner of Customs. It appears that Squire Cayley, or Captain Cayley, as he was alternatively called, had become the slave of a shameful passion towards Mrs Macfarlane, a woman of uncommon beauty, the wife of Mr John Macfarlane, Writer to the Signet in Edinburgh. One Saturday forenoon Mrs Macfarlane was exposed, by the treachery of Captain Cayley's landlady, with whom she was acquainted, to an insult of the most atrocious kind on his part, in the house where he lodged, which seems to have been situated in a close in the Cowgate, opposite to what where called the Back Stairs.* Next Tuesday Mr Cayley waited upon Mrs Macfarlane at her own house, and was shown into the drawing-room. According to an account given out by his friends, he was anxious to apologise for his former rudeness. From another account, it would appear that he had circulated reports derogatory to the lady's honour, which she was resolved to punish. A third story represents him as having repeated the insult which he had formerly offered; whereupon she went into another room, and presently came back with a pair of pistols in her hand. On her bidding him leave the house instantly, he said: 'What, madam, d'ye design to act a comedy?' To which she answered that '*he would find it a tragedy if he did not retire.*' The infatuated man

---

* The Back Stairs, built on the site of St Giles' Churchyard, gave direct communication between the Cowgate and Old Parliament Square. It was by this way that Robertson the smuggler escaped from the Tolbooth Church, where he and his accomplice Wilson had been taken, as was usual with condemned prisoners, the Sunday before their execution. It was Porteous's behaviour at the execution of Wilson that led to the riot and his own death in the Grassmarket.

not obeying her command, she fired one of the pistols, which, however, only wounded him slightly in the left wrist, the bullet slanting down into the floor. The mere instinct, probably, of self-preservation caused him to draw his sword; but before he could use it she fired the other pistol, the shot of which penetrated his heart. 'This dispute,' says a letter of the day, 'was so close that Mr Cayley's shirt was burnt at the sleeves with the fire of one of the pistols, and his cravat and the breast of his shirt with the fire of the other.' * Mrs Macfarlane immediately left the room, locking the door upon the dead body, and sent a servant for her husband, who was found at a neighbouring tavern. On his coming home about an hour after, she took him by the sleeve, and leading him into the room where the corpse lay, explained the circumstances which had led to the bloody act. Mr Macfarlane said: 'Oh, woman! what have you done?' But soon seeing the necessity for prompt measures, he went out again to consult with some of his friends. 'They all advised,' says the letter just quoted, 'that he should convey his wife away privately, to prevent her lying in jail, till a precognition should be taken of the affair, and it should appear in its true light. Accordingly [about six o'clock], she walked down the High Street, followed by her husband at a little distance, and now absconds.

'The thing continued a profound secret to all except those concerned in the house till past ten at night, when Mr Macfarlane, having provided a safe retreat for his wife, returned and gave orders for discovering it to the magistrates, who went and viewed the body of the deceased, and secured the house and maid, and all else who may become evidence of the fact.'

Another contemporary says: 'I saw his [Cayley's] corpse after he was cereclothed, and saw his blood where he lay on the floor for twenty-four hours after he died, just as he fell; so it was a difficulty to straight him.'

A careful investigation was made into every circumstance connected with this fatal affair, but without demonstrating anything except the passionate rashness or magnanimity of the fair homicide. Mr Macfarlane was discharged upon his own affirmation that he knew nothing of the deed till after it had taken place. A pamphlet was published by Mrs Murray, Mr Cayley's landlady, who seems to have kept a grocery shop in the Cowgate, vindicating herself from the imputation which Mrs Macfarlane's tale had thrown upon

* The pistols belonged to Mr Cayley himself, having been borrowed a few days before by Mr Macfarlane.

her character; but to this there appeared an answer, from some friend of the other party, in which the imputation was fixed almost beyond the possibility of doubt. Mrs Murray denied that Mrs Macfarlane had been in her house on the Saturday before the murder; but evidence was given that she was seen issuing from the close in which Mrs Murray resided, and, after ascending the Back Stairs, was observed passing through the Parliament Square towards her own house.

It will surprise every one to learn that this Scottish Lucrece was a woman of only nineteen or twenty years of age, and some months *enceinte*, at the time when she so boldly vindicated her honour. She was a person of respectable connections, being a daughter of Colonel Charles Straiton, 'a gentleman of great honour,' says one of the letters already quoted, and who further appears to have been entrusted with high negotiations by the Jacobites during the reign of Queen Anne. By her mother, she was granddaughter to Sir Andrew Forrester.

Of the future history of Mrs Macfarlane we have but one glimpse, but it is of a romantic nature. Margaret Swinton, who was the aunt of Sir Walter Scott's mother, and round whom he and his boy-brothers used to close to listen to her tales, remembered being one Sunday left by her parents at home in their house of Swinton in Berwickshire, while the rest of the family attended church. Tiring of the solitude of her little nursery, she stole quietly downstairs to the parlour, which she entered somewhat abruptly. There, to her surprise, she beheld the most beautiful woman she had ever seen, sitting at the breakfast-table making tea. She believed it could be no other than one of those enchanted queens whom she had heard of in fairy tales. The lady, after a pause of surprise, came up to her with a sweet smile, and conversed with her, concluding with a request that she would speak only to her mamma of the stranger whom she had seen. Presently after, little Margaret having turned her back for a few moments, the beautiful vision had vanished. The whole appeared like a dream. By-and-by the family returned, and Margaret took her mother aside that she might talk of this wonderful apparition. Mrs Swinton applauded her for thus observing the injunction which had been laid upon her. 'Had you not,' she added, 'it might have cost that lady her life.' Subsequent explanations made Margaret aware that she had seen the unfortunate Mrs Macfarlane, who, having some claim of kindred upon the Swinton family, had been received by them, and kept in a secret room till such time as she could venture to make her way out of the country. On Margaret looking away for a moment, the lady had glided by a sliding panel into her Patmos behind the wainscot, and thus unwittingly increased the child's apprehension of the whole being an event out of the course of nature.

THE CANONGATE.

Distinguished Inhabitants in Former Times—Story of a Burning—
Morocco's Land—New Street.

THE Canongate, which takes its name from the Augustine canons
of Holyrood (who were permitted to build it by the charter
of David I. in 1128, and afterwards ruled it as a burgh of regality),
was formerly the court end of the town. As the main avenue
from the palace into the city, it has borne upon its pavement the
burden of all that was beautiful, all that was gallant, all that has
become historically interesting in Scotland for the last six or seven
hundred years. It still presents an antique appearance, although
many of the houses are modernised. There is one with a date from
Queen Mary's reign,* and many may be guessed, from their appearance, to be of even an earlier era. Previously to the Union, when
the palace ceased to be occasionally inhabited, as it had formerly
been, by at least the vicar of majesty in the person of the Commissioner to the Parliament, the place was densely inhabited by
persons of distinction. Allan Ramsay, in lamenting the death of
Lucky Wood, says:

> 'Oh, Canigate, puir elrich hole,
> What loss, what crosses does thou thole!
> London and death gars thee look droll,
>   And hing thy head;
> Wow but thou has e'en a cauld coal
>   To blaw indeed;'

and mentions in a note that this place was 'the greatest sufferer
by the loss of our members of parliament, which London now
enjoys, many of them having had their houses there;' a fact which
Maitland confirms. Innumerable traces are to be found, in old
songs and ballads, of the elegant population of the Canongate in a
former day. In the piteous tale of Marie Hamilton—one of the
Queen's Maries—occurs this simple but picturesque stanza:

> 'As she cam' doun the Cannogait,
>   The Cannogait sae free,
> Mony a lady looked owre her window,
>   Weeping for this ladye.'

* A little below the church.

An old popular rhyme expresses the hauteur of these Canongate dames towards their city neighbours of the male sex :

> 'The lasses o' the Canongate,
>   Oh they are wondrous nice ;
> They winna gi'e a single kiss
>   But for a double price.
>
> Gar hang them, gar hang them,
>   Hich upon a tree ;
> For we 'll get better up the gate
>   For a bawbee !'

Even in times comparatively modern, this faubourg was inhabited by persons of very great consideration.* Within the memory of a lady living in 1830, it used to be a common thing to hear, among other matters of gossip, '*that there was to be a braw flitting* † *in the Canongate to-morrow ;*' and parties of young people were made up to go and see the fine furniture brought out, sitting perhaps for hours in the windows of some friend on the opposite side of the

---

* Subjoined is a list of persons of note who lived in the Canongate in the early days of the late Mr Chalmers Izett, whose memory extended back to 1769 :

'DUKES.	COUNTESSES.	BARONETS.	EMINENT MEN.
Hamilton.	Tweeddale.	Sir J. Grant.	Adam Smith.
Queensberry.	Lothian.	Sir J. Suttie.	Dr Young.
		Sir J. Whiteford.	Dugald Stewart.
EARLS.	LORDS.	Sir J. Stewart.	Dr Gardner.
Breadalbane.	Haddo.	Sir J. Stirling.	Dr Gregory.
Hyndford.	Colvill.	Sir J. Sinclair, Glorat.	
Wemyss.	Blantyre.	Sir J. Halkett.	BANK.
Balcarras.	Nairn.	Sir James Stirling.	Douglas, Heron, and
Moray.	Semple.	Sir D. Hay.	Company.
Dalhousie.	A. Gordon.	Sir B. Dunbar.	
Haddington.	Cranstoun.	Sir J. Scott, Ancrum.	LADIES' BOARDING-
Mar.		Sir R. Anstruther.	SCHOOL.
Srathmore.	L. OF SESSION.	Sir J. Sinclair, Ulbster.	Mrs Hamilton,
Traquair.	Eskgrove.		Chessels's Court.
Selkirk.	Hailes.		
Dundonald.	Prestongrange.	COMMANDERS-IN-CHIEF.	PRINCIPAL INNS.
Kintore.	Kames.	General Oughton.	Ramsay's, St Mary's
Dunmore.	Milton.	General Skene.	Wynd.
Seafield.	Montgomery.	Lord A. Gordon.	Boyd's, Head of
Panmure.	Bannatyne.	Lord Moira.	Canongate.

'Two coaches went down the Canongate to Leith—one hour in going, and one hour in returning.'

† Removal.

street, while cart after cart was laden with magnificence.* Many of the houses to this day are fit for the residence of a first-rate

Weir's Close, Canongate—wretchedly squalid.

family in every respect but *vicinage* and *access*. The last grand blow was given to the place by the opening of the road along the Calton Hill in 1817, which rendered it no longer the avenue of approach to the city from the east. Instead of profiting by the comparative retirement which it acquired on that occasion, it seemed to become the more wretchedly squalid from its being the less under notice— as a gentleman dresses the least carefully when not expecting visitors. It is now a secluded and, in general, meanly inhabited suburb, only accessible by ways which, however lightly our fathers and

* ' At a former period, when the Canongate of Edinburgh was a more fashionable residence than at present, a lady of rank who lived in one of the closes, before going out to an evening-party, and at a time when hairdressers and peruke-makers were much in demand, requested a servant (newly come home) to tell Tam Tough the hairdresser to come to her immediately. The servant departed in quest of Puff, but had scarcely reached the street before she forgot the barber's name. Meeting with a caddy, she asked him if he knew where the hairdresser lived. "Whatna hairdresser is 't?" replied the caddy. "I ha'e forgot his name," answered she. "What kind o' name wus 't?" responded Donald. "As near as I can mind," said the girl, "it was a name that wad neither *rug* nor *rive*." "The deil 's in 't," answered Donald, "but that 's a tam'd tough name." "Thank ye, Donald, that 's the man's name I wanted—*Tam Tough*." '—[*From an Edinburgh Newspaper.*]

grandfathers might regard them, are hardly now pervious to a lady
or gentleman without shocking more of the senses than one, besides
the difficulty of steering one's way through the herds of the idle
and the wretched who encumber the street.

One of the houses near the head of the Canongate, on the north
side of the street, was indicated to me by an old lady a few years
ago as that which tradition in her young days pointed to in connection with a wild story related in the notes to *Rokeby.* She had
often heard the tale told, nearly in the same manner as it has been
given by Scott, and the site of the house concerned in the tragedy
was pointed out to her by her seniors. Perhaps the reader will
again excuse a quotation from the writings of our late gifted fellow
townsman : if to be related at all—and surely in a work devoted
to Edinburgh popular legends it could not rightly be overlooked—
it may as well be given in the language of the prince of modern
conteurs :

' About the beginning of the eighteenth century, when the large
castles of the Scottish nobles, and even the secluded hotels, like
those of the French *noblesse,* which they possessed in Edinburgh
were sometimes the scenes of strange and mysterious transactions
a divine of singular sanctity was called up at midnight to pray
with a person at the point of death. This was no unusual summons
but what followed was alarming. He was put into a sedan-chair
and after he had been transported to a remote part of the town
the bearers insisted upon his being blindfolded. The request was
enforced by a cocked pistol, and submitted to ; but in the course
of the discussion, he conjectured, from the phrases employed by the
chairmen, and from some part of their dress, not completely concealed by their cloaks, that they were greatly above the menial
station they assumed. After many turns and windings, the chair
was carried upstairs into a lodging, where his eyes were uncovered
and he was introduced into a bedroom, where he found a lady
newly delivered of an infant. He was commanded by his attendant
to say such prayers by her bedside as were fitting for a person
not expected to survive a mortal disorder. He ventured to remon-
strate, and observe that her safe delivery warranted better hopes
But he was sternly commanded to obey the orders first given, and
with difficulty recollected himself sufficiently to acquit himself of
the task imposed on him. He was then again hurried into the
chair ; but as they conducted him downstairs he heard the report
of a pistol. He was safely conducted home ; a purse of gold was
forced upon him ; but he was warned, at the same time, that the

least allusion to this dark transaction would cost him his life. He betook himself to rest, and after long and broken musing, fell into a deep sleep. From this he was awakened by his servant, with the dismal news that a fire of uncommon fury had broken out in the house of ——, near the head of the Canongate, and that it was totally consumed; with the shocking addition that the daughter of the proprietor, a young lady eminent for beauty and accomplishments, had perished in the flames. The clergyman had his suspicions, but to have made them public would have availed nothing. He was timid; the family was of the first distinction; above all, the deed was done, and could not be amended. Time wore away, however, and with it his terrors. He became unhappy at being the solitary depositary of this fearful mystery, and mentioned it to some of his brethren, through whom the anecdote acquired a sort of publicity. The divine, however, had been long dead, and the story in some degree forgotten, when a fire broke out again on the very same spot where the house of —— had formerly stood, and which was now occupied by buildings of an inferior description. When the flames were at their height, the tumult which usually attends such a scene was suddenly suspended by an unexpected apparition. A beautiful female, in a nightdress extremely rich, but at least half a century old, appeared in the very midst of the fire, and uttered these tremendous words in her vernacular idiom: "*Anes* burned, *twice* burned; the *third* time I 'll scare you all!" The belief in this story was formerly so strong that on a fire breaking out, and seeming to approach the fatal spot, there was a good deal of anxiety testified, lest the apparition should make good her denunciation.'

A little way farther down the Canongate, on the same side, is an old-fashioned house called *Morocco's Land*, having an alley passing under it, over which is this inscription *—a strange cry of the spirit of man to be heard in a street:

MISERERE MEI, DOMINE: A PECCATO, PROBRO,
DEBITO, ET MORTE SUBITA, LIBERA ME.

From whom this exclamation proceeded I have never learned; but the house, which is of more modern date than the legend, has a story connected with it. It is said that a young woman belonging to Edinburgh, having been taken upon a voyage by an African rover, was sold to the harem of the Emperor of Morocco, with whom she became a favourite. Mindful, like her countrymen in

* The inscription is now removed.

general, of her native land and her relations, she held such a correspondence with home as led to a brother of hers entering into merchandise, and conducting commercial transactions with Morocco. He was successful, and realised a little fortune, out of which he built this stately mansion. From gratitude, or out of a feeling of vanity regarding his imperial brother-in-law, he erected a statue of that personage in front of his house—a black, naked figure, with a turban and a necklace of beads; such being the notion which a Scottish artist of those days entertained of the personal aspect of the chief of one of the Mohammedan states of Africa. And this figure, perched in a little stone pulpit, still exists. As to the name bestowed upon the house, it would most probably arise from the man being in the first place called *Morocco* by way of sobriquet, as is common when any one becomes possessed by a particular subject, and often speaks of it.

Morocco's Land.

A little farther along is the opening of New Street, a modern offshoot of the ancient city, dating from a time immediately before the rise of the New Town. Many persons of consequence lived here: Lord Kames, in a neat house at the top, on the east side—an edifice once thought so fine that people used to bring their country cousins to see it; Lord Hailes, in a house more than half-way down, afterwards occupied by Mr Ruthven, mechanist; Sir

Philip Ainslie, in another house in the same row. The passers-by were often arrested by the sight of Sir Philip's preparations for a dinner-party through the open windows, the show of plate being particularly great. Now all these mansions are left to become workshops. *Sic transit.** Opposite to Kames's house is a small circular arrangement of causeway, indicating where St John's Cross formerly stood. Charles I., at his ceremonial entry into Edinburgh in 1633, knighted the provost at St John's Cross.†

* With the exception of Lord Kames's house, all the others referred to have been swept away by the North British Railway and the Corporation Gasworks, which at one time occupied the eastern side of the street.

† Although it was outside the wall, the city authorities claimed jurisdiction over the Canongate as far as St John's Cross, notwithstanding that the Canongate was a separate burgh, which it continued to be till the middle of the nineteenth century. Proclamations were made at St John's Cross as well as at the Mercat Cross in the High Street, and at it the Canongate burgh officials joined the city fathers when paying ceremonial visits to Holyrood.

ST JOHN STREET.

**Lord Monboddo's Suppers—The Sister of Smollett—Anecdote
of Henry Dundas.**

ST JOHN STREET, so named with reference to St John's Cross
above mentioned, was one of the heralds of the New Town.   In
the latter half of the last century it was occupied solely by persons
of distinction—nobles, judges, and country gentleman ; now it is

possessed as exclusively by persons of the middle rank. In No. 13 lived that eccentric genius, Lord Monboddo, whose supper-parties, conducted in classic taste, frequented by the *literati*, and for a time presided over by an angel in the form of a daughter of his lordship, were of immense attraction in their day. In a stair at the head of this street lived the sister of the author of *Roderick Random*.

Smollett's life as a literary adventurer in London, and the full participation he had in the woes of authors by profession, have perhaps conveyed an erroneous idea of his birth and connections. The Smolletts of Dumbartonshire were in reality what was called in Scotland a good old family. The novelist's own grandfather had been one of the commissioners for the Union between England and Scotland. And it is an undoubted fact that Tobias himself, if he had lived two or three years longer, would have become the owner of the family estate, worth about a thousand a year. All this, to any one conversant with the condition of the Scottish gentry in the early part of the last century, will appear quite consistent with his having been brought up as a druggist's apprentice in Glasgow—'the bubbly-nosed callant, wi' the stane in his pouch,' as his master affectionately described him, with reference to his notorious qualities as a Pickle.

The sister of Smollett—she who, failing him, did succeed to the family property—was a Mrs Telfer, domiciled as a gentle widow in a common stair at the head of St John Street (west side), first door up. She is described as a somewhat stern-looking specimen of her sex, with a high cast of features, but in reality a good-enough-natured woman, and extremely shrewd and intelligent. One passion of her genus possessed her—whist. A relative tells me that one of the city magistrates, who was a tallow-chandler, calling upon her one evening, she said : ' Come awa, bailie, and take a trick at the cartes.'

' Troth, ma'am,' said he, ' I hav'na a bawbee in my pouch.'

' Tut, man, ne'er mind that,' replied the lady ; ' let 's e'en play for a pund o' candles ! '

During his last visit to Edinburgh (1766)—the visit which occasioned *Humphry Clinker*—Smollett lived in his sister's house. A person who recollects seeing him there describes him as dressed in black clothes, tall, and extremely handsome, but quite unlike the portraits at the front of his works, all of which are disclaimed by his relations. The unfortunate truth appears to be that the world is in possession of no genuine likeness of Smollett ! He was very peevish, on account of the ill-health to which he had been so long a martyr, and used to complain much of a severe ulcerous disorder in his arm.

His wife, according to the same authority, was a Creole, with a dark complexion, though, upon the whole, rather pretty—a fine lady, but a silly woman. Yet she had been the Narcissa of *Roderick Random.**

In *Humphry Clinker*, Smollett works up many observations of things and persons which he had made in his recent visit to Scotland. His relative Commissary Smollett, and the family seat near Loch Lomond, receive ample notice. The story in the family is that while Matthew Bramble was undoubtedly himself, he meant in the gay and sprightly Jerry Melford to describe his sister's son, Major Telfer, and in Liddy to depict his own daughter, who was destined to be the wife of the major, but, to the inexpressible and ineffaceable grief of her father, died before the scheme could be accomplished. Jerry, it will be recollected, ' got some damage from the bright eyes of the charming Miss R——n, whom he had the honour to dance with at the ball.' Liddy contracted an intimate friendship with the same person. This young beauty was Eleonora Renton, charming by the true right divine, for she was daughter of Mr Renton of Lamerton, by Lady Susan Montgomery, one of the fair offshoots of the house of Eglintoune, described in a preceding article. A sister of hers was married to Smollett's eldest nephew, Telfer, who became inheritor of the family estate, and on account of it took the surname of Smollett: a large modern village in Dumbartonshire takes its name from this lady. It seems to have been this connection which brought the charming Eleonora under the novelist's attention. She afterwards married Charles Sharpe of Hoddam, and became the mother of Charles Kirkpatrick Sharpe, the well-known antiquary. Strange to say, the lady whose bright eyes had flamed upon poor Smollett's soul in the middle of the last century, was living so lately as 1836.

When Smollett was confined in the King's Bench Prison for the libel upon Admiral Knowles, he formed an intimacy with the celebrated Tenducci. This melodious singing-bird had recently

---

* Strap in *Roderick Random* was supposed to represent one Hutchinson, a barber near Dunbar. The man encouraged the idea as much as possible. When Mr [Warren] Hastings (governor of India) and his wife visited Scotland, they sent for this man, and were so pleased with him that Mr Hastings afterwards sent him a couple of razors, mounted in gold, from London.

got his wings clipped by his creditors, and was mewed up in the same cage with the novelist. Smollett's friendship proceeded to such a height that he paid the vocalist's debts from his own purse, and procured him his liberty. Tenducci afterwards visited Scotland, and was one night singing in a private circle, when somebody told him that a lady present was a near relation of his benefactor; upon which the grateful Italian prostrated himself before her, kissed her hands, and acted so many fantastic extravagances, after the foreign fashion, that she was put extremely out of countenance.

On the west side of the street, immediately to the south of the Canongate Kilwinning Mason Lodge, there is a neat self-contained house of old fashion, with a flower-plot in front. This was the residence of —— Anderson, merchant in Leith, the father of seven sons, all of whom attained respectable situations in life : one was the late Mr Samuel Anderson of St Germains, banker. They had been at school with Mr Henry Dundas (afterwards Lord Melville); and when he had risen to high office, he called one day on Mr Anderson, and expressed his earnest wish to have the pleasure of dining with his seven school companions, all of whom happened at that time to be at home. The meeting took place at Mr Dundas's, and it was a happy one, particularly to the host, who, when the hour of parting arrived, filled a bumper in high elation to their healths, and mentioned that they were the only men who had ever dined with him since he became a public servant who had not asked some favour either for themselves or their friends.

The house adjoining to the one last mentioned—having its gable to the street, and a garden to the south—was, about 1780, the residence of the Earl of Wemyss. A Lady Betty Charteris, of this family, occupied the one farthest to the south on that side of the street. She was a person of romantic history, for, being thwarted in an affair of the heart, she lay in bed for twenty-six years, till dismissed to the world where such troubles are unknown.

MORAY HOUSE.

IN the Canongate there is a house which has had the fortune to be connected with more than one of the most interesting points in our history. It is usually styled Moray House, being the entailed property of the noble family of Moray. The large proportions and elegant appearance of this mansion distinguish it from all the surrounding buildings, and in the rear (1847) there is a fine garden, descending in the old fashion by a series of terraces. Though long deserted by the Earls of Moray, it has been till a recent time kept in the best order, being occupied by families of respectable character.*

This house was built in the early part of the reign of Charles I. (about 1628) by Mary, Countess of Home, then a widow. Her ladyship's initials, M. H., appear, in cipher fashion, underneath her coronet upon various parts of the exterior; and over one of the principal windows towards the street there is a lozenge shield, containing the two lions rampant which form the coat armorial of the Home family. Lady Home was an English lady, being the

* For many years the Practising School for Teachers under the management of the Free Church of Scotland, now the Training College for Teachers under the Provincial Council of Education.

daughter of Edward Sutton, Lord Dudley. She seems to have been unusually wealthy for the dowager of a Scottish earl, for in 1644 the English Parliament repaid seventy thousand pounds which she had lent to the Scottish Covenanting Government; and she is found in the same year lending seven thousand to aid in paying the detachment of troops which that Government had sent to Ireland. She was also a sufferer, however, by the civil war, in as far as Dunglass House, which was blown up in 1640, by accident, when in the hands of the Covenanters, belonged to her in liferent. To her affluent circumstances, and the taste which she probably brought with her from her native country, may be ascribed the superior style of this mansion, which not only displays in the outside many traces of the elegant architecture which prevailed in England in the reign of James I., but contains two state apartments, decorated in the most elaborate manner, both in the walls and ceilings, with the favourite stucco-work of that reign. On the death of Lady Home the house passed (her ladyship having no surviving male issue) to her daughters and co-heiresses, Margaret, Countess of Moray, and Anne, Countess (afterwards Duchess) of Lauderdale, between whom the entire property of their father, the first Earl of Home, appears to have been divided, his title going into another line. By an arrangement between the two sisters, the house became, in 1645, the property of the Countess of Moray and her son James, Lord Doune.

It stood in this condition as to ownership, though still popularly called 'Lady Home's Lodging,' when, in the summer of 1648, Oliver Cromwell paid his first visit to Edinburgh. Cromwell had then just completed the overthrow of the army of the *Engagement* —a gallant body of troops which had been sent into England by the more Cavalier party of the Scottish Covenanters, in the hope of rescuing the king from the hands of the sectaries. The victorious general, with his companion Lambert, took up his quarters in this house, and here received the visits of some of the leaders of the less loyal party of the Covenanters—the Marquis of Argyll, the Chancellor Loudoun, the Earl of Lothian, the Lords Arbuthnot, Elcho, and Burleigh, and the Reverend Messrs David Dickson, Robert Blair, and James Guthrie. 'What passed among them,' says Bishop Henry Guthrie in his *Memoirs*, 'came not to be known infallibly; but it was talked very loud that he did communicate to them his design in reference to the king, and had their assent thereto.' It is scarcely necessary to remark that this was probably no more than a piece of Cavalier scandal, for there is no reason to believe that Cromwell, if he yet contemplated the death of the king, would have disclosed his views to men still so far tinctured with loyalty as those enumerated. Cromwell's object in visiting Edinburgh on this occasion and in holding these conferences, was probably limited to the reinstatement of the ultra-Presbyterian party in the government, from which the Duke of Hamilton and other loyalists had lately displaced it.

When, in 1650, the Lord Lorn, eldest son of the Marquis of Argyll, was married to Lady Mary Stuart, eldest daughter of the Earl of Moray, the wedding feast ' stood,' as contemporary writers express it, at the Earl of Moray's house in the Canongate. The event so auspicious to these great families was signalised by a circumstance of a very remarkable kind. A whole week had been passed in festivity by the wedded pair and their relations, when, on Saturday the 18th of May, the Marquis of Montrose was brought to Edinburgh, an excommunicated and already condemned captive, having been taken in the north in an unsuccessful attempt to raise a Cavalier party for his young and exiled prince. When the former relative circumstances of Argyll and Montrose are called to mind—when it is recollected that they had some years before struggled for an ascendancy in the civil affairs of Scotland, that Montrose had afterwards chased Argyll round and round the Highlands, burned and plundered his country undisturbed, and on one occasion overthrown his forces in a sanguinary action, while Argyll looked on from a safe distance at sea—the present relative circumstances of the two chiefs become a striking illustration of the vicissitudes in personal fortune that characterise a time of civil commotion. Montrose, after riding from Leith on a sorry horse, was led into the Canongate by the Watergate, and there placed upon a low cart, driven by the common executioner. In this ignominious fashion he was conducted up the street towards the prison, in which he was to have only two days to live, and in passing along was necessarily brought under the walls and windows of Moray House. On his approach to that mansion, the Marquis of Argyll, his lady, and children, together with the whole of the marriage-party, left their banqueting, and stepping out to a balcony which overhangs the street, there planted themselves to gaze on the prostrated enemy of their house and cause. Here, indeed, they had the pleasure of seeing Montrose in all external circumstances reduced beneath their feet ; but they had not calculated on the strength of nature which enabled that extraordinary man to overcome so much of the bitterness of humiliation and of death. He is said to have gazed upon them with so much serenity that they shrank back with some degree of discomposure, though not till the marchioness had expressed her spite at the fallen hero by spitting at him—an act which in the present age will scarcely be credible, though any one well acquainted with the history of the seventeenth century will have too little reason to doubt it.

In a Latin manuscript of this period, the gardens connected with the house of the Earl of Moray are spoken of as ' of such elegance, and cultivated with so much care, as to vie with those of warmer countries, and perhaps even of England itself. And here,' pursues the writer, ' you may see how much the art and industry of man may avail in supplying the defects of nature. Scarcely any one would believe it possible to give so much beauty to a garden in this frigid clime.' One reason for the excellence of the garden may have been its southern exposure. On the uppermost of its terraces there is a large and beautiful thorn, with pensile leaves ; on the second there are some fruit-trees, the branches of which have been caused to spread out in a particular way, so as to form a kind of cup, possibly for the reception of a pleasure-party, for such fantastic twistings of nature were not uncommon among our ancestors. In the lowest level of the garden there is a little receptacle for water, beside which is the statue of a fishing-boy, having a basket of fish at his feet, and a *clam-shell* inverted upon his head.* Here is also a small building, surmounted by two lions holding female shields, and which may therefore be supposed contemporaneous with the house : this was formerly a summer-house, but has latterly been expanded into the character of a conservatory. Tradition vaguely reports it as the place where the Union between England and Scotland was signed ; though there is also a popular story of that fact having been accomplished in a *laigh shop* of the High Street (marked No. 117), at one time a tavern, and known as the *Union Cellar*.† Probably the rumour, in at least the first instance, refers only to private arrangements connected with the passing of the celebrated statute in question. The Chancellor Earl of Seafield inhabited Moray House at that

* The terraces have long since been deprived of their last semblance of the old gardens ; but while recent excavations were being made for an extension of the educational buildings, the statue of the boy was discovered underground in the lowest terrace. The statue is preserved, and forms a connecting link between ' My Lady Murray's Yards ' and the ' Yards ' of the modern school.

† On the north side of the High Street, opposite the Tron Church. The site is now covered by the opening of Cockburn Street.

time on lease, and nothing could be more likely than that he should there have after-dinner consultations on the pending measure, which might in the evening be adjourned to this garden retreat.

It would appear that about this period the garden attached to the house was a sort of a public promenade or lounging-place; as was also the garden connected with Heriot's Hospital. In this character it forms a scene in the licentious play called *The Assembly*, written in 1692 by Dr Pitcairn. *Will*, ' a discreet smart gentleman,' as he is termed in the prefixed list of *dramatis personæ*, but in reality a perfect debauchee, first makes an appointment with Violetta, his mistress, to meet her in this place; and as she is under the charge of a sourly devout aunt, he has to propound the matter in metaphorical language. Pretending to expound a particular passage in the Song of Solomon for the benefit of the dame, he thus gives the hint to her young protégée:

' *Will*. " Come, my beloved, let us walk in the fields, let us lodge in the villages." The same metaphor still. The kirk not having the liberty of bringing her servant to her mother's house, resolveth to meet him in the villages, such as the Canongate, in respect of Edinburgh; and the vineyard, such as *my Lady Murray's Yards*, to use a homely comparison.

' *Old Lady*. A wondrous young man this!

       *   *   *   *

' *Will*. The eighth chapter towards the close: " Thou that dwellest in the gardens, cause me to hear thy voice."

' *Violetta*. That's still alluding to the metaphor of a gallant, who, by some signs, warns his mistress to make haste—a whistle or so. The same with early in the former chapter; that is to say, to-morrow by six o'clock. Make haste to accomplish our loves.

' *Old L*. Thou art a hopeful girl; I hope God has blest my pains on thee.'

In terms of this curious assignation, the third act opens in a walk in Lady Murray's Yards, where Will meets his beloved Violetta. After a great deal of badinage, in the style of Dryden's comedies, which were probably Dr Pitcairn's favourite models, the dialogue proceeds in the following style:

' *Will*. I 'll marry you at the rights, if you can find in your heart to give yourself to an honest fellow of no great fortune.

' *Vio*. In truth. sir, methinks it were fully as much for my future comfort to bestow myself, and any little fortune I have, upon you, as some reverend spark in a band and short cloak, with the patrimony of a good gift of prayer, and as little sense as his father, who was hanged in the Grassmarket for murdering the king's officers, had of honesty.

' *Will.* Then I must acknowledge, my dear madam, I am most damnably in love with you, and must have you by foul or fair means ; choose you whether.

' *Vio.* I 'll give you fair-play in an honest way.

' *Will.* Then, madam, I can command a parson when I please ; and if you be half so kind as I could wish, we 'll take a hackney, and trot up to some honest curate's house : besides, a guinea or so will be a charity to him perhaps.

' *Vio.* Hold a little ; I am hardly ready for that yet,' &c.

After the departure of this hopeful couple, Lord Huffy and Lord Whigriddin, who are understood to have been intended for Lord Leven (son of the Earl of Melville) and the Earl of Crawford, enter the gardens, and hold some discourse of a different kind.

THE SPEAKING HOUSE.

THE mansion on which I venture to confer this title is an old one of imposing appearance, a little below Moray House. It is conspicuous by three gables presented to the street, and by the unusual space of linear ground which it occupies. Originally, it has had no door to the street. A *porte-cochère* gives admittance to a close behind, from which every part of the house had been admissible, and when this gateway was closed the inhabitants would be in a tolerably defensible position. In this feature the house gives a striking idea of the insecurity which marked the domestic life of three hundred years ago.

It was built in the year of the assassination of the Regent Moray, and one is somewhat surprised to think that, at so dark a crisis of our national history, a mansion of so costly a character should have taken its rise. The owner, whatever grade he held, seems to have felt an apprehension of the popular talk on the subject of his raising so elegant a mansion; and he took a curious mode of deprecating its expression. On a tablet over the ground-floor he inscribes: HODIE MIHI: CRAS TIBI. CUR IGITUR CURAS? along with the year of the erection, 1570. This is as much as to say: 'I am the happy man to-day; your turn may come to-morrow.

Why, then, should you repine?' One can imagine from a second tablet, a little way farther along the front, that as the building proceeded, the storm of public remark and outcry had come to be more and more bitter, so that the soul of the owner got stirred up into a firm and defying anger. He exclaims (for, though a lettered inscription, one feels it as an exclamation): UT TU LINGUÆ TUÆ, SIC EGO MEAR. AURIUM, DOMINUS SUM ('As thou of thy tongue, so I of my ears, am lord'); thus quoting, in his rage on this petty occasion, an expression said to have been used in the Roman senate by Titus Tacitus when repelling the charges of Lucius Metellus.* Afterwards he seems to have cooled into a religious view of the predicament, and in a third legend along the front he tells the world: CONSTANTI PECTORI RES MORTALIUM UMBRA ; ending a little farther on with an emblem of the Christian hope of the Resurrection, ears of wheat springing from a handful of bones. It is a great pity that we should not know who was the builder and owner of this house, since he has amused us so much with the history of his feelings during the process of its erection. A friend at my elbow suggests—a schoolmaster! But who ever heard of a schoolmaster so handsomely remunerated by his profession as to be able to build a house?

Nothing else is known of the early history of this house beyond the fact of the Canongate magistrates granting a charter for it to the Hammermen of that burgh, September 10, 1647.† It was, however, in 1753 occupied by a person of no less distinction than the Dowager Duchess of Gordon. ‡

In the alley passing under this mansion there is a goodly building of more modern structure, forming two sides of a quadrangle, with a small court in front divided from the lane by a wall in which there is a large gateway. Amidst filthiness inde-

---

* I was indebted to my friend Dr John Brown (*Horæ Subsecivæ*, p. 42) for drawing my attention to a quotation of Seneca by Beyerlinck (*Magn. Theatr. Vit. Human.*, tom. vi. p. 60), involving this fine expression. Some one, however, has searched all over the writings of Seneca for it in vain.

† The close entering by the archway at the east end of the house, now called 'Bakehouse Close,' was formerly 'Hammermen's Close.'

‡ 'The Speaking House' is now recognised as a town mansion of the Huntly family. It is said to be associated with the first marquis, who killed the 'Bonnie Earl of Moray' at Donibristle, and died in 1636 at Dundee on his way north to Aberdeenshire. His son, the second marquis, who was beheaded in 1649, was residing in this house ten years prior to his execution, and in it his daughter Lady Ann was married to Lord Drummond, third Earl of Perth.

scribable, one discerns traces of former elegance : a crest over the doorway—namely, a cock mounted on a trumpet, with the motto ' VIGILANTIBUS,' and the date 1633 ; over two upper windows, the letters ' S. A. A.' and ' D. M. H.'   These memorials, with certain references in the charter before mentioned, leave no room for doubt that this was the house of Sir Archibald

Acheson of Aber-cairny, Secretary of State for Scotland in the reign of Charles I., and ancestor to the Earl of Gosford in Ireland, who to this day bears the same crest and motto. The letters are the initials of Sir Archibald and his wife, Dame Margaret Hamilton. Here of course was the *court* of Scotland for a certain time, the Secretary of State being the grand dispenser of patronage in our country at that period — *here*, where nothing but the extremest wretchedness

Acheson House.

is now to be seen ! That boastful bird, too, still seeming to assert the family dignity, two hundred years after it ceased to have any connection with the spot ! Verily there are some moral preachments in these dark old closes if modern refinement could go to hear the sermon !

Sir Archibald Acheson acquired extensive lands in Ireland,* which have ever since been in the possession of his family. It was a descendant of his, and of the same name, who had the gratification of becoming the landlord of Swift at Market-hill,

---

* Which he named Gosford, after the estate in East Lothian, which was acquired by Sir Archibald's ancestor, a wealthy burgess in the reign of Queen Mary. The Viscounts Gosford take their title from the Irish estate.

and whom the dean was consequently led to celebrate in many of his poems. Swift seems to have been on the most familiar terms with this worthy knight and his lady; the latter he was accustomed to call *Skinnibonia, Lean,* or *Snipe,* as the humour inclined him. The inimitable comic painting of her ladyship's maid Hannah, in the debate whether Hamilton's Bawn should be turned into a malt-house or a barrack, can never perish from our literature. In like humour, the dean asserts the superiority of himself and his brother-tenant Colonel Leslie, who had served much in Spain, over the knight:

> 'Proud baronet of Nova Scotia,
> The dean and Spaniard much reproach ye.
> Of their two fames the world enough rings;
> Where are thy services and sufferings?
> What if for nothing once you kissed,
> Against the grain, a monarch's fist?
> What if among the courtly tribe,
> You lost a place and saved a bribe?
> And then in surly mood came here
> To fifteen hundred pounds a year,
> And fierce against the Whigs harangued?
> You never ventured to be hanged.
> How dare you treat your betters thus?
> Are you to be compared to us?'

Speaking also of a celebrated thorn at Market-hill, which had long been a resort of merry-making parties, he reverts to the Scottish Secretary of former days:

> 'Sir Archibald, that valorous knight,
>   The lord of all the fruitful plain,
> Would come and listen with delight,
>   For he was fond of rural strain:
>
> Sir Archibald, whose favourite name
>   Shall stand for ages on record,
> By Scottish bards of highest fame,
>   Wise Hawthornden and Stirling's lord.'

The following letter to Sir Archibald from his friend Sir James

Balfour, Lord Lyon, occurs amongst the manuscript stores of the latter gentleman in the Advocates' Library :

'To Sir ARCHIBALD ACHESONE,
  one of the Secretaries of Staite.

  'WORTHY SIR—Your letters, full of Spartanical brevity to the first view, bot, againe overlooked, Demosthenicall longe ; stuffed full of exaggerations and complaints ; the yeast of your enteirest affections, sent to quicken a slumbring friend as you imagine, quho nevertheless remains vigilant of you and of the smallest matters, which may aney wayes adde the least rill of content to the ocean of your happiness ; quherfor you may show your comerad, and intreat him from me, as from one that trewly loves and honors his best pairts, that now he vold refraine, both his tonge and pen, from these quhirkis and obloquies, quherwith he so often uses to stain the name of grate personages, for hardly can he live so reteiredly, in so voluble ane age, without becoming at one tyme or uther obnoxious to the blow of some courtier. So begging God to bless you, I am your—   JA. BALFOUR.
  'LONDON, 9 *Apryll* 1631.'

Twenty years before the Duchess of Gordon lived in the venerable house at the head of the close, a preceding dowager resided in another part of the town. This was the distinguished Lady Elizabeth Howard (daughter of the Duke of Norfolk, by Lady Anne Somerset, daughter of the Marquis of Worcester), who occasioned so much disturbance in the end of Queen Anne's reign by the Jacobite medal which she sent to the Faculty of Advocates. Her grace lived in a house at the Abbeyhill, where, as we are informed by Wodrow, in a tone of pious horror,* she openly kept a kind of college for instructing young people in Jesuitism and Jacobitism together. In this labour she seems to have been assisted by the Duchess of Perth, a kindred soul, whose enthusiasm afterwards caused the ruin of her family, by sending her son into the insurrection of 1745.† The Duchess of Gordon died here in 1732. I should suppose the house to have been that respectable old villa, at the extremity of the suburb of Abbeyhill, in which the late Baron Norton, of the Court of Exchequer, lived for many years. It was formerly possessed by Baron Mure, who, during the administration of the Earl of Bute, exercised the duties and dispensed the patronage of the *sous-ministre* for Scotland, under the Hon. Stuart Mackenzie, younger brother of the Premier. This

---

* In his MS. Diaries in the Advocates' Library.

† In an advertisement in a Jacobite newspaper, called *The Thistle*, which rose and sank in 1734, the house is advertised as having lately been occupied by the Duchesses of Gordon and Perth. [1868. It is in the course of being taken down to make way for a railway.]

was of course in its turn the *court* of Scotland; and from the description of a gentleman old enough to remember attending the levees (Sir W. M. Bannatyne), I should suppose that it was as much haunted by suitors of all kinds as ever were the more elegant halls of Holyrood House. Baron Mure, who was the personal friend of Earl Bute, died in 1774.

PANMURE HOUSE—ADAM SMITH.

AT the bottom of a close a little way below the Canongate Church, there is a house which a few years ago bore the appearance of one of those small semi-quadrangular manor-houses which were prevalent in the country about the middle of the seventeenth cen-

tury. It is now altered, and brought into jux-taposition with the coarse details of an ironfoundry, yet still is not without some traits of its original style. The name of Panmure House takes the mind back to the Earls of Panmure, the fourth of whom lost title and estates for his concern in the affair of 1715; but I am not certain of any earlier proprietor of this family than William Maule, nephew of the attainted earl, created Earl of Panmure as an Irish title in 1743. *He* possessed the house in the middle of the last century.

Back of Canongate Tolbooth—Tolbooth Wynd.

All reference to rank in connection with this house appears trivial in comparison with the fact that it was the residence of Adam Smith from 1778, when he came to live in Edinburgh as a commissioner of the customs, till his death in 1790, when he was interred in a somewhat obscure situation at the back of the Canongate Tolbooth. In his time the house must have seen the most intellectual company to be had in Scotland ; but it had not the honour of being the birthplace of any of Smith's great works. His last and greatest—the book which has undoubtedly done more for the good of the community than any other ever produced in Scotland—was the work of ten quiet, studious years previous to 1778, during which the philosopher lived in his mother's house in Kirkcaldy.

The gentle, virtuous character of Smith has left little for the anecdotist. The utmost simplicity marked the externals of the man. He said very truly (being in possession of a handsome library) that ' he was only a beau in his books.' Leading an abstracted, scholarly life, he was ill-fitted for common worldly affairs. Some one remarked to a friend of mine while Smith still lived : ' How strange to think of one who has written so well on the principles of exchange and barter—he is obliged to get a friend to buy his horse-corn for him ! ' The author of the *Wealth of Nations* never thought of marrying. His household affairs were managed to his perfect contentment by a female cousin, a Miss Jeanie Douglas, who almost necessarily acquired a great control over him. It is said that the amiable philosopher, being fond of a bit sugar, and chid by her for taking it, would sometimes, in sauntering backwards and forwards along the parlour, watch till Miss Jeanie's back was turned in order to supply himself with his favourite morsel. Such things are not derogatory to greatness like Smith's : they link it to human nature, and secure for it the love, as it had previously possessed the admiration, of common men.

The one personal circumstance regarding Smith which has made the greatest impression on his fellow-citizens is the rather too well-known anecdote of the two fishwomen. He was walking along the streets one day, deeply abstracted, and speaking in a low tone to himself, when he caught the attention of two of these many-petticoated ladies, engaged in selling their fish. They exchanged significant looks, bearing strong reference to the restraints of a well-managed lunatic asylum, and then sighed one to the other : ' Aih, sirs ; and he's weel put on too ! '—that is, well dressed ; his gentleman-like condition making the case appear so much the more piteous.

JOHN PATERSON THE GOLFER.

IN the Canongate, nearly opposite to Queensberry House, is a narrow, old-fashioned mansion, of peculiar form, having a coat-armorial conspicuously placed at the top, and a plain slab over the doorway containing the following inscriptions:

> 'Cum victor ludo, Scotis qui proprius, esset,
> Ter tres victores post redimitus avos,
> Patersonus, humo tunc educebat in altum
> Hanc, quæ victores tot tulit una, domum.'

> 'I hate no person.'

It appears that this quatrain was the production of Dr Pitcairn, while the sentence below is an anagram upon the name of JOHN PATERSONE. The stanza expresses that 'when Paterson had been crowned victor in a game peculiar to Scotland, in which his ancestors had also been often victorious, he then built this mansion, which one conquest raised him above all his predecessors.' We must resort to tradition for an explanation of this obscure hint.

Golfers' Land.

Till a recent period, golfing had long been conducted upon the Links of Leith.* It had even been the sport of princes on

* In 1864 this favourite Scottish pastime was resuscitated on Leith Links, and is now enjoyed with a relish as keen as ever.

that field. We are told by Mr William Tytler of Woodhouselee that Charles I. and the Duke of York (afterwards James II.) played at golf on Leith Links, in succession, during the brief periods of their residence in Holyrood. Though there is an improbability in this tale as far as Charles is concerned, seeing that he spent too short a time in Edinburgh to have been able to play at a game notorious for the time necessary in acquiring it, I may quote the anecdote related by Mr Tytler: 'That while he was engaged in a party at golf on the green or Links of Leith, a letter was delivered into his hands, which gave him the first account of the insurrection and rebellion in Ireland; on reading which, he suddenly called for his coach, and leaning on one of his attendants, and in great agitation, drove to the palace of Holyrood House, from whence next day he set out for London.' Mr Tytler says, regarding the Duke of York, that he 'was frequently seen in a party at golf on the Links of Leith with some of the nobility and gentry. I remember in my youth to have often conversed with an old man named Andrew Dickson, a golf-club maker, who said that, when a boy, he used to carry the duke's golf-clubs, and run before him, and announce where the balls fell.' *

Tradition reports that when the duke lived in Holyrood House he had on one occasion a discussion with two English noblemen as to the native country of golf; his Royal Highness asserting that it was peculiar to Scotland, while they as pertinaciously insisted that it was an English game as well. Assuredly, whatever may have been the case in those days, it is not now an English game in the proper sense of the words, seeing that it is only played to the south of the Tweed by a few fraternities of Scotsmen, who have acquired it in their own country in youth. However this may be, the two English nobles proposed, good-humouredly, to prove its English character by taking up the duke in a match to be played on Leith Links. James, glad of an opportunity to make popularity in Scotland, in however small a way, accepted the challenge, and sought for the best partner he could find. By an association not at this day surprising to those who practise the game, the heir-presumptive of the British throne played in concert with a poor shoemaker named John Paterson, the worthy descendant of a long line of illustrious golfers. If the two southrons were, as might be expected, inexperienced in the game, they had no chance against a pair,

* *Archæologia Scotica,* i.

one member of which was a good player. So the duke got the best of the practical argument; and Paterson's merits were rewarded by a gift of the sum played for. The story goes on to say that John was thus enabled to build a somewhat stylish house for himself in the Canongate, on the top of which, being a Scotsman, and having of course a pedigree, he clapped the Paterson arms—three pelicans vulned ; on a chief three mullets ; crest, a dexter hand grasping a golf-club; together with the motto—dear to all golfers—FAR AND SURE.

It must be admitted there is some uncertainty about this tale. The house, the inscriptions, and arms only indicate that Paterson built the house after being a victor at golf, and that Pitcairn had a hand in decorating it. One might even see, in the fact of the epigram, as if a gentleman wit were indulging in a jest at the expense of some simple plebeian, who held all notoriety honourable. It might have been expected that if Paterson had been enriched by a match in which he was connected with the Duke of York, a Jacobite like Pitcairn would have made distinct allusion to the circumstance. The tradition, nevertheless, seems too curious to be entirely overlooked, and the reader may therefore take it at its worth.

[LOTHIAN HUT.

THE noble family of Lothian had a mansion in Edinburgh, though of but a moderate dignity. It was a small house situated in a spare piece of ground at the bottom of the Canongate, on the south side. Latterly it was leased to Professor Dugald Stewart, who, about the end of the last century, here entertained several English pupils of noble rank—among others, the Hon. Henry Temple, afterwards Lord Palmerston.* About 1825 the building was taken down to make room for a brewery.

About the middle of the last century, Lothian Hut was occupied by the wife of the fourth marquis, a lady of great lineage, being the only daughter of Robert, Earl of Holderness, and great-granddaughter of Charles Louis, Elector Palatine. Her ladyship was a person of grand character, while yet admittedly very amiable. As a piece of very old gossip, the Lady Marchioness, on first coming to live in the Hut, found herself in want of a few trifling articles from a milliner, and sent for one who was reputed to be the first of the class then in Edinburgh—namely, Miss Ramsay. But there were two Miss Ramsays. They had a shop on the east side of the Old Lyon Close, on the south side of the High Street, and there made ultimately a little fortune, which enabled them to build the villa of Marionville, near Restalrig (called *Lappet Hall* by the vulgar). The Misses Ramsay, receiving a message from so grand a lady, instead of obeying the order implicitly, came together, dressed out in a very splendid style, and told the marchioness that every article they wore was 'at the very top of the fashion.' The marchioness, disgusted with their forward-

---

* A newspaper, giving an account of Lord Palmerston's visit to Edinburgh in 1865, mentions that his lordship, during his stay in the city, was made aware that an aged woman of the name of Peggie Forbes, who had been a servant with Dugald Stewart, well remembered his lordship when under the professor's roof in early days. Interested in the circumstance, Lord Palmerston took occasion to pay her a visit at her dwelling, No. 1 Rankeillor Street, and expressed his pleasure at renewing the acquaintance of the old domestic. Dr John Brown had discovered the existence of this old association, and with it a box of tools which were the property of 'young Maister Henry' of those days. The sight of them called up within the breast of the Premier further associations of days long bygone.

ness and affectation, said she would take their specimens into consideration, and wished them a good-morning. According to our gossiping authority, she then sent for Mrs Sellar, who carried on the millinery business in a less pretentious style at a place in the Lawnmarket where Bank Street now stands. (I like the localities, for they bring the Old Town of a past age so clearly before us.) Mrs Sellar made her appearance at Lothian Hut in a plain, decorous manner. Her head-dress consisted of a mob-cap of the finest lawn, tied under her chin; over which there was a hood of the same stuff. She wore a cloak of plain black silk without any lace, and had no bonnet, the use of which was supplied by the hood. Mrs Sellar's manners were elegant and pleasing. When she entered, the marchioness rose to receive her. On being asked for her patterns, she stepped to the door and brought in two large boxes, which had been carried behind her by two women. The articles, being produced, gave great satisfaction, and her ladyship never afterwards employed any other milliner. So the story ends, in the manner of the good-boy books, in establishing that milliners ought not to be too prone to exhibit their patterns upon their own persons.]

HENRY PRENTICE AND POTATOES.

NO doubt is entertained on any hand that the field-culture of the potato was first practised in Scotland by a man of humble condition, originally a pedlar, by name Henry Prentice. He was an eccentric person, as many have been who stepped out of the common walk to do things afterwards discovered to be great. A story is told that while the potatoes were growing in certain little fields which he leased near our city, Lord Minto came from time to time to inquire about the crop. Prentice at length told his lordship that the experiment was entirely successful, and all he wanted was a horse and cart to drive his potatoes to Edinburgh that they might be sold. 'I 'll give you a horse and cart,' said his lordship. Prentice then took his crop to market, cart by cart, till it was all sold, after which he disposed of *the horse and cart*, which he affected to believe Lord Minto had given him as a present.

Having towards the close of his days realised a small sum of money, he sunk £140 in the hands of the Canongate magistrates, as managers of the poorhouse of that parish, receiving in return seven shillings a week, upon which he lived for several years. Occasionally he made little donations to the charity. During his last years he was an object of no small curiosity in Edinburgh, partly on account of his connection with potato culture and partly by reason of his oddities. It was said of him that he would never shake hands with any human being above two years of age. In his bargain with the Canongate dignitaries, it was agreed that he should have a *good grave* in their churchyard, and one was selected according to his own choice. Over this, thinking it as well, perhaps, that he should enjoy a little quasi-posthumous notoriety during his life, he caused a monument to be erected, bearing this inscription ·

'Be not anxious to know how I lived,
But rather how you yourself should die.'

He also had a coffin prepared at the price of two guineas, taking the undertaker bound to screw it down gratis with his own hands. In addition to all this, his friends the magistrates were under covenant to bury him with a hearse and four coaches.

But even the designs of mortals respecting the grave itself are liable to disappointment. Owing to the mischief done by the boys to the premature monument, Prentice saw fit to have it removed to a quieter cemetery, that of Restalrig, where, at his death in 1788, he was accordingly interred.

Such was the originator of that extensive culture of the potato which has since borne so conspicuous a place in the economics of our country, for good and for evil.

It is curious that this plant, although the sole support of millions of our population, should now again (1846) have fallen under suspicion. At its first introduction, and for several ages thereafter, it was regarded as a vegetable of by no means good character, though for a totally different reason from any which affect its reputation in our day. Its supposed tendency to inflame some of the sensual feelings of human nature is frequently adverted to by Shakespeare and his contemporaries ; and this long remained a popular impression in the north.*

* Robertson, in his *Rural Recollections* (Irvine, 1829), says : ' The earliest evidence that I have met with of potatoes in Scotland is an old household book of the Eglintoune family in 1733, in which potatoes appear at different times as a dish at supper.' They appear earlier than this—namely, in 1701—in the household book of the Duchess of Buccleuch and Monmouth, where the price per peck is intimated at 2s. 6d.—See Arnot's *History of Edinburgh,* 4to, p. 201

THE DUCHESS OF BUCCLEUCH AND MONMOUTH.

IT is rather curious that one of my informants in this article should have dined with a lady who had dined with a peeress married in the year 1662.

This peeress was Anne, Duchess of Buccleuch and Monmouth, the wife of the unfortunate son of Charles II. As is well known, she was early deserted by her husband, who represented, not without justice, that a marriage into which he had been tempted for reasons of policy by his relations, when he was only thirteen years of age, could hardly be binding.

The young duchess, naturally plain in features, was so unfortunate in early womanhood as to become lame in consequence of some feats in dancing. For her want of personal graces there is negative evidence in a dedication of Dryden, where he speaks abundantly of her wit, but not a word of beauty, which shows that the case must have been desperate. [This, by the way, was the remark made to me on the subject by Sir Walter Scott, who, in the *Lay of the Last Minstrel*, has done what Dryden could not do—flattered the duchess :

> 'She had known adversity,
> Though born in such a high degree ;
> In pride of power and *beauty's bloom*,
> Had wept o'er Monmouth's bloody tomb.']

Were any further proof wanting, it might be found in the regard in which she was held by James II., who, as is well known, had such a tendency to plain women as induced a suspicion in his witty brother that they were prescribed to him by his confessor by way of penance. This friendship, in which there was nothing improper, was the means of saving her grace's estates at the tragical close of her husband's life.

It is curious to learn that the duchess, notwithstanding the terms on which she had been with her husband, and the sad stamp put upon his pretensions to legitimacy, acted throughout the remainder of her somewhat protracted life as if she had been the widow of a true prince of the blood-royal. In her state-rooms she had a canopy erected, beneath which was the only seat in the apartment, everybody standing besides herself. When

Lady Margaret Montgomery, one of the beautiful Countess of Eglintoune's daughters, was at a boarding-school near London— previous to the year *Thirty*—she was frequently invited by the duchess to her house; and because her great-grandmother, Lady Mary Leslie, was sister to her grace's mother, *she* was allowed a chair; but this was an extraordinary mark of grace. The duchess was the last person of quality in Scotland who kept *pages*, in the proper acceptation of the term—that is, young gentlemen of good birth, who acquired manners and knowledge of the world in attending upon persons of exalted rank. The last of her grace's pages rose to be a general. When a letter was brought for the duchess, the domestic gave it to the page, the page to the waiting-gentlewoman (always a person of birth also), and she at length to her grace. The duchess kept a tight hand over her clan and tenants, but was upon the whole beloved.

She was buried (1732) on the same day with the too-much-celebrated Colonel Charteris. At the funeral of Henry, Duke of Buccleuch, in the year 1812, in the aisle of the church at Dalkeith, my informant (Sir Walter Scott) was shown an old man who had been at the funeral of both her grace and Colonel Charteris. He said that the day was dreadfully stormy, which all the world agreed was owing to the devil carrying off Charteris. The mob broke in upon the mourners who followed this personage to the grave, and threw cats, dogs, and a pack of cards upon the coffin; whereupon the gentlemen drew their swords, and cut away among the rioters. In the confusion one little old man was pushed into the grave; and the sextons, somewhat prompt in the discharge of their duty, began to shovel in the earth upon the quick and the dead. The grandfather of my informant (Dr Rutherford), who was one of the mourners, was much hurt in the affray; and my informant has heard his mother describe the terror of the family on his coming home with his clothes bloody and his sword broken.

As to pages—a custom existed among old ladies till a later day of keeping such attendants, rather superior to the little polybuttoned personages who are now so universal. It was not, however, to be expected that a pranksome youth would behave with consistent respect to an aged female of the stiff manners then prevalent. Accordingly, ridiculous circumstances took place. An old lady of the name of Plenderleith, of very stately aspect and grave carriage, used to walk to Leith by the Easter Road with her little foot-page behind her. For the whole way, the young rogue would be seen projecting burs at her dress, laughing immoderately, but silently, when one stuck. An old lady and her sequel of a page was very much like a tragedy followed by a farce. The keeping of the rascals in order at home used also to be a sad problem to a quiet old lady. The only expedient which Miss ———— could hit upon to preserve her page from the corruption of the streets was, in her own phrase, to *lock up his breeks*, which she did almost every evening. The youth, being then only presentable at a window, had to content himself with such chat as he could indulge in with his companions and such mischief as he could execute from that loophole of retreat. So much for the parade of keeping pages.

CLAUDERO.

EDINBURGH, which now smiles complacently upon the gravities of her reviews and the flippancies of her magazines, formerly laughed outright at the coarse lampoons of her favourite poet and pamphleteer, Claudero. The distinct publications of this witty and eccentric personage (whose real name was James Wilson) are well known to collectors; and his occasional pieces must be fresh in the remembrance of those who, forty or fifty years ago (1824), were in the habit of perusing the *Scots Magazine*, amidst the general gravity of which they appeared, like the bright and giddy eyes of a satyr, staring through the sere leaves of a sober forest scene.

Claudero was a native of Cumbernauld, in Dumbartonshire, and at an early period of his life showed such marks of a mischief-loving disposition as procured him general odium. The occasion of his lameness was a pebble thrown from a tree at the minister, who, having been previously exasperated by his tricks, chased him to the end of a closed lane, and with his cane inflicted such personal chastisement as rendered him a cripple, and a hater of the clergy, for the rest of his life.

In Edinburgh, where he lived for upwards of thirty years previous to his death in 1789, his livelihood was at first ostensibly gained by keeping a little school, latterly by celebrating what were called *half-mark marriages*—a business resembling that of the Gretna blacksmith. It is said that he, who made himself the terror of so many by his wit, was in his turn held in fear by his wife, who was as complete a shrew as ever fell to the lot of poet or philosopher.

He was a satirist by profession; and when any person wished to have a squib played off upon his neighbours, he had nothing to do but call upon Claudero, who, for half a crown, would produce the desired effusion, composed, and copied off in a fair hand, in a given time. He liked this species of employment better than writing upon speculation, the profit being more certain and immediate. When in want of money, it was his custom to write a sly satire on some opulent public personage, upon whom he called with it, desiring to have his opinion of the work, and his countenance in favour of a subscription for its publication. The object of his ridicule, conscious-struck by his own portrait, would wince and be civil, advise him to give up thoughts of publishing so hasty a production, and conclude by offering a guinea or two to keep the poet alive till better times should come round. At that time there lived in Edinburgh a number of rich old men who had made fortunes in questionable ways abroad, and whose characters, labouring under strange suspicions, were wonderfully susceptible of Claudero's satire. These the wag used to bleed profusely and frequently by working upon their fears of public notice.

In 1766 appeared *Miscellanies in Prose and Verse, by Claudero, Son of Nimrod the Mighty Hunter, &c., &c.*, opening with this preface: 'Christian Reader—The following miscellany is published at the desire of many gentlemen, who have all been my very good friends; if there be anything in it amusing or entertaining, I shall be very glad I have contributed to your diversion, and will laugh as heartily at your money as you do at my works. Several of my pieces may need explanation; but I am too cunning for that: what is not understood, like Presbyterian preaching, will at least be admired. I am regardless of critics; perhaps some of my lines want a foot; but then, if the critic look sharp out, he will find that loss sufficiently supplied in other places, where they have a foot too much: and besides, men's works generally resemble themselves; if the poems are lame, so is the author—CLAUDERO.'

The most remarkable poems in this volume are: 'The Echo of the Royal Porch of the Palace of Holyrood House, which fell under Military Execution, anno 1753;' 'The Last Speech and Dying Words of the Cross, which was Hanged, Drawn, and Quartered on Monday the 15th of March 1756, for the horrid crime of being an Incumbrance to the Street;' 'Scotland in Tears for the horrid Treatment of the Kings' Sepulchres;' 'An Elegy on the much-lamented Death of Quaker Erskine;'* 'A Sermon on the Condemnation of the Netherbow;' 'Humphry Colquhoun's Last Farewell,' &c. Claudero seems to have been the only man of his time who remonstrated against the destruction of the venerable edifices then removed from the streets which they

---

* A noted brewer, much given to preaching. Of him Claudero says:

'Our souls with gospel he did cheer,
Our bodies, too, with ale and beer;
Gratis he gospel got and gave away;
For ale and beer he only made us pay.'

ornamented, to the disappointment and indignation of all future antiquaries. There is much wit in his sermon upon the destruction of the Netherbow. 'What was too hard,' he says, 'for the great ones of the earth, yea, even queens, to effect, is now accomplished. No patriot duke opposeth the scheme, as did the great Argyll in the grand senate of our nation ; therefore the project shall go into execution, and down shall Edina's lofty porches be hurled with a vengeance. Streets shall be extended to the east, regular and beautiful, as far as the Frigate Whins ; and Portobello * shall be a lodge for the captors of tea and brandy. The city shall be joined to Leith on the north, and a procession of wise masons shall there lay the foundations of a spacious harbour. Pequin or Nanquin shall not be able to compare with Edinburgh for magnificence. Our city shall be the greatest wonder of the world, and the fame of its glory shall reach the distant ends of the earth.†

But lament, O thou descendant of the royal Dane, and chief of the tribe of Wilson ; for thy shop, contiguous to the porch, shall be dashed to pieces, and its place will know thee no more ! No more shall the melodious voice of the loyalist Grant ‡ be heard in the morning, nor shall he any more shake the bending wand towards the triumphal arch. Let all who angle in deep waters lament, for Tom had not his equal. The Netherbow Coffee-house of the loyal Smeiton can now no longer enjoy its ancient name

* This thriving parliamentary burgh originated in a cottage built, and long inhabited, by a retired seaman of Admiral Vernon's squadron, who gave it this name in commemoration of the triumph which his commander there gained over the Spaniards in 1739. There must have been various houses at the spot in 1753, when we find one 'George Hamilton, in Portobello,' advertising in the *Edinburgh Courant* that he would give a reward of three pounds to any one who should discover the author of a scandalous report, which represented him as harbouring robbers in his house. The waste upon which Portobello is now partly founded was dreadfully infested at this time with robbers, and resorted to by smugglers ; see *Courant*. [Portobello, while remaining one of the 'Leith burghs' for parliamentary purposes, was municipally incorporated with Edinburgh in 1896. Claudero's 'Frigate Whins' are better known as the 'Figgate Whins.']

† Claudero could have little serious expectation that several of these predictions would come to pass before he had been forty years in his grave.

‡ A celebrated and much-esteemed fishing-rod maker, who afterwards flourished in the old wooden *land* at the head of Blackfriars Wynd. He survived to recent times, and was distinguished for his adherence to the cocked hat, wrist ruffles, and buckles of his youth. He was a short, neat man, very well bred, a great angler, intimate with the great, a Jacobite, and lived to near a century. He had fished in almost every trouting stream in the three kingdoms, and was seen skating on Lochend at the age of eighty-five.

with propriety ; and from henceforth *The Revolution Coffee-house* shall its name be called. Our gates must be extended wide for accommodating the gilded chariots, which, from the luxury of the age, are become numerous. With an impetuous career, they jostle against one another in our streets, and the unwary foot-passenger is in danger of being crushed to pieces. The loaded cart itself cannot withstand their fury, and the hideous yells of *Coal Johnie* resound through the vaulted sky. The sour-milk barrels are overturned, and deluges of Corstorphin cream run down our strands, while the poor un-happy milk-maid wrings her hands with sorrow.' To the sermon are appended the 'Last Speech and Dying Words of the Nether-bow,' in which the following laughable de-claration oc-curs: 'May my clock be struck dumb in the other

Netherbow.

world, if I lie in this! and may MACK, the reformer of Edina's lofty spires, never bestride my weathercock on high, if I deviate from truth in these my last words! Though my fabric shall be levelled with the dust of the earth, yet I fall in hope that my weathercock shall be exalted on some more modern dome, where it shall shine like the burnished gold, reflecting the rays of the sun to the eye of ages unborn. The daring Mack shall yet look down from my cock, high in the airy region, to the brandy-shops below, where large graybeards shall appear to him no bigger than mutchkin-bottles, and mutchkin-bottles shall be in his sight like the spark of a diamond.' One of Claudero's versified compositions, ' Humphry Colquhoun's Farewell,' is remarkable as a kind of coarse prototype of the beautiful lyric entitled ' Mary,' sung in *The Pirate* by Claud Halcro. One wonders to find the genius of Scott refining upon such materials :

> ' Farewell to Auld Reekie,
>   Farewell to lewd Kate,
> Farewell to each ——,
>   And farewell to cursed debt ;
> With light heart and thin breeches,
>   Humph crosses the main ;
> All worn out to stitches,
>   He 'll ne'er come again.
>
> Farewell to old Dido,
>   Who sold him good ale ;
> Her charms, like her drink,
>   For poor Humph were too stale ;
> Though closely she urged him
>   To marry and stay,
> Her Trojan, quite cloyed,
>   From her sailed away.
>
> Farewell to James Campbell,
>   Who played many tricks ;
> Humph's ghost and Lochmoidart's *
>   Will chase him to Styx ;
> Where in Charon's wherry
>   He 'll be ferried o'er
> To Pluto's dominions,
>   'Mongst rascals great store.
>
> Farewell, pot-companions,
>   Farewell, all good fellows ;
> Farewell to my anvil,
>   Files, pliers, and bellows :
> Sails, fly to Jamaica,
>   Where I mean long to dwell,
> Change manners with climate—
>   Dear Drummond, farewell.'

It is not unworthy of notice that the publication of Dr Blair's *Lectures on Rhetoric and the Belles-lettres* was hastened by Claudero, who, having procured notes taken by some of the students, avowed an intention of giving these to the world. The reverend author states in his preface that he was induced to publish the

* This seems to bear some reference to the seizure of young Macdonald of Kinlochmoidart at Lesmahagow in 1745.

lectures in consequence of some surreptitious and incorrect copies finding their way to the public; but it has not hitherto been told that this doggerel-monger was the person chiefly concerned in bringing about that result.

Claudero occasionally dealt in whitewash as well as blackball, and sometimes wrote regular panegyrics. An address of this kind to a *writer* named Walter Fergusson, who built St James's Square, concludes with a strange association of ideas :

> 'May Pentland Hills pour forth their springs,
>   To water all thy square !
> May Fergussons still bless the place,
>   Both gay and debonnair !'

When the said square was in progress, however, the water seemed in no hurry to obey the bard's invocation; and an attempt was made to procure this useful element by sinking wells for it, despite the elevation of the ground. Mr Walter Scott, W.S., happened one day to pass when Captain Fergusson of the Royal Navy—a good officer, but a sort of Commodore Trunnion in his manners—was sinking a well of vast depth. Upon Mr Scott expressing a doubt if water could be got there, 'I will get it,' quoth the captain, 'though I sink to hell for it !' 'A bad place for water,' was the dry remark of the doubter.

QUEENSBERRY HOUSE.

IN the Canongate, on the south side, is a large, gloomy building, enclosed in a court, and now used as a refuge for destitute persons. This was formerly the town mansion of the Dukes of Queensberry, and a scene, of course, of stately life and high political affairs. It was built by the first duke, the willing minister of the last two Stuarts—he who also built Drumlanrig Castle in Dumfriesshire, which he never slept in but one night, and with regard to which it is told that he left the accounts for the building tied up with this inscription: 'The deil pyke out his een that looks herein!' Duke William was a noted money-maker and land-acquirer. No little laird of his neighbourhood had any chance with him for the retention of his family property. He was something still worse in the eyes of the common people —a *persecutor*; that is, one siding against the Presbyterian cause. There is a story in one of their favourite books of his having died of the *morbus pediculosus*, by way of a judgment upon him for his wickedness. In reality, he died of some ordinary fever. It is also stated, from the same authority, that about the time when his grace died, a Scotch skipper, being in Sicily, saw one day a coach-and-six driving to Mount Etna, while a diabolic voice exclaimed: 'Open to the Duke of Drumlanrig!'—'which proves, by the way,' says Mr Sharpe, 'that the devil's porter is no herald. In fact,' adds this acute critic, 'the legend is borrowed from the story of Antonio the Rich, in George Sandys's *Travels*.' *

It appears, from family letters, that the first duchess often resided in the Canongate mansion, while her husband occupied Sanquhar Castle. The lady was unfortunately given to drink, and there is a letter of hers in which she pathetically describes her situation to a country friend, left alone in Queensberry House with only a few bottles of wine, one of which, having been drawn, had turned out sour. Sour wine being prejudicial to her health, it was fearful to think of what might prove the quality of the remaining bottles.

The son of this couple, James, second duke, must ever be memorable as the main instrument in carrying through the

* Introduction to Law's *Memorials*, p. lxxx.

Union. His character has been variously depicted. By Defoe, in his *History of the Union*, it is liberally panegyrised. 'I think I have,' says he, 'given demonstrations to the world that I will flatter no man.' Yet he could not refrain from extolling the 'prudence, calmness, and temper' which the duke showed during that difficult crisis. Unfortunately the author of *Robinson Crusoe*, though not a flatterer, could not insure himself against the usual prepossessions of a partisan. Boldness the duke must certainly have possessed, for during the ferments attending the parliamentary proceedings on that occasion, he continued daily to drive between his lodgings in Holyrood and the Parliament House, notwithstanding several intimations that his life was threatened. His grace's eldest son, James, was an idiot of the most unhappy sort—rabid and gluttonous, and early grew to an immense height, which is testified by his coffin in the family vault at Durisdeer, still to be seen, of great length and unornamented with the heraldic follies which bedizen the violated remains of his relatives. A tale of mystery and horror is preserved by tradition respecting this monstrous being. While the family resided in Edinburgh, he was always kept confined in a ground apartment, in the western wing of the house, upon the windows of which, till within these few years, the boards still remained by which the dreadful receptacle was darkened to prevent the idiot from looking out or being seen. On the day the Union was passed, all Edinburgh crowded to the Parliament Close to await the issue of the debate, and to mob the chief promoters of the detested measure on their leaving the House. The whole household of the commissioner went *en masse*, with perhaps a somewhat different object, and among the rest was the man whose duty it was to watch and attend Lord Drumlanrig. Two members of the family alone were left behind—the madman himself, and a little kitchen-boy who turned the spit. The insane being, hearing everything unusually still around, the house being deserted, and the Canongate like a city of the dead, and observing his keeper to be absent, broke loose from his confinement, and roamed wildly through the house. It is supposed that the savoury odour of the preparations for dinner led him to the kitchen, where he found the little turnspit quietly seated by the fire. He seized the boy, killed him, took the meat from the fire, and spitted the body of his victim, which he half-roasted, and was found devouring when the duke, with his domestics, returned from his triumph. The idiot survived his father many years, though he did not succeed him upon his death in 1711, when the titles devolved upon Charles, the younger brother. He is known to have died in England. This horrid act of his child was, according to the common sort of people, the judgment of God upon him for his wicked concern in the Union—the greatest blessing, as it has happened, that ever was conferred upon Scotland by any statesman.

Charles, third Duke of Queensberry, who was born in Queensberry House, resided occasionally in it when he visited Scotland; but as he was much engaged in attending the court during the earlier part of his life, his stay here was seldom of long continuance. After his grace and the duchess embroiled themselves with the court (1729), on account of the support which they gave to the poet Gay, they came to Scotland, and resided for some time here. The author of the *Beggar's Opera* accompanied them, and remained about a month, part of which was given to Dumfries-

Allan Ramsay's Shop, High Street.

shire. Tradition in Edinburgh used to point out an attic in an old house opposite to Queensberry House, where, as an appropriate abode for a poet, his patrons are said to have stowed him. It was said he wrote the *Beggar's Opera* there—an entirely gratuitous assumption. In the progress of the history of his writings, nothing of consequence occurs at this time. He had finished the second part of the opera a short while before. After his return to the south, he is found engaged in 'new-writing a damned play, which he wrote several years before, called *The Wife of Bath;* a task which he accomplished while living with the Duke of Queensberry in Oxfordshire, during the ensuing months of August, September, and October.'* It is known, however, that while in

* See letters of Gay, Swift, Pope, and Arbuthnot, in Scott's edition of Swift.

Edinburgh, he haunted the shop of Allan Ramsay, in the Lucken-booths—the flat above that well-remembered and classical shop so long kept by Mr Creech, from which issued the *Mirror, Lounger,* and other works of name, and where for a long course of years all the *literati* of Edinburgh used to as-semble every day, like merchants at an Ex-change. Here Ramsay amused Gay by pointing out to him the chief public characters of the city as they met in the forenoon at the Cross. Here, too, Gay read the *Gentle Shepherd,* and studied the Scottish lan-guage, so that upon his return to England he was enabled to make Pope

Jenny Ha's Ale-House.

appreciate the beauties of that delightful pastoral. He is said also to have spent some of his time with the sons of mirth and humour in an alehouse opposite to Queensberry House, kept by one Janet Hall. *Jenny Ha's,* as the place was called, was a noted house for drinking claret from the butt within the recollection of old gentlemen living in my time.

While Gay was at Drumlanrig, he employed himself in picking out a great number of the best books from the library, which were sent to England, whether for his own use or the duke's is not known.

Duchess Catherine was a most extraordinary lady, eccentric to a degree undoubtedly bordering on madness. Her beauty has been celebrated by Pope not in very elegant terms :

'Since Queensberry to strip there's no compelling,
''Tis from a handmaid we must take a Helen.'

Prior had, at an early period of her life, depainted her irrepress-ible temper :

'Thus Kitty, beautiful and young,
    And wild as colt untamed,
Bespoke the fair from whom she sprang,
    By little rage inflamed :
Inflamed with rage at sad restraint,
    Which wise mamma ordained ;
And sorely vexed to play the saint,
    Whilst wit and beauty reigned.

"Shall I thumb holy books, confined
    With Abigails forsaken ?
Kitty's for other things designed,
    Or I am much mistaken.
Must Lady Jenny frisk about,
    And visit with her cousins ?
At balls must she make all the rout,
    And bring home hearts by dozens ?

What has she better, pray, than I ?
    What hidden charms to boast,
That all mankind for her should die,
    Whilst I am scarce a toast ?
Dearest mamma, for once let me,
    Unchained, my fortune try ;
I 'll have my earl as well as she,
    Or know the reason why.

I 'll soon with Jenny's pride quit score,
    Make all her lovers fall ;
They 'll grieve I was not loosed before,
    She, I was loosed at all."
Fondness prevailed, mamma gave way ;
    Kitty, at heart's desire,
Obtained the chariot for a day,
    And set the world on fire !'

It is an undoubted fact that, before her marriage, she had been confined in a *strait-jacket* on account of mental derangement ; and her conduct in married life was frequently such as to entitle her to a repetition of the same treatment. She was, in reality, at all times to a certain extent insane, though the politeness of fashionable society and the flattery of her poetical friends seem to have succeeded in passing off her extravagances as owing to an agreeable freedom of carriage and vivacity of mind. Her brother was as clever and as mad as herself, and used to amuse himself by hiding a book in his library, and hunting for it after he had forgot where it was deposited.

Her grace was no admirer of Scottish manners. One of their habits she particularly detested—the custom of eating off the end of a knife. When people dined with her at Drumlanrig, and began to lift their food in this manner, she used to scream out and beseech them not to cut their throats; and then she would confound the offending persons by sending them a silver spoon or fork upon a salver.*

When in Scotland her grace always dressed herself in the garb of a peasant-girl. Her object seems to have been to ridicule and put out of countenance the stately dresses and demeanour of the Scottish gentlewomen who visited her. One evening some country ladies paid her a visit, dressed in their best brocades, as for some state occasion. Her grace proposed a walk, and they were of course under the necessity of trooping off, to the utter discomfiture of their starched-up frills and flounces. Her grace at last pretended to be tired, sat down upon the dirtiest dunghill she could find, at the end of a farmhouse, and saying, 'Pray, ladies, be seated,' invited her poor draggled companions to plant themselves round about her. They stood so much in awe of her that they durst not refuse; and of course her grace had the satisfaction of afterwards laughing at the destruction of their silks.

When she went out to an evening entertainment, and found a tea-equipage paraded which she thought too fine for the rank of the owner, she would contrive to overset the table and break the china. The forced politeness of her hosts on such occasions, and the assurances which they made her grace that no harm was done, &c., delighted her exceedingly.

Her custom of dressing like a *paysanne* once occasioned her grace a disagreeable adventure at a review. On her attempting to approach the duke, the guard, not knowing her rank or relation to him, pushed her rudely back. This threw her into such a passion that she could not be appeased till his grace assured her that the men had all been soundly flogged for their insolence.

* In a letter from Gay to Swift, dated February 15, 1727-8, we find the subject illustrated as follows: 'As to my favours from great men, I am in the same state you left me; but I am a great deal happier, as I have expectations. The Duchess of Queensberry has signalised her friendship to me upon this occasion [the bringing out of the *Beggar's Opera*] in such a conspicuous manner, that I hope (for her sake) you will take care to put your fork to all its proper uses, and suffer nobody for the future to put their knives in their mouth.'

In the *P.S.* to a letter from Gay to Swift, dated Middleton Stoney, November 9, 1729, Gay says: 'To the lady I live with I owe my life and fortune. Think of her with respect—value and esteem her as I do—and never more despise a fork with three prongs. I wish, too, you would not eat from the point of your knife. She has so much goodness, virtue, and generosity, that if you knew her, you would have a pleasure in obeying her as I do. She often wishes she had known you.'

An anecdote scarcely less laughable is told of her grace as occurring at court, where she carried to the same extreme her attachment to plain-dealing and plain-dressing. An edict had been issued forbidding the ladies to appear at the drawing-room in aprons. This was disregarded by the duchess, whose rustic costume would not have been complete without that piece of dress. On approaching the door she was stopped by the lord in waiting, who told her that he could not possibly give her grace admission in that guise, when she, without a moment's hesitation, stripped off her apron, threw it in his lordship's face, and walked on, in her brown gown and petticoat, into the brilliant circle!

Her caprices were endless. At one time when a ball had been announced at Drumlanrig, after the company were all assembled her grace took a headache, declared that she could bear no noise, and sat in a chair in the dancing-room, uttering a thousand peevish complaints. Lord Drumlanrig, who understood her humour, said: 'Madam, I know how to cure you;' and taking hold of her immense elbow-chair, which moved on castors, rolled her several times backwards and forwards across the saloon, till she began to laugh heartily—after which the festivities were allowed to commence.

The duchess certainly, both in her conversation and letters, displayed a great degree of wit and quickness of mind. Yet nobody perhaps, saving Gay, ever loved her. She seems to have been one of those beings who are too much feared, admired, or envied, to be loved.

The duke, on the contrary, who was a man of ordinary mind, had the affection and esteem of all. His temper and dispositions were sweet and amiable in the extreme. His benevolence, extending beyond his fellow-creatures, was exercised even upon his old horses, none of which he would ever permit to be killed or sold. He allowed the veterans of his stud free range in some parks near Drumlanrig, where, retired from active life, they got leave to die decent and natural deaths. Upon his grace's decease, however, in 1778, these luckless pensioners were all put up to sale by his heartless successor; and it was a painful sight to see the feeble and pampered animals forced by their new masters to drag carts, &c., till they broke down and died on the roads and in the ditches.

Duke Charles's eldest son, Lord Drumlanrig, was altogether mad. He had contracted himself to one lady when he married another. The lady who became his wife was a daughter of the Earl of Hopetoun, and a most amiable woman. He loved her

tenderly, as she deserved ; but owing to the unfortunate contract
which he had engaged in, they were never happy. They were
often observed in the beautiful pleasure-grounds at Drumlanrig
weeping bitterly together. These hapless circumstances had such
a fatal effect upon him that during a journey to London in 1754
he rode on before the coach in which the duchess travelled, and
shot himself with one of his own pistols. It was given out that
the pistol had gone off by chance.

There is just one other tradition of Drumlanrig to be noticed.
The castle, being a very large and roomy mansion, had of course
a ghost, said to be the spirit of a Lady Anne Douglas. This
unhappy phantom used to walk about the house, terrifying everybody, with her head in one hand and her fan in the other—are
we to suppose, fanning her face ?

On the death of the Good Duke, as he was called, in 1778, the
title and estates devolved on his cousin, the Earl of March, so
well remembered as a sporting character and debauchee of the old
school by the name of *Old Q.* In his time Queensberry House
was occupied by other persons, for he had little inclination to
spend his time in Scotland. And this brings to mind an anecdote
highly illustrative of the wretchedness of such a life as his. When
professing, towards the close of his days, to be eaten up with
ennui, and incapable of any longer taking an interest in anything,
it was suggested that he might go down to his Scotch estates and
live among his tenantry. ' I 've tried that,' said the *blasé* aristo-
crat ; ' it is not amusing.' In 1801 he caused Queensberry House
to be stripped of its ornaments and sold. With fifty-eight fire-
rooms, and a gallery seventy feet long, besides a garden, it was
offered at the surprisingly low upset price of £900. The Government purchased it for a barrack. Thus has passed away the [home
of the] Douglas of Queensberry from its old place in Edinburgh,
where doubtless the money-making duke thought it would stand
for ever.

TENNIS COURT.

Early Theatricals—The Canongate Theatre—Digges and Mrs Bellamy—A Theatrical Riot.

'JUST without the Water-gate,' says Maitland, 'on the eastern side of the street, was the Royal Tennis Court, anciently called the Catchpel [from Cache, a game since called *Fives*, and a favourite amusement in Scotland so early as the reign of James IV.].' The house—a long, narrow building with a court—was burned down in modern times, and rebuilt for workshops. Yet the place continues to possess some interest as connected with the early and obscure history of the stage in Scotland, not to speak of the tennis itself, which was a fashionable amusement in Scotland in the seventeenth century, and here played by the Duke of York, Law the financial schemer, and other remarkable persons.

The first known appearance of the post-reformation theatre in Edinburgh was in the reign of King James VI., when several companies came from London, chiefly for the amusement of the Court, including one to which Shakespeare is known to have belonged, though his personal attendance cannot be substantiated. There was no such thing, probably, as a play acted in Edinburgh from the departure of James in 1603 till the arrival of his grandson, the Duke of York, in 1680.

Threatened by the Whig party in the House of Commons with an exclusion from the throne of England on account of his adherence to popery, this prince made use of his exile in Scotland to conciliate the nobles, and attach them to his person. His beautiful young wife, Mary of Modena, and his second daughter, the *Lady Anne*, assisted by giving parties at the palace—where, by the bye, tea was now first introduced into Scotland. Easy and obliging in their manners, these ladies revived the entertainment of the masque, and took parts themselves in the performance. At length, for his own amusement and that of his friends, James had some of his own company of players brought down to Holyrood and established in a little theatre, which was fitted up in the Tennis Court. On this occasion the remainder of the company playing at Oxford apologised for the diminution of their strength in the following lines written by Dryden :

'Discord and plots, which have undone our age,
With the same ruin have o'erwhelmed the stage.
Our house has suffered in the common woe ;
We have been troubled with Scots rebels too.
Our brethren have from Thames to Tweed departed,
And of our sisters, all the kinder-hearted
To Edinburgh gone, or coached or carted.
With bonny *Blew cap* there they act all night,
For Scotch half-crowns—in English threepence hight.
One nymph to whom fat Sir John Falstaff's lean,
There, with her single person, fills the scene.
Another, with long use and age decayed,
Died here old woman, and there rose a maid.
Our trusty door-keeper, of former time,
There struts and swaggers in heroic rhyme.
Tack but a copper lace to drugget suit,
And there's a hero made without dispute ;
And that which was a capon's tail before,
Becomes a plume for Indian emperor.
But all his subjects, to express the care
Of imitation, go like Indians bare.
Laced linen there would be a dangerous thing,
It might perhaps a new rebellion bring ;
The Scot who wore it would be chosen king.'

We learn from Fountainhall's *Diary* that on the celebration of
the king's birthday, 1681, the duke honoured the magistrates of
the city with his presence in the theatre—namely, this theatre in
the Tennis Court.

No further glimpse of our city's theatrical history is obtained till
1705, when we find a Mr Abel announcing a concert in the Tennis
Court, under the patronage of the Duke of Argyll, then acting as
the queen's commissioner to the Parliament. It is probable that
the concert was only a cloak to some theatrical representation.
This is the more likely from a tradition already mentioned of
some old members of the Spendthrift Club who once frequented
the tavern of a Mrs Hamilton, whose husband recollected having
attended the theatre in the Tennis Court at Holyrood House,
when the play was *The Spanish Friar*, and many members of the
Union Parliament were present in the house.

Theatrical amusements appear to have been continued at the
Tennis Court in the year 1710, if we are to place any reliance
upon the following anecdote : When Mrs Siddons came to Edinburgh in 1784, the late Mr Alexander Campbell, author of the
History of Scottish Poetry, asked Miss Pitcairn, daughter of Dr
Pitcairn, to accompany him to one of the representations. The
old lady refused, saying with coquettish vivacity : 'Laddie, wad
ye ha'e an auld lass like me to be running after the play-actors—

me that hasna been at a theatre since I gaed wi' papa to the Canongate in the year *ten?*' The theatre was in those days encouraged chiefly by such Jacobites as Dr Pitcairn. It was denounced by the clergy as a hotbed of vice and profanity.

After this we hear no more of the theatre in the Tennis Court. The next place where the drama set up its head was in a house in Carrubber's Close, under the management of an Italian lady styled Signora Violante, who paid two visits to Edinburgh. After her came, in 1726, one Tony Alston, who set up his scenes in the same house, and whose first prologue was written by Ramsay : it may be found in the works of that poet. In 1727 the Society of High Constables, of which Ramsay was then a member, endeavoured to 'suppress the abominable stage-plays lately set up by Anthony Alston.' * Mr Alston played for a season or two, under the fulminations of the clergy and a prosecution on their part in the Court of Session.

CANONGATE THEATRE.

From a period subsequent to 1727 till after the year 1753, the Tailors' Hall in the Cowgate † was used as a theatre by itinerating companies, who met with some success notwithstanding the incessant hostility of the clergy. ‡ It was a house which in

* Record of that Society.

† The date over the exterior gateway of the Tailors' Hall, towards the Cowgate, is 1644 ; but it is ascertained that the corporation had its hall at this place at an earlier period. An assembly of between two and three hundred clergymen was held here on Tuesday the 27th of February 1638 in order to consider the National Covenant, which was presented to the public next day in the Greyfriars Church. We are informed by the Earl of Rothes, in his *Relations* of the transactions of this period, in which he bore so distinguished a part, that some few objected to certain points in it ; but being taken aside into the garden attached to this hall, and there lectured on the necessity of mutual concession for the sake of the general cause, they were soon brought to give their entire assent.

‡ The announcements of entertainments given at this fashionable place of amusement in the eighteenth century make amusing reading to-day. 'February 17, 1743. We hear that on Monday 21st instant, at the Tailors' Hall, Cowgate, at the desire of several ladies of distinction, will be performed a concert of vocal and instrumental music. After which will be given gratis *Richard the Third*, containing several historical passages. To which will be added gratis "The Mock Lawyer." Tickets for the Concert (on which *are* [sic] printed a new device called Apology and Evasion) to be had at the Exchange and John's Coffee-houses, and at Mr Este's lodgings at Mr Monro's, musician in the Cowgate, near Tailors' Hall. As Mrs Este's present condition will not admit a personal application, she hopes the ladies notwithstanding will grace her concert.'

theatrical phrase, could hold from £40 to £45. A split in the company here concerned led to the erection, in 1746–7, of a theatre at the bottom of a close in the Canongate, nearly opposite to the head of New Street. This house, capable of holding about £70—the boxes being half-a-crown and pit one and sixpence—was for several years the scene of good acting under Lee, Digges, Mrs Bellamy, and Mrs Ward. We learn from Henry Mackenzie that the tragedy of *Douglas*, which first appeared here in 1756, was most respectably acted—the two ladies above mentioned playing respectively Young Norval and Lady Randolph.* The personal elegance of Digges—understood to be the natural son of a man of rank—and the beauty of Mrs Bellamy were a theme of interest amongst old people fifty years ago; but their scandalous life

Entrance to Tailors' Hall, Cowgate.

* Among the audience on the first night of the performance of *Douglas* were the two daughters of John and Lady Susan Renton, one of whom, Eleanor, was the mother of Charles Kirkpatrick Sharpe, to whom the author in his 'Introductory Notice' expresses his indebtedness for assistance on the first appearance of this work. And it was for attending one of the performances that the minister of Liberton Church brought himself under sentence of six weeks' suspension by the Presbytery of Edinburgh—a sentence modified in consideration of his plea that though he attended the play, 'he concealed himself as well as he could to avoid giving offence.'

was of course regarded with horror by the mass of respectable society. They lived in a small country-house at Bonnington, between Edinburgh and Leith. It is remembered that Mrs Bellamy was extremely fond of singing-birds, and kept many about her. When emigrating to Glasgow, she had her feathered favourites carried by a porter all the way that they might not suffer from the jolting of a carriage. Scotch people wondered to hear of ten guineas being expended on this occasion. Persons under the social ban for their irregular lives often win the love of individuals by their benevolence and sweetness of disposition—qualities, it is remarked, not unlikely to have been partly concerned in their first trespasses. This was the case with Mrs Bellamy. Her waiting-maid, Annie Waterstone, who is mentioned in her *Memoirs*, lived many years after in Edinburgh, and continued to the last to adore the memory of her mistress. Nay, she was, from this cause, a zealous friend of all kinds of players, and never would allow a slighting remark upon them to pass unreproved. It was curious to find in a poor old Scotchwoman of the humbler class such a sympathy with the follies and eccentricities of the children of Thespis.

While under the temporary management of two Edinburgh citizens extremely ill-qualified for the charge—one of them, by the bye, a Mr David Beatt, who had read the rebel proclamations from the Cross in 1745—a sad accident befell the Canongate playhouse. Dissensions of a dire kind had broken out in the company. The public, as usual, was divided between them. Two classes of persons —the gentlemen of the bar and the students of the university *— were especially zealous as partisans. Things were at that pass when a trivial incident will precipitate them to the most fearful conclusion. One night, when *Hamlet* was the play, a riot took place of so desperate a description that at length the house was set on fire. It being now necessary for the authorities to interfere, the Town-guard was called forth, and marched to the scene of disturbance; but though many of that veteran corps had faced the worst at Blenheim and Dettingen, they felt it as a totally different thing to be brought to action in a place which they regarded as a peculiar domain of the Father of Evil. When ordered, therefore, by their commander to advance into the house and across the stage,

* Maitland, in his *History of Edinburgh*, 1753, says that the encouragement given to the diversions at the house 'is so very great, 'tis to be feared it will terminate in the *destruction of the university*. Such diversions,' he adds, 'are noways becoming a seat of the Muses.'

the poor fellows fairly stopped short amidst the scenes, the glaring colours of which at once surprised and terrified them. Indignant at their pusillanimity, the bold captain seized a musket, and placing himself in an attitude equal to anything that had ever appeared on those boards, exclaimed : 'Now, my lads, follow *me !*' But just at the moment that he was going to rush on and charge the rioters, a trap-door on which he trod gave way, and in an instant the heroic leader had sunk out of sight, as if by magic. This was too much for the excited nerves of the guard ; they immediately vacated the house, leaving the devil to make his own of it ; and accordingly it was completely destroyed. It is added that when the captain by-and-by reappeared, they received him in the quality of a gentleman from the other world ; nor could they all at once be undeceived, even when he cursed them in vigorous Gaelic for a pack of cowardly scoundrels.

Old Playhouse Close.

The Canongate theatre revived for a short time, and had the honour to be the first house in our city in which the drama was acted with a license. It was opened with this privilege by Mr Ross on the 9th December 1767, when the play was *The Earl of Essex*, and a general prologue was spoken, the composition of James Boswell. Soon after, being deserted for the present building in the New Town,* it fell into ruin ; in which state it formed the subject of a mock elegy to the muse of Robert Fergusson. The reader will perhaps be amused with the following extract from that poem :

> 'Can I contemplate on those dreary scenes
> Of mouldering desolation, and forbid
> The voice elegiac, and the falling tear !
> No more from box to box the basket, piled

* The Theatre Royal in Shakespeare Square, where the General Post Office now stands.

With oranges as radiant as the spheres,
Shall with their luscious virtues charm the sense
Of taste or smell. No more the gaudy beau,
With handkerchief in lavender well drenched,
Or bergamot, or [in] rose-waters pure,
With flavoriferous sweets shall chase away
The pestilential fumes of vulgar cits,
Who, in impatience for the curtain's rise,
Amused the lingering moments, and applied
Thirst-quenching porter to their parched lips.
Alas! how sadly altered is the scene!
For lo! those sacred walls, that late were brushed
By rustling silks and waving capuchines,
Are now become the sport of wrinkled Time!
Those walls that late have echoed to the voice
Of stern King Richard, to the seat transformed
Of crawling spiders and detested moths,
Who in the lonely crevices reside,
Or gender in the beams, that have upheld
Gods, demigods, and all the joyous crew
Of thunderers in the galleries above.'

MARIONVILLE—STORY OF CAPTAIN MACRAE.

BETWEEN the eastern suburbs of Edinburgh and the village of Restalrig stands a solitary house named Marionville, enclosed in a shrubbery of no great extent, surrounded by high walls. Whether it be that the place has become dismal in consequence of the rise of a noxious fen in its neighbourhood, or that the tale connected with it acts upon the imagination, I cannot pretend to decide, but unquestionably there is about the house an air of depression and melancholy such as could scarcely fail to strike the most unobservant passenger. Yet, in 1790, this mansion was the abode of a gay and fashionable family, who, amongst other amusements, indulged in that of private theatricals, and

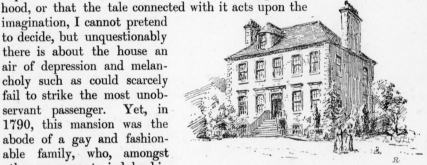

Marionville.

in this line were so highly successful that admission to the Marionville theatre became a privilege for which the highest in the land would contend. Mr Macrae, the head of this family, was a man of good fortune, being the proprietor of an estate in Dumfriesshire, and also of good connections—the Earl of Glencairn, whom Burns has so much celebrated, being his cousin, while by his mother he was nearly related to Viscount Fermoy and the celebrated Sir Boyle Roche. He had been for some years retired from the Irish Carabiniers, and being still in the prime of life, he was thinking of again entering the army, when the incident which I am about to relate took place. He was a man of gentlemanlike accomplishments and manners, of a generous and friendly disposition, but marked by a keen and imperious sense of the deference due to a gentleman, and a heat of temper which was apt to make him commit actions of which he afterwards bitterly repented. After the unfortunate affair which ended his career in Scotland, the public, who never make nice distinctions as to the character of individuals, adopted the idea that he was as inhumane as rash, and he was reported to

be an experienced duellist.   But here he was greatly misrepresented.
Mr Macrae would have shrunk from a deliberate act of cruelty ;
and the only connection he had ever had with single combat was
in the way of endeavouring to reconcile friends who had quarrelled
—an object in which he was successful on several memorable
occasions.   But the same man—whom all that really knew him
allowed to be a delightful companion and kind-hearted man—was
liable to be transported beyond the bounds of reason by casual and
trivial occurrences.   A messenger of the law having arrested the
Rev. Mr Cunningham, brother of the Earl of Glencairn, for debt,
as he was passing with a party from the drawing-room to the
dining-room at Drumsheugh House, Mr Macrae threw the man
over the stair.   He was prompted to this act by indignation at the
affront which he conceived his cousin, as a gentleman, had received
from a common man.   But soon after, when it was represented to
him that every other means of inducing Mr Cunningham to settle
his debt had failed, and when he learned that the messenger had
suffered severe injury, he went to him, made him a hearty apology,
and agreed to pay three hundred guineas by way of compensation.
He had himself allowed a debt due to a tailor to remain too long
unpaid, and the consequence was that he received a summons for
it before the sheriff-court.   With this document in his hand, he
called, in a state of great excitement, upon his law-agent, to whom
he began to read : ' Archibald Cockburn of Cockpen, sheriff-depute,'
&c., till he came to a passage which declared that ' he, the said
James Macrae, had been oft and diverse times desired and required,'
&c.   ' The greatest lie ever uttered ! ' he exclaimed.   ' He had
never heard a word of it before ; he would instantly go to the
sheriff and horsewhip him.'   The agent had at the time letters of
horning against a very worthy baronet lying upon his table—that
is to say, a document in which the baronet was denounced as a
rebel to the king, according to a form of the law of Scotland, for
failing to pay his debt.   The agent took up this, and coolly began
to read : ' George III. by the grace of God,' &c.   Macrae at once
saw the application, and fell a-laughing at his own folly, saying he
would go directly and give the sheriff tickets for the play at
Marionville, which he and his family requested.   It will be seen
that the fault of this unfortunate gentleman was heat of temper,
not a savage disposition ; but what fault can be more fatal than
heat of temper ?

Mr Macrae was married to an accomplished lady, Maria Cecilia
le Maitre, daughter of the Baroness Nolken, wife of the Swedish

ambassador. They occasionally resided in Paris, with Mrs Macrae's relations, particularly with her cousin, Madame de la Briche, whose private theatricals in her elegant house at the Marais were the models of those afterwards instituted at Marionville. It may not be unworthy of notice that amongst their fellow-performers at Madame de la Briche's was the celebrated Abbé Sieyès. When Mr Macrae and his lady set up their theatre at Marionville, they both took characters, he appearing to advantage in such parts as that of Dionysius in the *Grecian Daughter*, and she in the first line of female parts in genteel comedy. Sir David Kinloch and a Mr Justice were their best male associates; and the chief female performer, after Mrs Macrae herself, was Mrs Carruthers of Dormont, a daughter of the celebrated artist Paul Sandby. When all due deduction is made for the effects of complaisance, there seems to remain undoubted testimony that these performances involved no small amount of talent.

In Mr and Mrs Macrae's circle of visiting acquaintance, and frequent spectators of the Marionville theatricals, were Sir George Ramsay of Bamff and his lady. Sir George had recently returned, with an addition to his fortune, from India, and was now settling himself down for the remainder of life in his native country. I have seen original letters between the two families, showing that they lived on the most friendly terms and entertained the highest esteem for each other. One written by Lady Ramsay to Mrs Macrae, from Sir George's country-seat in Perthshire, commences thus: 'My dear friend, I have just time to write you a few lines to say how much I long to hear from you, and to assure you how sincerely I love you.' Her ladyship adds: 'I am now enjoying rural retirement with Sir George, who is really so good and indulgent, that I am as happy as the gayest scenes could make me. He joins me in kind compliments to you and Mr Macrae,' &c. How deplorable that social affections, which contribute so much to make life pass agreeably, should be liable to a wild upbreak from perhaps some trivial cause, not in itself worthy of a moment's regard, and only rendered of consequence by the sensitiveness of pride and a deference to false and worldly maxims!

The source of the quarrel between Mr Macrae and Sir George was of a kind almost too mean and ridiculous to be spoken of. On the evening of the 7th April 1790, the former gentleman handed a lady out of the Edinburgh theatre, and endeavoured to get a chair for her, in which she might be conveyed home. Seeing two men approaching through the crowd with one, he called to ask if it was disengaged, to which the men replied with a distinct affirmative. As Mr Macrae handed the lady forward to put her into it, a footman, in a violent manner, seized hold of one of the poles, and insisted that it was engaged for his mistress. The man seemed disordered by liquor, and it was afterwards distinctly made manifest that he was acting without the guidance of reason. His lady had gone home some time before, while he was out of the way. He was not aware of this, and, under a confused sense of duty, he was now eager to obtain a chair for her, but in reality had not bespoken that upon which he laid hold. Mr Macrae, annoyed at the man's pertinacity at such a moment, rapped him over the knuckles with a short cane to make him give way ; on which the servant called him a scoundrel, and gave him a push on the breast. Incensed overmuch by this conduct, Mr Macrae struck him smartly over the head with his cane, on which the man cried out worse than before, and moved off. Mr Macrae, following him, repeated his blows two or three times, but only with that degree of force which he thought needful for a chastisement. In the meantime the lady whom Mr Macrae had handed out got into a different chair, and was carried off. Some of the bystanders, seeing a gentleman beating a servant, cried shame, and showed a disposition to take part with the latter ; but there were individuals present who had observed all the circumstances, and who felt differently. One gentleman afterwards gave evidence that he had been insulted by the servant, at an earlier period of the evening, in precisely the same manner as Mr Macrae, and that the man's conduct had throughout been rude and insolent, a consequence apparently of drunkenness.

Learning that the servant was in the employment of Lady Ramsay, Mr Macrae came into town next day, full of anxiety to obviate any unpleasant impression which the incident might have made upon her mind. Meeting Sir George in the street, he expressed to him his concern on the subject, when Sir George said lightly that the man being his lady's footman, he did not feel any concern in the matter. Mr Macrae then went to apologise to Lady Ramsay, whom he found sitting for her portrait in the lodgings of the young artist Raeburn, afterwards so highly distinguished. It has been said that he fell on his knees before the lady to entreat her pardon for what he had done to her servant. Certainly he left her with the impression that he had no reason to expect a quarrel between himself and Sir George on account of what had taken place.

James Merry—this was the servant's name—had been wounded

in the head, but not severely. The injuries which he had sus-
tained—though nothing can justify the violence which inflicted
them—were only of such a nature as a few days of confinement
would have healed. Such, indeed, was the express testimony
given by his medical attendant, Mr Benjamin Bell. There was,
however, a strong feeling amongst his class against Macrae, who
was informed, in an anonymous letter, that a hundred and seven
men-servants had agreed to have some revenge upon him. Merry
himself had determined to institute legal proceedings against Mr
Macrae for the recovery of damages. A process was commenced
by the issue of a summons, which Mr Macrae received on the 12th.
Wounded to the quick by this procedure, and smarting under the
insolence of the anonymous letter, Mr Macrae wrote next day a
note to Sir George Ramsay, in which, addressing him without any
term of friendly regard, he demanded that either Merry should
drop the prosecution or that his master should turn him off. Sir
George temperately replied 'that he had only now heard of the
prosecution for the first time; that the man met with no encouragement from him ; and that he hoped that Mr Macrae, on further
consideration, would not think it incumbent on him to interfere,
especially as the man was at present far from being well.'

On the same evening Mr Amory, a military friend of Mr
Macrae, called upon Sir George with a second note from that
gentleman, once more insisting on the man being turned off, and
stating that in the event of his refusal Mr Amory was empowered
to communicate his opinion of his conduct. Sir George did
refuse, on the plea that he had yet seen no good reason for his
discharging the servant ; and Mr Amory then said it was his duty
to convey Mr Macrae's opinion, which was 'that Sir George's
conduct had not been that of a gentleman.' Sir George then
said that further conversation was unnecessary ; all that remained
was to agree upon a place of meeting. They met again that
evening at a tavern, where Mr Amory informed Sir George that
it was Mr Macrae's wish that they should meet, properly attended,
next day at twelve o'clock at Ward's Inn, on the borders of
Musselburgh Links.

The parties met there accordingly, Mr Macrae being attended
by Captain Amory, and Sir George Ramsay by Sir William
Maxwell ; Mr Benjamin Bell, the surgeon, being also of the party.
Mr Macrae had brought an additional friend, a Captain Haig, to
favour them with his advice, but not to act formally as a second.
The two parties being in different rooms, Sir William Maxwell

came into that occupied by Mr Macrae, and proposed that if Mr Macrae would apologise for the intemperate style of his letters demanding the discharge of the servant, Sir George would grant his request, and the affair would end. Mr Macrae answered that he would be most happy to comply with this proposal if his friends thought it proper ; but he must abide by their decision. The question being put to Captain Haig, he answered, in a deliberate manner : 'It is altogether impossible ; Sir George must, in the first place, turn off his servant, and Mr Macrae will then apologise.' Hearing this speech, equally marked by wrong judgment and wrong feeling, Macrae, according to the testimony of Mr Bell, shed tears of anguish. The parties then walked to the beach, and took their places in the usual manner. On the word being given, Sir George took deliberate aim at Macrae, the neck of whose coat was grazed by his bullet. Macrae had, if his own solemn asseveration is to be believed, intended to fire in the air ; but when he found Sir George aiming thus at his life, he altered his resolution, and brought his antagonist to the ground with a mortal wound in the body.

There was the usual consternation and unspeakable distress. Mr Macrae went up to Sir George and 'told him that he was sincerely afflicted at seeing him in that situation.' * It was with difficulty, and only at the urgent request of Sir William Maxwell, that he could be induced to quit the field. Sir George lingered for two days. The event occasioned a great sensation in the public mind, and a very unfavourable view was generally taken of Mr Macrae's conduct. It was given out that during a considerable interval, while in expectation of the duel taking place, he had practised pistol-shooting in his garden at a barber's block ; and he was also said to have been provided with a pair of pistols of a singularly apt and deadly character ; the truth being that the interval was a brief one, his hand totally unskilled in shooting, and the pistols a bad brass-mounted pair, hastily furnished by Amory. We have Amory's testimony that as they were pursuing their journey to another country, he was constantly bewailing the fate of Sir George Ramsay, remarking how unfortunate it was that he took so obstinate a view about the servant's case. The demand, he said, was one which he would have thought it necessary to comply with. He had asked Sir George nothing but what he would have done had it been his own case. This is so consonant with what appears otherwise respecting his character

* Letter of Captain Amory, MS.

that we cannot doubt it.   It is only to be lamented that he should not have made the demand in terms more calculated to lead to compliance.

The death of an amiable man under such deplorable circumstances roused the most zealous vigilance on the part of the law authorities ; but Mr Macrae and his second succeeded in reaching France.   A summons was issued for his trial, but he was advised not to appear, and accordingly sentence of outlawry was passed against him.   The servant's prosecution meanwhile went on, and was ultimately decided against Mr Macrae, although, on a cool perusal of the evidence on both sides, there appears to me the clearest proof of Merry having been the first aggressor.   Mr Macrae lived in France till the progress of the Revolution forced him to go to Altona.   When time seemed to have a little softened matters against him, he took steps to ascertain if he could safely return to his native country.   It was decided by counsel that he could not.   They held that his case entirely wanted the extenuating circumstance which was necessary—his having to contemplate degradation if he did not challenge.   He was under no such danger ; so that, from his letters to Sir George Ramsay, he appeared to have forced on the duel purely for revenge.   He came to see the case in this light himself, and was obliged to make up his mind to perpetual self-banishment.   He survived thirty years. A gentleman of my acquaintance, who had known him in early life in Scotland, was surprised to meet him one day in a Parisian coffee-house after the peace of 1814—the wreck or ghost of the handsome, sprightly man he had once been.   The comfort of his home, his country, and friends, the use of his talents to all these, had been lost, and himself obliged to lead the life of a condemned Cain, all through the one fault of a fiery temper.

ALISON SQUARE.

THIS is a large mass of building between Nicolson Square and the Potterrow, in the south side of the town. It was built about the middle of the eighteenth century, upon venture, by one Colin Alison, a joiner, who in after-life was much reduced in his circumstances, not improbably in consequence of this large speculation. In his last days he spent some of his few remaining shillings in the erection of two boards, at different parts of his buildings, whereon was represented a globe in the act of falling, with this inscription:

> 'If Fortune smile, be not puffed up,
> And if it frown, be not dismayed;
> For Providence governeth all,
> Although the world's turned upside down.'

Alison Square * has enjoyed some little connection with the Scottish muses. It was in the house of a Miss Nimmo in this place that Burns met Clarinda. It would amuse the reader of the ardent letters which passed between these two kindred souls to visit the plain, small, dusky house in which the lady lived at that time, and where she received several visits of the poet. It is situated in the adjacent humble street called the Potterrow, the first floor over the passage into General's Entry, accessible by a narrow spiral stair from the court. A little parlour, a bedroom, and a kitchen constituted the accommodations of Mrs M'Lehose; now the residence of two, if not three, families in the extreme of humble life. Here she lived with a couple of infant children, a young and beautiful woman, blighted in her prospects in consequence of an unhappy marriage (her husband having deserted her, after using her barbarously), yet cheerful and buoyant, through constitutional good spirits and a rational piety. To understand her friendship with Burns and the meaning of their correspondence, it was almost necessary to have known the woman. Seeing her and hearing her converse, even in advanced life, one could penetrate the whole mystery very readily, in appreciating a spirit

---

* The north and south sides only of this square now remain. The east was removed to make a thoroughfare—Marshall Street, connecting Nicolson Square and Potterrow.

unusually gay, frank, and emotional. The perfect innocence of the woman's nature was evident at once; and by her friends it was never doubted.

In Alison Square Thomas Campbell lived while composing his *Pleasures of Hope*. The place where any deathless composition took its shape from the author's brain is worthy of a place in the chart. A lady, the early friend of Campbell and his family, indicates their residence at that time as being the second door in the stair, entered from the east side, on the north side of the arch, the windows looking partly into Nicolson Square and partly to the Potterrow. The same authority states that much of the poem was written in the middle of the night, and from a sad cause. The poet's mother, it seems, was of a temper so extremely irritable that her family had no rest till she retired for the night. It was only at that season that the young poet could command repose of mind for his task.

LEITH WALK.

UP to the period of the building of the North Bridge, which connects the Old with the New Town of Edinburgh, the Easter Road was the principal passage to Leith. The origin of Leith Walk was accidental. At the approach of Cromwell to Edinburgh, immediately before the battle of Dunbar, Leslie, the Covenanting general, arranged the Scottish troops in a line, the right wing of which rested upon the Calton Hill, and the left upon Leith, being designed for the defence of these towns. A battery was erected at each extremity, and the line was itself defended by a trench and a mound, the latter composed of the earth dug from the former. Leslie himself took up his head-quarters at Broughton, whence some of his despatches are dated. When the war was shifted to another quarter, this mound became a footway between the two towns. It is thus described in a book published in 1748 : 'A very handsome gravel walk, twenty feet broad, which is kept in good repair at the public charge, and no horses suffered to come upon it.' When Provost Drummond built the North Bridge in 1769, he contemplated that it should become an access to Leith as well as to the projected New Town. Indeed, he seems to have been obliged to make it pass altogether under that semblance in order to conciliate the people ; for upon the plate sunk under the foundations of the bridge it is solely described as the opening of a road to Leith. At that time the idea of a New Town seemed so chimerical that he scarcely dared to avow his patriotic intentions. After the opening of the bridge, the *Walk* seems to have become used by carriages, but without any regard being paid to its condition or any system established for keeping it in repair. It consequently fell into a state of disorder, from which it was not rescued till after the commencement of the present century, when a splendid causeway was formed at a great expense by the city of Edinburgh, and a toll erected for its payment.

One terrible peculiarity attended Leith Walk in its former condition. It was overhung by a gibbet, from which were suspended all culprits whose bodies at condemnation were sentenced to be hung in chains. The place where this gibbet stood, called the Gallow Lee, is now a good deal altered in appearance. It was a slight rising ground immediately above the site of the toll * and on the west side of the road, being now partly enclosed by the precincts of a villa, where the beautiful Duchess of Gordon once lived. The greater part of the Gallow Lee now exists in the shape of mortar in the walls of the houses of the New Town. At the time when that elegant city was built, the proprietor of this redoubtable piece of ground, finding it composed of excellent sand, sold it all away to the builders, to be converted into mortar, so that it soon, from a rising ground, became a deep hollow. An amusing anecdote is told in connection with this fact. The honest man, it seems, was himself fully as much of a sand-bed as his property. He was a big, voluminous man, one of those persons upon whom drink never seems to have any effect. It is related that every day, while the carts were taking away his sand, he stood regularly at the place receiving the money in return, and every little sum he got was immediately converted into liquor and applied to the comfort of his inner man. A public-house was at length erected at the spot for his particular behoof; and, assuredly, as long as the Gallow Lee lasted this house did not want custom. Perhaps, familiar as the reader may be with stories of sots who have drunk away their last acre, he never before heard of the thing being done in so literal a manner.

If my reader be an inhabitant of Edinburgh of any standing, he must have many delightful associations of Leith Walk in connection with his childhood. Of all the streets in Edinburgh or Leith, the *Walk* in former times was certainly the street for boys and girls. From top to bottom, it was a scene of wonders

---

* The site was midway between Edinburgh and Leith, now represented by Shrub Place.

T.E.   24

and enjoyments peculiarly devoted to children. Besides the panoramas and caravan-shows, which were comparatively transient spectacles, there were several shows upon Leith Walk, which might be considered as regular fixtures and part of the *country-cousin sights* of Edinburgh. Who can forget the waxworks of 'Mrs Sands, widow of the late G. Sands,' which occupied a *laigh* shop opposite to the present Haddington Place, and at the door of which, besides various parrots and sundry birds of Paradise, sat the wax figure of a little man in the dress of a French courtier of the *ancien régime*, reading one eternal copy of the *Edinburgh Advertiser?* The very outsides of these wonder-shops was an immense treat; all along the Walk it was one delicious scene of squirrels hung out at doors, and monkeys dressed like soldiers and sailors, with holes behind where their tails came through. Even the half-penniless boy might here get his appetite for wonders to some extent gratified.

Besides being of old the chosen place for shows, Leith Walk was the Rialto of *objects*. This word requires explanation. It is applied by the people of Scotland to persons who have been born with or overtaken by some miserable personal evil. From one end to the other, Leith Walk was garrisoned by poor creatures under these circumstances, who, from handbarrows, wheelbarrows, or iron legs, if peradventure they possessed such adjuncts, entreated the passengers for charity—some by voices of song, some by speech, some by driddling, as Burns calls it, on fiddles or grinding on hand-organs—indeed, a complete continuous ambuscade against the pocket. Shows and *objects* have now alike vanished from Leith Walk. It is now a plain street, composed of little shops of the usual suburban appearance, and characterised by nothing peculiar, except perhaps a certain air of pretension, which is in some cases abundantly ludicrous. A great number, be it observed, are mere tiled cottages, which contrive, by means of lofty fictitious fronts, plastered and painted in a showy manner, to make up a good appearance towards the street. If there be a school in one of those receptacles, it is entitled an *academy*; if an artisan's workshop, however humble, it is a *manufactory*. Everything about it is still showy and unsubstantial; it is still, in some measure, the type of what it formerly was.

Near the bottom of Leith Walk is a row of somewhat old-fashioned houses bearing the name of Springfield. A large one, the second from the top, was, ninety years ago, the residence of Mr M'Culloch of Ardwell, a commissioner of customs, and noted as a man of pleasantry and wit. Here, in some of the last years of his life, did Samuel Foote occasionally appear as Mr M'Culloch's guest—*Arcades ambo et respondere parati.* But the history of their intimacy is worthy of being particularly told ; so I transcribe it from the recollection of a gentleman whose advanced age and family connections could alone have made us faithfully acquainted with circumstances so remote from our time.

In the winter of 1775–6 [more probably that of 1774–5], Mr M'Culloch visited his country mansion in the stewartry of Kirkcudbright, in company of a friend named Mouat, in order to be present at an election. Mr M'Culloch was a man of joyous temperament and a good deal of wit, and used to amuse his friends by spouting half-random verses. He and his friend spent a week or two very pleasantly in the country, and then set out on their return to Leith ; Mr M'Culloch carrying with him his infant son David, familiarly called *Wee Davie,* for the purpose of commencing his education in Edinburgh. To pursue the narrative of my correspondent : ' The two travellers got on pretty well as far as Dumfries ; but it was with difficulty, occasioned by a snowstorm, that they reached Moffat, where they tarried for the night.

' Early on a January morning, the snow having fallen heavily during the preceding night, they set off in a post-chaise and four horses to proceed on their perilous journey. Two gentlemen in their own carriage left the *King's Arms Inn* (then kept by James Little) at the same time. With difficulty the first pair of travellers reached the top of Erickstane, but farther they could not go. The parties came out of their carriages, and, aided by their postillions, they held a consultation as to the prudence of attempting to proceed down the vale of Tweed. This was considered as a vain and dangerous attempt, and it was therefore determined on to return to Moffat. The turning of the carriages having become a dangerous undertaking, Wee Davie had to be taken out of the chaise and laid on the snow, wrapped in a blanket, until the business was accomplished. The parties then went back to Moffat, arriving there between nine and ten in the morning. Mr M'Culloch and his friend then learned that, of the two strangers who had left the inn at the same time, and had since returned, one was the celebrated Foote, and the other either Ross or Souter, but which of the two favourite sons of Thalia I cannot remember at this distant period of time. Let it be kept in mind that Foote had lost a leg, and walked with difficulty.

'Immediately on returning Foote had entered the inn, not in good-humour, to order breakfast. His carriage stood opposite the inn door, in order to get the luggage taken off. While this was going on a paper was placarded on one of the panels. The wit came out to see how all matters were going on, when, observing the paper, he in wrath exclaimed : " What rascal has been placarding his ribaldry on my carriage ? " He had patience, however, to pause and read the following lines :

> " While Boreas his flaky storm did guide,
> Deep covering every hill, o'er Tweed and Clyde,
> The north-wind god spied travellers seeking way ;
> Sternly he cried : 'Retrace your steps, I say ;
> Let not *one foot*, 'tis my behest, profane
> The sacred snows which lie on Erickstane.' "

The countenance of our wit now brightened, as he called out, with an exclamation of surprise : " I should like to know the fellow who wrote that ; for, be he who he may, he 's no mean hand at an epigram." Mrs Little, the good but eccentric land-lady, now stepped forward and spoke thus : " Trouth, Maister Fut, it 's mair than likely that it was our *frien'* Maister M'Culloch of Ardwell that did it ; it 's weel kent that he 's a poyet ; he 's a guid eneugh sort o' man, but he never comes here without poyet-teasing mysel' or the guidman, or some ane or other about the house. It wud be weel dune if ye wud speak to him." Ardwell now came forward, muttering some sort of apology, which Foote instantly stopped by saying : " My dear sir, an apology is not necessary ; I am fair game for every one, for I take any one for game when it suits me. You and I must become acquainted, for I find that we are brother-poets, and that we were this morning companions in misfortune on ' the sacred snows of Erick-stane.' " Thus began an intimacy which the sequel will show turned out to be a lasting one. The two parties now joined at the breakfast-table, as they did at every other meal for the next twenty days.

'Foote remained quiet for a few hours after breakfast, until he had beat about for game, as he termed it, and he first fixed on worthy Mrs Little, his hostess. By some occult means he had managed to get hold of some of the old lady's habiliments, particularly a favourite night-cap—provincially, a *mutch*. After attiring himself *à la* Mrs Little, he went into the kitchen and through the house, mimicking the garrulous landlady so very exactly in giving orders, scolding, &c. that no servant doubted as to its being the mistress *in propriâ personâ*. This kind of amusement went on for several days for the benefit of the people in Moffat. By-and-by the snow allowed the united parties to advance as far as the Crook, upon Tweed, and here they were again storm-stayed for ten days. Nevertheless, Foote and his companion, who was well qualified to support him, never for a moment flagged in creating merriment or affording the party amusement of some sort. The snow cleared away at last, so as to enable the travellers to reach Edinburgh, and there to end their journey. The intimacy of Foote and Ardwell did not end here, but continued until the death of Foote.

'After this period Foote several times visited Scotland : he always in his writings showed himself partial to Scotland and to the Scotch. On every visit which he afterwards made to the northern metropolis, he set apart a night or two for a social meeting with his friend Ardwell, whose family lived in the second house from the head of that pretty row of houses more than half-way down Leith Walk, still called Springfield. In the parlour, on the right-hand side in entering that house, the largest of the row, Foote, the celebrated wit of the day, has frequently been associated with many of the Edinburgh and Leith worthies, when and where he was wont to keep the table in a roar.

'The biography of Foote is well known. However, I may add that Mr Mouat and Mr M'Culloch died much lamented in the year 1793. David M'Culloch (Wee Davie) died in the year 1824, at Cheltenham, much regretted. For many years he had resided in India. In consequence of family connection, he became a familiar visitor at Abbotsford, and a favourite acquaintance of Sir Walter Scott.* Mr Lockhart tells us that, next to Tom Moore, Sir Walter thought him the finest warbler he had ever heard. He was certainly an exquisitely fine singer of Scotch songs. Sir Walter Scott never heard him sing until he was far advanced in life, or until his voice had given way to a long residence in India. Mr Lockhart also tells us that David M'Culloch in his youth was an intimate and favourite companion of Burns, and that the poet hardly ventured to publish many of his songs until he heard them sung by his friend. I will only add that the writer of this has more than once heard Burns say that he never fully knew the beauty of his songs until he heard them sung by David M'Culloch.'

* Sir Walter's brother Thomas was married to a sister of Mr M'Culloch.

[GABRIEL'S ROAD.

PREVIOUS to 1767 the eye of a person perched in a favourable situation in the Old Town surveyed the whole ground on which the New Town was afterwards built. Immediately beyond the North Loch was a range of grass fields called Bearford's Parks, from the name of the proprietor, Hepburn of Bearford in East Lothian. Bounding these on the north, in the line of the subsequent Princes Street, was a road enclosed by two dry-stone walls, thence called the Lang Dykes; it was the line by which the Viscount Dundee rode with his small troop of adherents when he had ascertained that the Convention was determined to settle the crown upon the Prince of Orange, and he saw that the only duty that remained for him was to raise the Highland clans for King James.* The main mass of ground, originally rough with whins and broom, but latterly forming what was called Wood's Farm, was crossed obliquely by a road extending between Silvermills, a rural hamlet on the mill-course of the Leith, and the passage into the Old Town obtained by the dam of the North Loch at the bottom of Halkerston's Wynd. There are still some traces of this road. You see it leave Silvermills behind West Cumberland Street. Behind Duke Street, on the west side, the boundary-wall of the Queen Street Garden is oblique in consequence of its having passed that way. Finally it terminates in a short, oblique passage behind the Register House, wherein stood till lately a tall building containing a famous house of resort, Ambrose's Tavern. This short passage bore the name of Gabriel's Road, and it was supposed to do so in connection with a remarkable murder, of which it was the scene.

The murderer in the case was in truth a man named Robert Irvine. He was tutor to two boys, sons of Mr Gordon of Ellon. In consequence of the children having reported some liberties they saw him take with their mother's maid, he conceived the horrible design of murdering them, and did so one day as he was leading them for a walk along the rough ground where the

---

* It was also along this road that the anxious citizens, watching on the Castle esplanade, saw the royalist cavalry retiring at full gallop from Coltbridge on the approach of Prince Charlie and his Highland army.

New Town is now situated. The frightful transaction was beheld from the Castle-hill; he was pursued, taken, and next day but one hanged by the baron of Broughton, after having his hands hacked off by the knife with which he had committed the deed. The date of this off-hand execution was 30th April 1717. Both the date and the murderer's name have several times been misstated.[*]

Adjacent to this road, about the spot now occupied by the Royal Bank, stood a small group of houses called Mutrie's Hill, some of which professed to furnish curds and cream and fruits in their seasons, and were on these accounts resorted to by citizens and their families on summer evenings. One in particular bore the name of 'Peace and Plenty.'

The village of Silvermills, for the sake of which, as an access to the city, Gabriel's Road existed, still maintains its place amidst the streets and crescents of the New Town. It contains a few houses of a superior cast; but it is a place sadly in want of the *sacer vates*. No notice has ever been taken of it in any of the books regarding Edinburgh, nor has any attempt ever been made to account for its somewhat piquant name. I shall endeavour to do so.

In 1607 silver was found in considerable abundance at Hilderstone, in Linlithgowshire, on the property of the gentleman who figures in another part of this volume as Tam o' the Cowgate. Thirty-eight barrels of ore were sent to the Mint in the Tower of London to be tried, and were found to give about twenty-four ounces of silver for every hundredweight. Expert persons were placed upon the mine, and mills were erected on the Water of Leith for the melting and fining of the ore. The sagacious owner gave the mine the name of *God's Blessing*. By-and-by the king heard of it, and thinking it improper that any such fountain of wealth should belong to a private person, purchased God's Blessing for £5000, that it might be worked upon a larger scale for the benefit of the public. But somehow, from the time it left the hands of the original owner, God's Blessing ceased to be anything like so fertile as it had been, and in time the king withdrew from the enterprise a great loser. The Silvermills I conceive to have been a part of the abandoned plant.[†]]

---

[*] In Mr Lockhart's clever book, *Peter's Letters to his Kinsfolk*, the murderer is called Gabriel. A work called *Celebrated Trials* (6 vols. 1825) gives an erroneous account of the murder, styling the murderer as the Rev. Thomas Hunter.

[†] See *Domestic Annals of Scotland*, i. 407.

INDEX.

THE END